Introducing Revit® Architecture 2009

Introducing Revit® Architecture 2009

BIM FOR BEGINNERS

GREG DEMCHAK | TATJANA DZAMBAZOVA | EDDY KRYGIEL

Wiley Publishing, Inc.

Acquisitions Editor: WILLEM KNIBBE
Development Editor: DICK MARGULIS
Technical Editor: PHIL READ
Production Editor: DASSI ZEIDEL
Copy Editor: LIZ WELCH
Production Manager: TIM TATE
Vice President and Executive Group Publisher: RICHARD SWADLEY
Vice President and Executive Publisher: JOSEPH B. WIKERT
Vice President and Publisher: NEIL EDDE
Book Designer: CARYL GORSKA
Compositor: KATE KAMINSKI, HAPPENSTANCE TYPE-O-RAMA
Proofreader: NANCY BELL
Indexer: NANCY GUENTHER
Cover Designer: RYAN SNEED
Front Cover Images: ANDREA SADER AND INES MAGRI, UNIVERSIDAD ORT, URUGUAY (TOP IMAGE), KUBIK+NEMETH+VLKOVIC (FAR LEFT AND FAR RIGHT IMAGES), GREG DEMCHAK (MIDDLE IMAGE)
Back Cover Images: GENSLER (LEFT IMAGE), KUBIK+NEMETH+VLKOVIC (MIDDLE IMAGE), HOK (RIGHT IMAGE)

Library of Congress Cataloging-in-Publication Data

Demchak, Greg.

   Introducing Revit architecture 2009 : BIM for beginners / Greg Demchak, Eddy Krygiel, Tatjana Dzambazova. — 1st ed.

      p. cm.

   ISBN 978-0-470-26098-2 (paper/website)

   1. Architectural drawing—Computer-aided design. 2. Architectural design—Data processing. I. Krygiel, Eddy, 1972– II. Dzambazova, Tatjana. III. Title.

   NA2728.D45 2008

   720'.285—dc22

                              2008012003

Dear Reader,

Thank you for choosing *Introducing Revit® Architecture 2009: BIM for Beginners.* This book is part of a family of premium quality Sybex books, all written by outstanding authors who combine practical experience with a gift for teaching.

Sybex was founded in 1976. More than thirty years later, we're still committed to producing consistently exceptional books. With each of our titles we're working hard to set a new standard for the industry. From the authors we work with to the paper we print on, our goal is to bring you the best books available.

I hope you see all that reflected in these pages. I'd be very interested to hear your comments and get your feedback on how we're doing. Feel free to let me know what you think about this or any other Sybex book by sending me an e-mail at nedde@wiley.com, or if you think you've found a technical error in this book, please visit http://sybex .custhelp.com. Customer feedback is critical to our efforts at Sybex.

Best regards,

Neil Edde
Vice President and Publisher
Sybex, an Imprint of Wiley

Sybex®
An Imprint of
Ⓦ**WILEY**

Dedication

For Gage
—Greg

For Thea and Michael, who brought love and laughter in my life
—Tanja

For my beautiful daughters, Zoë and Maya
—Eddy

Acknowledgments

Hats off to the innovators who conceptualized, designed, and made Revit happen. You have changed the world! ■ Huge thanks to all the faithful followers! Without you, Revit wouldn't be what it is today. ■ Personal thanks to the grand masters Philippe Drouant and Phil Read for their heroic dedication and help; to Simone Cappochin and Kubik+Nemeth+Vlkovic, who keep on doing beautiful architecture with Revit and are willing to share it with us; and to our friends, Martin Taurer, Paul Woddy, and Emmanuel Di Giacommo, for their contributions A final thank-you to BNIM Architects, who continue to let us use their Revit models to help raise the knowledge base of the design community. ■ To Tsvetan Tsvetanov, whose dedication and hard work was essential to providing Revit with its great new rendering capabilities. ■ Sincere thanks to all the hardworking developers, product designers, and quality assurance testers from the development team of Revit, for their dedication, passion, and love of Revit. ■ And finally, thanks are due to our excellent support team at Sybex, who helped us develop and focus the content; Dick Margulis, for making a philosopher, nonnative English speaker, and a dyslexic look good in print; Liz Welch for making it grammatically correct; Dassi Zeidel for keeping tabs on all the parts and pieces; Eric Charbonneau for keeping things on track; and a special thanks to Willem Knibbe, for his willingness to go to bat for us and deal with our high-maintenance attitudes.

About the Authors

Greg Demchak is a designer, a technology advocate, urban explorer, and post-apocalyptic film producer. He holds architectural degrees from the University of Oregon and Massachusetts Institute of Technology. He is a product designer for Autodesk and has been working with Revit since 2000. He has been teaching at the Boston Architectural College since 2003 and is currently the principal investigator for the 2009 Solar Decathlon competition. He resides in Massachusetts.

Tatjana Dzambazova was the product manager for Revit Architecture between 2005 and 2007, after which she moved into global sales development management for the AEC industry. Before joining Autodesk in 2000, she practiced architecture for 12 years in Vienna and London. At Autodesk, she has focused on evangelizing technology and established herself as an internationally renowned speaker who has fostered relationships with architects and industry leaders from all around the globe. Powered with seemingly unlimited sources of energy and passion, Tanja manages to make three days out of one, always on the hunt of what's new and exciting in the world of architecture and technology; and when she is not working or coauthoring technology books, she is advocating wildlife conservation, reading books like a maniac, getting inspired in the theaters, and playing Scrabble and Texas Hold 'Em.

Eddy Krygiel is a registered architect, a LEED Accredited Professional, and an Autodesk Authorized Author at BNIM Architects headquartered in Kansas City, Missouri. He has been using Revit since version 5.1 to complete projects ranging from single-family residences and historic remodels to 1.12-million-square-foot office buildings. Eddy is responsible for implementing BIM at his firm and also consults for other architecture and contracting firms around the country looking to implement BIM. For the last four years, he has been teaching Revit to practicing architects and architectural students in the Kansas City area and has lectured around the nation on the use of BIM in the construction industry. Eddy also coauthored *Green BIM: Successful Sustainable Design with Building Information Modeling*, a book on sustainability and BIM, with Bradley Nies (Sybex, 2008).

CONTENTS AT A GLANCE

Contents

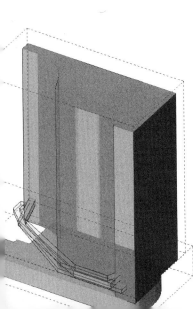

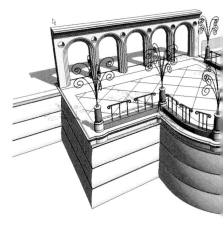

Introduction

Welcome to the second edition of *Introducing Revit Architecture*, which was written based on the 2009 release of the software.

It was great fun re-visiting our first book—we worked hard to polish it up, and capture the new features in the 2009 release of Revit Architecture. We enjoyed the synergy of three friends, three architects, three authors collaborating to bring this project into reality. But mostly, we were all driven by the feeling that we're doing something great: introducing Revit to those who have not been acquainted with its incredible power and its ability to put some fun back into using software and designing architecture.

This book is written for beginners who have never seen or may have just heard about Revit. It's for architects of any generation—you don't need to be a high-tech wizard to get into Revit. Toward that end, we wanted to make a book that is as much about architecture as it is about software. We've added many timesaving and inspiring concepts to the book to get you motivated and to help you on your journey into the new era of building information modeling (BIM). We think we've succeeded, because the book is full of real-world examples that show how to use Revit practically and creatively based on all of our experiences out there in professional practice.

This book will help you learn Revit and BIM basics easily and efficiently via straightforward explanations, real-world examples, and practical tutorials that focus squarely on accomplishing vital Revit tasks.

Our book begins with an overview of BIM concepts before introducing the Revit interface. You'll start working with basic modeling features, learning how to create walls, floors, roofs, and stairs. The book then explains how to use components and provides descriptions and examples of Revit's suite of editing tools.

The book continues by looking deeper into the capabilities of core modeling elements. We explain how Revit works with other applications, show you how to document the model for construction, and explore how you can integrate annotations into the model.

After we discuss printing to paper and files, we explore worksets and team collaboration, followed by a look at some of Revit's more advanced options. The book concludes with a chapter on troubleshooting and best practices; that's where we try to share our practical experience with you so you can avoid some of the common beginner pitfalls (and enjoy beginner's luck). Also featured is a new full-color gallery containing inspirational Revit projects from around the globe.

The book's companion web page, at `www.wiley.com/go/introducingrevit2009`, features all the tutorial files necessary to complete the book's exercises, plus sample families and a trial version of the Revit software.

Enjoy! Revit has changed our lives. Maybe it will change yours as well.

We welcome your feedback! Please feel free to e-mail us at `GoRevit@gmail.com`.

Greg Demchak
Tatjana Dzambazova
Eddy Krygiel

CHAPTER 1

Understanding BIM

A great building must begin with the unmeasurable, must go through measurable means when it is being designed and in the end must be unmeasurable.

—Louis Kahn

Building information modeling (BIM) is an emerging approach to the design, analysis, and documentation of buildings. At its core, BIM is about the management of information throughout the entire lifecycle of a design process, from early conceptual design through construction administration, and even into facilities management. By information we mean all the inputs that go into a building design: the number of windows, the cost of materials, the size of heating and cooling equipment, the total energy footprint of the building, and so on. This information is captured in a digital model that can then be presented as coordinated documents, be shared across disciplines, and serve as a centralized design management tool. With a tool like Revit, you will reap the benefits of fully coordinated documents, but this represents just the tip of the BIM iceberg.

In this chapter, we'll present the basics of BIM and summarize how BIM differs from traditional 2D drafting–based methodologies. We will explain the key characteristics of Revit and how Revit is truly designed to deliver the benefits of building information modeling.

Topics we'll cover include:

- **A brief history of architectural documentation**
- **Advantages of a BIM approach**
- **How BIM is different from CAD**
- **Why Revit?**
- **Revit concepts**
- **Types of elements in Revit**
- **Tips for getting started in Revit**

A Brief History of Architectural Documentation

The production of design documents has traditionally been an exercise in making drawings to represent a building. These drawings become instruction document sets: an annotated booklet that describes how the building is to be built. The plan, section, and elevation—all skillfully drafted, line by line, drawing by drawing. Whether physical or digital, these traditional drawing sets are composed of graphics where each line is part of a larger abstraction meant to convey design intent so that a building can eventually be constructed. When Filippo Brunelleschi drew the plans for Santa Maria del Fiore (Figure 1.1) in Renaissance Italy, the drawings represented ideas of what the building would look like. They were simplified representations of a completed project, used to convey ideas to the patron. In those days, the architect also played the role of builder, so there was no risk of losing information between the documentation of the building and the actual building of it. This was the age of the master builder, where architect and builder shared the same responsibility and roles. Even so, Brunelleschi still needed to communicate his vision to his patrons and his workers, and he not only produced beautiful drawings but also built elaborate scale models so that others could easily visualize the project.

Figure 1.1

Santa Maria del Fiore; *image courtesy of Laura Lesniewski*

As buildings became increasingly complex, specialization in the design and construction process emerged. In turn, this led to the need for more elaborate forms of information exchange. One person was no longer responsible for both the design and construction phases, so it became necessary for designers to convey design intent with richer amounts of information and instructions.

Jump ahead in time to the twentieth century. The use of steel had been fully embraced, thus allowing buildings to reach higher than ever before; the age of the skyscraper and modern construction was in full force. The Power and Light Building (Figure 1.2) was erected in Kansas City, Missouri, in only 19 months. An Art Deco testament to the boldness of the times, the building was built without the use of modern earthmoving machinery or other heavy equipment. The drawing set for a building of this size in the 1930s would have been about 35 pages long. The Power and Light Building was more complex than its predecessors but far simpler than today's large commercial projects. There were no data or telecom systems, no air conditioning other than operable windows, and no security systems other than locks on the doors.

Figure 1.2

Power and Light Building, Kansas City, MO

Fast-forward to late twentieth century buildings. Buildings are more complex than ever before. Documentation sets span all disciplines and are hundreds of pages long. The number of people who will touch a set of drawings—to produce them, evaluate them, or use them to build the building—has become huge. Integrated building systems continue to expand with the growth of technology. Today, we have more security, electrical, data, telecom, HVAC, and energy requirements than ever before (see Figure 1.3). The quality and quantity of information that goes into a documentation set can no longer be thought of as abstract approximations—the cost of error is far too high, and fully coordinated drawings are expected. The use of computer-based technology has replaced pen and paper, yet documents are still largely generated in 2D. Drawing and editing lines has become faster and more efficient, but in the end, they are still collections of manually created, nonintelligent lines and text.

Figure 1.3

Layers of design

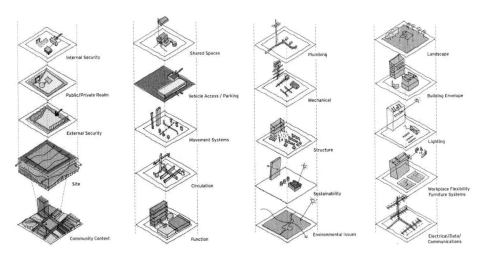

The year 1998—dawn of the Internet boom. Technology companies are flourishing, and start-ups are a dime a dozen. In the suburbs of Boston, a new approach to architectural documentation is about to be launched. The premise is simple: model the building once, and let architects view, edit, and annotate the model from any point of view, at any time. A change to the model from any view simultaneously updates all other views. Drawings cease to be separate, uncoordinated collections of lines and become by-products of a model-based design approach. Revit is born, and with it the foundation for a new approach to how buildings are designed, evaluated, represented, and documented (see Figure 1.4). In 2002, Revit Technology is acquired by Autodesk and continues to be developed. Welcome to the world of building information modeling.

Figure 1.4

The founders and some original members of Revit technology, having a tug-of-war at a release party, circa 2000

Advantages of a BIM Approach

The ultimate benefits of BIM are still emerging in the market and will radically change the way buildings are designed and built. A shift in process and expectation is happening in the construction market, and architects are stepping up to the challenge. The focus is shifting from traditional 2D abstractions to on-demand simulations of building performance, usage, and cost. This is no longer a futuristic fantasy but a practical reality. In the age of information-rich digital models, we can now have all disciplines involved with a project sharing a single database. Architecture, structure, mechanical, infrastructure, and construction are tied together and able to coordinate in ways never before possible. Models can now be sent directly to fabrication machines, bypassing the need for traditional shop drawings. Energy analysis can be done at the outset of design, and construction costs are becoming more and more predictable. These are just a few of the exciting opportunities that a BIM approach offers.

BIM has shifted how designers and contractors look at the entire building process, from preliminary design through construction documentation, into actual construction, and even into postconstruction building management. With BIM, a parametric 3D model is used to generate traditional building abstractions such as plans, sections, elevations, details, and schedules. Drawings produced using BIM are not just discrete collections of manually coordinated lines but interactive representations of a model.

Working in a model-based framework guarantees that a change in one view will propagate to all other views of the model. As you shift elements in plan, they change in elevation and section. If you remove a door from your model, it simultaneously gets removed from all views, and your door schedule is updated. This enhanced document delivery system allows unprecedented control over the quality and coordination of the document set.

With the advent of BIM, designers and builders have a better way to create, control, and display information. Some of the advantages that first-time users can expect to realize are as follows:

- Three-dimensional design visualization improves understanding of the building and its spaces and gives you the ability to show a variety of design options to both the team and the client.

- Integrated design documents minimize errors in documentation cross-referencing and keynoting, allowing clearer, more precise documents.

- Interference checking permits you to immediately see conflicts between architectural, structural, and mechanical elements in 3D and to avoid costly errors on site.

- Automated, always up-to-date schedules of building components (like door and room-area schedules) are data-driven and can drive data and improve the visibility of costs and quantities.

- Material quantity take-offs allow better predictability and planning.

- Sustainable strategies are easier to explore, enabling you to design better buildings and make a better world.

How BIM Is Different from CAD

The key difference between BIM and computer-aided design (CAD) is that a traditional CAD system uses many separate (usually 2D) documents to explain a building. These documents are created separately and have little to no intelligent connection between them. A wall in a plan view is represented with two parallel lines, with no understanding that those lines represent the same wall in a section. The possibility of uncoordinated data is very high. BIM takes the opposite approach: it assembles all information into one location and cross-links that data among associated objects. (See Figures 1.5 and 1.6.)

By and large, CAD is strictly a 2D technology with a specific need to output a collection of lines and text on a page. These lines have no inherent meaning, whether inside the computer or on the printed sheet. CAD drafting has its efficiencies and advantages over pen and paper, but it is really just a simulation of the act of drafting. This form of drawing is how architects and other designers have worked for the last couple of hundred years. Historically, the designer drew a set of plans and then used those plans to manually derive sections, elevations, and details. During the development of a project, if any of those items changed, the designer had to modify each of the other drawings that were affected to take the change into account. For a long time, this meant getting out an eraser and an eraser shield and spending days picking up changes. Today, you can use the Delete key, but the goal is fundamentally the same. This is where BIM makes a significant departure from legacy CAD platforms.

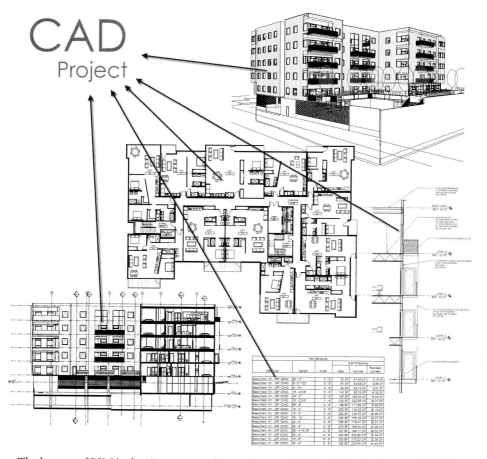

Figure 1.5

Typical CAD outputs

The beauty of BIM is that it manages change for you. Unlike CAD, the intent of BIM is to let the computer take responsibility for interactions and calculations (something computers are good at), providing you—the designer—with more time to design and evaluate your decisions. A core feature of BIM is that it allows you to create and modify everything in one design context. When a change to a project is done by the user in one place, the system will propagate that change to all relevant views and documents of the project. As you model in plan, the elevations, sections, and details are also being generated. Where you make the change is up to you, and the system will take care of the rest. With a BIM tool such as Revit, if you change the size of a window opening in elevation, this change is made throughout the entire model: sections, floor plans, schedule tables, and quantity take-offs.

Figure 1.6
Typical BIM outputs

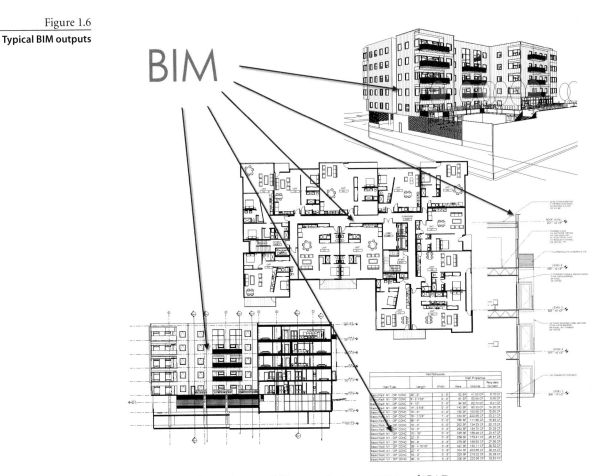

Here are a few other big differences between BIM and CAD:

BIM adopts a task-oriented rather than an object-oriented methodology. In 2D drafting CAD, you draw two lines (objects) to represent a wall. In BIM, the task of creating a wall is presented in the form of an interactive tool named Create Wall. This wall has properties like width, height, bearing or nonbearing, demolished or new, interior or exterior, fire rating, and materials (such as boards or brick). The wall interacts with other walls to automatically join geometries and clean up connections, showing how the walls will be built. Similarly, if you add a door, it's more than four lines and an arc; it's a door in plan and elevation. Adding it to the wall automatically creates an opening in the wall in all views where the door is visible. As we will discover, the tools available for walls are specific to walls, allowing you to attach walls to roofs and floors, punch openings, and change the layered construction of the wall. Again, all of these interactions are not just properties; they are focused on specific tasks associated with architectural walls.

BIM keeps you honest.   An additional advantage of a BIM methodology is that you can't cheat your design. Because the elements have properties based on real-life properties, you'll find it difficult to fake elements within the design. If you have a door in plan, it automatically appears in the other associated views such as elevation or section. In a CAD-based system this can be easy to overlook because the door has to be manually transcribed from plan to section and elevation and is easily forgotten or drawn at a wrong location. Because BIM is based on actual assemblies, it's difficult to misrepresent dimensions or objects within the model.

BIM is more than a modeler.   Other software packages, like SketchUp, Rhinoceros, and 3ds Max, are excellent modeling applications. However, these modeling applications don't have the ability to document your design for construction or to be leveraged downstream. This is not to say these tools don't play a part in a BIM workflow. Many architects use these tools to generate concept models, which can then be brought into a BIM application and progress through design, analysis, and documentation.

BIM is a data-driven design tool.   BIM lets you create custom content and libraries throughout the course of your project. This content contains rich amount of data that will inform schedules, quantity take-offs, and analysis. Again, it's not just 3D—it's 3D with intelligent information (metadata).

BIM is based on an architectural classification system, not "layers."   Because a building model is an assembly of meaningful, to-be-built objects, you control visibility and graphics of objects using a rational list of well-understood categories. This is different from CAD, where every line belongs to a layer, and it is up the user to manage all these layers. For example, in Revit there is no way to accidentally place a window into the "wall" layer. In a BIM world, layers become obsolete; after all, in the real world buildings are not made of abstract color-coded layers.

Potential Hazards

One of the powers of Revit is the ability to work in a single-file environment where the design and documentation of the building happens on a holistic model. This can also be a disadvantage if you do not take it seriously and give it full consideration. Users who may be quick to make changes without thinking how such a change will ripple through the model can cause unintended problems if they're not careful. Revit is a parametric modeler: it creates relationships between building elements in order to streamline the design process. For example, if you delete a level from your model, then all the walls, doors, and furniture on that level will also be deleted. Likewise, if you delete a wall, all the doors and windows in that wall will be deleted. If you underlay the roof in your second floor so that you can see the extents of the roof overhang, deleting the lines that represent the roof overhang actually means deleting the roof! These are basic mistakes that new users might encounter as they readjust their mental model and come to see the model as not just lines but actual building elements. A nice consequence of this is that Revit will not let you leave elements floating around in an abstract 3D vacuum. You will not have views cluttered with fragmented geometry from some other file, exploded blocks, or mysterious lines. At the same time, you must take care when making large-scale changes to a model, especially the further along in the design process you go.

Anticipate that tasks will take different amounts of time when compared to a CAD production environment. It isn't an apples-to-apples equation. You'll perform tasks in Revit that you never had in CAD; conversely, some of the CAD tasks that took weeks (chamfering and trimming thousands of lines to draw walls properly or making a door schedule) take almost no time using Revit.

If you've never worked in a 3D model–based environment, it can be frustrating at first to move from a strictly 2D world into the 3D BIM. At the same time, it's really quite nice to have immediate access to perspective views at any time! The Revit world is one with a white screen, no layers, and no x-references. This often leads to generic comparisons and some growing pains—but just stick with it, be patient, and you'll be hooked in no time at all. With any transition there is a learning curve; as you begin to use Revit, you'll quickly see the benefits.

Why Revit?

Revit is the newest and most technologically advanced BIM application. Currently, a number of BIM applications are on the market, provided by a host of different software vendors. Although most other products in today's market are based on technology that is 20-plus years old, Revit was designed from the ground up as a BIM platform to specifically address problem areas of the architecture, engineering, and construction (AEC) industry: communication, coordination, and change management. As you complete more projects with Revit, you'll begin to understand some of its advanced functionality. Being able to go direct to fabrication with your designs, provide digital shop drawing submittals, and execute 4D construction planning are just a few of the possibilities.

Revit is a technological platform that currently supports architectural, structural, and mechanical disciplines, but the possibilities for extending these are immense. It's supported by a patented parametric change engine that is unmatched in sophistication within the AEC world of applications. It's also the leading software package in the international market.

Revit Concepts

The name Revit comes from "Revise Instantly"; Revit is built for managing change, something that we architects have to do in our practice all the time.

Parametric Objects and Parametric Relationships

We all hear about *parametric objects*, but what makes an object parametric? A parametric object is a smart object that can change its size, materials, and graphic look but is consistently the same object. For example, think of a door. A single flush door can be 32″, 34″, or 36″ (70, 75, 80, 85, or 90cm). It can also be painted or solid wood. All of these sizes and colors can be part of the same door family, with different parametric values applied.

Or consider a table: it can be the same shape but made out of wood or metal, with a glass or wood top, and with the top extending over the legs or flush with them. Again, they're all in the same table family; only the parametric values are different. The parameters are meaningful ways to create variations of an element. And most importantly, this information is always accessible, reversible, editable, and schedulable.

In most CAD systems, to accommodate all the types of doors mentioned previously, you need to make not only a separate block for each representation (thus, plan, elevation, and section typically comprise 7 or 8 blocks) but also as many blocks as sizes you need. If you then wish to make a table that is 4′-0″ square (50/50) to 5′-0″ square (70/70), you use the Scale command, which unfortunately makes the table legs bigger than needed because they resize along with the table top! A parametric object allows you to effect a change on each parameter without affecting the others unless desired. So, you can change the size of the table legs independent from the table top, and so on.

Bidirectional Associativity

Objects with parameters that can be edited are nothing new in the world of software. But what makes Revit unique is its ability to create relationships within objects and *between* objects. This ability has been referred to as the *parametric change engine*, and is a core technological advantage built into Revit. Walls, for example, can be attached to roofs, so when the roof changes to a new shape or size, all walls attached to the roof automatically adapt to the new roof shape. Walls, floors, roofs, and components all have explicit relationships to levels. If a level changes height, all elements associated with that level will update automatically: the walls below the level will extend to the new height of the level above, and so forth. When you change the size of a room by moving a wall, you are changing not only the wall, but everything that wall affects in the model as well: the size of the room, color-fill diagrams, ceilings, floors, the doors and windows in the wall, and any dimensions to that wall, area, volume.

The parametric relationships are extended to annotations and sheet management as well. Tags are not simple graphics with a text notation; they are interactive graphical parameters that read the information directly from the characteristics and parameters of the element being tagged. To edit a tag is to edit the element, and vice versa. When you're laying out sheets and a section view is placed onto a sheet, the section key automatically references the sheet number and detail number on the sheet. Change the sheet number, and the section tag updates instantly. *This* is what a real parametric engine is and what ensures total coordination of your documentation. This parametric engine guarantees that a "change anywhere is a change everywhere."

Embedded Relationships

Revit has embedded logical relationships among elements, so that when one is modified, all related objects follow the change. To illustrate this, let's try a *smart move*. Look at Figures 1.7 and 1.8. To make one of the rooms smaller and move the south wall 3′-0″ (1m), you select the wall and drag it. The four walls perpendicular to and intersecting this wall adapt themselves, and the room area updates automatically. All you do is move the one wall. There is no need to create a complex series of selections; no need to use trim and extend tools, and no need to recompute room areas. Revit does all of this for you with a few mouse clicks.

Figure 1.7

The floor plan before the change

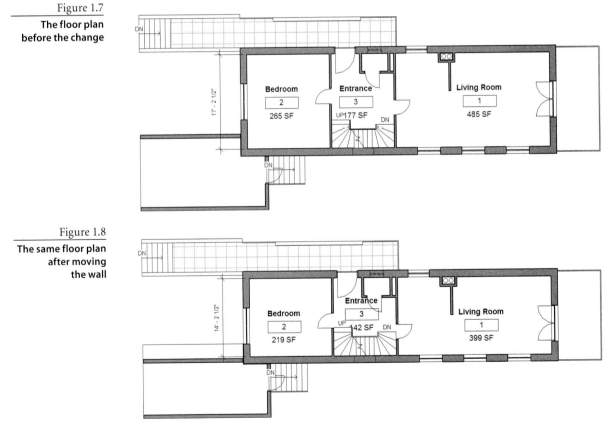

Figure 1.8

The same floor plan after moving the wall

If for some reason this automatic behavior is not to your liking—for example, when you are dealing with a renovation project and do not want to have existing conditions be affected by new construction—this is not a problem. Revit will not force you to do something you don't intend to: it allows you to break the "smart" relationships if needed by disallowing the joins between the walls. Hover the mouse over the end of a selected wall, right-click, and choose Disallow Join from the context menu. Only that one wall will be modified, and the others will not be affected.

You can also lock elements in place to prevent unintended consequences. You'll notice locks when aligning elements or selecting dimensions; these locks allow you to create hard constraints between elements in the model. For the most part, you'll find the default embedded behaviors make sense, and you'll not have to lock everything with explicit dimensions.

User-Defined Rules

During the design phase, you may want to maintain some dimensional rules and make sure these are not violated. Requirements like keeping the structural gridlines fixed (pin) or keeping a hallway a fixed width (lock) are some typical examples. You want to lock this rule down and keep it persistent as the design evolves. Such design rules are used all the time, but not many software applications let you capture this design intent and apply it in the model. For instance, you may want your door jamb always positioned 4″ (25cm) from the wall corner, or you may want three windows in a room to be always positioned at equal distances and the sill height for your windows to always be 4′-0″ (1.20m) above the floor. You want the rules and relationships to be remembered regardless of how many changes occur in the design process. Revit allows you to define and *lock* these relationships with *constraints*: explicit dimensional rules that keep elements locked to one another.

Types of Elements in Revit

Every parametric object in Revit is considered a *family*. In this section, we'll discuss how Revit organizes all these families and the data associated with them. Then we'll explain the available types of families, the principles of their behavior, how to create them, and where to find them. The categories are divided into two primary buckets: *model* categories and *annotation* categories.

How Revit Organizes Data

Revit organizes all the data in the model using building-industry–specific classifications. This system of organization manages relationships among classes of elements as well as their graphical display. At the top of this organization is a fixed list of categories into which all elements ultimately belong and a generic category to which unusual, nonstandard elements can be assigned. Every element you select in Revit belongs to one of these fixed categories.

Model Categories

Model categories include all physical object types typically found in buildings. All 3D families will use one of these categories, making them easy to schedule and control graphically. Also included are 2D elements that need to be represented in 3D views and that are used to add more detail to the model, such as floor patterns, ceiling hatch, and construction details. For elements that don't fit into the Revit categorization system, the generic model category can be used.

Annotation Categories

Annotation categories are all the annotations, symbols, text, and other 2D data added to a view to describe how the building is to be constructed. For example, all wall tags are members of the annotation category Wall Tags. Annotation categories also include 2D graphics overlaid on the model to convey additional information about the model. These annotations are view-specific and appear only in the view they were created in. The one exception to this rule is entities created in dependent views. Examples include dimensions, tags, callouts, section marks, and text notes.

To view all the model and annotation categories, select Settings → Object Styles. The table of categories is shown in Figure 1.9.

Figure 1.9

In the Object Styles dialog box, you set the graphics for all categories and subcategories in the project.

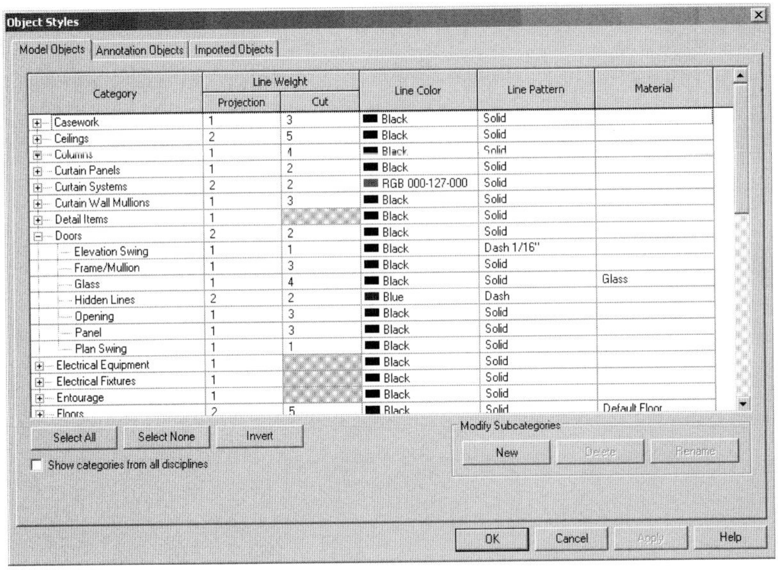

Annotation categories don't appear in 3D views.

Subcategories

Below each category can be many subcategories. Within the Door category you'll see subcategories for elevation swing, frame/mullion, glass, opening, panel swing, and other user-defined elements. You can add or remove subcategories when creating or editing families. The beauty of this system is that you can control the visibility and graphics of each subcategory independently. This allows you to use different line weights for different subcomponents of families. So, in our door example, you can independently control the graphics for the door leaf, frame, mullions, and glass. Figures 1.10 through 1.12 show how different subcomponents of a door can be turned on and off in a view.

Figure 1.10

A door family at fine level of detail

Figure 1.11

The same door with hardware not visible at medium level of detail

Controlling the Visibility of Elements in Revit

As you learned earlier in this chapter, there are no layers in Revit. You may be asking yourself, "Just a second! How will I live without layers? How will I control the visibility of what I want to present in different drawings at different scales?"

Let's look at the origin of layers. In the predigital era (and still, in some offices) projects were drawn manually on translucent paper called *trace*. Multiple layers of that trace paper were stacked and shuffled to create different representations of the same plan. Furniture might be drawn on one sheet of trace paper, mechanical systems on another, and so forth. In a paper-based workflow, to make a change you erased something on one sheet and redrew it on another.

CAD applications use layers as a digital version of trace paper to control the visibility of elements. These digital layers let you control the visibility of the elements representing your designs.

Instead of using layers, Revit uses object categories' view-specific settings to control how a drawing looks (see Figure 1.13). For example, instead of putting door handles on their own layer so they show only in high-scaled detailed views, Revit has commands to control the visibility of elements per view. If you don't want to show the fine-grain details of an element, such as door handles and hardware, you can change the level of detail for your view, as shown earlier in Figure 1.10 and Figure 1.11.

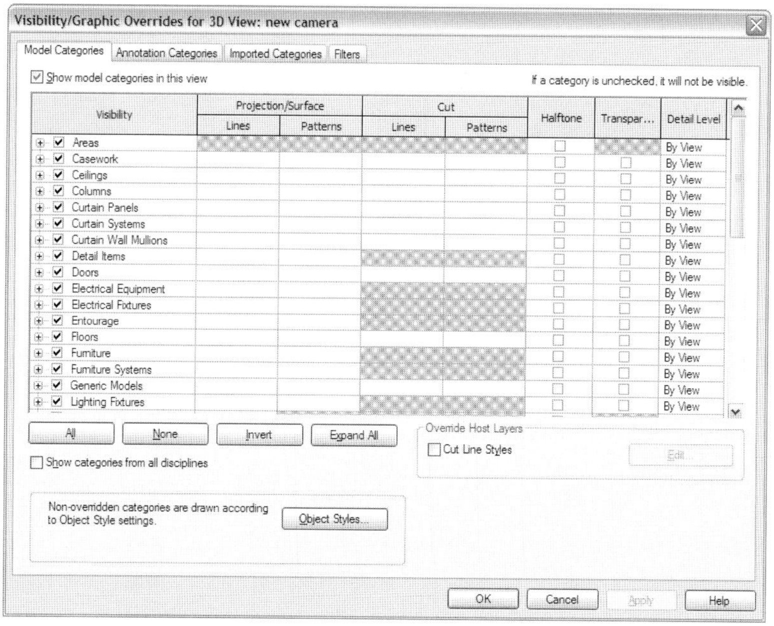

Figure 1.13

**The Visibility/
Graphic Overrides
dialog box lets you
control visibility
of categories on a
view-by-view basis.**

Families in Revit

Independently of whether it's a model or annotation category, a Revit family can be a *system family*, a *standard family*, or an *in-place family*.

System Families

Examples of system families are walls, roofs, stairs, railings, ramps, and mullions. To create such a family, you must be in the project environment (you will not be able to create system families in the Family Editor). To make additional types of these families, you need to duplicate an existing family of the same type and modify it. So to create a new wall type, for example, you must duplicate an existing wall, change its name, and then change the properties of the wall.

This method of duplicating a type to create new types is used frequently in Revit, so get used to this concept. While you cannot save a system family to a shared library as a standalone component, it is possible to transfer these families between projects. To reuse system families from one project to another, select File → Transfer Project Standards, then choose the category you want to transfer. We'll go into more detail about creating and using system families later in this book.

Standard Families

Standard families are created outside of the project environment—still in Revit, but in a specific environment called the Family Editor. Standard families have their own file format extension (.rfa) and can be stored or edited as separate files independent of a model and then loaded at any time into a project.

To see how Revit organizes standard families, choose File → Load from Library → Load Family. You'll see the folders in which these families are stored.

To create a new standard family, you can either duplicate an existing one in Windows Explorer and modify it in the Family Editor or create a new one in the Family Editor, using the family templates included with each copy of Revit. An important advantage to using Revit is that you are not required to know any programming or scripting language to create new smart, parametric families. This is an important advantage of Revit.

To open a template, choose File → New → Family. Embedded in each template are smart behavior characteristics of the family you're creating. Doors, windows, balusters, casework, columns, curtain wall panels, entourage, furniture, massing elements, generic objects, and plantings are all examples of standard Revit families.

In-Place Families

In-place families are custom objects that are specific to a certain context within the model. A complex sweep, such as a railing fence on a site, is an example of an in-place family. These families use the same functionality available in the Family Editor, but are made available in the context of a project file. Avoid making in-place families if you plan to reuse the family, or have multiple instances of it in the project.

Tips for Getting Started in Revit

Knowing how and where to begin your journey can be a challenge, and we want to give you a few pointers to help you get started. Although this list isn't complete by any means, it should help steer you in the right direction:

Begin with the end in your mind. When you begin any project, planning is always a good way to start. You can set yourself up for a successful implementation from the beginning by using a bit of forethought about your process, workflow, and desired outcome.

Get your project and office standards in place early. As design professionals, we have a tendency to develop unique graphic conventions and styles for our documents. This is a specific area where good planning leads to a good project. If possible, get your standards in place before you begin a project. Revit does an excellent job of getting you started with a good template of graphic standards to work with. However, if you're like most architects, an application right out of the box is never quite nice enough. Revit provides a good starting point for customization, and with some up-front time, you soon can have your project and office standards up and running. Once you nail down your standards, they can be easily applied to your project using Transfer Project Standards.

Remember that the first project you do in Revit is a change in methodology. You're leveraging technology to help you change the way you approach design and documentation. Don't expect the process to have the same workflow as it did in a CAD-based system. Try to stay flexible in your expectations and schedule and allow yourself time to adapt to the change.

Don't try to conquer the world on the first project. There are many advantages to using BIM as a design and documentation methodology. As this process becomes more mainstream within the industry, those benefits will only increase. All of these things and more are possible with the use of Revit, but it will take a couple of projects to get there. Tailor the use of BIM to the project, and use the features that will maximize the benefits of using BIM. Choose your goals realistically based on the expertise of your project team, and plan ahead so those goals can be met successful. Consider a project that is less complex for your initial pilot.

> One of the most important rules to follow as you begin your project is to model the building as it will be built, but keep in mind that you do not need to model every condition three-dimensionally. Use Revit to get the essential dimensions and building form coordinated. You can then embellish the model with 2D details to convey the fine grain.

Model correctly from the beginning. We can't stress this enough. As you refine your design, it's critical to model correctly right from the beginning so you don't have to fix things later. What does this mean? As an example, think of a wall. Does it sit on the floor, or does the floor attach to the wall? If you can begin to think about how your project will be assembled, it will save you a lot of time at the end. It's good practice to plan ahead, but remember that Revit will allow you to make major changes at any stage in the process and still maintain coordination. If you are still in early phase of design and do not know the exact wall type, use generic walls to capture your design intent; changing these later will be simple.

Get information into the project as soon as it is known. A key advantage of using Revit is the ability to change your project schedule. In a traditional design process, most of the effort on a project is realized during the construction-document phase. At that time, a typical project has the most staff working on the project, and it can be fairly difficult to implement major changes to the project design. This is due to the complexity of the documents by this time and the amount of effort for the team to redraw all the changed information. You'll find that with Revit, design change is largely managed by the software itself. This gives you a great deal of flexibility in both your design and documentation. Take advantage of this shift in the process, and add information to your model early. It can be in the form of more detailed content or showing the material construction of your wall system. Remember that you can change all this information much more quickly and easily than you ever could in CAD, so don't assume you're locked into the information you displayed early in the design process.

Plan for better communication among team members early in the process. Communication within a team is critical for understanding a project and documenting it successfully. One of the downfalls inherent in a CAD-based system is that there is no connection among the different files that make up the drawing set. This phenomenon carries through to the project team and is a function of project workflow and project management. In CAD, it's possible for team members to work in some degree of isolation. They aren't forced to immediately reconcile their changes with changes made by their teammates. Revit's single-file environment forces a much higher degree of team communication between not only the architects but also your structural and mechanical engineers.

Don't try to model everything. Most of us have drafted in a 2D environment until now. Moving to a 3D world is a significant change. Do you have to model every single screw? Every mullion? Every stud? That's a good question. The simple answer is no, you don't have to, and in fact you should not attempt to do so. Like any BIM system, Revit isn't 100 percent 3D information. Typical workstations aren't capable of handling all the data of a building in model form. Additionally, few projects have the time in their schedule to model the screws in a sheet of gypsum board or the sealant around all the windows; some of that information is best presented in 2D or in the specifications. This still leaves you with a wide range of options for modeling. In the beginning, err on the side of simplicity. It's far easier to add complexity to your model later on as you gain experience and confidence than it is to troubleshoot overconstrained parameters early in the process. Start with the big ideas: walls, openings, roofs, and so forth. Work your way down to a comfortable level of detail for both you and your computer.

Organize your team. A BIM project team includes three basic technical roles. These roles are interchangeable, especially on smaller projects with fewer team members. However small the team, it's useful to make sure all these roles are filled:

Building designer This is the person or team whose primary responsibility is to figure out what the project will look like and how it will be made. They create walls, floors, and roofs and locate windows, doors, and other building elements.

Content/family creator The family creator's primary role is to create the parametric content in the Revit model. This is typically someone with 3D experience who also has a firm understanding of Revit and Revit families. The families, as you'll see later, have parameters that can control visibility, size, color, proportion, and a number of other things.

Documenter This role supplies the bulk of the documentation. It consists of drafting some of the 2D line work over portions of the 3D model to show detail, adding annotations and keynotes, and creating details.

Ask for help. If you get stuck along the way, don't assume you're alone. There are myriad resources to help you find a specific solution to your problem. Chances are, someone has tried the same thing before. In our digital age, a wealth of information is available online; powerful communities of passionate users are out there willing to help. So before you spend hours trying to work through a particular problem on your own, try tapping some of the existing resources:

Revit Help menu Your first stop, if or when you get stuck, should be the Revit Help menu. It's one of the easier and more robust help menus out there, and it can give you a lot of useful information very quickly. It's also the most accessible help source. As with most applications, it's at the far right of the menu bar.

Subscription Support If you have bought Revit on subscription, Revit Subscription Support offers an exemplary web-based support system. Their responses are speedy, and their advice is top-notch. If you need information more quickly, Revit also has an online knowledge base of FAQs that is available without a subscription. Both of these resources can be accessed at www.autodesk.com/revit.

AUGI Autodesk User Group International (AUGI) is also an excellent source for tips and tricks. It's an online user community free to participate in, ask questions, get answers, and share families and examples. To get the benefit of this fantastic online resource, go to www.augi.com and look for Revit Architecture as a product. If you never logged in, you will have to registered once; from then on it's easy!

Revit City Looking for content and families? Revit City, another free online service, has a growing database of free families posted by other users. Its address is www.revitcity.com.

Autodesk Discussion Groups These pages offer insightful discussions and some great Q&A threads: http://discussion.autodesk.com/.

AECbytes A website dedicated to following and reporting on the trends in the AEC industry, with a strong focus on BIM, technology, and the direction of the industry—put together by Lachmi Khemlani: www.aecbytes.com.

Blogs Revit OpEd is a blog with some great information, useful links, and helpful tips and tricks. Put together by a longtime Revit guru, and fellow author, Steve Stafford: http://revitoped.blogspot.com/. And there are numerous blogs from passionate, experienced Revit aficionados such as these:

- www.allthingsbim.blogspot.com/ (James Vandezande)
- www.bimx.blogspot.com (Laura Handler)
- www.dorevit.blogspot.com
- www.greenrevit.blogspot.com

- `www.revitbeginners.blogspot.com` (Bradley Hartnagle)
- `www.revitcoaster.blogspot.com` (Troy Gates)
- `www.revitfamilies.blogspot.com` (Shaun Van Rooyen)
- `www.revit-alize.blogspot.com` (Bruce Gow)
- `www.revitrants.blogspot.com`
- `www.blog.reviteer.com` (Tom Dorner)
- `www.revitlution.blogspot.com` (Christopher Zoog)
- `www.revit-up.blogspot.com` (The PPI Group's Revit evangelist)
- `www.revitup.co.za` (Justin Taylor)
- `www.autodesk-revit.blogspot.com` (David Light)
- `www.auservice-bim.blogspot.com` (Simone Cappochin, Italian)
- `www.cmotion.net/products/revit-tools.html` (Siggi Pfundt and Gotthard Lanz, German and Italian)

CHAPTER 2

Getting Acquainted with the Revit Interface and File Types

In this chapter you'll become acquainted with the graphical user interface (GUI) of Revit Architecture. We explain terminology, menu arrangements, tools, views, common commands, and the basics to get you up and running. Topics we'll cover include:

- Overview of the Revit user interface
- Modifying and personalizing the interface
- Selection and view navigation
- Using keyboard shortcuts
- Setting up your project environment
- Revit file formats

Overview of the Revit User Interface

In this section we look at how Revit appears when first opened, out of the box, and familiarize you with how the interface is organized. We explore the use of some standard-looking toolbars and menus, as well as some features that are unique to Revit. One of the things you'll notice from the beginning is that Revit is tailored for the architectural design community. The tools, commands, and objects that you use in Revit are based on tasks and requirements taken directly from the practice of architecture.

> Throughout this book, when we say Revit we're referring to Revit Architecture. It's simpler this way!

Starting Revit

There are several ways to start Revit: by double-clicking the Revit icon that was automatically created on your desktop during installation, by going to `C:\Program Files\Revit Architecture 2009\Program` and double-clicking `Revit.exe`, or by double-clicking on any file with the `.rvt` extension.

The Basic Screen

When you start Revit, you see the screen shown in Figure 2.1.

Figure 2.1

Starting Revit

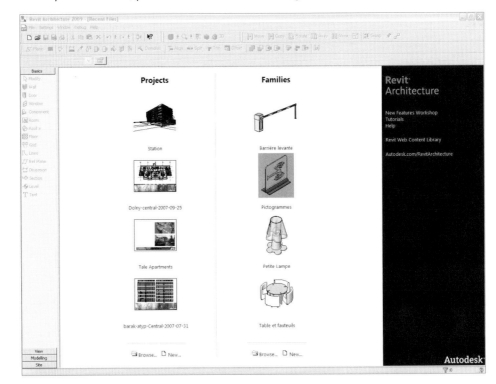

The start page is new to this release of Revit. In previous releases, when you opened a new session of Revit you always opened a default template, which would take unnecessary time and did not allow you to simply open a recent file. Starting with Revit 2009, instead of the opening a new project, Revit opens this new window that offers the following possibilities:

- Open a recent project (select one of the preview thumbnails)
- Open a recently created or modified family
- Create a new project (click the New button)
- Create a new family (click the New button)

Once you click New Project and select a starting template, a new Revit project opens; it looks like Figure 2.2. (There may be slight differences depending on which language version you have installed.)

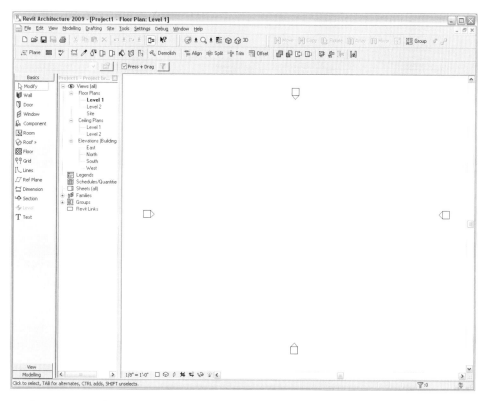

Figure 2.2

The Revit interface

The Revit interface is composed of multiple components:

Title bar This is displayed at the top of the entire Revit application frame, as in other Windows applications. In the title bar (Figure 2.3), you see the version of Revit that you're running as well as the name of the project that is currently active. If a single view is open in the main view window, the name of that view is displayed after the filename. If more than one view is open in the View window, the view name is not shown.

Figure 2.3
The title bar

Revit Architecture 2009 - [Project1 - Floor Plan: Level 1]

The title bar in Figure 2.2 indicates that Revit Architecture 2009 is running, the name of the open file is Project1, and the name of the active view is Floor Plan: Level 1.

Menu bar The menu bar (Figure 2.4) contains drop-down menus for all features and settings available in Revit. Many of the commonly used commands located in the menus are also accessible via toolbars and the Design bar (described shortly). However, some tools are exclusively accessible from these drop-down menus.

Figure 2.4

The menu bar

File   Edit   View   Modelling   Drafting   Site   Tools   Settings   Window   Help

Toolbars Revit provides toolbars with standard Windows tools (Save, Delete, New, Copy, etc.), as well as Revit-specific tools. The default toolbar settings used at startup (Figure 2.5) do not display all available tools. New to 2009, you will see a Content Search tool at the far right. This will take you to a new online content search tool developed by Autodesk. To hide or unhide tools, right-click an empty area in the toolbar. The context menu allows you toggle tools on and off.

Figure 2.5

Default toolbar settings

Type Selector The Type Selector (Figure 2.6) is a drop-down list of element types available in the project. The content of the list changes depending on the type of element that is selected or being created. For example, if you select the Wall tool from the Basic or Modeling tab of the Design bar, the Type Selector shows you a list of all available types of walls in your project. If you select a wall from within the project (the drawing area) you are working on, the Type Selector displays the type of that wall and again allows you to select a different wall type from the list. This works with just about any element you can select in Revit, and is an extremely powerful way to make easy and fast changes to the model.

Figure 2.6

The Type Selector

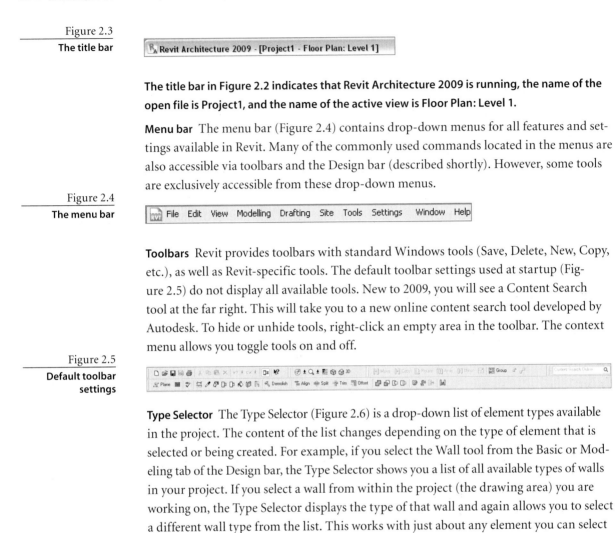

Properties button The Properties button ⬚ is located next to the Type Selector and becomes active when an element or tool is selected. Clicking this opens the Element Properties dialog box, where all instance and type parameters of selected elements are displayed and can be edited. You can also open this dialog box by right-clicking an element and selecting Element Properties from the context menu (Figure 2.7).

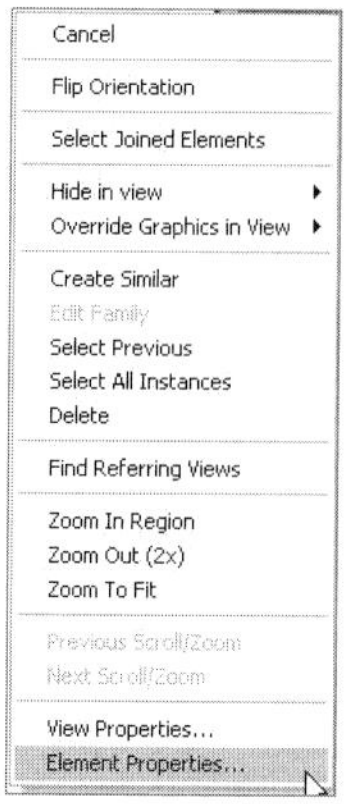

Options bar The Options bar changes depending on the type of element being created or selected and displays context-sensitive options relevant to that tool only. In Figure 2.8, you can see several states of the Options bar displayed when different elements or tools are being selected.

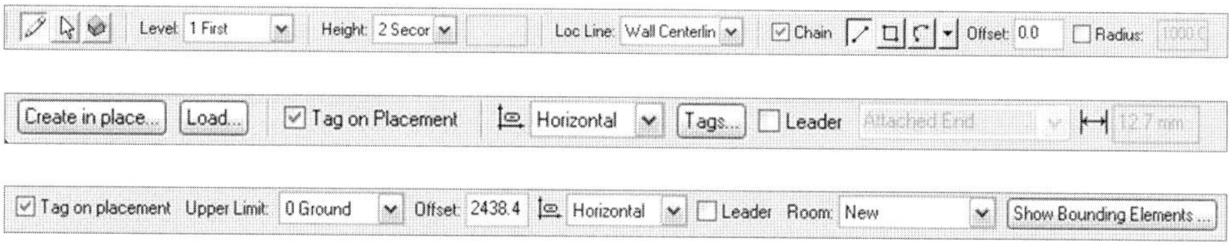

Figure 2.7

Context menu that appears when you right-click elements

Figure 2.8

The Options bar changes for (top) walls, (center) doors, and (bottom) rooms.

Status bar The status bar is located at the very bottom of the application window, on the far left. Here you will see helpful text that describes what you have selected and what you should do when in a command. Whenever you aren't sure what the next step should be, look at the status bar. See Figure 2.9 for a sample of the status bar in action.

New in Revit 2009 is the Count Selection tool. This is on the far right in the same zone as the status bar. The Count Selection tool gives information about the number of Revit elements currently selected.

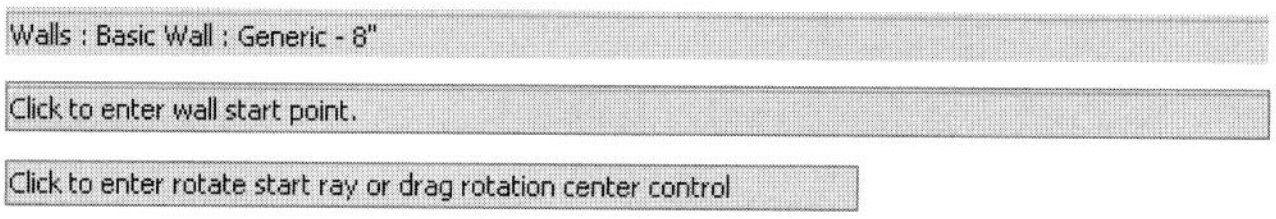

Double-clicking anywhere in the count box invokes the selection Filter dialog box, where you can narrow down a selection if needed. You can also access the Count Selection tool by directly invoking the Filter dialog box from the Options bar (Figure 2.10).

Next to the Count Selection tool is a symbol resembling a satellite dish. This is the link to the Communication Center. You will find more information about the Communication Center later in this chapter.

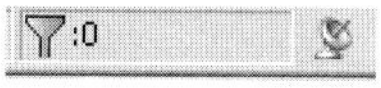

Design bar The Design bar (Figure 2.11) is a set of tabs containing tools related to common tasks that occur in a project. Some tools are repeated on multiple tabs because they're used in various tasks. The Dimension tool is an example: dimensions are used when you're modeling, drafting, and laying out structures.

Figure 2.9

The status bar when (top) selecting or hovering over a wall, (center) drawing a wall, and (bottom) using the Rotate command

Figure 2.10

At the far right on the status bar is the new Count Selection tool.

Figure 2.11

Design bar

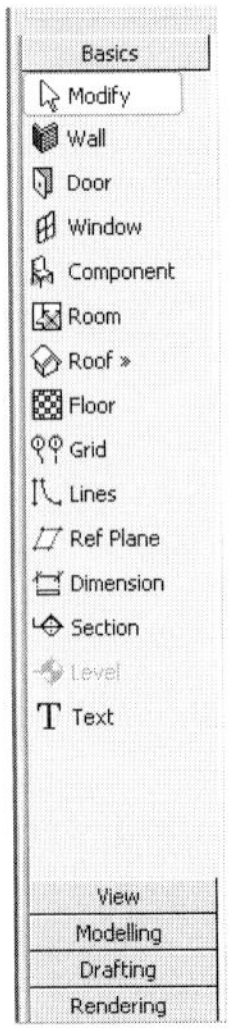

Figure 2.12

**Context menu
for a view**

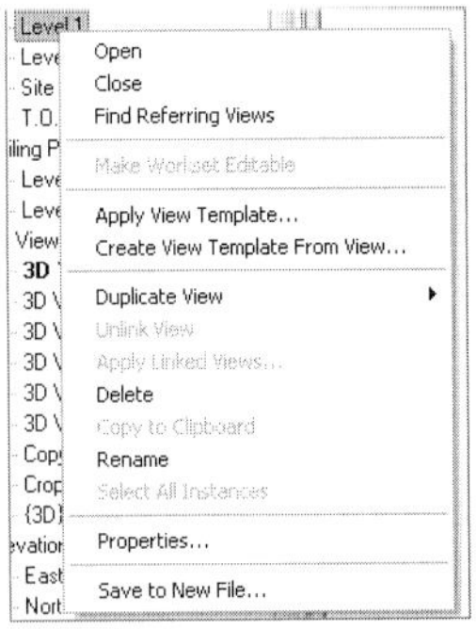

Figure 2.13

**Context menu for a
family**

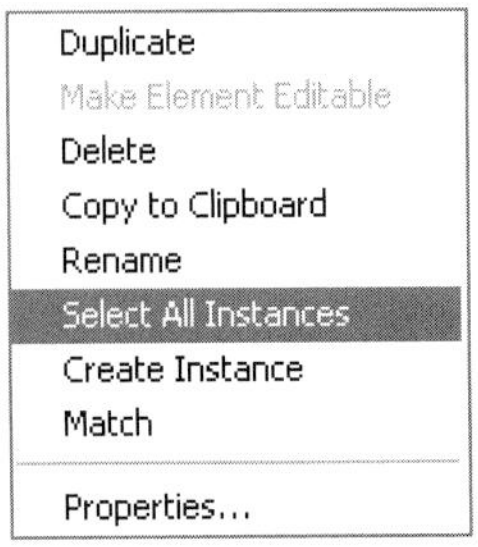

When you start Revit, by default only few of the tabs are visible (in the U.S. version, for example, only the Basics, View, Modeling, and Room and Area tabs are visible). But that's not all! There are many other tabs with tools that you can activate by clicking anywhere on an empty space on the Design bar and then right-clicking to bring up options for more tabs. On some smaller monitor resolutions (less than 1280×1024), it's possible you won't see all the tools available in a tab. To access those nondisplayed tools, click the More Tools flyout at the bottom of the tab.

Project Browser This is the heart and soul of the Revit user interface. From the Project Browser, you can navigate to all your views, create new views, access element properties, and place all forms of content in your project, ranging from linked Revit files to rendered images. Let's take a moment to explore the various parts of the Project Browser:

Views There are many types of views in which building information can be represented in Revit. These views are listed and organized in the Project Browser using a collapsible tree navigation framework. Types of views include plans, ceiling plans, sections, elevations, 3D views, animations, schedule tables, legends, and sheets. Once a view has been created, it can be duplicated to create a similar view and then modified to fit the requirements of different design deliverables. As an example, you can create a plan view of a first floor of a building with furniture layout and then duplicate it to make an electric layout plan. Every view allows you to control which elements will be visible and how will they will be visible. Elements also have additional view-related parameters, such as scale, name, and visibility and graphics settings. You can access these properties by right-clicking on the view name in the Project Browser (Figure 2.12) and selecting Properties from the context menu.

Families In the Project Browser, you can also see all the loaded families (library elements) in your project. *Loaded* means that they are a part of the project library, not necessarily that they have been used in the project. From here, you can drag and drop those families into the drawing area, query their properties, create new types of elements, and even select all instances of a given element in the model in order to perform wholesale changes. The right-click menu for families in the Project Browser (Figure 2.13) is different from that for views. Use the keyboard shortcut V-P for quick access to View Properties.

Revit links Revit links are other Revit projects that are referenced (linked) into your current project. If they are present in a project, they are listed in the Project Browser. From here you can reload, unload, open, copy, and visually identify the links in your project (Figure 2.14).

Using the Select All Instances command from the Families context menu in the Project Browser is a great way to instantly change all instances of a particular family from one type to another. For example, if you have placed a series of 2′ × 2′ (60 × 60cm) windows in your project and need to swap them with windows of another size or type, you can choose Select All Instances and choose a new size from the Type Selector. With that one click you will change all the instances throughout the entire model.

Navigating Through a Project

To open views listed in the Project Browser, double-click the name of the view you wish to open. The name of the open and active view is displayed in bold letters in the Project Browser. The Project Browser makes navigating through a project easy—all views are at your fingertips and organized into familiar categories. We'll discuss views in more detail in Chapter 3.

Figure 2.14

Links appear in the Project Browser.

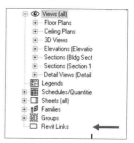

Organization of the Project Browser

The Project Browser ⬚ displays views in an organized tree structure that is predefined. The default organization shows views grouped by view type (plan views, ceiling plans, sections, and so on). Additional predefined organizations are also provided, and you can customize these to suit your specific needs. You can also create completely new view organizations in the Project Browser. When you click the Project Browser title bar, the Type Selector shows the list of all predefined organizational types (Figure 2.15). Try them out—swap from one to another to notice the different organizations of the project that they offer. To explore how these are set up or to make your own Project Browser organization, click the Properties button and check out the rules used to structure views.

View Window

The View window is the area where the model is generated graphically. It's where all the action takes place. The View window can show just one view, or it can be tiled in several windows to arrange as many views as you need when working on a project (as an example: you can split the view window into two windows—one showing a plan view and another showing a section view). One of the functions unique to Revit is that when you work in a window showing multiple views, whenever you modify or create an element in one view, all other views update concurrently, reflecting the change instantaneously and without any need for a manual refresh.

Figure 2.15

Using the Type Selector

Browser - Views : all
Browser - Views : all
Browser - Views : Discipline
Browser - Views : not on sheets
Browser - Views : Presentation Sheets
Browser - Views : Type/Discipline

GETTING ACQUAINTED WITH THE VIEW WINDOW

In this simple exercise, we are going to open a project file, open some common views, and then tile the views. When you select something, note how it gets selected in all views. This is a core concept when working in an integrated 3D model.

1. Open the file `Residence_Taurer_1.rvt` at the book's companion web page, `www.wiley.com/go/introducingrevit2009`.

2. Open the plan view (ground floor), section view, and 3D axonometric view.

3. Select Window Tile or press the keyboard shortcut WT.

4. Select a wall—notice how it turns red (indicating selection) in all open views.

    The View window shows three views: plan view (ground floor), section view, and a 3D axonometric view. Revit allows you to open and work in as many views as needed for clarity of the task. You can also simultaneously view changes taking place as the model is edited.

Figure 2.16 shows three open views that have been cascaded, stacking one view behind another. The Cascade Views function is another way to display multiple views simultaneously. You will find the Cascade tool under the Window menu or via the keyboard shortcut WC.

Figure 2.16

Cascaded views

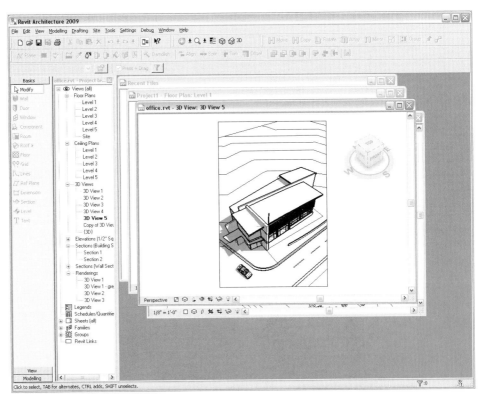

It's quite usual to open many views when working. So, how do you return to a single view window once you have opened and tiled several? To see just one view again, select the view and maximize it the way you would any window, using the control at the top right of the View window. Doing this, however, does not close all other views that were open—they are still open in the background and affect the performance of Revit. To make sure all open views are closed in the background, choose Window → Close Hidden Windows.

Notice that when you are working in multiple views, one of the title bars of the tiled views is blue. This denotes this view as the active one. Any activity that you do (such as draw, modify, or delete) takes place in the active view (Figure 2.17). The name of the active view is displayed in the Project Browser in bold letters.

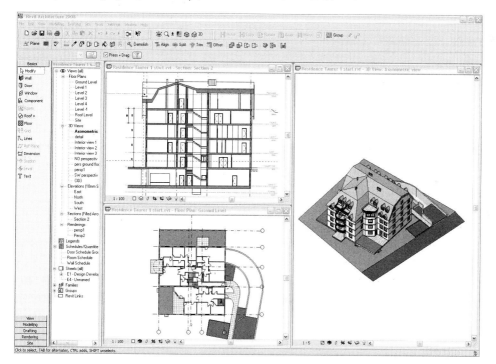

Figure 2.17

Tiled views

While Revit allows you to open and work in as many views as you wish, you will need to be prudent about how you use this capability: having too many open views can affect Revit's overall performance (speed). The relationship between the number of views you can open and your performance will depend on the speed of your computer and the amount of RAM it has.

Communication Center

You're familiar with the Communication Center 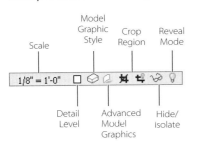 if you've used applications such as AutoCAD. When connected to the Internet, the Communication Center delivers information and announcements about new software updates, product support information, tips and tricks, and industry news. You can access and activate the Communication Center by clicking the satellite-dish icon at the bottom right of the Revit window.

View Control Bar

A view in Revit can be represented in many different scales, levels of detail, and model graphic styles. Shadows can be turned on and off; crop regions can be used to limit what portion of the model you wish to be visible; and the view can also hide elements and categories of elements. The View Control bar (Figure 2.18) contains shortcuts to many of the tools you'll use most often; the following sections look at some of these tools.

Figure 2.18

The View Control bar

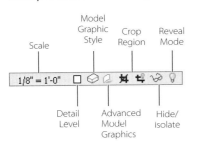

SCALE

The first tool indicates the scale in which the drawing will be printed. Clicking the Scale tool gives you a standard set of scales to choose from. The scale of the view determines how big your drawing will be when printed and also creates a visual relationship between annotations and the model. Annotations are always shown in paper size, and the model adjusts its graphics according to the view scale. Put simply, a plan view at ¼″ = 1′-0″ (1:50) will be twice as large as a plan view at ⅛″ = 1′-0″ (1:100) when printed, but in each view the text notes will be the same size.

In Revit you can create your own custom scales. Revit 2009 features some neat improvements that add new qualities to this functionality. To create your own custom scale, click the Scale button (the first one) on the View bar. In the drop-down menu, select Custom. A new Custom Scale dialog box opens (Figure 2.19). You can create your custom scale and assign a specific name to it. The name you give to the custom scale appears on the View Control bar, view title, or title block. If you do not give a specific name to the custom scale you create, then the numeric value of the scale is displayed.

Figure 2.19

Custom scale options

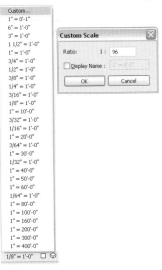

THIN LINE MODE

By default Revit displays real line weights of the model. Sometimes, though, this can make it hard to read the model, especially when working in high scales and zooming close to a detail. In such cases, for visual clarity, you can use the Thin Line mode tool ⊞ , which lets you see all lines drawn a single pixel wide.

Once active, this feature affects all views. As the following graphic demonstrates, when selected, Thin Line mode displays all lines as being a single pixel wide, regardless of view scale. When this tool is deselected, the line thickness corresponds to the thickness you have assigned to the elements and shows how the drawings will look when printed.

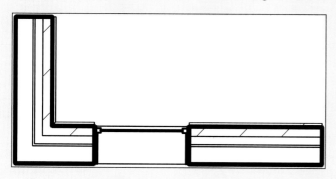

Note that this command affects only how Revit appears in the screen views and not how Revit prints. Thin Line mode is located in the View toolbar because it affects all views, not just the active view.

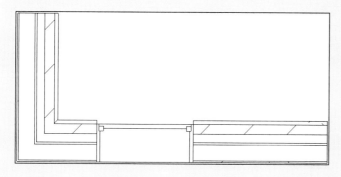

While we are talking about line thickness display, we should also mention a change introduced in Revit 2009. The following types of graphics are now drawn independently of any zoom scale:

- Reference Planes
- Workplane grids

- Snap lines

- Alignments

- Selection bounding box

- Group boundaries

- Measure tool lines

These lines are drawn with a consistent screen-based line style.

DETAIL LEVEL

This icon indicates the level of detail assigned to the view. There are three levels of detail in Revit, as illustrated in Figure 2.20, which can be used to show more or less information and detail in a view: Coarse, Medium, and Fine.

Depending on the type of drawing and where in the process your project is, you can use the level-of-detail options to expose more or less information in your documents. At 1″ = 50′ (1:600 scale, for example, you may represent a wall as a solid fill, regardless of the number of layers in the wall construction. At ¼″ = 1′-0″ (1:50), you probably want to show the different layers of the wall assembly. The same applies to a door or window. A door is represented with different levels of abstraction depending on the scale. Figure 2.21 illustrates a standard door shown in three levels of detail.

Figure 2.20

Detail level in the View Control bar

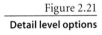

Figure 2.21

Detail level options

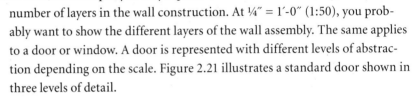

Coarse

Medium

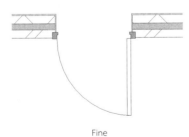

Fine

When using a computer-aided design (CAD) system, you use separate blocks for each of these symbolic representations. In the case of a door, you would have to create three different symbols that are drawn in different levels of detail. In 2D CAD, you would also need separate symbols for the section and elevation of a door. In Revit, the door is modeled once and can be designed so that it can show itself in meaningful representations for different scales as well as view types. The trick is that it's always the same object—it's just showing different levels of information about itself.

MODEL GRAPHIC STYLE

You may already be acquainted with this type of graphic display from using other design applications. The options shown in Figure 2.22 allow you to display the model in one of four modes: Wireframe, Hidden Line, Shading, and Shading with Edges. These are demonstrated in Figure 2.23.

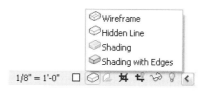

Figure 2.22

Model graphic style in the View Control bar

Figure 2.23

Model graphic styles demonstrated

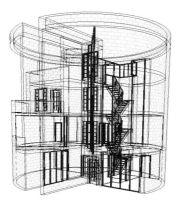

Wireframe

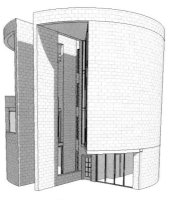

Hidden Line

Shading

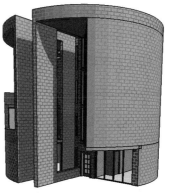

Shading with Edges

PROJECT COURTESY OF PAUL WODDY

ADVANCED MODEL GRAPHICS

Advanced Model Graphics is a set of view options that let you control shadow and silhouette settings. Here you can fine-tune the sun angle, time of day, intensity, and other variables. The settings shown in Figure 2.24 let you add graphic embellishments, such as brightness of the sun, contrast of the shadows, and the style of the silhouette outlines:

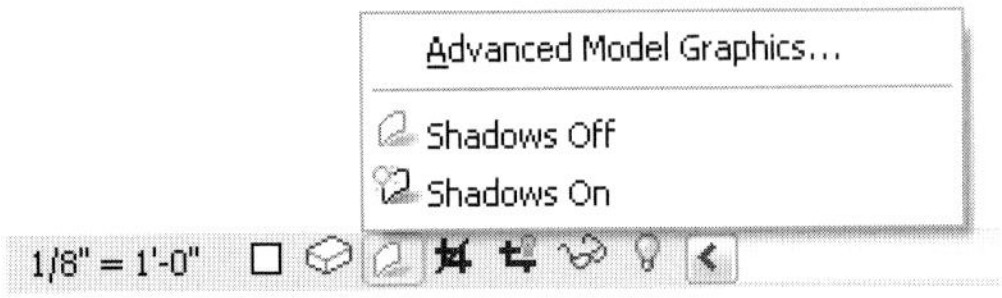

Figure 2.24

Advanced Model
Graphics in the View
Control bar

Shadows and sun Shadows can be turned on or off using the button from the View bar. The location of the sun can be relative to your model (summer solstice) or relative to the view (sun from top right, for example). Using the Sun and Shadows settings in the Advanced Model Graphics Settings dialog box shown in Figure 2.25, you can create accurate sun-angle studies by locating the model on the earth and dialing in various times and dates. The controls become available from the Advanced Model Graphics Settings dialog box whenever the Cast Shadows option is selected. You'll learn how to create sun studies in Chapter 8. Some examples of sun studies are shown in Figure 2.26.

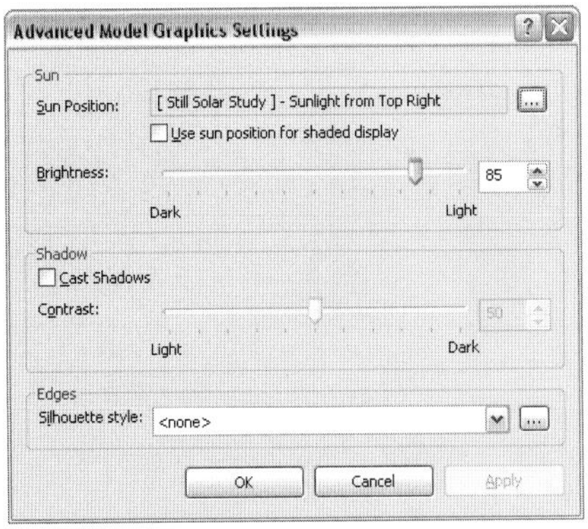

Figure 2.25

Advanced Model
Graphics Settings
dialog box

Silhouette edges Creating silhouette effects can give a nice artistic touch to your perspective or axonometric views, as shown in Figure 2.27. Silhouette edges can be applied only to the Hidden Line and Shading with Edges graphic styles.

> **USE CAUTION WITH SHADOWS**
>
> When you're working on bigger projects, shadows can affect performance significantly. Try to keep this feature turned off while you work, and activate it only when you need to validate your design or print the documents.

Figure 2.26

Sun studies

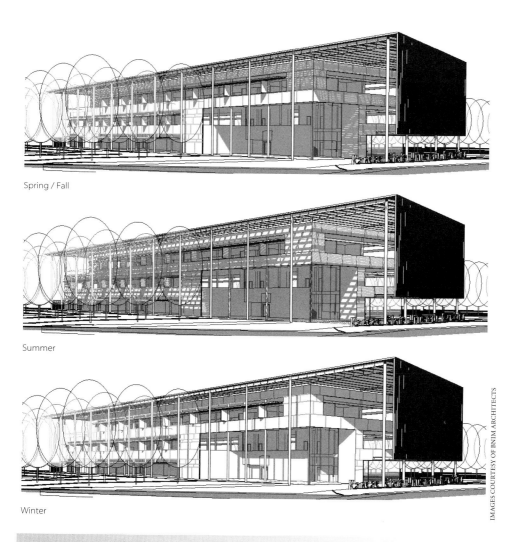

Spring / Fall

Summer

Winter

> When creating a silhouette edge, you can use any line style as a silhouette edge style—those offered by Revit as well as custom-created lines. Should you wish to emphasize some corners more than others, you can additionally use the Linework tool and override different lines with stronger or weaker line types as a final touch on the final image.

CROP REGION

The Crop Region tool allows you to limit what part of the model is visible. To better understand it, imagine that you have a piece of paper in which you have cut a rectangular hole and you are viewing the model through that hole. Crop region can be applied to all interactive views. The boundary of the region can be visible or invisible depending

Figure 2.27

Shadow view with silhouette edges

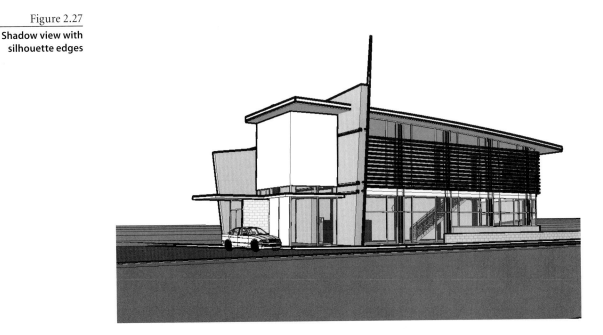

on how the view was generated: when making sections and callout views, a crop region is automatically visible by default in those views; plan views, on the other hand, do not show their crop regions by default. The Crop Region tool is accessible from the View Control bar, as shown in Figure 2.28. Some examples of the Crop Region are shown in Figure 2.29.

The Crop View toggle makes the Crop Region active and it crops the view; Do Not Crop View keeps the crop boundary but it does *not* crop anything. (This is useful for the

Figure 2.28

Crop Region options in the View Control bar

dependent views, which we will cover later).

You can toggle the visibility of the crop region (its boundary) using the Show/Don't Show Crop button. You'll notice a boundary around your model when the region is visible. You can change the size of this boundary by selecting it and dragging it with the blue arrows. The crop region can also be activated through View → Properties and is applicable in both 2D and 3D views.

HIDE AND ISOLATE

Hiding and isolating elements is a useful way to work with a model when it starts to get more complex. These tools will help you isolate problems, and get clutter out of the way when working.

Temporary hide and isolate The Hide/Isolate tool in the View Control bar allows you to temporarily change the visibility of elements in a view. Please note the meaning of the word *temporarily*: it indicates that the changes following the activation of this functionality are visible on screen but will not save nor print. This temporary mode is useful in visually cluttered situations when you want to isolate an object in order to work undistracted and freely with it, or when you need to view a portion of the model without the presence of certain elements. This feature allows you to change the visibility of a view independent of object types.

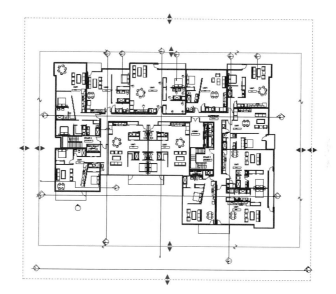

Figure 2.29

Crop region examples

To hide or isolate an element or an entire category of elements, first select the elements and choose among the options under the eyeglasses icon 👓. Figure 2.30 shows the different options available with the Hide/Isolate tool. Keep the following in mind:

- Isolating an element isolates only the selected element in that view.
- Hiding an element hides only the selected element in that view.
- Isolate Category isolates the entire category in that view.
- Hide Category hides the entire category in that view.

Once you've hidden an element, the eyeglasses icon turns cyan and a cyan border is drawn around the view, both indicating that something is temporarily hidden in this view. To reset the view to the normal state, select Reset Temporary Hide/Isolate. The temporary hide or isolate state is applied to *one* view only and is instantly lost when you press Esc, change a view, or reopen a project. The state isn't saved and is not printable.

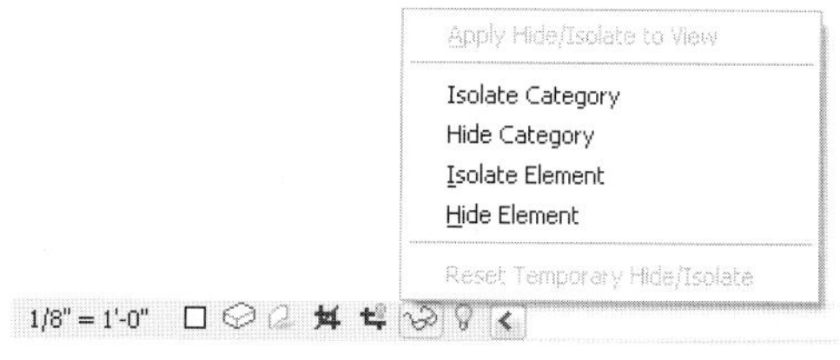

Figure 2.30

Hide/Isolate options in the View Control bar

Apply Hide/Isolate to View

Isolate Category
Hide Category
Isolate Element
Hide Element

Reset Temporary Hide/Isolate

1/8" = 1'-0"

TOOLS FOR CONTROLLING THE DISPLAY OF ANNOTATIONS IN A CROPPED VIEW

Note the difference between the two dialog boxes shown here. The first one is the View Properties dialog box of a 2D view; the second is for a 3D view. Some tools are specific to certain type of views. Let's review them.

Parameter	Value
Title on Sheet	
Referencing Sheet	
Referencing Detail	
Default View Template	None
Extents	
Crop View	
Crop Region Visible	
Annotation Crop	
View Range	Edit...
Associated Level	Level 1
Scope Box	None
Phasing	
Phase Filter	Show All
Phase	New Construction

Parameter	Value
Identity Data	
View Name	{3D}
Dependency	Independent
Title on Sheet	
Default View Template	None
Documentation Category	Construction Documentation
Extents	
Crop View	
Crop Region Visible	
Annotation Crop	
Far Clip Active	
Section Box	
Camera	
Render Scene	None
Render Image Size	Edit...

Extended view properties

ANNOTATION CROP

If you need to show only a portion of a floor plan that contains text, dimensions, and key-notes and use the Crop tool, it will crop the model elements but not the annotations. The Annotation Crop option makes the crop region aware of annotations as well as the model

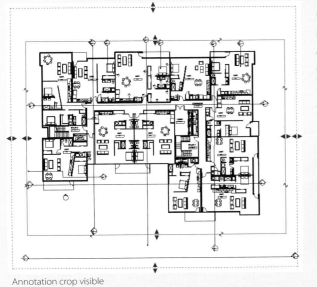

and lets you crop them with an additional crop region. The Annotation Crop option is turned off by default. Select View Properties to enable it. This creates a second crop region in the same view. Note that the model and annotation crop are separately controlled, and you can change their extents using the blue arrows when the border of the crop is activated. This is shown by the outer dashed box. It is important to know that the annotation crop can never be smaller than the model crop. The offset between the annotation crop and model crop can be preset by selecting the crop region and clicking the Size button in the Options bar. This opens the Crop Region Size dialog box, where you can present the offset for the annotation crop.

Annotation crop visible

The Apply Hide/Isolate to View option allows you to convert a temporarily hidden or isolated element into a permanently hidden element in the active view that saves and prints.

Permanent hide/isolate The permanent Hide/Isolate tools allows for elements to be hidden in a view that can be saved and printed.

There are two ways to permanently hide or isolate elements:

1. Convert a temporarily hidden or isolated element in a view to a permanent state using the Apply Hide/Isolate button.

2. Select an element in the drawing area, right-click, select Hide in View from the context menu, and choose Element or Category from the menu (shown in Figure 2.31).

Figure 2.31

Hide/Isolate context menu options

> Both the temporary and the permanent Hide and Isolate tools affect the current view only.

REVEAL MODE

When you're working in a team, some members of a team may hide certain elements in a view and leave them hidden when they leave the view. To make sure you can quickly assess what is going on and have an instant view of all the information you should, use the Reveal Mode tool. This tool offers a special way to display the view: after activating the Reveal mode, the model will be represented as halftone, and hidden elements or categories are shown in a bold magenta color that pops out and indicates what has been hidden.

In this mode, the temporarily hidden elements and categories (if any) are represented with cyan and the permanently hidden elements are with magenta, as shown in Figure 2.32. To indicate that you're in a Reveal mode, the drawing window has a magenta line around the drawing area. The light bulb icon 🔍 is changed as well.

Figure 2.32

Reveal mode options in the View Control bar

Figure 2.33 shows a sample plan and the same plan with Reveal mode turned on. Unlike when using temporarily hidden elements, Reveal mode allows you to add elements or categories to or remove them from the permanently hidden mode. To do this, select any element (regardless of its state), right-click, and select Hide or Unhide from the context menu. You can also use the Options bar to unhide elements or categories.

CONTROLLING THE EXTENT OF A 3D VIEW: SECTION BOX

For 3D views, an additional cropping feature is available that allows you to crop the model with a 3D clipping box. This option, named Section Box, cuts through your model like a cake, vertically and horizontally, and is available in both axonometric and perspective (camera) views. This tool is effective for creating perspective sections that are highly informative, creative, and appealing, showing what's going on in your model, or for isolating in 3D a portion of the model that you wish to indicate a detail solution for. To enable the Section Box tool, use the check box option in View Properties. If you orient the 3D view to another view (View → Orient → To Other View), a section box will be turned on and automatically initialized.

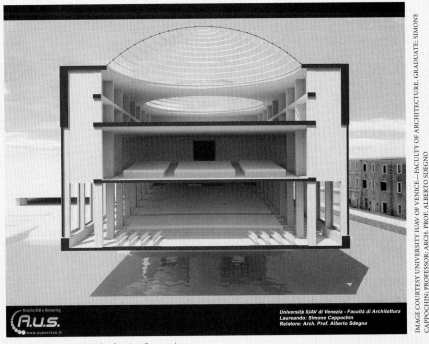

IMAGE COURTESY UNIVERSITY IUAV OF VENICE—FACULTY OF ARCHITECTURE. GRADUATE: SIMONE CAPPOCHIN; PROFESSOR: ARCH. PROF. ALBERTO SDEGNO

A rendered view using the Section Box tool

TOOLTIPS

When you hover over an element in the view, Revit helps you identify that object with a tooltip. You can read the name of the object and the type of family to which it belongs. The same information is also displayed in the status bar.

Tooltip

Consistent with Microsoft conventions, tooltips also appear when hovering over any button in the UI, helping new users to identify what the button is used for.

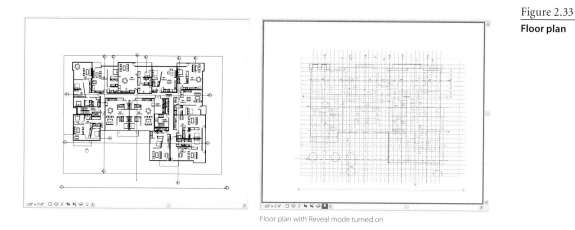

Figure 2.33

Floor plan

Floor plan with Reveal mode turned on

Modifying and Personalizing the Interface

If you expected to be able to modify the interface and move around or create your own toolbars in Revit, you may be disappointed. Revit doesn't allow you to customize the interface *ad infinitum*. Here are some of the allowed modifications available:

Button display Right-clicking any of the toolbar icons drops down a list where you can choose to turn text labels on or off. When turned on, some of the toolbar icons display an image and text; when off, only an icon with image is displayed. See Figure 2.34 for clarification.

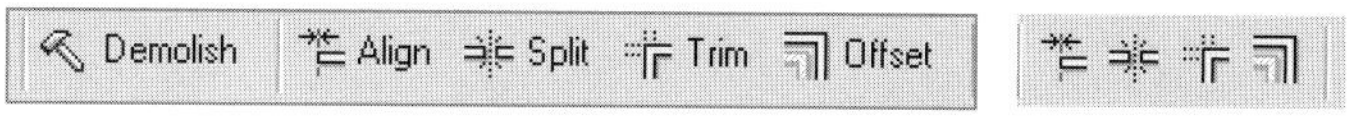

Figure 2.34

Button display with text turned on and off

Project Browser The Project Browser can be undocked and moved around on the screen (Figure 2.35). To do this, grab it by clicking in the title bar of the Project Browser and dragging it to the desired place. After its position is modified, if you close and then reopen Revit, the Project Browser defaults back to its standard position. If for some reason you don't see the Project Browser, this is because it has been turned off. To turn on the Project Browser, use the icon in the Standard toolbar.

You can also close the Project Browser by clicking the X in the upper-right corner. To open it again, click the Browser icon in the toolbar (Figure 2.36); the Project Browser will reappear at its standard position at the right of the Design toolbar.

Keyboard shortcuts (accelerators) Computer users like using keyboard shortcuts to speed up common commands and minimize the need to interrupt workflow. When you open any of the menus in the menu bar, the keyboard shortcut is indicated to the right of each tool name (Figure 2.37). Revit contains preset keyboard shortcuts when installed, but

Figure 2.35
**Undocking the Proj-
ect Browser**

Figure 2.36
**Project Browser
undocked**

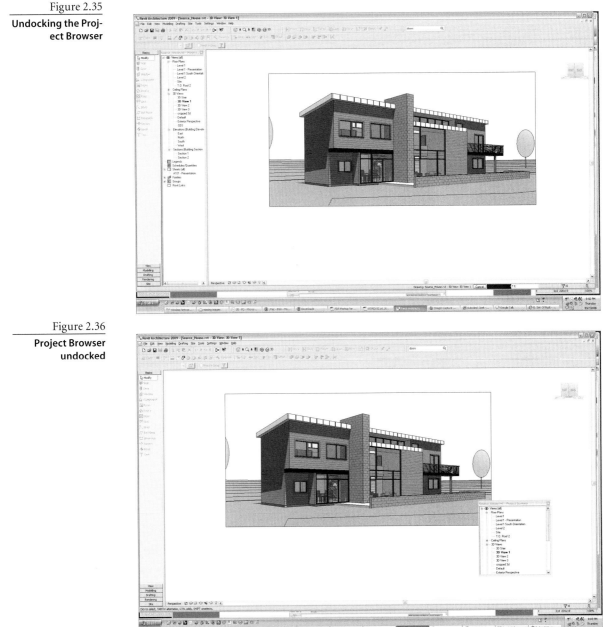

you can modify the default shortcuts by editing the keyboard.txt file located in the C:\
Program Files\Revit Architecture 2009\Program folder. Be aware that Revit's shortcuts are
two-key shortcuts and are available only for commands that already
exist in the user interface. As you change the shortcuts in the
keyboard.txt file, Revit also changes the abbreviations shown in
the menus.

Figure 2.37

**Keyboard shortcuts
indicated**

Wall	WA
Door	DR
Window	WN
Column	

EXERCISE: OPENING VIEWS

To get a feel for how to use the Project Browser, follow these few simple steps:

1. Open Botta.rvt from the Chapter 2 folder on the book's companion web page.

   You'll see a 3D axonometric view of the project you're viewing, as in the one shown here:

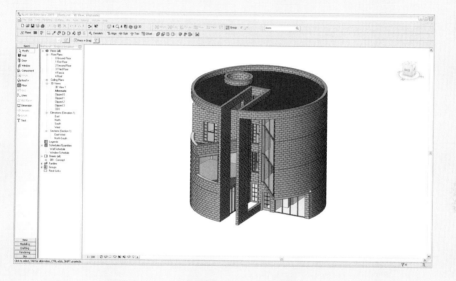

2. To see the plan views, double-click 0-Ground Floor in the Project Browser. The 0-Ground
   Floor name is now displayed in bold, indicating that it is the active view in the project.

3. Following the same logic, double-click 1 First Floor and 4 Roof Floor or any of the 3D views
   or elevations. Double-click the Wall Schedule to open a schedule view of all walls in the
   project. Or double-click the Sheet List to view the sheets prepared to be printed and sent
   out to the owner.

   In Revit, all the documents you just opened are called views, and they show different representations of information from the underlying database of this building. You'll learn how to create and
   manage different views, and many other things about the Project Browser, in Chapter 3.

4. Close the file without saving.

Selection and View Navigation

Now that you are familiar with the interface, it's important to understand what common tools you will use when working with Revit.

Using the Mouse

Figure 2.38

Windows mouse
with a scroll wheel

Although using the mouse cursor may seem like a fairly basic function of any software, Revit has some built-in functionality that lets you take full advantage of the graphical interface. Revit was built around the use of a Windows mouse like that shown in Figure 2.38. Additional options include some keyboard and mouse routines to allow you to maximize workflow.

Left Mouse Button

To select an object, use the left mouse button 🖰 . This button also allows you to specify a starting point when drawing an element, navigate through the user interface, and select different tools.

Right Mouse Button

Figure 2.39

A context menu
with view-specific
information and
options

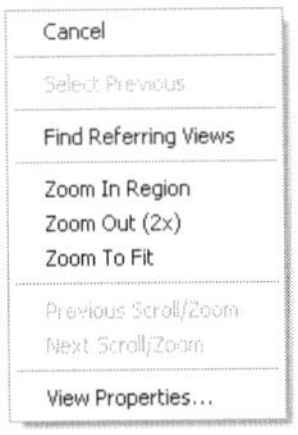

Cancel
Select Previous
Find Referring Views
Zoom In Region
Zoom Out (2x)
Zoom To Fit
Previous Scroll/Zoom
Next Scroll/Zoom
View Properties...

Right-clicking 🖰 an object opens a context menu with various additional tools specific to the selected object.

Anywhere in the free space of the View window, right-clicking opens a menu specific to the navigation of the particular view (Figure 2.39). Note the View Properties option. This is something you'll use regularly, and we'll go into more detail about its specific functions later.

Zooming, Panning, and Scrolling in a View

Mouse Scroll Wheel

The scroll wheel 🖰 can be rolled, held while moving the mouse, or used with modifier keys to alter your view:

Zoom Scrolling the mouse wheel while in a view invokes the Zoom command so you can zoom in and zoom out, depending on the scrolling direction. Pressing the wheel while holding down the key (Ctrl+mouse wheel) also invokes Zoom but with a slightly smaller zoom factor.

Pan Moving the mouse while pressing and holding the mouse wheel invokes the Pan command.

Spin When in a 3D axonometric view, holding the Shift key with the mouse wheel pressed allows you to spin the entire model. When an element is selected, the model spins around that element.

These last three functionalities (Zoom, Pan, and Spin) are also available in the newly introduced SteeringWheel and ViewCube tools, which we cover next.

SteeringWheels

A three-button scroll mouse is recommended for effective use and navigation in Revit, but you can achieve all of the needed behaviors with a two-button mouse as well. We will explain that and all navigation possibilities in this section.

Let us first take a look at the SteeringWheels: you can access the wheels from the toolbar ⊙ ⬙ ⬙ ⬙ ⬙ ⬙ 3D .

Upon selection, the SteeringWheel appears on the screen; it follows (travels with) the mouse to provide quick access to the navigation tools in the context of the work you do. When placed in 2D view, the wheel looks as shown in Figure 2.40 and offers three functionalities.

> For users accustomed to previous versions of Revit, note that there are some changes in the viewing terminology.

Figure 2.40

SteeringWheel tool in 2D view allows for zoom, pan, and rewind.

ZOOM

The Zoom option in the SteeringWheel has the following behavior:

- When used in a 3D context, Zoom dollies the camera in and out.
- When used in a 2D context, Zoom moves up and down, perpendicular to the view.

PAN

- Panning the view has several meanings: When used in a 3D context, Pan dollies the camera left and right.
- When used in a 2D context, Pan means one of two things:
  - When using the 2D SteeringWheel in any 2D view, Pan means *scroll*.
  - When in a sheet view with an active 2D view, Pan allows you to scroll the sheet view on the sheet.

REWIND

The Rewind History stack is view specific and is persistent for each view throughout the session, until the file is closed. It is a practical tool that allows you to go back to a previous camera state quickly. Figure 2.41 shows the Rewind tool in process.

Figure 2.41

Rewind allows a one-click access to different previous camera states of the model.

Here are general guidelines for all SteeringWheels:

1. Click on different regions of the SteeringWheel, keep the left button pressed, and move the mouse to navigate in the view.

2. Click the arrow or right-click the Navigation Wheel to access the context menu.

Navigation in 3D views

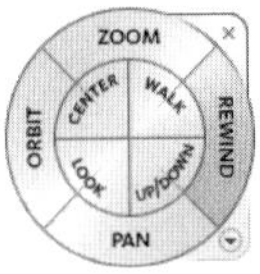

The SteeringWheel in 3D view looks slightly different, as shown on Figure 2.42.

You will find additional tools in this wheel:

Orbit Replaces the old Spin command.

Look Replaces the old Turn command.

Walk Click and hold the left mouse button on this tool and start moving the mouse in a direction you wish to walk through the model. Using Ctrl+> and Ctrl+< lets you increase or decrease walk speed in Walk mode.

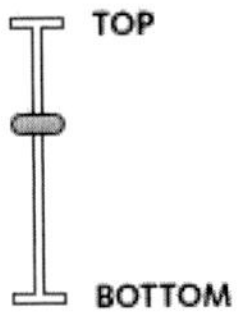

Center Lets you define a pivot point around which all other movements will be oriented.

Top Down Click and drag this tool; it initiates a slider (Figure 2.43) that, when moved up or down, moves the view of the model in those directions.

When starting the SteeringWheels in a 3D view for a first time, you will be offered a SteeringWheels wizard that teaches you interactively all the possibilities of the tools. The wizard considers whether you are an experienced 3D user or new to 3D and teaches you accordingly. We strongly recommend that you try out all the options: 1,000 words will not be enough to explain what this interactive wizard will help you learn (Figure 2.44).

Figure 2.42

SteeringWheel tool in Rewind

Figure 2.43

Use the on-screen controls to move camera.

Figure 2.44

Use the Try Me buttons to get familiar with SteeringWheels controls.

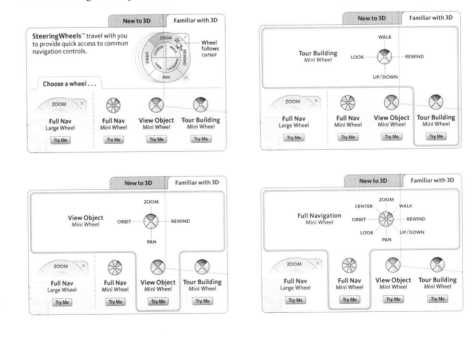

Before you continue, try this behavior on any of the sample files you've used up to now. Open a 3D view, and using the mouse and keyboard combinations or the SteeringWheels, familiarize yourself with the navigation commands. You'll use them frequently throughout the model and documentation process.

You will notice that the SteeringWheel will also be present in the preview window of the Element Properties dialog box of any element in Revit (Figure 2.45).

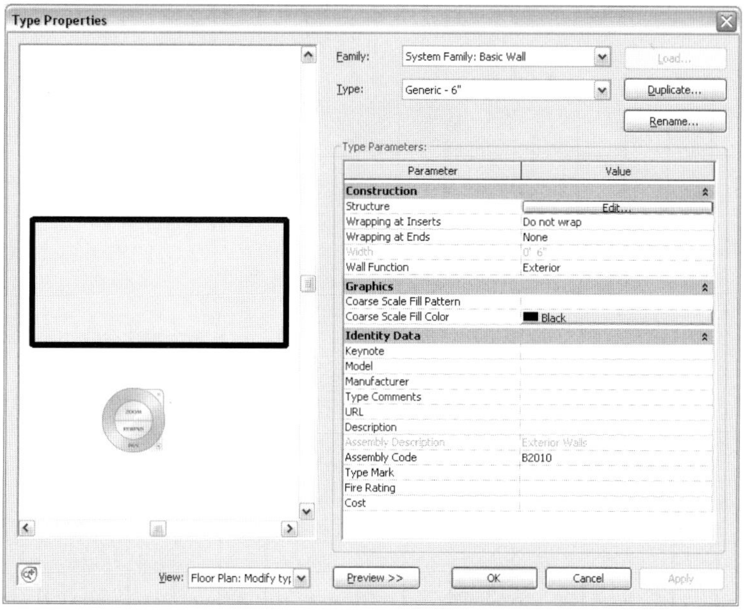

Figure 2.45

SteeringWheel tool in the preview window

ViewCube

For even easier navigation in 3D views, there is another new navigation tool in Revit 2009: the ViewCube (Figure 2.46).

The ViewCube allows for intuitive and easy navigation through 3D views. It appears in the top-right corner of all 3D views, both in Revit and the Family Editor.

To use the ViewCube, click its icon to orient the view to a direction of your choice. To rotate the view, drag the ViewCube in one direction. The right-click menu of the View-Cube will let you reset the Home camera, reset the Front direction, lock to the current selection, and orient the current view to an existing view or a predefined standard direction. Right-click the ViewCube and click Properties to set the ViewCube properties. Figure 2.47 shows an example of the ViewCube reorienting a 3D view to Top.

Figure 2.46

ViewCube tool

Figure 2.47

**A 3D view oriented
to Top using the
ViewCube**

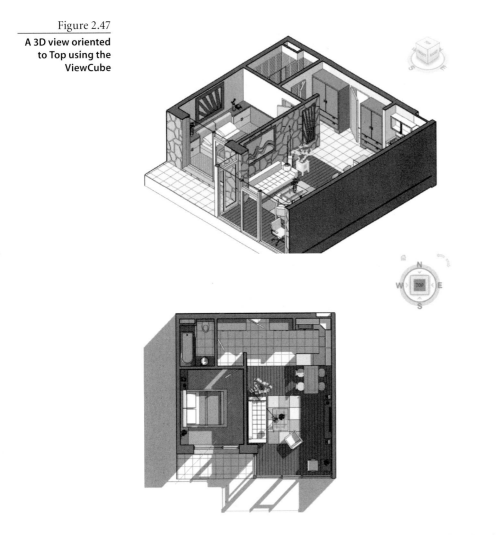

Using the ViewCube you can with one click orient any 3D view into a Top view or Elevation view, as shown in Figure 2.48.

Try this out! You will be surprised at the ease of use and the speed with which you can access specific views of your model.

Selecting Objects

To select an individual element, click on it. To select multiple elements, several options are available. The easiest way to select multiple elements is with a selection window. Depending on the direction that you drag the mouse, you can select different elements. If you are an AutoCAD user, this will be very familiar.

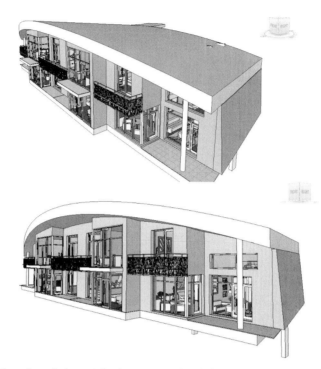

Figure 2.48

The ViewCube in perspective view—dragging the corners of the View-Cube you can easily orient the view in a direction of your choice.

Dragging a selection window from left to right (Figure 2.49), while holding down the left mouse button, results in the selection of only those elements that are entirely within in the selection window.

Figure 2.49

Left-to-right window selection

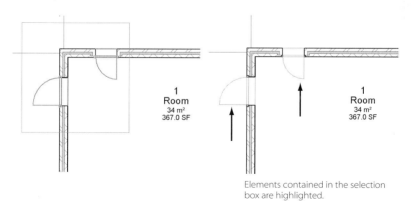

Elements contained in the selection box are highlighted.

Dragging the selection window from right to left (Figure 2.50) results in the selection of elements that intersect or are entirely within the selection window. Note that enabling the option Press + Drag in the Options bar lets you drag an element when you hold down the left mouse button while dragging. If you find that you accidentally drag an element when creating a window selection, deselect this option to avoid dragging elements.

Figure 2.50

Right-to-left window selection

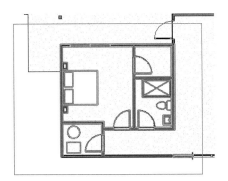

Figure 2.50

Right-to-left window selection

To be more specific about what you want to select, you can select all elements of a particular type by using the right-click menu when an element is selected. Choose Select All Instances from the menu, and all elements in the model of that type will become selected. You can then make changes, delete all the elements, or swap the element with a new type.

You can also limit selection to categories by using the Filter tool, located in the Options bar. Once you've selected some elements, click the Filter button, which opens a dialog box that shows the selected categories. To deselect categories, uncheck them.

Manipulating Objects

Many elements can be edited directly in the view using graphical controls. Let's take a look at these.

Grip Editing

Figure 2.51

Dragging a grip enables a preview of the movement's outcome.

Many elements display blue grips when selected that allow you to modify their size or location. Selecting and dragging the grip provides a preview (like the one in Figure 2.51) of the final outcome prior to completing the drag operation.

For walls and lines, blue-filled grips are displayed at the ends of selected element in plan view, and along the ends, bottoms, and tops of selected walls in Elevation and 3D views, where they're labeled as shape handles. You can click and drag these controls to resize an element, as shown in Figure 2.52.

The blue grips also have additional functionality. With walls, by right-clicking and accessing the context menu, you can control the wall joins (the way the walls connect) by using the grips to disallow joins between two walls. By default, the walls join automatically, but this behavior may be undesirable in some conditions (see Figure 2.53).

> You can right-click the wall-end controls and use the context menu to allow or disallow wall joins. Once a wall end join is disallowed, an icon shows up when that wall is selected, indicating that the end is disallowed. Clicking that icon reestablishes the join.

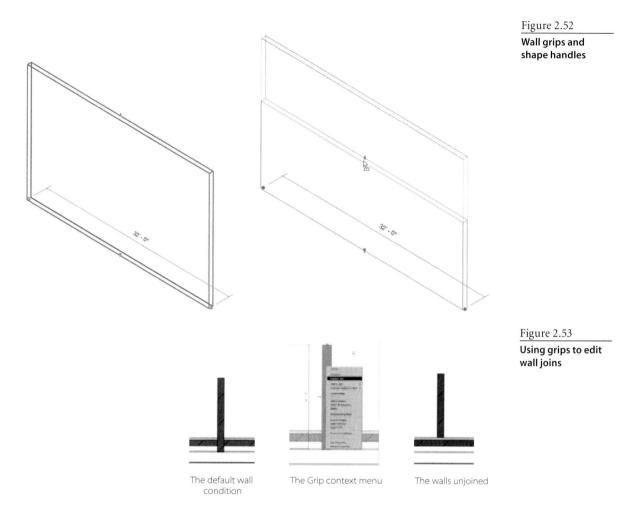

Figure 2.52

Wall grips and shape handles

Figure 2.53

Using grips to edit wall joins

The default wall condition	The Grip context menu	The walls unjoined

Figure 2.54

Wall grip when multiple walls are selected

When a chain of walls or lines is selected (Figure 2.54), drag controls are displayed at the coincident endpoints; you can drag these to change the layout of the chain. Touching walls are selected at the same time, and the filled blue grip turns into an empty blue grip. Dragging this grip drags both walls at the same time, as shown in Figure 2.55.

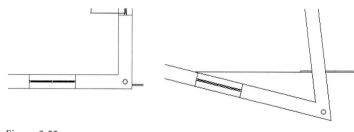

Figure 2.55

Manipulating multiple walls using the grips

Move

Each object, when selected, can be moved without invoking the Move command in the toolbars. When you move your mouse close to the element, a set of crosshairs appears. By clicking and holding the left mouse button, you can dynamically move the element selected.

Smart Constraints

Revit has many embedded help tools to make your life easier when creating or editing objects. One of these is the dashed blue line shown in Figure 2.57. This line displays each time a movement is constrained to a plane, as with walls and lines in plan views.

Figure 2.56

Manipulating the wall constrained to a plane

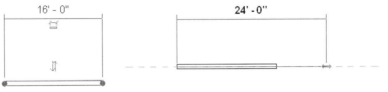

The line helps you maintain the same plane of the wall when extending it, without the necessity of holding down the Shift key or using any other auxiliary tool.

A similar dashed line helps you place a new element, similar to an adjacent one, by taking a reference from the nearby element. Figure 2.57 shows how placing new level lines in section or elevation references the start or end of an existing level line.

Figure 2.57

Referencing similar elements

When you're drawing or editing elements, Revit lets you orient them with respect to other elements without changing coordinate systems. This is a neat advantage of Revit.

If you want to draw a wall parallel to another that is already drawn, Revit recognizes the angle of that wall and offers it as a constraint. This lets you draw the second element, keeping it parallel to the first wall during its creation (see Figure 2.58).

Figure 2.58

A new element is constrained when created near a similar one.

Using the spacebar also helps you orient elements during creation or while editing them. During placement, pressing the spacebar lets you rotate elements at 90-degree intervals. However, if you mouse over a nonorthogonal reference (such as the wall in Figure 2.59), the spacebar starts rotating the element, adding the angle for reference. For example, a bed placed next to a nonorthogonal wall can be quickly oriented to the angle of the wall. Just imagine how cool this is after all the trouble you may have had in the past defining locations!

Figure 2.59

Use the spacebar to rotate elements during placement.

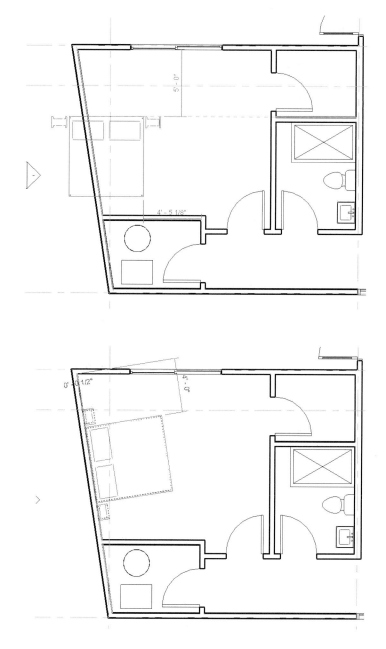

Flip Controls

You click a flip control ⇕ to change the orientation of an element. Flip controls are shown by two opposing blue arrows. For example, when you flip a wall, you reverse the order of its component layers. Figure 2.60 demonstrates how to use a flip control.

Figure 2.60

Editing a wall using a flip control

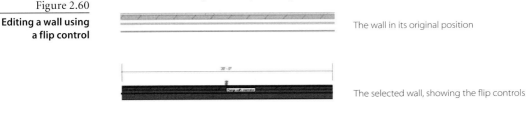

The wall in its original position

The selected wall, showing the flip controls

The finished wall, modified

Figure 2.61

Door flip controls

Swinging doors have two flip controls: Flip Facing (which controls whether the door swings in or out) and Flip Hand (which controls whether the door swings right or left, as shown in Figure 2.61).

The flip control applies not only during creation of an element but also when an element is edited later. Note that flip controls are displayed only when applicable: they don't appear for items that don't need to be flipped (a table, for example).

Manipulating Objects Using Dimensions

In Revit, dimensions are much more than static forms of documentation. They can be used to interactively adjust the model at any time. Temporary dimensions are displayed each time an object is selected, inserted, or edited. Revit allows you to type a value in the temporary dimension string that determines the position or size of an object. Permanent dimensions work the same way: you can edit the location of elements directly by changing dimensional values.

A wall 32′ (10m) long displays a 32′ (10m) temporary dimension. However, if you enter a 20′ (6m) dimension, the wall becomes 20′ (6m) long (see Figure 2.62).

New Revit users are sometimes confused about which elements change or move when you use temporary dimensions. When you use temporary dimensions to change distances between elements, the selected element moves. If you select the wall on the right in Figure 2.63 and type a value in the temporary dimension area, the wall at the right moves, not the left one.

It works the same way for levels. If you need to modify the height between levels, select the level you wish to move, and modify the temporary dimension. Regardless of whether you're changing the upper dimension or the lower dimension, in each case Level 2 is modified, as shown in Figure 2.64.

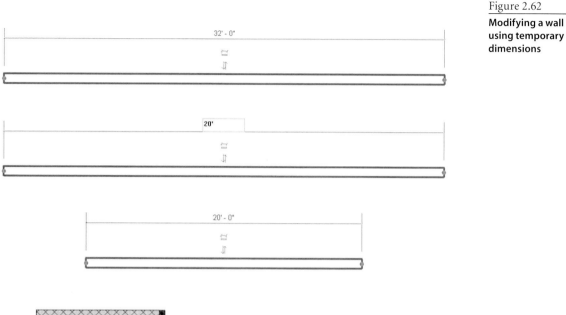

Figure 2.62

**Modifying a wall
using temporary
dimensions**

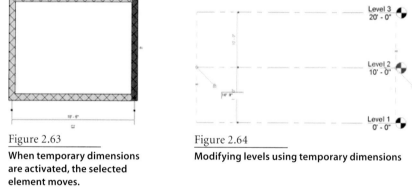

Figure 2.63

**When temporary dimensions
are activated, the selected
element moves.**

Figure 2.64

Modifying levels using temporary dimensions

Padlocks

Revit is one of the rare architectural authoring applications that allow you to embed
your design intent in the form of locks and constraints that persist until you consciously
remove them. Here are a few examples:

- You can tell a door to be a certain distance from a wall so it fits a closet and lock
  that relationship so that when you move the wall or the door, that relationship is
  maintained.

- You can space windows equidistant along an exterior wall so that even if you change
  the length of the façade, the windows keep their positions relative to the wall's length.

- You can keep an exterior wall attached to the roof so that if you change the height of
  the roof, the walls also move, reflecting that change.

In the example in Figure 2.65, the door is constrained to a 1′-4″ (40cm) distance from the wall to accommodate a cupboard. To constrain a distance, you set it by placing a dimension, selecting the dimension, and locking it with the Padlock command. After having locked the door to the wall (Figure 2.66) at a distance of 1′-4″ (40cm), if you move the wall in the drawing, the door will always move with it, retaining the locked distance.

Figure 2.65

Temporary dimensions at a closet door

Figure 2.66

Locking the door location

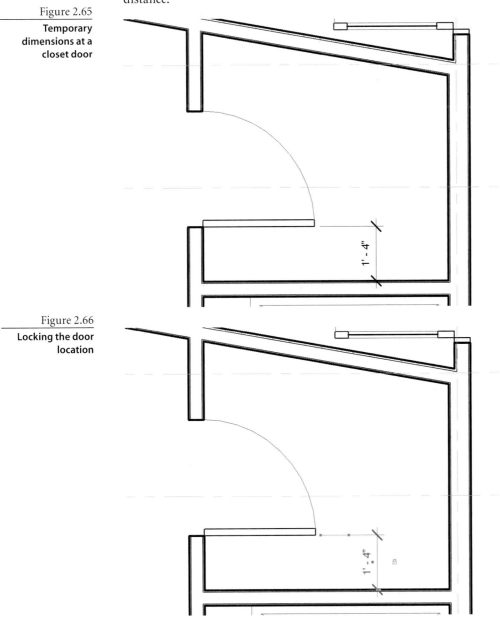

Keeping Objects from Moving—the Pin

The Pin tool is another way to set a constraint for an element. In this case, the element is constrained not with respect to another element in the model but geospatially. You can pin your grid system so it doesn't move from its location or pin elements from an existing building so they aren't mistakenly modified while you're working on new additions. You'll find the Pin command 📌 in the editing toolbar.

Pin also appears in element types like the predefined curtain walls shown in Figure 2.67. By default, the pins exist here because there are embedded rules in a type-based curtain wall that you don't want to inadvertently change. If, however, you consciously decide to change the type or a distance (like the space between the mullions), you can unlock the pin at any time by clicking it. This undoes the constraint and allows you to freely change the element from now on. Locked and unlocked pins in a curtain wall are shown in Figure 2.68.

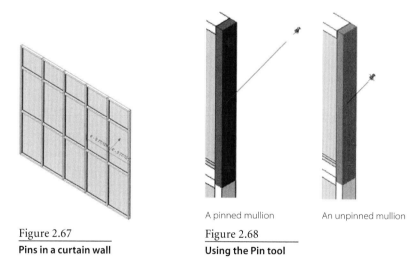

A pinned mullion   An unpinned mullion

Figure 2.67   Figure 2.68

Pins in a curtain wall   **Using the Pin tool**

Moving with Nearby Elements

Another type of constraint is designed for logical relationships between elements. When furnishing a space, you probably want to align the bed or dresser with a wall. If you change your design, you want the furniture to follow the wall to the new location. For this purpose, Revit has a command called Move with Nearby Elements. When you select a furniture element, like the bed in Figure 2.69, this option appears in the Options bar. It lets you check a box to move the associated elements. By selecting this option, you create an invisible relationship between the bed and the wall so that each time you move the wall, the bed moves with it.

Figure 2.69

**Moving an element
with nearby
elements**

Using Instance Parameters to Change Size

When elements appear with editable drag controls, these are considered *instance parameters*. This means you can modify the geometry on an instance-by-instance bases rather than change the definition of a type and have all occurrences of the type in the model update at once. Many elements in Revit are driven by type parameters, but this doesn't restrict making and using content that is more flexible and driven only at the individual instance level.

This type of instance-level behavior may be desirable for windows and doors. Once a window or door is placed in a wall, there seems to be no way to change its size aside from opening the properties of that object and changing type parameters. When you select a window, blue grip controls do not appear as they do when you select walls. You might wonder: why can I not drag windows and doors to be any width and height I want? Essentially, the dimensions of windows and doors are defined as type parameters by default, and Revit does not let you manipulate these dimensions on a per-instance basis. This is done intentionally, because you typically want to use a standard range of door sizes and keep this information stable and predictable. Nonetheless, it is possible to create windows and doors that vary in size and shape on a per-instance basis. Remember that Revit makes some assumptions about desired behavior, but in most cases it lets you move beyond the typical and not be hindered.

Should you want the ability to change the dimensions of windows and doors with direct editing (using the blue grips), you must change the parameters for width and height from *type parameters* to *instance parameters*. This can be done in the Family Editor with a few clicks. Note that this method of working takes away the advantage of having all windows and doors changed at once via a single parameter change. You also need to be careful not to create any odd custom sizes unintentionally. Figure 2.70 shows an example of a window as a type and an instance.

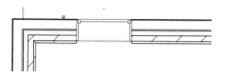

A window as a type parameter

A window as an instance parameter has arrows to dynamically modify its size

Figure 2.70

Type and instance parameters

Using Keyboard Shortcuts

Out of the box, Revit automates a variety of common commands using preset keyboard shortcuts:

Tab The Tab key is similar to the Cycle command you may know from AutoCAD. It allows you to cycle through various elements near the cursor when more than one is present. In Revit this can happen frequently, so get used to using this key. The Tab key is useful when you're dimensioning because it allows you to cycle through various references of the elements dimensioned (dimension to wall center instead of wall face; opening of a door instead of outer frame; and so on). The Tab key is also used to select chains of connected lines and walls.

Shift+Tab This shortcut reverses the default order in which the Tab command cycles.

Ctrl The Ctrl key is used to add multiple objects to a selection at the same time.

Ctrl+Tab This keyboard shortcut will cycle though open views. Use this to quickly move from view to view.

Shift Unlike Microsoft conventions, which use the Ctrl key to deselect, Revit uses the Shift key to deselect an element.

Some elements in Revit are constrained to move horizontally or vertically only. Revit gives you visual clues indicating which way a selected element can move. You can remove this constraint by holding the Shift key while repositioning the element. At the same time, some elements can move in any direction by default, but holding the Shift key while moving them constrains their direction. For example, you can move a window freely in any direction in an Elevation or a 3D view, but holding down the Shift key constrains the movement of the window so that it moves only horizontally. Likewise, you can normally move walls, lines, or gridlines freely in any direction, but the Shift key lets you constrain their movement to directions perpendicular to the wall or line.

Delete The Delete key is used to delete selected elements from the model. You can also use the Backspace key to delete elements.

Undo and Redo Commands can be undone and restored using Ctrl+Z (undo) and Ctrl+Y (redo). These shortcuts are standard in many Windows applications.

Multiple undo operations (Figure 2.71) can also be performed from the toolbar using the list of recent commands. Dragging the mouse down this list undoes all selected commands in one step.

Figure 2.71

Multiple undo

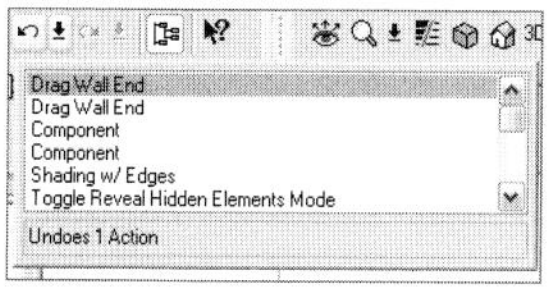

Spacebar The spacebar is mostly used to cycle through rotation of an element during or after placement. For instance, when you set a door in a wall, you can use the spacebar to cycle through choices, including having the door open into or out of the room, and having it open from the left or right. The spacebar is also used to identify the direction in which walls will be placed and to edit their position after placement.

F1 This is a quick way to call the Help function. (Revit's embedded help menus are getting better with each release!)

Setting Up Your Project Environment

Now that you have an initial idea about the user interface and the tools available, let's look at how to predefine some settings in Revit. Many definitions and global settings are stored under the Settings menu. We'll cover some of the more important settings in this section.

Project Units

Revit has its default units fairly well defined; however, local standards or various projects may ask for different ways of documenting length, area, and other measurements. In the Settings → Project Units dialog box (Figure 2.72), you can set the measurement units, rounding convention (number of decimals), and suffixes for length, area, volume, and angle. You can also define the way you measure slopes—in rise or angle degrees—as well as the symbol used for the decimal division (point or comma).

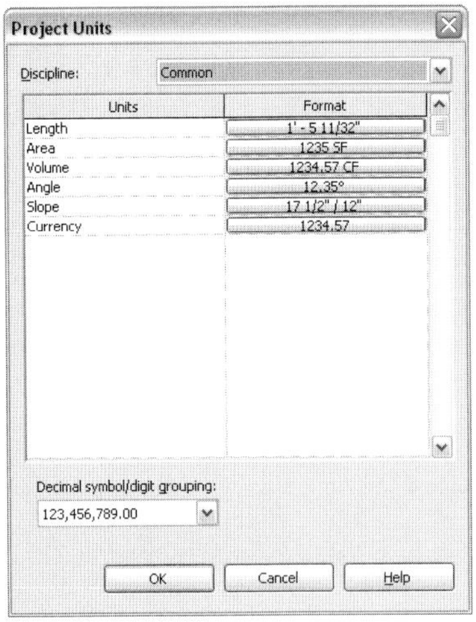

Figure 2.72

The Project Units dialog box

As a rule, you should define all your units prior to starting a project, but if necessary, you can change any of them on the fly later in the development of the project.

Slope

Various settings for slope have been added in Revit 2009 as a tab, Format, in the Project Units dialog box. You can control units, rounding, and digit grouping, as shown in Figure 2.73.

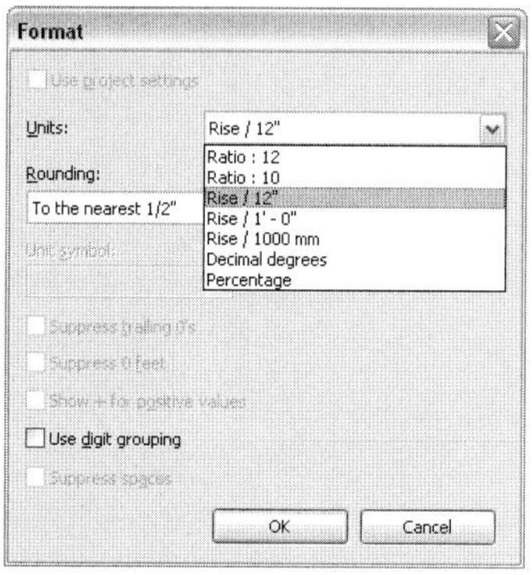

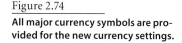

Figure 2.73

Slope settings in the Project Units dialog box

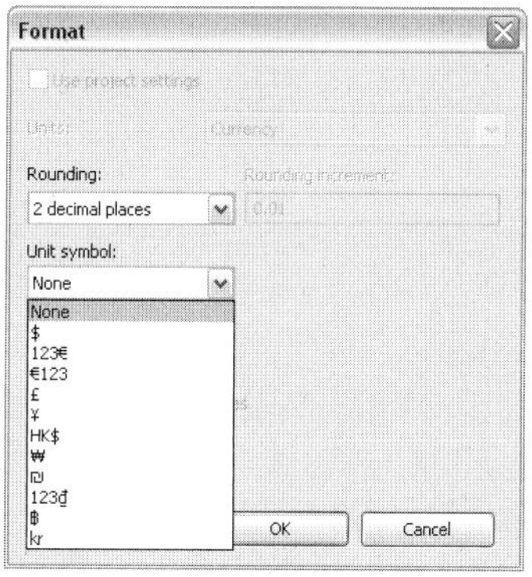

Figure 2.74

All major currency symbols are provided for the new currency settings.

Ratio, rise, decimal degrees, and percentage are the available options for units.

Currency

Setting currency is a new option in the Revit 2009. When making schedules, architects often have the need to add currency information when calculating cost, and this improvement accommodates that need. Currency formatting allows you to format costs using common currency symbols.

In the Format dialog box you can choose any of the 10-plus major worldwide currencies, suppress trailing zeros,), and decide to use grouping that replaces decimal symbol setting (comma separators in 1,234,567).

You will access the same settings when you make a cost schedule and access the Field Format under the Format tab of the schedule (Figure 2.74).

Additional Formatting

Suppressing zeros is often desired, for example: if the value of the cost is 2756.400, checking the suppressing trailing zeros will result in 2756.4. For drawings, you can suppress spaces—for example, in the value 1′ - 2″, the result is 1′-2″.

Digit grouping options set the separator, the decimal symbol, and how many digits to group by.

By default, Revit inputs and displays in feet (U.S. customary) or millimeters (metric). To change the input value to something you may be more familiar with, under Settings → Project Units, choose Length, and change the setting to fractional inches. Click OK. Next, choose the Dimension tool, and open the Properties dialog box. Click Edit → New. Then, choose Units → Format. Deselect the Use Project Settings option, and change the units to read Feet and Fractional Inches from the drop-down list at the top.

Snaps

Snaps are a great help for precise placement and modification of elements. In Revit, you can define snaps by choosing Settings → Snaps. In the resulting dialog box, you can turn the snaps on or off globally, set a variety of snap types, and specify the angular and length increments at which the system will snap. For the most part, these settings are adequate. Although they aren't represented in this dialog box (Figure 2.75), different graphics and tooltips for each snap type appear in the view when you're drawing.

In Revit 2009, a Snap Overrides submenu has been added in the context menu during creation of elements. Right-click when drawing a wall, and you can override any of the project definitions for Snap by choosing Snap Overrides and selecting the option you need. See Figure 2.76.

Figure 2.75

The Snaps dialog box

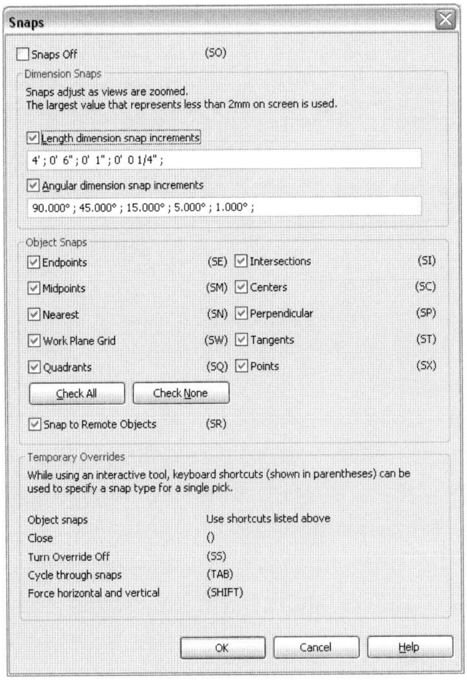

Revit has a limitation that you should be aware of: the system is preset to straighten out lines or walls drawn in small angles. This is helpful when creating new projects, but it can be an issue when you're working with existing projects, especially surveyed properties or old buildings. If you import a .dwg from such a project, Revit will, without prompting, make something like a 0.00005-degree angle a 0- or 90-degree angle—and this might affect the final precision of your outcome. So be aware of this limitation.

Helpful hint: Snap is on by default. If you are creating a project of an existing building and are drawing it directly in Revit, turning off Snap will be helpful; otherwise, Revit will force you to round angles to the first minimum snap angle defined.

Close

If an element you're drawing is part of a chain (connected lines or walls) and is a valid open loop, you can close it by selecting the Close command from the context menu: Snap Shortcuts Close. This is a long-desired functionality that AutoCAD users are accustomed to having.

You can access the same function with the keyboard shortcut SZ.

Line Weights

Revit has a global setting to display line thicknesses on the screen and the printed page. Revit provides independent control over cut and projected line weights on a per-category basis, giving you a great deal of flexibility. For example, cut lines for walls are often represented with thicker lines than walls in elevation. You can choose from 16 preset line weights that range from very thin to very thick.

Revit does an excellent job of presetting these line weights to produce a good graphical display of your model on the printed page. We don't recommend manipulating the dialog box shown in Figure 2.77; however, if you're unhappy with the print quality of the line weights, you can access the values in this dialog box and make changes by selecting Settings → Line Weights.

Object Styles

Line colors and styles are defined in the Object Styles dialog box, which you can access by choosing Settings → Object Styles. As you'll notice in the Object Styles dialog box (Figure 2.78), each Revit element has an assigned line weight number that corresponds to what is defined in the Line Weights dialog box. The line weights chosen for Projection (elevation) and Cut can vary depending on your requirements. You can also define line color and line pattern for each category here. We'll dig deeper into these settings in the next few chapters.

Figure 2.76

Snap Overrides appears in the context menu.

Figure 2.77
The Line Weights dialog box

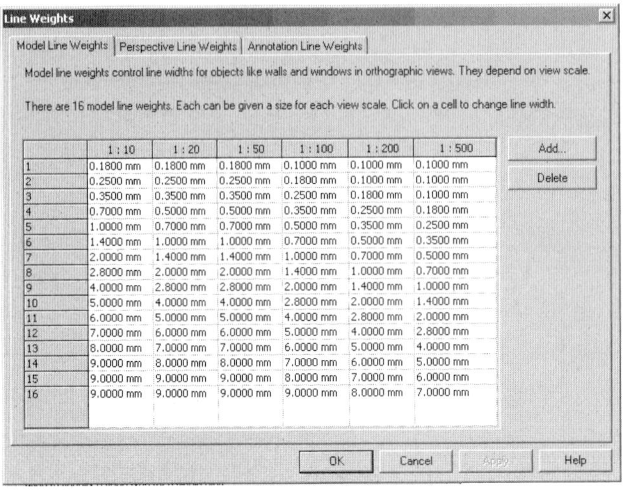

Line Weights

Model Line Weights | Perspective Line Weights | Annotation Line Weights

Model line weights control line widths for objects like walls and windows in orthographic views. They depend on view scale.

There are 16 model line weights. Each can be given a size for each view scale. Click on a cell to change line width.

	1 : 10	1 : 20	1 : 50	1 : 100	1 : 200	1 : 500
1	0.1800 mm	0.1800 mm	0.1800 mm	0.1000 mm	0.1000 mm	0.1000 mm
2	0.2500 mm	0.2500 mm	0.2500 mm	0.1800 mm	0.1000 mm	0.1000 mm
3	0.3500 mm	0.3500 mm	0.3500 mm	0.2500 mm	0.1800 mm	0.1000 mm
4	0.7000 mm	0.5000 mm	0.5000 mm	0.3500 mm	0.2500 mm	0.1800 mm
5	1.0000 mm	0.7000 mm	0.7000 mm	0.5000 mm	0.3500 mm	0.2500 mm
6	1.4000 mm	1.0000 mm	1.0000 mm	0.7000 mm	0.5000 mm	0.3500 mm
7	2.0000 mm	1.4000 mm	1.4000 mm	1.0000 mm	0.7000 mm	0.5000 mm
8	2.8000 mm	2.0000 mm	2.0000 mm	1.4000 mm	1.0000 mm	0.7000 mm
9	4.0000 mm	2.8000 mm	2.8000 mm	2.0000 mm	1.4000 mm	1.0000 mm
10	5.0000 mm	4.0000 mm	4.0000 mm	2.8000 mm	2.0000 mm	1.4000 mm
11	6.0000 mm	5.0000 mm	5.0000 mm	4.0000 mm	2.8000 mm	2.0000 mm
12	7.0000 mm	6.0000 mm	6.0000 mm	5.0000 mm	4.0000 mm	2.8000 mm
13	8.0000 mm	7.0000 mm	7.0000 mm	6.0000 mm	5.0000 mm	4.0000 mm
14	9.0000 mm	8.0000 mm	8.0000 mm	7.0000 mm	6.0000 mm	5.0000 mm
15	9.0000 mm	9.0000 mm	9.0000 mm	8.0000 mm	7.0000 mm	6.0000 mm
16	9.0000 mm	9.0000 mm	9.0000 mm	9.0000 mm	8.0000 mm	7.0000 mm

Add... | Delete | OK | Cancel | Apply | Help

Figure 2.78
The Object Styles dialog box

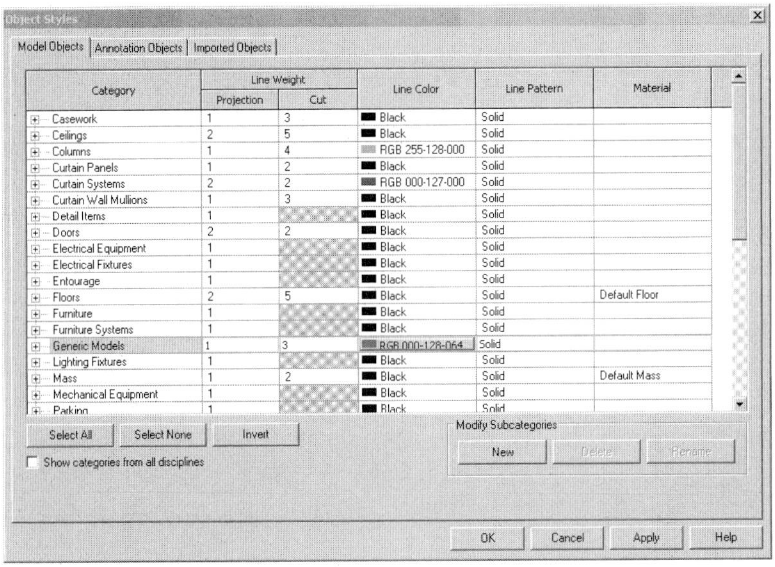

Object Styles

Model Objects | Annotation Objects | Imported Objects

Category	Line Weight		Line Color	Line Pattern	Material
	Projection	Cut			
Casework	1	3	Black	Solid	
Ceilings	2	5	Black	Solid	
Columns	1	4	RGB 255-128-000	Solid	
Curtain Panels	1	2	Black	Solid	
Curtain Systems	2	2	RGB 000-127-000	Solid	
Curtain Wall Mullions	1	3	Black	Solid	
Detail Items	1		Black	Solid	
Doors	2	2	Black	Solid	
Electrical Equipment	1		Black	Solid	
Electrical Fixtures	1		Black	Solid	
Entourage	1		Black	Solid	
Floors	2	5	Black	Solid	Default Floor
Furniture	1		Black	Solid	
Furniture Systems	1		Black	Solid	
Generic Models	1	3	RGB 000-128-064	Solid	
Lighting Fixtures	1		Black	Solid	
Mass	1	2	Black	Solid	Default Mass
Mechanical Equipment	1		Black	Solid	
Parking	1		Black	Solid	

Select All | Select None | Invert

Show categories from all disciplines

Modify Subcategories: New | Delete | Rename

OK | Cancel | Apply | Help

Options

The Settings → Options dialog box (Figure 2.79) has a variety of other options for using Revit. The tabs for this function include the following:

General Here you can set your save-reminder intervals and your username. By default, your username is the same as your Windows login name.

Graphics This is where you can change some of the settings for your graphics card and the screen colors in Revit. As you may have noticed, Revit by default has a white screen with black lines (the inverse of AutoCAD).

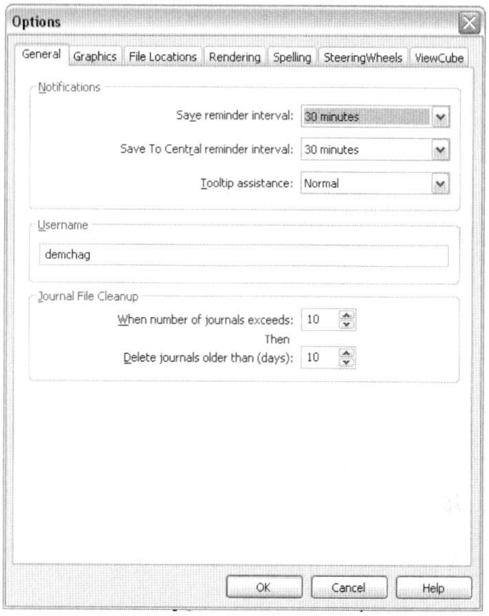

Figure 2.79

The Options dialog box

File Locations This tab stores the location of your default paths for templates, user files, and most importantly paths to your family libraries. Selecting File → Load from Library → Load Family lets you see all available folders in which families are logically stored. You can add libraries to that menu here. If you create new file locations, they will show up as quick links in the left pane of the standard File → Open dialog box.

Rendering This tab shows you the default installation path to the new rendering library, used when you render views. This is also where you can add additional material libraries, as well as licenced ArchVision (photorealistic rendering entourage) content.

Spelling This tab allows you to specify various settings for automated spelling and indicate the dictionary that you want to be used. You can leave the default Revit dictionary or switch to a Microsoft Office dictionary, change the language settings, and add other dictionaries.

SteeringWheels This tab is new in Revit 2009 and offers various controls over the visibility of the SteeringWheel, its size and opacity on the screen, and some additional settings, such as the Zoom and Orbit settings.

You can also access these settings by clicking Options in the Wheel context menu (the Options dialog box opens with the SteeringWheels tab selected). You can adjust any of the parameters shown in Figure 2.80.

ViewCube This tab is also newly introduced in Revit 2009 and allows you to set the appearance of the ViewCube as well as some behavioral and scene settings, as shown in Figure 2.81.

Figure 2.80
The new SteeringWheels tab allows you to control various aspects of the visibility of the wheels as well as additional Zoom and Orbit settings.

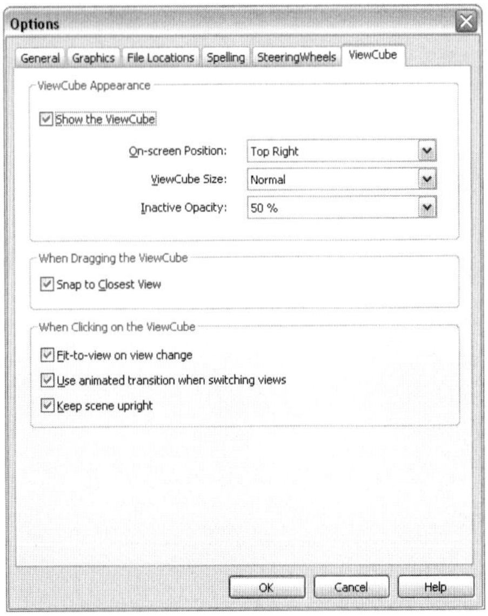

Figure 2.81
The new ViewCube tab lets you specify appearance and behavioral settings of the ViewCube.

Revit File Formats

The Revit-specific file formats are:

- .rvt

- .rfa

- .rvg

- .rft

- .rte

RVT: Revit File

Each Revit project is saved with the file extension .rvt. When you save a project using the .rvt extension, all project information is saved in that one file. This file includes all library components used in the project and imported DWG, DGN, or image files. Don't be too surprised to see the size of your project file grow significantly as you begin adding more details to the model. It isn't unusual for file sizes to exceed 50MB or even 100MB. If you want to share your project with another person or office, you won't need to send them any files other than your project *.rvt file. Note that all flavors of Revit (Revit Architecture, Revit MEP, and Revit Structure) use the same file format (.rvt).

If you have linked files to a project, regardless of whether they are DWG or RVT files, you will need to send them along with the project if you are sending files.

RFA: Revit Family

The RFA file format is used for Revit library elements that can be loaded into a project. These are also referred to as *families* in the Project Browser. A small subset of loaded families is already available in the templates that come with Revit out of the box. Another, bigger library of loadable content has been provided with the standard Revit installation and is accessible via File → Load from Library → Load Family. These libraries are starting points, and represent only a small sampling of what is possible to create in Revit.

All these library elements have been created in a designated content-creation environment known as the Family Editor. The Family Editor comes along with the installation of Revit and is an integral part of it. You don't need any other software or knowledge of scripting or programming languages to build your own content in the Revit Family Editor. Once created, Revit families are loaded into a project, where you can edit and make modifications to them from within the project environment at any time, thus minimizing workflow interruptions.

Unless you changed the default installation, Revit installs all library objects in the directory C:\Documents and Settings\All Users\Application Data\Autodesk\Revit Architecture 2009.This is the location of the default content that ships with Revit, and where the File → Load from Library → Load Family dialog box will take you (see Figure 2.82).

You can also browse for, and download content from, the new Autodesk Seek beta website. Type in a search term in the Search field in the main tool bar and press the magnifying glass icon. You will be taken to a website where you can search for a wide range of content in various formats, including .rfa files.

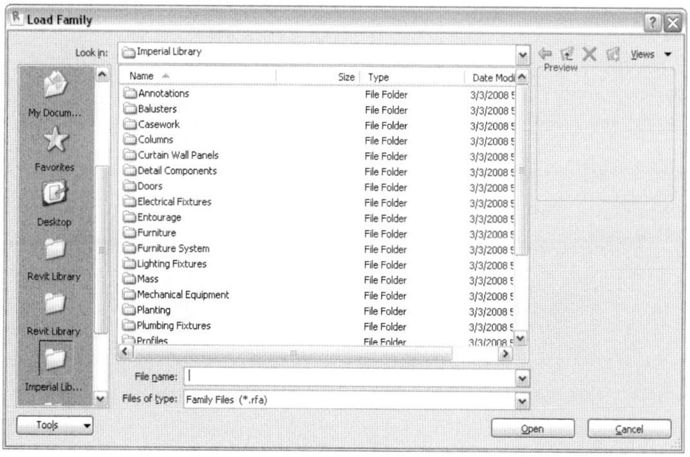

Figure 2.82
Revit library-object library

Figure 2.83

Autodesk content
website

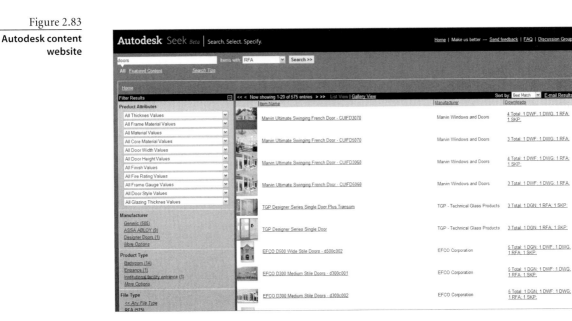

Revit families can be two-dimensional (2D) or three-dimensional (3D). Annotations and title blocks are obviously 2D, but you're welcome to create (or reuse from your CAD libraries) 2D symbols for real objects as well (toilets, furniture, and so on).

Double-clicking an RFA file from Windows opens the family file in the Revit Family Editor.

RVG: Revit Group

The Revit Group file format was made obsolete with the Revit 2008 release. We mention it here, however, so that if you use a project created in an earlier release of Revit, you understand what to do with any .rvg file that is included.

To group elements together and repeat them throughout a project (imagine a table with chairs, or typical bathroom or hotel room fixtures), Revit has a tool called Group ▦ Group . It's somewhat similar to the Block concept in AutoCAD, but with a higher level of intelligent behavior. You create a group in Revit by selecting several objects and then clicking the Group button on the menu bar. The file extension in which Revit groups were saved before Revit 2008 was .rvg. When a group is saved in Revit 2008 and later, it's saved as an RVT file. However, groups created in previous versions of Revit that are still in the RVG file format can be used and loaded in a project.

RFT: Family Template

Family template files are used to create custom families. The family templates are hard-coded in Revit. To see the full selection of available templates, choose File → New → Family. The principle is simple: if you wish to create a new table design, you use the Furniture template; for a door, use the Door template. These templates have embedded behavior and intelligent parameters relevant to the type of object you're creating. For example, a template for creating a window has a different set of available parameters and behaviors than a template for creating a door. You can't create your own family template as you can a project template. If you cannot find an appropriate template for a new object you wish to create (a fireplace, for example), you should use the generic family or a more appropriate hosted family.

RTE: Revit Template

Templates are preconfigured empty drawings in which standard settings and content can be predefined so that each time you start a new project using that template, you have a predictable starting point that incorporates your office standards.

A template file allows many users working in the same company to start with a baseline set of graphic standards and a preloaded set of commonly used model and annotation elements. This is crucial for achieving a similar look and feel for all documents produced by your office. Architectural firms can have one office template or many different ones, depending on the type of job they're engaged in. For example, a residential template may have different content preloaded than a commercial template, but the annotation and line style standards may be identical. Templates allow this kind of flexibility when defining a starting point for any given project. From what we have heard and seen from many offices that have used Revit for some time already, they usually stick to one to three templates and use more only if the office is not focused on one type of job.

You can preset the following in a template:

- Default title blocks used for your sheets
- Loaded families
- Line styles
- Line weights
- Line patterns
- Fill patterns
- Materials
- Units
- Snaps
- Dimension styles
- Temporary dimensions
- Object styles

The location and selection of the default template used in Revit is defined in Settings → Options → File, as discussed earlier in this chapter.

Only one template at the time can be set as a default template. If you've created a few templates and you want to start a new project using a template other than the default one, you can choose File → New → Project and select from the drop-down list or browse to another template. Revit includes a selection of preloaded templates, but in practice every office creates their own custom templates that will also appear in this list. Note that clicking the New button ☐ opens the default template and won't offer you the option of choosing or browsing to a different template file. Therefore, we suggest that at the beginning you use the File → New menu option.

To create and save your own template, open any of the existing template files and save it as a new name. Next, modify the settings, units, fonts, and load library objects that you want to see each time you open a new project using that template. Starting a new project in Revit is easy. Choose File → New → Project, and Revit will open a dialog box with the following options:

Browse From here, you can change the default template predefined in the Settings options and select another template.

Project This option is selected by default. It means you're starting a new project using one of the templates selected.

Project Template Choose this option if you want to create your own template. Under Create New, select Project Template and under Template File, select the template that is most similar to what you want to create so that it serves as a basis for the new template. Make additional changes to that template, change settings, add or remove content, and save it under another name.

CHAPTER 3

Views

This chapter discusses how to look at a Revit model using the views set up in the default template, as well as how to create new views. We'll explore how to create plan, section, elevation, and 3D views. This chapter also discusses how to quickly create simple schedules and how to customize a schedule to show a wide range of information available in a building information model.

Topics we'll cover include:

- Visualizing a Revit model
- Creating views
- Working with views
- Schedules

Visualizing a Revit Model

In Chapter 2, we discussed the basics of the Revit interface. Let's now dive into the primary data visualization components of Revit. You'll notice immediately that Revit is designed with architectural drawing conventions in mind. The various views that Revit generates should be familiar: floor plans, sections, elevations, details, perspectives, and even schedules. Each of these is a way to display the building model in what Revit calls *views*. The view typology follows a long tradition; however, the act of creating them with Revit is quite new and can be very different from traditional drafting and CAD practices.

There is an important difference between Revit and CAD applications to keep in mind as we delve into documenting and viewing a building information model. In Revit, views are dynamic, living images taken from the same database that you created as you built your model. In CAD, views are represented by line drawings created manually from scratch and are independent of one another. Each drawing is a manually generated artifact. In Revit, you build your building by making a digital model. Then when you create a view, be it plan, section, or whatever, you don't need to redraw. It's as if you're taking a snapshot of the very same 3D model from various vantage points.

As you learned in Chapter 1, in Revit a wall drawn in any view is represented in other views automatically. For example, the wall is drawn in plan view, and it shows automatically in 3D, section, and elevation view. There is no need to draw the wall in separate views as you'd need to in CAD. This feature is incredibly powerful because it allows you to rapidly generate your building geometry and have all the information necessary to begin laying out a drawing set much earlier in the design process. From an early stage, you have enough information to generate plans, sections, elevations, and details and place them onto sheets for documentation. From that point forward, sheets on which such views have been placed will update automatically as the design progresses and moves through the many changes and iterations that are typical in an architecture project. When the design solidifies, you'll add the necessary level of construction detail and annotations to your views.

Creating Views

Views are best understood as live snapshots of the same 3D model from various vantage points. There are many view types in Revit: plans, sections, elevations, schedule tables, lists, 3D views, and sheets. These are easily recognized and organized in the Project Browser. Each view type provides control over values such as view depth, scale, display style, visibility of elements, and level of detail. Right-clicking any view in the Project Browser lets you access the properties of that view and change any of these values. As you'll see, View Properties let you be extremely versatile in how you represent a view.

The majority of the tools for view creation can be found under the View Tab in the Design bar (shown in Figure 3.1). There are some additional ways to create views, which we'll be exploring throughout this chapter. Any view can be preset using project templates; this assures consistency across teams and projects when new projects are started. When you use Revit's default templates, a number of views are already established when you start a new project. As you develop your own graphic standards, you'll be able to create your own starting project templates. Throughout this book, we will primarily be using the default templates. Customization of templates is covered extensively in the book *Mastering Revit Architecture 2009* (Sybex, 2008).

Navigating Views

As new views are created, they appear instantly in the Project Browser. When you create new views or delete views, they're added to or removed from this list automatically. Double-clicking on the name of any view in the Project Browser opens that view in the drawing area and makes it active. An active view can be closed later using the Close button in the upper-right corner of the view. Note that this will not delete the view—it will just close it in the drawing area. To delete a view, use the right-click menu when the mouse is over the view name in the Project Browser, or delete the view symbol (such as the section mark or elevation tag) in another view where mark is available.

In addition to using the Project Browser, you can use view reference graphics, including section marks, elevation tags, and levels, as hyperlinks to navigate between views. When a view such as a section is created, the section view tag in Revit will be displayed in blue in other views—such as floor plans and other sections. This blue tag can be double-clicked to take you directly to the view it references. You must double-click the arrow (in the case of elevations) or the flag (for sections and callouts). Figure 3.2 shows that tag in black and white.

Figure 3.1

The View tab

Figure 3.2

Section flag

To toggle through multiple open views, press Ctrl+Tab on the keyboard. To view all open views, go to the Window menu—they will be listed at the bottom of the list.

Make sure you double-click within the blue section tag to open the corresponding view (see Figure 3.3). Double-clicking the section line will not open the associated section. You can also use the right-click menu when hovering your mouse over view tags, and choose Go to View (or Go to *Specific View* when one unique link is available) from the context menu to navigate to a new view.

The hyperlinking of section and elevation tags via double-click works only when they are not selected or highlighted. If they're selected (highlighted red within Revit), no matter how many times you double-click, it won't lead you to another view.

Figure 3.3

Where to click

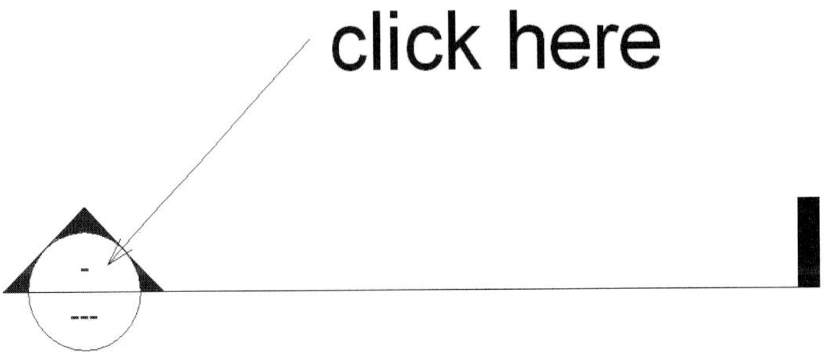

click here

Working with Views

This section discusses a few tasks and challenges you may encounter in your first Revit projects when adding or manipulating views.

Creating New Plan Views with Levels

Let's start with the first view you'll typically use: a plan view. In Revit, the default plan view is referred to as a Level 1 view and is organized under Floor Plans in the Project Browser. A level typically represents one story in a building, but as you'll see later, a level can also be used to reference the position or height of other elements (split levels, roof edges, and so on). Levels are typically created for each story in the building model.

Creating Levels

Figure 3.4

Choose the Level command from the Drafting (or Basics) tab in the Design bar.

You can select the Level command from either the Drafting or Basics tab in the Design bar (Figure 3.4). When selected, this command allows you to draw a level using two mouse clicks to define the start and end point of the level graphics—this will add a new level and plan view to the model. It's important to note that the Level command is disabled unless you're actively in an elevation or section view.

To create a level, select the Level tool, click on a point that will define the height of the level, and then drag the mouse horizontally to complete the command. The interaction is similar to drawing a line and will create a 3D level (story) in the project. When a level is drawn, Revit automatically generates a floor plan and a reflected ceiling plan for that level, and lists them in the Project Browser. To add another story, repeat the process.

You can also create a level by copying an existing one. If you are starting with a default Revit template, usually at least two levels are predefined. To create additional levels, open a section or elevation view; select the level line in the view; and, using the Copy command, copy the existing level, thus creating a new one.

Copied levels react differently from those drawn with the Level command. The critical difference is that the level symbol will appear black instead of blue. This isn't just a graphic change: the copied level doesn't automatically create a new view (you will see in the Project Browser that no new plan has been added); it only gives you another level graphic in the project that shows in elevation or in section. This is intentional, and it's useful when you need another benchmark in elevation to show heights or want to associate geometry to a level but you don't necessarily want to generate an associated plan view. A good example is the top of a parapet wall.

Adding a Plan View

What do you do when you have created a level using the copy method and it isn't associated with a plan view, and you later decide that you want it to become a plan view? It's not too late. Go to View → New → Floor Plan. A dialog box opens that allows you to select a level and create a new floor plan based on that level (Figure 3.5). Check Do Not Duplicate Existing Views at the bottom of the dialog box (this process is the same for ceiling plans). The level symbol will then change to blue, indicating that it is a hyperlink to a plan view.

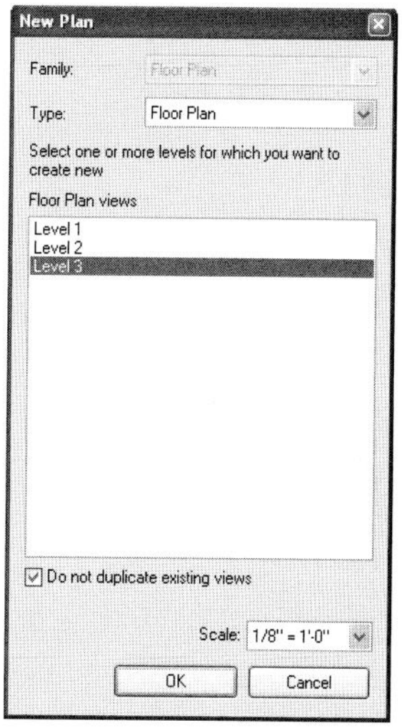

Figure 3.5

New Plan dialog box

Duplicating Views

What happens when you want to create a new view based on an existing floor plan? Say you already have a design plan of Level 1 but also need a presentation plan and a fully annotated plan for your documentation set. You can achieve this in Revit by duplicating views. To duplicate a view, right-click the view's name in the Project Browser (Level 1 for example), and choose Duplicate View from the context menu (see Figure 3.6).

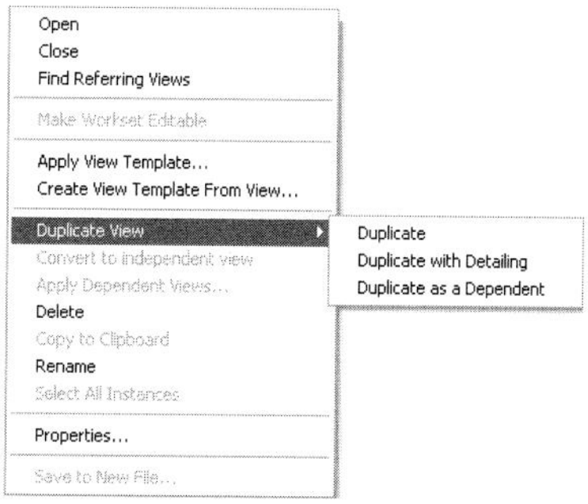

Each command on the Duplicate View submenu makes a duplicate view of the model from the same vantage point. There are three different ways to duplicate a view:

Figure 3.6

Duplicate View submenu

Duplicate Makes a duplicated view in which only the model data of that view is copied. This can be useful when you don't wish to copy any tags, dimensions, or annotations from one view to the next. Keep in mind that the model is not copied— you're just creating a duplicate view of the model without bringing along any 2D graphics.

Duplicate with Detailing Makes a copy of the model data and any 2D information (such as text, dimensions, or keynotes) in the view. When this method is used, annotations and detailing that are added or edited in the original view after the duplication aren't propagated in the duplicated view. Only model-data modifications are propagated in the duplicated view. The copied annotations are not linked.

Duplicate as a Dependent Not only creates a duplicate of all the model and drafting data, but also creates a dependency between the detailing information of the duplicate view and the original view. When this type of duplication is used, changes of both model (3D) and drafting (2D) elements in the original view will propagate in the duplicate view. A use case for this type of duplication would be in a project with a big floor plate that you need to split in separate segments for printing, or if you need to place the very same view on multiple sheets.

> *Dependent views* created with the third method must always remain in the same scale as the original.

Types of Views in Revit

Revit provides many types of views for documenting and representing your building designs. This section lists the commonly used views.

Plans

All plan views are horizontal slices through the building. Each plan shows the model as cut but can also show information above and below the cut. To control how the plan is represented, a *view range* is defined that is a combination of settings to help you create exactly what you need when creating a floor plan. Most of the time, Revit's default settings are sufficient. However, there are situations in which you may want (or need) to modify the view range settings to get correct representation.

When working in a modeling environment, a plan view is nothing but a horizontal slice of your building. Architects slice the building at what is called a *cut plane*. The value varies slightly in different regions, but it usually is about 4′-0″ (1.20m). So far, so good. But once you cut the building, how deep do you want to see? Only to the first floor you hit with your eyes? Or do you need to see beyond that? How do you want to represent the objects below the cut plane: Hidden? Cut through? Dashed? What about the objects above you: Do you want to see the beams above your cut height dashed? Or not at all? This is where the view range options come in handy.

These options are applicable only to floor and ceiling views. Modifying these options influences the visibility and appearance of the elements in the project. To access the View Range dialog box, shown in Figure 3.7, right-click in the Drawing area and choose View Properties → View Range.

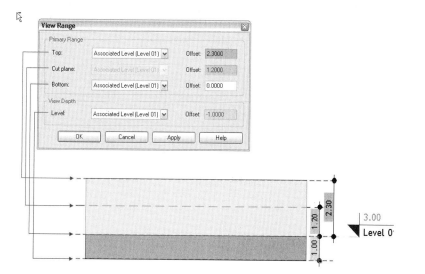

Figure 3.7

Accessing the View Range dialog box

The following list describes the Primary Range features in the View Range dialog box (see Figure 3.8). These features can be a little complex to understand initially, but as you modify them and see the results in your model, they will become easier to understand:

Top plane The top plane defines the uppermost plane above the cut plane up to which elements will be considered. If an element is above the cut plane but still in the primary range (partially or fully), the element is visible in the plan view as if it were seen from below the element.

Figure 3.8

View Range dialog box

Cut plane The cut plane defines the height at which the 3D elements of the model are physically cut, as shown in Figure 3.9.

Figure 3.9

Cut plane functionality

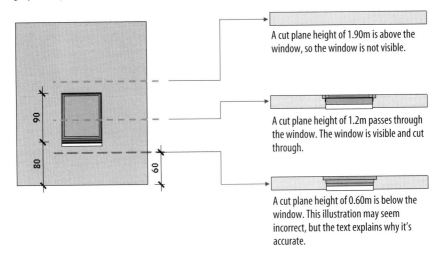

A cut plane height of 1.90m is above the window, so the window is not visible.

A cut plane height of 1.2m passes through the window. The window is visible and cut through.

A cut plane height of 0.60m is below the window. This illustration may seem incorrect, but the text explains why it's accurate.

Bottom plane By default, the bottom plane is coincident with the view depth plane, but it doesn't have to be. If an element is below the cut plane and is wholly in the primary range, it's still shown. Note that only a few Revit elements are considered here: windows, furniture systems, and generic models.

View depth View depth defines the extent to which you want to view what is below the cut plane.

Figures 3.10 through 3.13 demonstrate the use of the view range. Different settings for the bottom plane and cut plane result in different ways to see a split view.

Figure 3.10

Cut plane and bottom plane shown at the upper floor level

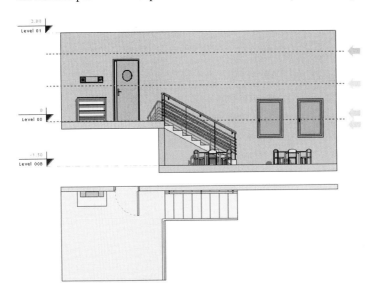

Revit doesn't cut all 3D elements. When you cut furniture, regardless of the cut plane, the furniture is not cut. Some Revit families are never cut: to understand which Revit elements are cuttable and which not, choose Settings → Object Styles, and note that some elements are grayed out in the Cut column (see Figure 3.14). These objects aren't affected by a change of cut height.

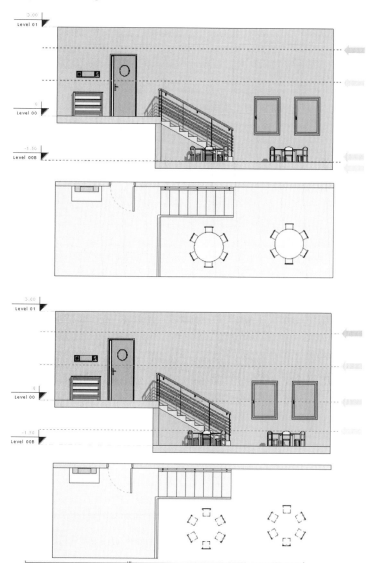

Figure 3.11

Cut plane and bottom plane shown at the lower floor level

Figure 3.12

Cut plane and bottom plane shown at 1 meter above the lower floor level

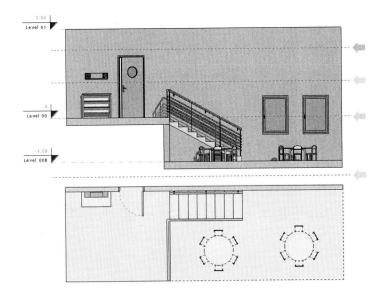

Category	Line Weight	
	Projection	Cut
⊞ Furniture	1	
⊞ Furniture Systems	1	
⊞ Generic Models	1	1
⊞ Lighting Fixtures	1	
⊞ Mass	1	2

FLOOR PLANS

Floor plans are horizontal slices through the building and are associated with levels. These views typically cut the model at 4′ (1.2m) above the level line.

CEILING PLANS

Ceiling-plan views behave in a similar fashion to floor plans, with the exception that they give a view upward to the ceiling of a level (you look up instead of down as in a standard floor plan).

SITE PLANS

Site plans by default are at 1″=20′ (1:250) scale and are views from above your model. The site plan typically shows the physical and topographic features of the model and doesn't show certain annotations that normally would not appear at scales greater than 1/16″=1′ 0″ (1:200).

AREA PLANS

Area plans can be used for gross area, rentable, or Building Owners and Managers Association (BOMA) area calculations, to name a few. To create one of these types of plans, click the Room and Area tab and choose Area Plan. Area plans are most effective when you have areas that span multiple rooms.

CALLOUTS

A *callout* is a detail view that can be placed in plan, section, or elevation views. Callouts are used to show a larger-scale cutout of a view that is dependent on the parent view from which it was placed. This is important to note: if the parent view is deleted, any callout view or views dependent on that parent view will also be deleted. For example, if you have a plan view of a kitchen and you want to create another plan view that represents only part of the kitchen at a larger scale to show more detail, you use this command. There are two possible types of callout views (see the Type Selector upon selection of the Callout tool): Floor Plan or Detail View: Detail. You can select the one you want to make and, depending on that selection, the new callout will show up in the Project Browser under either Floor Plans or Callouts.

Elevations

Elevations show your model projected onto a vertical plane, so you can evaluate and annotate building facades and interior wall elevations. Elevations are created by placing elevation tags into your model. These are orthogonal projection views (of the exterior façades of the building or of interior elevations). What's great about Revit is that when you insert an elevation tag, it dynamically positions itself perpendicular to any wall. This speeds up the process of making as many elevations as you need, even in projects that have complex floor plans. Once an elevation has been placed, you can duplicate any elevation by right-clicking the view name in the Project Browser and choosing Duplicate View → Duplicate. This will make a new nondependent elevation view.

Try drawing a few nonorthogonal walls. From the View tab on the Design bar, select Elevation and start placing the elevation tag at various places around the walls, moving the mouse around the plan. See how the elevation tag orients itself automatically according to the wall that it references or is nearby. If you have a series of walls at different angles to each other, it selects the one closest to being perpendicular to it.

Each elevation symbol is capable of creating four elevation views at once, each facing a different direction. This is designed for interior elevations. If you place an elevation symbol in the middle of a room, by inserting the tag and then highlighting the center of it, you see check boxes that can be used to activate the other elevations. Check or uncheck one of the boxes to turn the elevation on or off (see Figure 3.15).

Figure 3.15

A highlighted elevation tag. Note that the active elevations' associated boxes are checked.

Revit understands the differences between interior and exterior elevations. When creating interior elevations (placing an elevation tag in the middle of a room), Revit draws the elevation of the room in a way that it cuts it where the bounding walls, floors, and ceilings are located. The interior elevation tags in Revit are capable of generating four orthogonal elevations at a time: to do that, you select the tag and check all four sides of the elevation arrows.

Selecting an activated elevation arrow gives you additional options and displays the width and depth of the elevation. In Figure 3.16, the bar represents the width of the elevation, and the dashed line shows the depth. Both of these properties can be modified either in plan or in the actual elevation.

Figure 3.16

Elevation width and depth

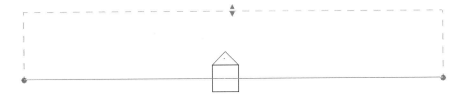

You can double-click any of the elevation arrows to navigate directly to the corresponding elevation view, or you can open the elevation views from the Project Browser. Once the elevation is placed on a sheet, the sheet number appears inside the elevation box (Figure 3.17), and the view number appears in the elevation arrow. Deleting the elevation tag deletes all the corresponding elevations from the model.

Figure 3.17

Elevation tag with its corresponding sheet marker

Sections

Sections show a vertical slice through the model. The properties of section tags are similar to those of elevation tags. The view width and depth are defined by the dashed lines when a section is selected, as in the elevation. Use the opposing arrow drag controls to adjust the crop boundary of the section (Figure 3.18).

Figure 3.18

A typical section symbol

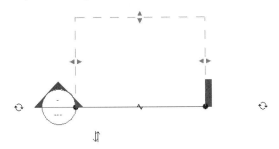

You often need a jointed section cut through a project—for example, when you want to cut through a building but jog the section line to pass through a staircase that isn't in the cut line of the initially desired section. To accommodate this, the section tool has the capability of splitting such that it allows for staggered section lines.

To stagger a section line, first draw a section line where you need to establish a view. Next, select the section, and choose Split Segment [Split Segment] from the Options bar. This enables the Split tool and allows you to split the section line at any point. Note that now each segment of the section cut can be adjusted for location and depth. Grab a portion of a section line that you've segmented, and move it up or down to achieve the desired position. A section line can be cut multiple times if need be.

> For best performance, be sure to limit the depth of your section and elevation cuts only to what you really want to see. For example, if you are cutting a wall section, there is no reason to set the section depth past the back wall of the room in which you are cutting the section. Revit will calculate all of the information whether or not you see it, so make your section depth as shallow as possible in order to gain on performance and not force Revit to calculate what you do not need to see.

Drafting Views

Drafting views are 2D views specifically designed to show information that is not generated directly from the model. They're usually used to show standardized details or information that is typical of a certain area but doesn't necessarily have a connection with the model. Drafting views can also be used to display detailed 2D information about something in the model.

A plenitude of 2D details and elements by various manufacturers is available on the Web, usually in DWG or DXF format. You can use these resources to enrich your Revit model. You can also reuse 2D details from previous CAD projects. Drafting views let you import CAD files of standard details or create 2D details by drawing with drafting tools such as lines and fill patterns.

It is very important to understand that drafting views created separately from the model or imported can be referenced in the model and linked to a callout so your drawing sheets always maintain a parametric relationship to their associated details. You should also understand that using the Callout Detail tool allows you to create dynamic details that are generated out of the model with 2D drafting elements overlaid on top. Unlike drafting details, these details are connected with the model elements, so any model changes are reflected in the details.

Drafting views can be inserted onto sheets and can also be referenced to sections or elevations as a similar (SIM) condition. To reference a drafting view to a model, follow these steps:

1. Create your new drafting view from the View → New → Drafting View menu, or choose Drafting View from the View menu bar.

2. Import a DWG file, or draft your detail using detail lines, filled regions, and other drafting tools in the Drafting tab of the Design bar, to create the 2D detail.

3. Select the View tab and choose Callout ⬚ Callout .

4. Prior to drawing the callout bubble in the model where the detail explains the condition, from the Options bar select Reference Other View and choose the drafting view you just created (see Figure 3.19). Now draw the callout bubble where you wish the drafting view to be referenced.

Figure 3.19

**Selecting Reference
Other View**

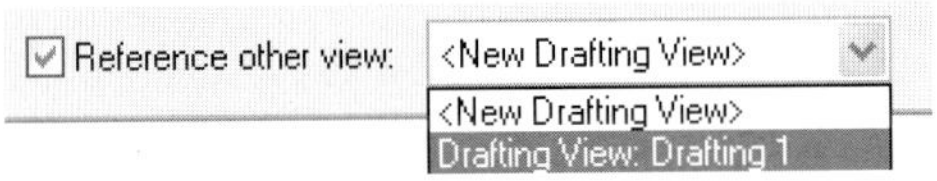

> ☑ Reference other view: <New Drafting View> ▼
> <New Drafting View>
> Drafting View: Drafting 1

The resulting reference brings you to more detailed information about the portion of the model that you describe in the drafting view.

As discussed in Chapter 1, you don't need to model every detail of the building. Each project needs to define an acceptable level of detail to model, based on the project parameters.

We've just covered the main types of views in Revit. Now let's take a look at some additional tools that fine-tune how we look at the model.

Legends

Legends are a special type of view in Revit that allow you to place graphic representations of elements in the model to explain the symbology used in the project. Examples include a key to symbols in a site plan; typical wall, door, or window types used in a project; or demolition notes on a title block. Unlike all other views, which you can place only once on a sheet, legends are used for views you want to have appear on multiple sheets. Legends are 2D elements derived from the components used in your project. Elements in a legend have no effect on scheduling quantities of elements. For example, adding a door symbol to a legend view will not increase the number of instances of that door in the overall project and thus won't be reflected in the schedule of the door totals. This is one of Revit's more sophisticated and unique features (see Figures 3.20 and 3.21).

Legends are the only view type in Revit that can be placed on multiple sheets.

To create a legend view, click the View tab on the Design bar and select the Legend tool. You can then give the legend view a name and associated scale, and you will be presented with an empty view window. To start creating the legend and add content to this view, go to the Drafting tab of the Design bar and, using the Legend Components or Symbols tool, start generating the legend as per your needs.

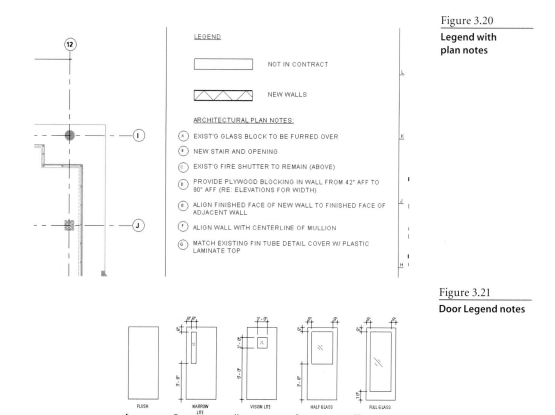

Figure 3.20

Legend with plan notes

Figure 3.21

Door Legend notes

3D View—Axonometric Views

Axonometric views of the entire project model can be generated by clicking the 3D button on the toolbar (Figure 3.22).

Figure 3.22

Click the 3D button on the toolbar to create a 3D view of the model.

Once a 3D view is created, you can orbit around the model to get a visual feel for your building. Once you like the view, rename it so it gets stored under a recognizable name in the Project Browser and you can easily get back to it later. Once you've renamed the default {3D}, any time you next click the 3D button from the tool bar it will create a new default 3D view for you to use again (Figure 3.22). To orbit and pan around the model, use the newly introduced View cube (see figure 3.23) that appears in the top-right corner of any 3D view. Clicking on faces, edges, and corners of the view cube will spin the model (actually the camera) accordingly.

This tool is also accessible from the pull-down menu named Dynamically Modify View (which you access by pressing F8).

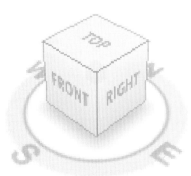

Details of how to use the mouse, the View cube, and the navigation wheels are covered in Chapter 2. Figure 3.24 shows an axonometric view of a house.

Figure 3.24

Axonometric view of a house

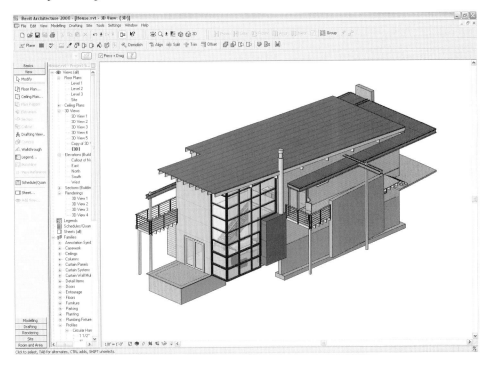

3D View—Perspective (Camera) Views

Another type of 3D view is the perspective view (Figure 3.25). Once created, these views appear in the 3D Views folder in the Project Browser. These views can be taken from anywhere in the model. Be sure to give your views unique names, as you will find yourself making many perspective views in a project. This will save time later when you are hunting for views to open or place on sheets.

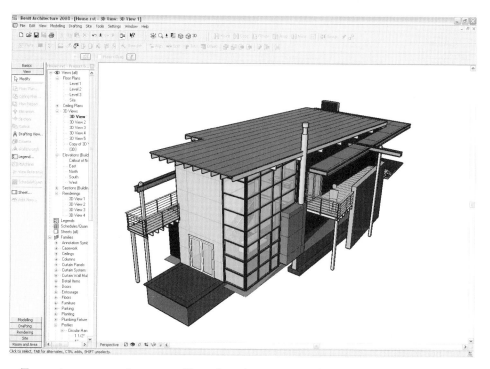

Figure 3.25

Perspective view of a house

To create a camera view, you will need to place a camera in a view: open a floor plan view or level where you want the camera to be placed. By default, the camera view is 5'-6" (1750mm) above the floor and looks straight ahead.

To create a camera view, follow these steps:

1. Make sure you're in a floor plan view. Click the View tab and choose Camera 🖥 Camera .

2. Click on the location where you'd stand in the model and then click again to set the direction in which you want to look. The second click will determine the visual focal point and the center of rotation for the camera when you orbit the view. You can manipulate the view size, width, height, and clipping plane once the camera is placed. Figure 3.26 shows the camera after it has been placed in a view.

3. When your camera is placed, it automatically opens the 3D view of the model that you just created. At this point, you can expand the view boundary vertically and horizontally using the blue drag grips to show more or less of the model.

4. Once you are in a perspective view, the camera you have placed will not be visible in other views. To see the camera placement, open the perspective view and select the crop region surrounding the view (the border of the view), or right-click the view

name in the Project Browser and choose Show Camera. Back in the plan where you created the camera view, the camera will be highlighted in red. The extent of the new view range is shown graphically in this view.

5. To modify it numerically, select the camera and right-click to select its properties. Doing so pulls up the view properties for the view and allows you to modify the camera's head height, target height, and far clipping (this sets the farthest point to which the camera can see).

Figure 3.26

A camera view placed within the model

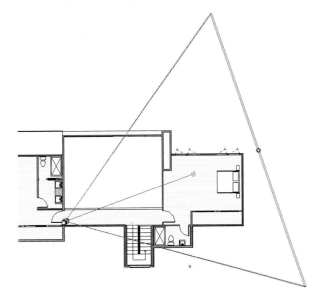

Walkthroughs

A *walkthrough* is an animation of a camera that follows a path. It's an effective method to create a sense of walking through a building that you can communicate to a client.

You create a walkthrough by placing a series of keyframes (camera positions) in a chosen order along a path in plan view. You can then walk through each keyframe and adjust the camera to change where the view is being directed. Once the keyframes have been set, you can then export an animation that takes the camera along the path. Revit automatically makes transitions between keyframes smooth and seamless. You can export the walkthrough view as an AVI file to share with your clients or team members.

Schedules

Schedules are lists of entities and objects within the model. They enumerate things that can range from building objects such as walls, doors, and windows to drawing sheets, text notes, and keynotes. The ability to dynamically create and update schedules as well as drive or locate model information from within a schedule is a core aspect of BIM and Revit.

Creating schedules of objects, areas, or material quantities in a project is one of the most painful tasks for architects. A manual calculation takes a long time and can result in errors. And those painfully created manual calculations are good until the next change, when the work needs to start over. Using CAD systems, this process may be partially automated, but the calculation can only reflect the number of blocks that are predefined in a file. In Revit, all elements have information about their physical properties, and you can add information to individual elements. For example, doors can have properties like width and height as well as material, color, fire rating, exterior or interior, and so forth.

Revit lets you schedule any element based on the properties of the element. Any geometric element placed in a Revit view can be scheduled. Additionally, because the schedule is linked to the objects in the model, you can use the schedule to locate objects within the model and change their types or properties. As we often state, it does not matter in which view you add or change something in Revit; the changes will be reflected in all the views. Schedules are easy to create and use, and they are intuitive.

To create a schedule, select the View tab and choose Schedule/Quantities ⊞ Schedule/Quantities... .

Not All Schedules Need to Appear on Sheets

You can use a schedule to document doors and windows within a project, but you can also use a schedule to look for inconsistencies within your model. For instance, you can keep a schedule of text notes only within a model and not use them on sheets. This schedule can then be used to look for odd items inserted into the model. You can schedule the text note name and the number of times it appears in the model. Perhaps the schedule indicates that a particular note is used only one or two times in the model. You can then decide if the note was inserted incorrectly into the project and determine whether it's inconsistent with the other notes in the model. The same thing can be done for wall types or anything else you can schedule.

Creating Schedules

To create a schedule, go to the View Tab in the Design Bar. This will open a dialog box that lists several possibilities, starting with the following:

Multi-category This schedule is for objects that don't normally appear together. For example, you may want to create a schedule of fire-rated windows and doors combined. You may also want a schedule showing all the casework and furniture in a project. A multi-category schedule allows you to combine a number of different items in separate categories into one schedule.

Area (Gross Building) This schedule lists the gross building areas created with the area plans.

Areas (Rentable) Rentable area plans can be created with a rentable plans schedule.

The following is a list of categories that you can schedule in Revit:

Casework	Plumbing fixtures
Ceilings	Property line segment
Curtain panels	Property lines
Curtain systems	Railings
Curtain wall mullions	Ramps
Doors	Roofs
Electrical equipment	Rooms
Electrical fixtures	Site
Fascias	Slab edges
Floors	Specialty equipment
Furniture	Stairs
Furniture systems	Structural columns
Gutters	Structural foundations
Lighting fixtures	Structural framing
Mass	Structural trusses
Mechanical equipment	Topography
Parking	Walls
Planting	Windows

Material Take-off   This type of schedule can list all the materials and subcomponents of any Revit family and allow an enhanced level of detail for each assembly. You can use a material take-off to schedule any material that is placed in a component. For example, you might want to know the cubic yardage of concrete within the model. Regardless of whether the concrete is in a wall or floor or column, you can tell the schedule to report the total amount of that material in the project.

View List   This schedule shows a list of all the views in the Project Browser and their properties.

Drawing List   This schedule shows a list of all the sheets in the project, sorted alphabetically.

> The drawing list can also be used as a sheet index to the documents. Because Revit sorts sheets alphabetically, it's typically not desirable to prepare the sheet index in the traditional fashion, with civil sheets first, then architectural, and so on. One way to customize sheet sorting is to add a field to the schedule and number the sheets so civil is 1, architectural 2, and so on. You can then sort by that number column.

Note Block   This schedule lists the notes that are applied to elements and assemblies in your project. You can also use a note block to list the annotation symbols (centerlines, north arrows) used in a project.

Keynote Legend This schedule lists all the keynotes that have been applied to materials and objects in the model. You can either use this list as a complete index of all the notes in the drawing set or filter it by sheet. This legend can then be placed on multiple sheets. For more about keynote legends, see Chapter 10.

The views listed in the View pull-down menu don't appear in the regular Schedule tool in the Design bar because they aren't as commonly used in building documentation. These schedules are primarily for data coordination that happens outside the project documentation.

Making a Simple Schedule

Now that we've discussed the variety of schedule types, let's make a simple schedule. When you begin a new schedule, you're presented with a number of format and selection choices. These will help you organize and filter the data shown in the schedule but also set the graphical aspects of the schedule, such as font style and text alignment. Remember that Revit at its core is a database, so many of the same functionalities that are available in database queries are also available in Revit. If you're unfamiliar with database concepts, don't worry; we'll explain the options as they appear in the New Schedule dialog box.

The schedule choices for a new schedule in Revit are shown in Figure 3.27.

You're first given the option of choosing a category to schedule from the menu. You're also prompted for a name for the schedule (you can change this later) and given the option of a phase filter. This filter allows you to schedule new construction or existing construction in conditions where you may be working on a renovation and want to schedule only the new or existing materials.

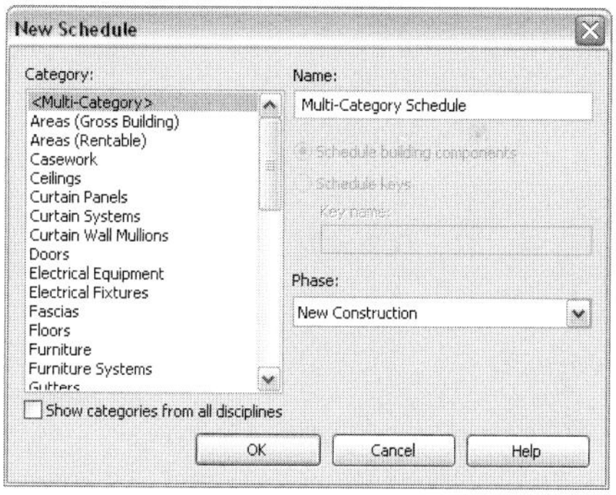

Figure 3.27

New Schedule dialog box

The following example of creating a new door schedule walks through the options in the New Schedule dialog box:

1. Open the Station.rvt file found on the book's companion web page, www.wiley.com/go/introducingrevit2009.

2. Navigate to the View design bar → Schedule/Quantities ⊞.

3. Choose Doors from the Category menu, and name the schedule **Door Schedule.**

4. Click OK. You'll see a series of tabs that allow you to choose the graphics of the schedule and exactly what data is shown. We'll discuss these tabs and how they control the information and visibility in the schedule in Chapter 10. For the time being, we'll only discuss the use of the Fields tab.

5. You can add fields either by double-clicking the name of the field or by highlighting the field and clicking the Add button. Doing so moves the field from the left to the right column. You can also remove a field by highlighting it in the right column and clicking Remove.

6. Choose the fields Family and Type, Type Mark, and Level, described in Table 3.1.

Table 3.1

Some Door Schedule Fields

FIELD	DESCRIPTION
Family and Type	The name of the door family and its type name
Type Mark	The number or letter that appears in the door tag
Level	The level of the model on which the door appears

7. Click OK. Revit will show you the complete schedule in table form (see Figure 3.28).

Figure 3.28

Schedule in table form

Door Schedule		
Family and Type	Mark	Level
04106-pocket_door_658: G.1	1727	LEVEL 4
04106-pocket_door_658: G.1	1736	LEVEL 5
04106-pocket_door_658: G.1	1745	LEVEL 6
04106-pocket_door_658: G.1	1722	LEVEL 3
04106-pocket_door_658: G.1	1730	LEVEL 2
04106-pocket_door_658: G.2 Pocket Door	805	LEVEL 5
04106-pocket_door_658: G.2 Pocket Door	838	LEVEL 6
04106-pocket_door_658: G.2 Pocket Door	839	LEVEL 6
04106-pocket_door_658: G.2 Pocket Door	759	LEVEL 2
04106-pocket_door_658: G.2 Pocket Door	782	LEVEL 2
04106-pocket_door_658: G.2 Pocket Door	783	LEVEL 2
04106-pocket_door_658: G.2 Pocket Door	784	LEVEL 2
04106-pocket_door_658: G.2 Pocket Door	804	LEVEL 2
04106-pocket_door_658: G.2 Pocket Door	820	LEVEL 2
04106-pocket_door_658: G.2 Pocket Door	822	LEVEL 2
04106-pocket_door_658: G.2 Pocket Door	939	LEVEL 5
04106-pocket_door_658: G.2 Pocket Door	957	LEVEL 5
04106-pocket_door_658: G.2 Pocket Door	958	LEVEL 6
04106-pocket_door_658: G.2 Pocket Door	968	LEVEL 6
04106-pocket_door_658: G.2 Pocket Door	977	LEVEL 6
04106-pocket_door_658: G.2 Pocket Door	978	LEVEL 6
04106-pocket_door_658: G.2 Pocket Door	1060	LEVEL 2
04106-pocket_door_658: G.2 Pocket Door	914	LEVEL 4
04106-pocket_door_658: G.2 Pocket Door	917	LEVEL 4
04106-pocket_door_658: G.2 Pocket Door	1076	LEVEL 5
04106-pocket_door_658: G.2 Pocket Door	1115	LEVEL 6
04106-pocket_door_658: G.2 Pocket Door	1118	LEVEL 6

You've just created a schedule that shows all the doors in the project and the levels they appear on. As you can see, it is very easy to create simple schedules in Revit. These schedules can be modified, re-sorted, filtered, or copied at any time in the process—and they will always be up to date.

CHAPTER 4

Modeling Basics

This chapter focuses on the creation of the basic modeling elements—walls, floors, and roofs, as well as windows, curtain walls, doors, stairs, and railings. We'll take you through an exercise where you'll build a small house that touches the following basics:

- Levels and grids
- Basic walls
- Floors, roofs, and ceilings
- Doors and windows
- Components
- Stairs and railings
- Getting started with a project

Levels and Grids

Levels and grids are the horizontal and vertical planes that represent major floor-to-floor divisions (levels) in a building as well as the vertical division of the building into structural bays (grids). In Revit, levels are powerful elements, as just about every model element in Revit has a relationship to a level. When a level elevation is changed, all elements associated with that level also change. Elements such as walls have top and bottom relationships to levels, so that when floor-to-floor heights change in the model, walls won't start to stick through floors or appear too short but will instead adjust to the new base or height of the floor. These smart relationships with the levels reduce the need to manage the vertical position of elements in the model on an individual basis (see Figure 4.1).

Figure 4.1

Levels drive floor-to-floor heights.

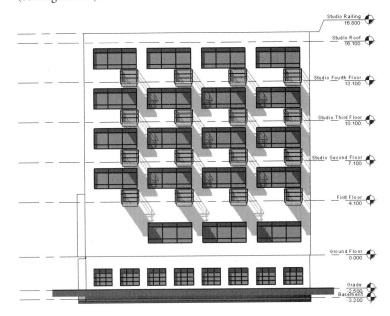

To find out what level an element is associated with, select the element and check its element properties. The word *Level* will appear for most content. You can see this readily by looking at the element properties of walls, where there are two constraints to levels: one for the base of the wall and one for the top. These parameters are named Base Constraint and Top Constraint, as shown in Figure 4.2. Furniture and fixtures all have a relationship to a level as well. Figure 4.3 shows the element properties of a desk family and its constraint to Level 1.

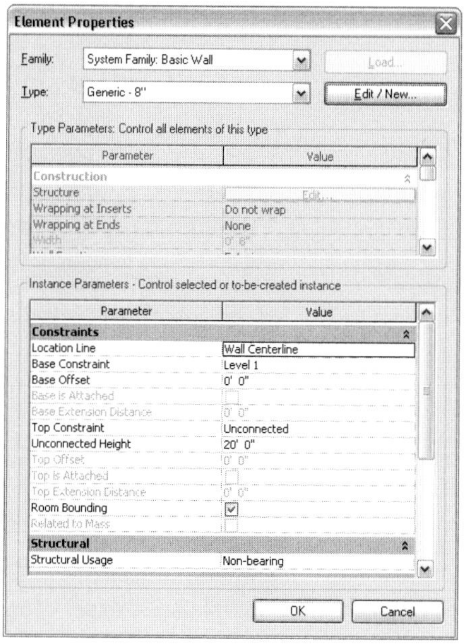

Figure 4.2

Base and top constraints of a wall

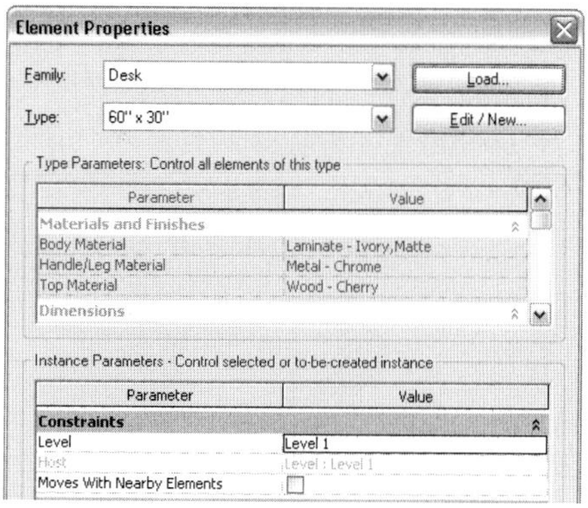

Figure 4.3

Level parameter for a desk

Creating Levels and Grids

Levels generate new plan and ceiling views when created using the Level tool 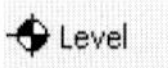 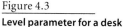 located in the Basics and Drafting tabs of the Design bar. Levels are displayed and created in the model in perpendicular sections and elevation views as lines with a symbol and name attached to them. To draw a level, you have to be in section or elevation view. You'll enter a two-click placement mode where your first click defines the beginning of the level graphic, and your second click defines the end. At the end of the level is a symbol with the name and an elevation value.

Creating grids uses the same method. The Grid tool ⁹⁹ Grid is located in the Basics and Drafting tabs of the Design bar. Grids, unlike levels, can be created in plan view as well as section or elevation view.

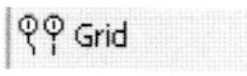

Graphical Editing Controls

When a level or grid is selected some text turns blue, and some additional controls will appear:

Blue text indicates that text is editable. Clicking the text allows you to edit values directly.

Drag controls 🔵 are blue dots that allow you to drag elements interactively, and are used throughout Revit. With your cursor over the control dot, drag the mouse: the level line will dynamically adjust its length with the mouse movements. With levels and grids, dragging a control often drags other aligned levels and grids.

Break controls ⌁ allow you to break lines and adjust the graphic representation of the line. For levels and grids, this will allow you to *kink* the end of the line (make an elbow) to make room for symbols. This control is also used for section lines, but clicking the break will remove the middle segment of the section line, not kink it.

Locks and implicit alignment lines 🔒- are used to keep elements aligned when dragged. When something is locked, then when one control dot is dragged, other controls will also move with it. You will see a dashed blue line when elements are in alignment. To free a level from this implicit constraint, click the lock icon.

Check box icons ☑ turn the symbol and associated text on or off. You can turn the symbol on or off at either end of the level line using the check box, as shown in Figure 4.4. The same icon can be found on grids, where it will toggle the grid bubble on or off. New to Revit 2009, these check boxes appear in section and elevation views for grids. (In previous releases, the grid bubbles in section view were always there and had limited controls.)

Figure 4.4

Symbol visibility

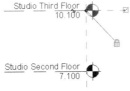

The 2D/3D extents ²ᴰ ³ᴰ icon is a toggle that lets you control either the 2D or 3D end of the line. When the toggle is set to 2D, the changes to the line length are only applied to the view you are actively working on. When you toggle to the 3D extents and change the line, the line will change in all views. In general, plan and elevation views use 3D extents, while sections, callouts, and details use 2D extents.

Grids and Structural Elements

Grids are vertical planes used as standard references in the construction industry for creating location grids on the site. These construction planes are used to accurately define

Figure 4.5

A selected grid symbol

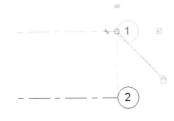

locations for elements such as columns and beams. In Revit, when columns and beams are placed on grids, they're automatically constrained to grids and grid intersections. As with a level, when a grid is moved, associated elements move with the grid. As you can see, the creation, graphic representation, and control editing of grids is similar to that of levels (Figure 4.5).

A grid is composed of a line, a symbol, and a unique grid number or letter. Revit does not let you give two separate grids the same name, just as it won't let you name two separate levels with the same name. This reduces the possibility of generating uncoordinated data.

Basic Walls

Walls are one of the basic building blocks of architecture, and they are easily constructed with Revit. Walls are built up from layers of materials that give the wall thickness—they aren't a mere collection of parallel lines. Each material has a user-definable representation for cut and projected geometry, which makes it possible for walls to be represented properly depending on the type of view the wall appears in. For example, when you draw walls in plan view (see Figure 4.6), you see the wall as if it were being cut, with materials represented as abstract hatch patterns. When you look at the same wall from an elevation or in 3D view, you see materials represented with a more realistic expression. You can see how materials are defined by opening the Settings → Materials dialog box. You'll see that each material has a projection and cut pattern associated with it. Any of these materials can be used in the construction of your walls. You can also define your own materials here, for use in your project.

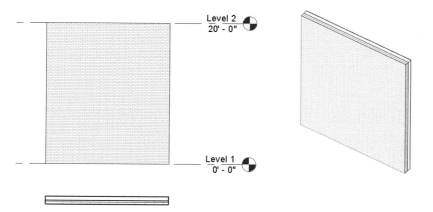

Figure 4.6

Wall representations

The materials in walls can be designed to provide automatic layer routing, greatly reducing the need to manually deal with wall intersections. Stud layers connect with other stud layers and bypass finish layers, creating clean join representations.

Wall layers are properties of each wall type (see Figure 4.7) and can be accessed through the Element Properties dialog box. When the Properties dialog box is open, click the Edit/New button to access type properties. From this dialog box, you can the access the Edit Wall Assembly dialog box by editing the Structure parameter (see Figure 4.8).

Figure 4.7
Wall properties

Figure 4.8
**Wall layers and
materials**

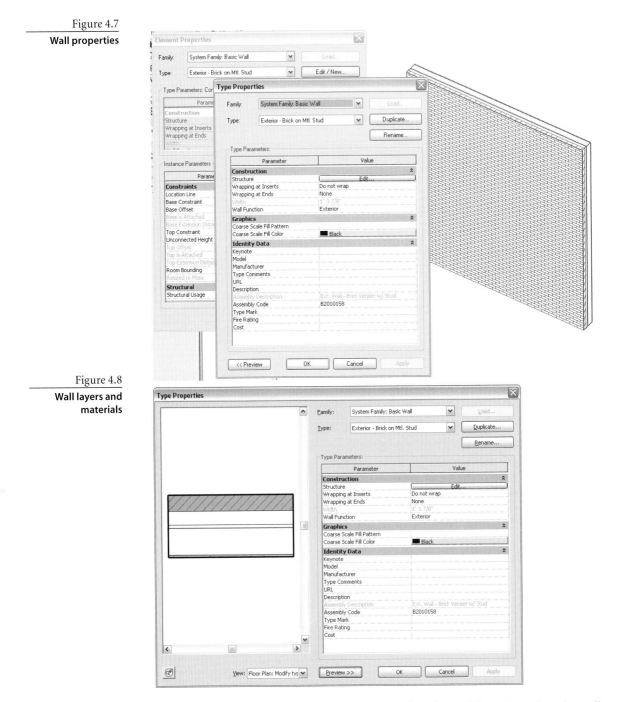

These properties allow you to define a hierarchy of materials so that when the walls
in Revit dynamically join (see Figure 4.9), Revit knows how to properly show the joint
condition.

Figure 4.9

A stud wall joining to a brick wall in plan

Curtain Walls

Curtain walls are a special type of wall (usually known as a hung façade) that allows you to divide the wall into a grid that regulates panel and mullion placement. An example curtain wall is shown in Figure 4.10. Panels and mullions can be customized to meet most design requirements, from metal panels to structural glazing. As with basic walls, curtain wall height is controlled by setting base and top constraints to levels or offsets from specific levels. See Chapter 6 for more details on curtain walls.

Figure 4.10

A customized curtain wall

Creating Walls

The Wall tool 🪵 Wall   is located in the Basics and Modeling tabs of the Design bar. With this tool, you can create basic walls, curtain walls, and stacked walls in plan and 3D views. Making a wall involves using one of three methods:

- ✏️ Draw
- 🔖 Pick line
- ◈ Pick face

The most common method is to draw walls using a multipick interaction—defining a start and end point for each wall as if you were drawing it. You can also pick existing lines and generate walls with a single pick. Using the pick face method, it's possible to place walls on more complex geometric shapes with a single pick. The specific methodologies are covered in more detail in exercises throughout the book.

Floors, Roofs, and Ceilings

Floors, roofs, and ceilings are similar to walls in that they're built of layers of materials and are constrained to levels. The interface for creating and editing layers of construction is nearly identical, as you'll see in this chapter's exercises. Floors and roofs also use the same material layer routing as walls, making connections between walls, floors, and roofs appear correctly (shown in Figure 4.11).

Figure 4.11

Walls join with floors and roofs.

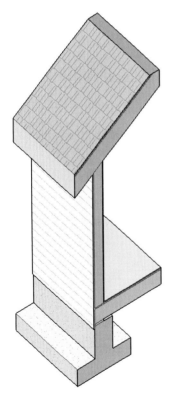

Creating Floors, Roofs, and Ceilings

These tools can be accessed from either the Basics or Modeling tab in the Design bar. All of these elements are sketch-based elements in that they are made by first defining a 2D boundary in the Sketch Editor. When you activate these tools, the Design bar is replaced with a set of tools specific to sketching 2D shapes. In this mode, you draw lines that represent the extent of the element as if it were projected onto a 2D plane. When you draw a closed loop of lines and finish the sketch, Revit generates 3D geometry for you.

In the case of floors, the geometry is coplanar with the sketch and has a predictable outcome. With more complex forms, such as hipped roof configurations, the resulting geometry is less obvious from within the Sketch mode. Nonetheless, the underlying 2D sketch is always just a click away and can be easily manipulated to achieve your design objectives. To change the shape of an already created floor, roof, or ceiling, you need to get back to its sketch: to do that, select the element, then click the Edit button in the Options bar. Figure 4.12 shows some common roof forms that can be made using Sketch mode.

Roofs can also be made by picking faces or by extrusion. These methods are suited for arc roof forms and more complex shapes that cannot be reduced to a 2D projected sketch plane.

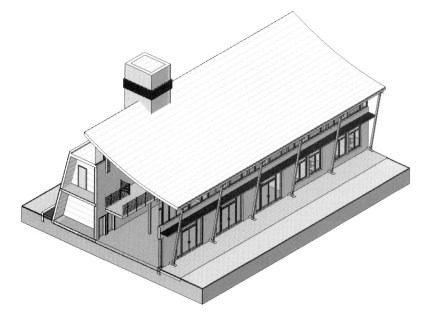

Figure 4.12

The flat roof is by footprint on the left, and arc roof by extrusion on the right.

Doors and Windows

Revit makes adding doors and windows to your model a snap. The key thing to understand about windows and doors is that they're hosted by walls. Without a host wall, doors and windows can't exist in your model. Figure 4.13 shows a window hosted by a wall.

Figure 4.13

Example showing a window hosted by a wall

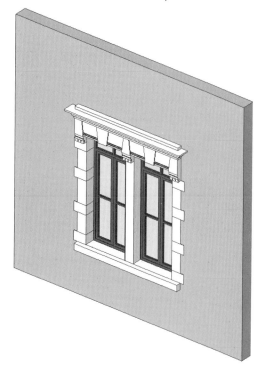

Windows and doors always stay in line with a wall; when the wall is moved or rotated, the windows and doors also move and rotate. Likewise, if a wall is copied, all hosted elements in the wall are copied. Like everything else in Revit, windows and doors are associated with a level in order to streamline the design process and remove obstacles to iteration by reducing the need to manually fix the model. Changing floor-to-floor heights will always keep your windows and doors in proper relation to the floor they belong to.

Windows and doors have specialized representations that are specific to the view in which they're placed. For example, in plan view, a door can be shown as open with an abstract door-swing graphic, whereas in elevation it appears closed and the door swing is shown as diagonal lines indicating the hinge side (see Figure 4.14). Given the fact that graphical symbology varies across the world, Revit is designed to allow you to represent these however you see fit; whether you want a door swing to be an arc or a straight line, or to be shown at all, is at your discretion. Customizing content to suit your needs is always just a few clicks away.

Creating Doors and Windows

Figure 4.14
Door representations

To place a window or door, use the tools in the Basics or Modeling tab in the Design bar. Windows and doors can be placed in any view except perspective view. Move your cursor into the view. A preview graphic of the element appears on your cursor when it hovers over valid hosts. Pressing the spacebar will rotate the element prior to placement. When you're ready to place the window, click to place it; it will automatically cut out material from the host wall. If you need to change the swing direction, press the spacebar when the door is selected, and it will cycle through all possible configurations.

Components

Figure 4.15
Wall-mounted light fixture

Windows and doors are just a subset of the possible components that can be created using Revit. Revit allows you to design, create, and place just about any kind of component you can dream up. The predefined categories of component types include everything from casework to structural framing. Components are a bit more flexible than windows and doors in that they are not required to be hosted by a wall in order to exist in the model. A piece of furniture, for example, does not need a wall in order to be placed. At the same time, you can design components with the same dependency as windows or doors. For example, with a wall-mounted light fixture (Figure 4.15), you'd expect it to move with the wall and get deleted with the wall just like a window or door would. Revit allows for this flexibility when designing components.

To place components, use the Component tool in the Modeling tab of the Design bar. You can also drag and drop components from the Families node in the Project Browser.

When placing components, you'll get helpful snapping and alignment graphics. Pressing the spacebar before placing a component will rotate it.

Stairs and Railings

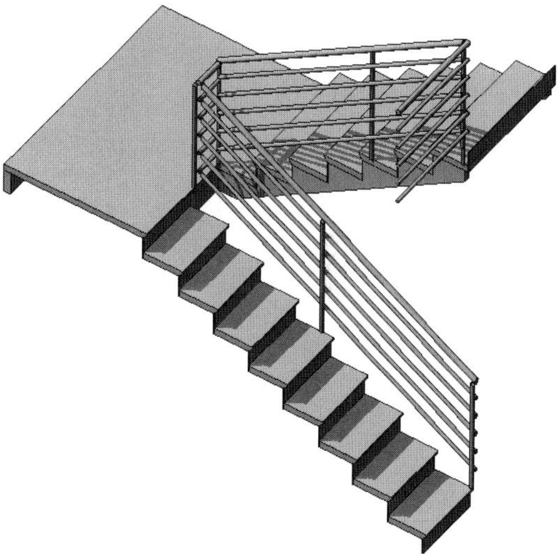

Most buildings have stairs, and where there is a stair, you're likely to encounter a railing. Revit provides specially designed tools for the creation of stairs and railings that give you control over their basic constructive parts. With stairs, you set up design rules for elements such as stringers, treads, and risers; then Revit goes to work building the 3D geometry for you. The same is true for railings. Using design rules, you establish a pattern of rails and balusters and then draw a simple 2D path. Revit fills in the path with 3D geometry based on the rules you establish. Figure 4.16 shows a typical Revit stair.

Figure 4.16

A stair

The Stair ✐ and Railing ▦ tools are located in the Modeling tab of the Design bar. When you activate these tools, you enter a special Sketch mode where you sketch 2D lines. The lines used to construct stairs define the boundary and the risers. When you finish, Revit builds the 3D geometry for you. Changing the appearance and design rules for stairs and railings is done through the Element Type Properties dialog box.

Stairs can be set to be multistory, so that if your building is a six-story building out of which five have the same floor-to-floor height, you can draw the stair and the railing once and have it automatically repeat through multiple levels. This is an instance property of any stair (see Figure 4.17). If the stair is drawn with a railing, the railing is also drawn on all multistory stairs. If you later decide to make any changes to the stair, you'll need to change it only once, and the change will propagate throughout all floors. Figure 4.18 shows a staircase (one element) spanning multiple floors.

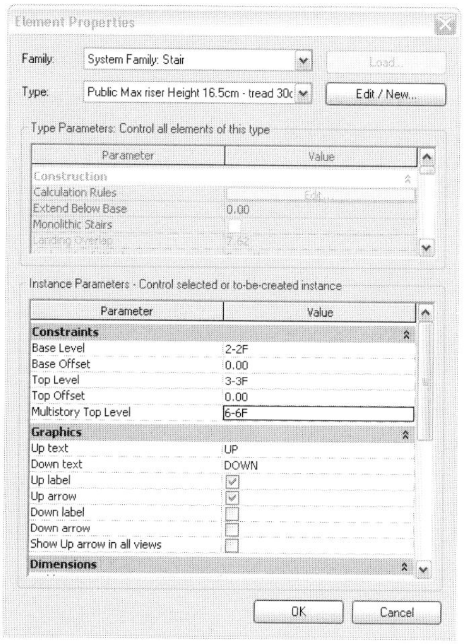

Figure 4.17

The Multistory parameter

Figure 4.18

**A multistory stair
example**

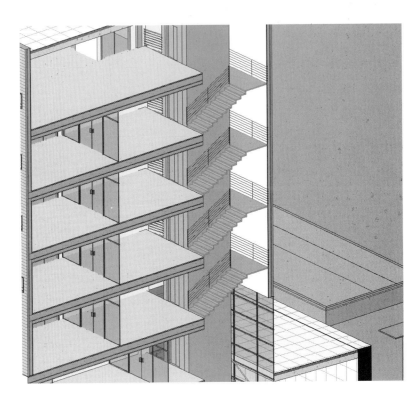

Getting Started with a Project

In the following exercise, you'll use some pre-drawn lines to help you begin laying
out exterior and interior walls. This does not mean that you'll always need or have
such lines to begin using Revit. We do it here so you can move through the exercise
efficiently and to avoid burdening you with typing in every dimension value. In real
life, there are many different ways to start a project—from an existing 2D import
(covered in Chapter 7), from a conceptual massing form, from an imported image, or
from scratch. As you will see, Revit has many useful features when laying out walls,
especially the smart temporary dimensions that let you see and edit dimensions of
elements before and during creation.

In the exercise, we will start with a set of lines, and construct 3D walls using these
lines as guides. In fact, the lines are named guides, and are located in the Line Styles
dialog box, if you feel the need to edit their appearance. To follow along with the process of building exterior and interior walls throughout the rest of this chapter, open the
exercise base file named Source_House_Walls_Start.rvt at the book's companion web
page, www.wiley.com/go/introducingrevit2009. The model opens with the Level 1 plan
view active. Several levels are predefined for first and second floors as well as for some
roof planes.

Wall Options Bar

Click the Wall tool in the Basics tab to begin the process of drawing a wall. Before you start drawing anything, focus your attention on the horizontal Options bar (Figure 4.19) just above the view. The options you see here are always specific to the selected tool—in this case, the Wall tool. Get accustomed to looking at the Options bar for tool-specific options, because many features show up in this thin strip of interface. We covered some of the basics of the available options in Chapter 2, but the following paragraphs talk more about the wall-specific options.

Figure 4.19

Wall Options bar

The first part of the Options bar is the Type Selector, which lets you choose the type of wall element to create. Go ahead and choose the Basic Wall: Exterior Wall. The nice thing about the type-selection list is that even if you place a generic wall initially, you can change the type of wall later by selecting it and changing the type with the same mechanism. When new users start using Revit, they often wonder what level of detail they should model when starting out. It's OK to not know that right from the start. Revit is designed to easily change any wall type to another later in the process without losing any intelligence or relationships with other elements. It's natural to use more generic, abstract wall types when beginning a design process and refine the model later. At the same time, Revit also allows you to be specific from the get-go. If you know your interior walls are wood studs with gypsum wallboard, you can start placing those immediately.

The next set of options is the methods for making the wall 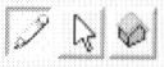 . You'll use the default option, which uses a drawing metaphor and allows you to draw walls as you would lines. The next two options let you select existing lines or geometric faces to auto-generate a wall without drawing. These options are generally used if you're working from an imported set of lines, an imported solid geometry, or a massing form made of geometric faces.

Next you need to define the height of your wall  . You define which level the top of the wall is constrained to, or if you want the wall to have a specific fixed height that isn't tied to a level. In Revit, when the top of a wall is not tied to a level, this is referred to as its unconnected height. A knee wall is an example of a wall that isn't necessarily tied to a level at the top but needs an explicit height from the base level.

Next on the Options bar is the Loc Line parameter. This is short for Location Line, which is really the wall's justification. The Loc Line allows you to set a fixed axis for the wall based on the built-up construction of the wall. The most common use of this is to draw with either the interior or exterior core boundary (as in Figure 4.20) or structural layer when laying out walls. For example, you can draw walls relative to the stud face, rather than the finish face, of gypsum board. Whatever is set here determines where your cursor is relative to the wall construction during creation. You'll notice this when walls are selected as well: the drag control is located at the location line. Note that you can change the wall location line at any point using the Element Properties dialog box for walls.

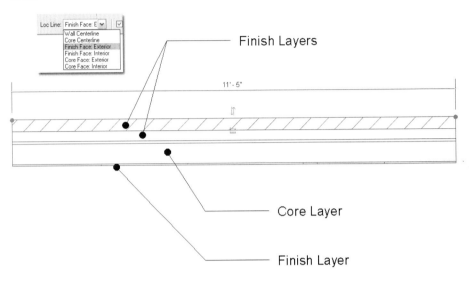

Next is the Chain check box 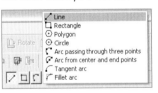. When this is selected, it means you can keep making connected walls after every click of the mouse. When it's deselected, extra clicks are needed to snap to the end of the previous wall in order to start the next wall. Chain is selected by default, based on the assumption that when you're making walls (and, as you'll see later, this is the case for sketch lines as well), you generally make a series of connected walls. If this isn't the case, deselect the box, and Revit will remember this setting the next time you use the Wall tool.

Finally, we get to some options for different types of wall shapes you can draw, shown in Figure 4.21. This includes an obvious suite of line-generation options: lines, rectangles, polygons, circles, and various types of arcs.

Exterior Walls: Drawing Exterior Walls

Let's start the exercise. For the remainder of this chapter you'll make the small house shown in Figure 4.22. Make sure you've got the file, `Source_House_Walls_Start.rvt`, open. Follow these steps:

1. Select the Wall tool from the Basics tab of the Design bar. From the Type Selector, set the wall type to Basic Wall: Exterior Wall.

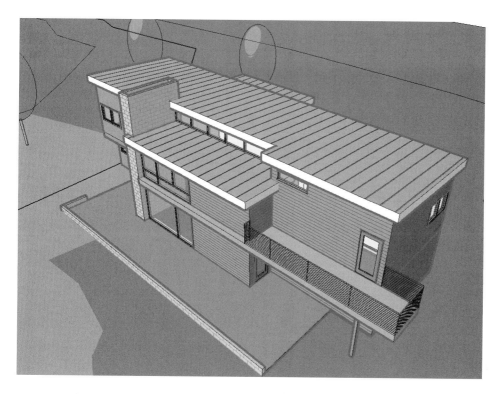

Figure 4.22

Here's the house you'll be designing.

2. Using the Options bar, set the Loc Line to Core Face: Exterior. This will allow you to draw the wall using the structural core edge as a baseline, rather than a finish layer or wall centerline.

3. Starting in the upper-left corner of the sketch, begin tracing the outer edge of lines with your wall. Move in a clockwise direction, drawing walls from left to right (see Figure 4.23). As you do this, take note of snapping as you move the cursor from point to point. Snap your walls to intersection points of the guidelines. Zoom and pan while drawing walls—try this by scrolling the middle mouse button zoom, and holding the middle mouse button down to pan while drawing your walls. To avoid snapping to the wrong points, zoom in and trace the sketch. Revit provides snapping that lets you be precise in your wall creation by looking for endpoints, midpoints, and perpendicular edges (among others).

   Notice the dimension strings that appear as you draw the walls. These are temporary dimensions that indicate the dimensions of the objects you're drawing and, more important, can be used to specify explicit length and angular values. (To try them, click one point as the start of a wall and start typing a value on the keyboard. Revit won't need any units or X–Y coordinates.) Use snap intersections to place walls.

Temporary dimensions can be used to get a more precise placement, as shown in Figure 4.24.

Figure 4.23

Starting a sketch

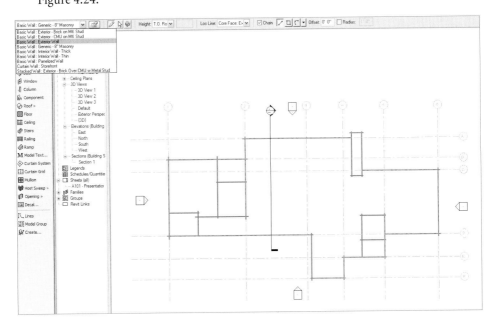

Figure 4.24

Snaps and temporary dimensions

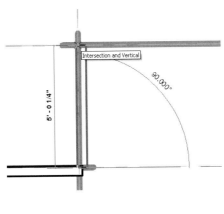

Note that the blue guidelines are obscured by the wall as you draw the walls. This is because the walls you're drawing have a physical height in the model and are being represented as if cut at 4′ (1.2 m) above Level 1. What you see isn't just lines, but the cut face of the wall geometry, which obscures the lines below. This type of display is called *hidden line*. It means that geometry is displayed relative to your point of view: elements closer to you will obscure elements farther away.

4. Continue drawing walls until you complete a circuit of lines around the perimeter. If you want to stop drawing walls, press the Esc key twice, or click the Modify tool in the Design bar. If you misdraw a wall, you can select the wall and use the drag controls to snap it to the correct location.

Drawing walls from left to right on the screen places the exterior face of the wall facing the top of your screen by default. If this isn't the desired orientation, press the spacebar while drawing the wall, and it will flip. The flip controls are always drawn on the exterior side of walls.

5. Once you complete the walls around the perimeter, toggle the view display to Shading with Edges using the keyboard shortcut SD (press S, then D); the display mode will change to Shading with Edges. This option also appears at the bottom of each view in the View Control bar, as shown in Figure 4.25.

6. Use the Tab-selection method by hovering the mouse over one of the walls without clicking it, and then press the Tab key once. You'll see the chain of connected walls highlight. Click once to select the walls. Use this method to quickly select connected walls rather than picking walls individually (see Figure 4.26). Now that all these walls are selected, you can change the wall type with one click (Figure 4.27). To see this, Tab-select all exterior walls, and then use the Type Selector and change them from Basic: Exterior Wall to Basic: Exterior—Brick on Mtl. Stud.

Figure 4.25

View-display modes can be changed using the View Control bar.

| Wireframe |
| Hidden Line |
| Shading |
| Shading with Edges |

1/8" = 1'-0"

7. All the walls became thicker. These aren't the walls you want, so press Ctrl+Z to undo the type change.

Figure 4.26

Connected walls can be selected by using the Tab key prior to selecting.

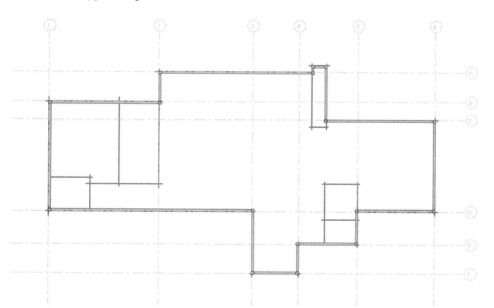

Figure 4.27

**Swapping
wall types**

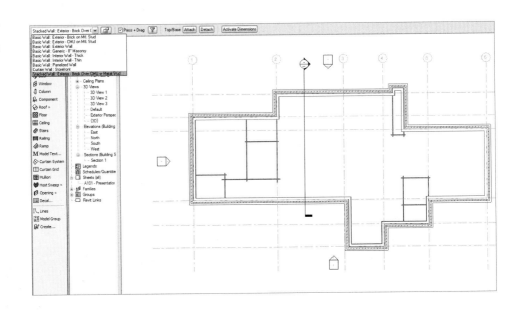

Drawing the Fireplace Walls

Let's use a similar method to make the fireplace walls:

1. Zoom into the area between gridlines 4 and 5, where we will put the fireplace (see Figure 4.28). Hold down the Ctrl key and select the three walls. Note that the cursor changes to show a plus symbol (+), indicating that each selection will add to the current selection.

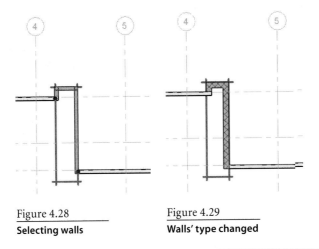

Figure 4.28

Selecting walls

Figure 4.29

Walls' type changed

To remove elements from a selection, press Shift and then pick elements that are already selected. To add new elements to a selection, use the Ctrl key when making selections.

2. Use the Type Selector to change the walls to Generic – 8″ (20cm) Masonry. The walls maintain their exterior face justification and expand inward. Notice that the cut graphic changes as well—to a diagonal crosshatch. See Figure 4.29.

3. Select the far-left shortest segment of the fireplace wall and extend it by dragging the blue end grip control (Figure 4.30).

4. Continue by selecting each wall individually and dragging the end controls until they snap to the guideline intersections (Figure 4.30).

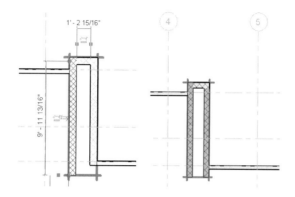

Figure 4.30

Extending walls

5. All that's left to do is draw the last segment and close the fireplace walls. To do that, select only one of the masonry walls of the fireplace and right-click to open the context menu, and select Create Similar (Figure 4.31). This command puts you directly into drawing mode. Draw the remaining section of the fireplace. If you start drawing from the left corner, the wall is drawn inside-out. To resolve this, press the spacebar to flip the wall on its location line while drawing. Figure 4.32 shows the wall before it's flipped and after it has been corrected.

> Even if you draw the wall inside-out to begin with, you can always flip it later by selecting it and pressing the spacebar. The spacebar is a generic method for flipping objects about one or more axes. This is one of the beauties of Revit: there are no rules for when you do what; everything is changeable and replaceable later.

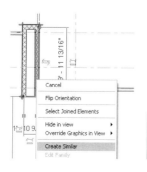

Figure 4.31

Choosing Create Similar using the context menu and the toolbar

Figure 4.32

Flipping a wall

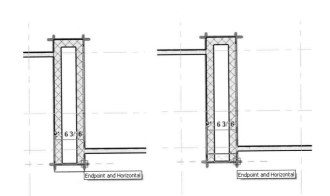

6. Let's change the height of the fireplace walls to go up to a predefined level in the model. Using the chain selection method mentioned earlier, hover the cursor over one of the masonry walls and press Tab once. The four walls forming the fireplace highlight. (If this doesn't happen, select the walls individually by pressing the Ctrl key or box-select them—whichever method works best for you.) Click to select them.

7. Right-click the fireplace walls and choose Element Properties from the context menu.

8. Change the top constraint parameter to T.O. Chimney, as shown in Figure 4.33.

9. Click the Modify button, or press the Esc key twice to exit the wall creation mode.

Figure 4.33

Select T.O. Chimney in the Element Properties dialog box.

Changing Wall Types

Let's assume we are now at a stage of our design where we know exactly which type of walls we are using. We will change some walls to more specific types using the Type Selector. You'll see how easy it is to deal with design changes using Revit. Follow these steps:

1. Select the walls as indicated in Figure 4.34, and change them from Basic Wall: Exterior to Basic Wall: Panelized Wall using the Type Selector.

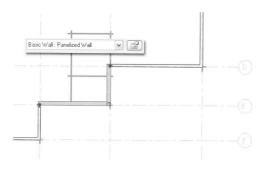

Figure 4.34

Changing to panel-ized walls

2. Let's see what the 3D view looks like. Click the 3D button ⊕ 3D at the top of the toolbar to open the default 3D view (see Figure 4.35).

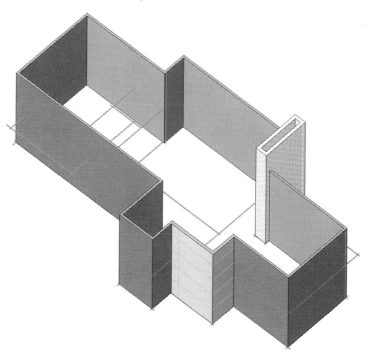

Figure 4.35

The default 3D view

Exterior Walls: Level 2

We are now moving to the second level and will start by adding exterior walls to it:

1. From the 3D view, select the wall running into the fireplace, as shown earlier in Figure 4.31. Open the Element Properties dialog box, and change the top constraint to Level 2. You do this because the bedroom on Level 2 needs to cantilever over Level 1, and you don't want that wall going through the bedroom. Figure 4.36 shows the wall before and after the constraints have been changed.

Figure 4.36

Modifying the top constraint

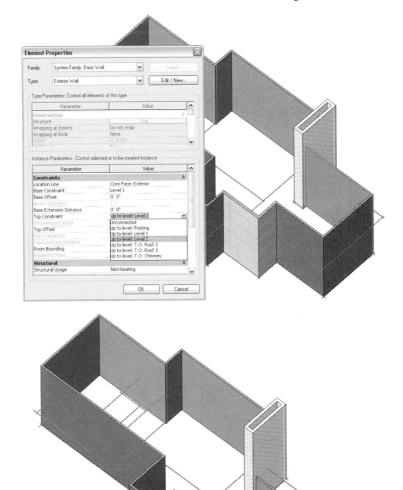

2. You can add some walls to the model directly from the 3D view—a nice benefit of working with a building model. Activate the Wall tool and choose Basic Wall: Exterior Wall. Using the Options bar, set the level to Level 2, and set the height to T.O. Roof 3 (see Figure 4.37). Make sure the Loc Line is still set to Core Face: Exterior.

Figure 4.37

Set the wall parameters before drawing the wall.

3. Start drawing the wall from the intersection of the guideline and the fireplace, and turn the corner to meet the other wall, as shown in Figure 4.38.

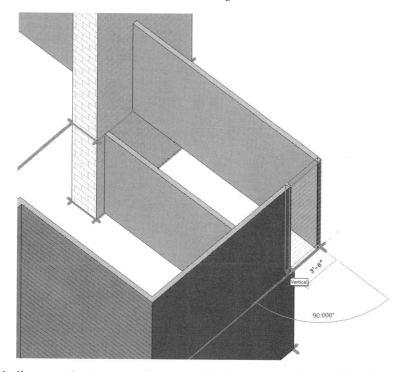

Figure 4.38

Adding walls to Level 2

4. Perform a similar operation to create a bump-out for the master bedroom; this will become a closet later (see Figure 4.39). Before you start drawing, make the wall type Basic Wall: Panelized Wall, and draw it from right to left so that the panel material faces the exterior.

5. To give the house a bit more variation, let's bring down the height of walls for the front entry and the walls in the back, as shown in Figure 4.40. Multiselect the walls as indicated, using the Ctrl key, and then open the Element Properties dialog box and change the top constraint to T.O. Roof 2.

Figure 4.39

Adding closet walls

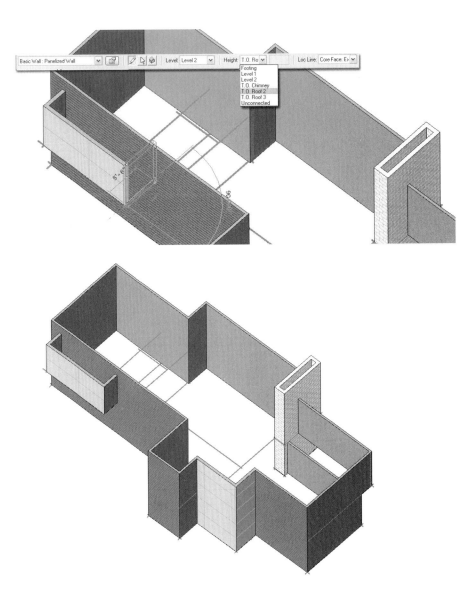

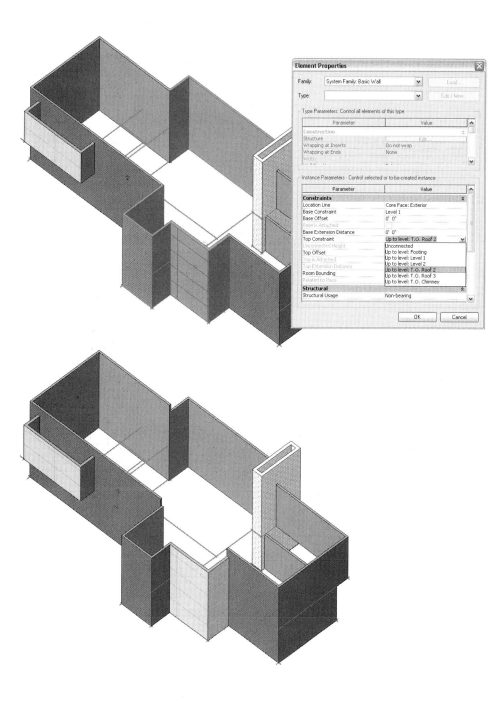

Figure 4.40

**Modifying wall
height**

Interior Walls: Level 1

Everything's looking good so far. Now let's add some interior walls to the project:

1. Open the Level 1 plan.

2. Select the Wall tool and choose Basic Wall: Interior – Thin.

3. In the Options bar, set the height to Level 2 and the Loc Line to Wall Centerline. Begin laying out the interior walls using the guidelines provided in the view, as shown in Figure 4.41.

Figure 4.41

Creating interior walls

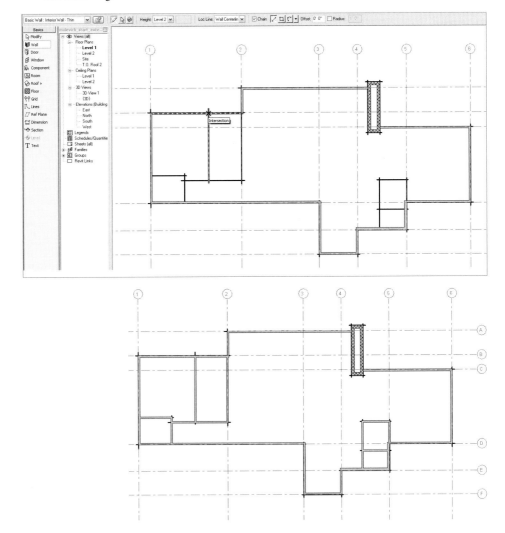

Wall Join and Face Resolution

Not all of the interior walls are lining up neatly with exterior walls. Let's fix that. You'll first change to a thicker wall and then unjoin the wall. You'll use the Align tool to make things line up, and then rejoin the walls. Follow these steps:

1. Zoom into the grid 2 join condition where the interior wall hits the exterior, as shown in Figure 4.42. You need to clean this up.

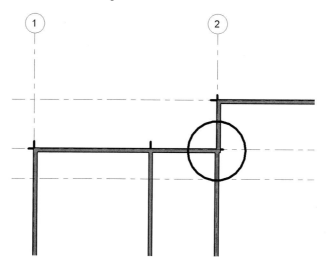

Figure 4.42

An example of a bad wall join

2. Change the wall type to Basic Wall: Interior Wall – Thick. You do so because this wall will span two levels and also act as a plumbing cavity.

3. Grab the wall-end control and drag it away from the join, as shown in Figure 4.43.

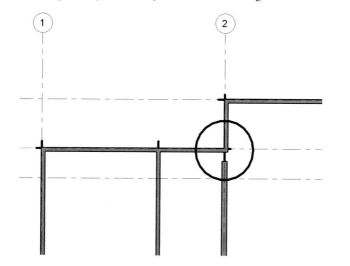

Figure 4.43

Modifying the wall join

If you don't detach the join, then you won't be able to realign the walls to the finish face. When you're dealing with complex joins such as this, the best practice is to pull the walls away from the join, make proper alignments, and then rejoin the walls.

4. Select the Align tool in the toolbar. You'll use it to align the finish faces of the two walls. This tool allows you to make alignments between elements and constrain that alignment if you desire. Walls that are connected automatically attempt to stay aligned. (Users often comment that the Align tool is one of the most useful tools in Revit. The thing to remember is that the first pick is where you want to align to, and the second pick chooses which element you want to move [align].)

5. Select the geometry (the horizontal wall) that you want to align. This is the target that you want other geometry to align with. Then, choose the geometric edge that you want to align, as shown in Figure 4.44—in this case, the thick interior wall face.

Figure 4.44

Aligning the wall

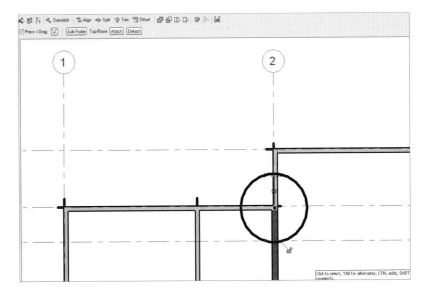

6. Drag the wall end back into the join. The walls clean up, and you get a nice-looking image like the one in Figure 4.45.

7. Now that the wall looks good, change its height so that its top constraint is T.O. Roof 3. Check out your results in the 3D view; see Figure 4.46.

8. Using the technique you just went through, clean up the condition shown in Figure 4.47.

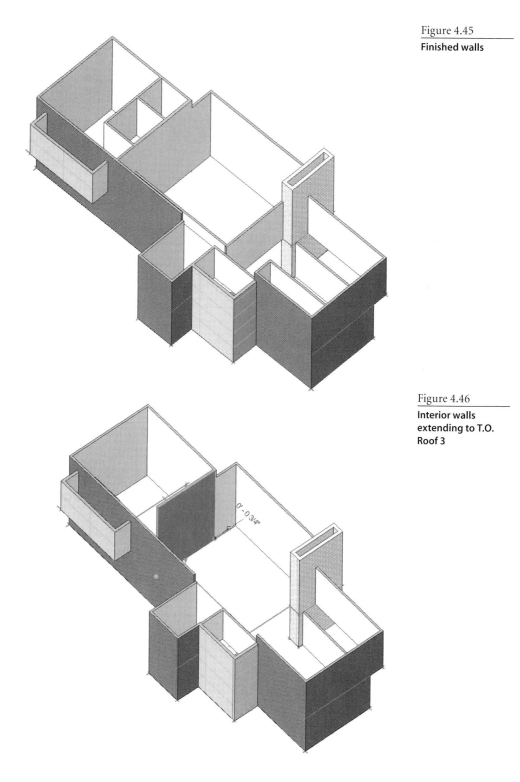

Figure 4.45

Finished walls

Figure 4.46

**Interior walls
extending to T.O.
Roof 3**

Figure 4.47

**Clean up this join
condition also.**

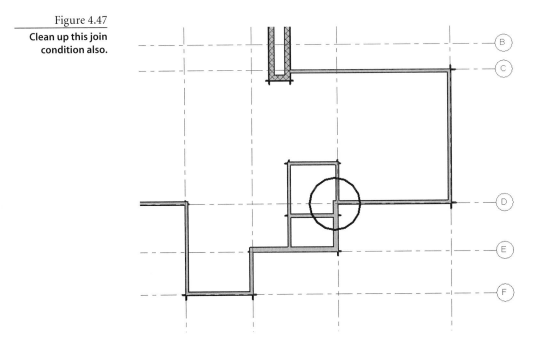

Interior Walls: Level 2

Let's continue to add interior walls, this time to Level 2:

1. Open the Level 2 Floor plan and place Basic Wall: Interior Wall – Thin walls using the guidelines as placement aids.

2. Using the Basic Wall: Interior Wall – Thin wall type and the Pick tool, pick the lines in the view. Before picking, use the Options bar to set the Loc Line to Wall Centerline and the height to T.O. Roof 3.

3. Be sure to clean up the walls highlighted in Figure 4.48 to achieve aligned walls and clean joins. Use the same technique used in Level 1 by pulling the join apart and then using the Align tool as shown in the figure.

4. The model has a large double-height volume for the main living space. A knee wall will be used to bridge the two bedrooms on either side of the volume. To change the height of the wall, select it and change its top constraint from T.O. Roof 3 to Unconnected (see Figure 4.49).

5. Set the Unconnected parameter value to 3′-0″ (1m).

   Excellent job! Now you have the beginnings of a small house (see Figure 4.50). The next exercise will pick up from this point and continue to add more detail to the model.

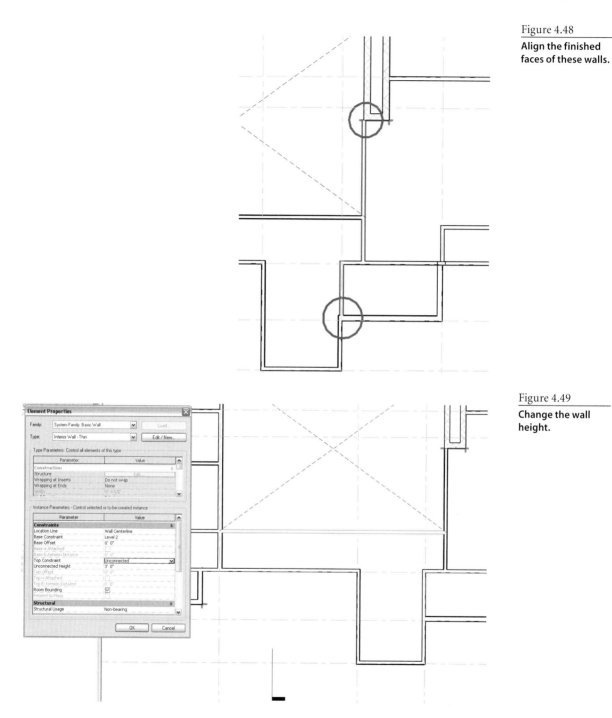

Figure 4.48

Align the finished faces of these walls.

Figure 4.49

Change the wall height.

Figure 4.50

The walls of the house

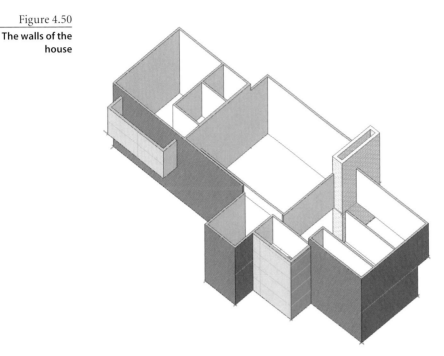

Adding a Floor to Level 1

Now that you've built the exterior and interior walls, let's add floors and roofs. You can continue where you stopped on your file, or open the file Source_House_Floor-Roofs_ Start.rvt.

1. Open floor plan Level 1. From the Basics tab in the Design bar, select the Floor tool  . The view and interface change into Sketch mode.

   In Sketch mode, the model becomes halftone and noneditable. A specialized set of tools replaces the normal Design bar. Depending on the type of element that is being edited, different options appear in the Sketch tab. The Sketch tab for floors looks like Figure 4.51.

   The default state puts you into the Pick Walls command. This allows you to create the sketch of the floor by picking walls in the model to create a parametrically associated floor boundary. A sketch is a series of connected lines that form closed shapes. Sketches can form multiple closed shapes, but lines can't intersect or be left unconnected at an end. Revit uses the term *loop* to define a closed sketch.

Figure 4.51

Sketch tab for floors

A sketch must follow some basic rules in order to generate geometry. It needs to form a closed loop of lines that do not overlap or have unconnected ends. Lines cannot be left floating around, overlapped, or disconnected, and the sketch cannot be finished. If your sketch is invalid, Revit will warn you and even highlight the problem areas so that you can fix them on the fly (close the loop) and finish your sketch.

2. Using the Pick Walls option, hover your cursor over an exterior wall but don't click on it. Press the Tab key; the chain of all connected walls highlights. Now click once on the wall. Sketch lines will be generated from the walls, as shown in Figure 4.52.

Figure 4.52

Walls used to generate sketch lines

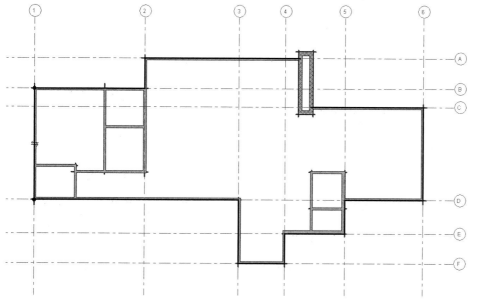

3. Not all the walls along the perimeter were selected. This is because the fireplace walls aren't connected at their ends with other walls in the selection. To finish the sketch into a closed loop of connected sketch lines that define the shape of the floor to be, you need to select the fireplace walls; this will generate sketch lines over those walls. Finally you will need to clean up the sketch. Trim the lines so they don't overlap and trim perfectly in a closed loop. If you attempt to finish the sketch without adding lines around the fireplace or without trimming and connecting them, your sketch will be invalid and you'll get the warning shown in Figure 4.53.

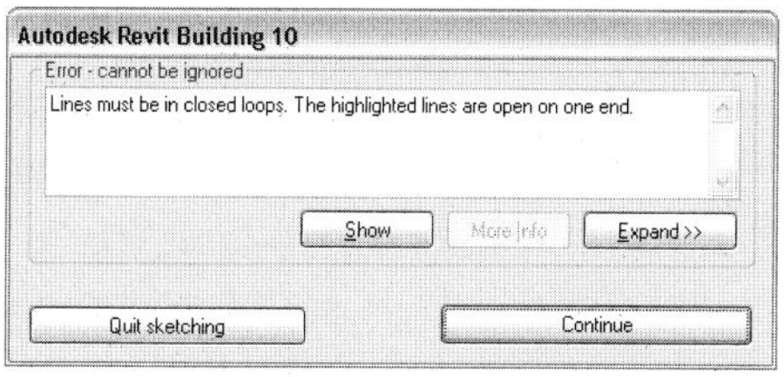

Figure 4.53

The warning if lines don't form closed loops

Autodesk Revit Building 10

Error - cannot be ignored

Lines must be in closed loops. The highlighted lines are open on one end.

Show   More Info   Expand >>

Quit sketching   Continue

4. The final sketch should look like Figure 4.54.

The lines in our sketch intersect and will need to be cleaned up in order to complete the sketch. The Trim tool ⊤ is great for these conditions. Let's continue:

5. Select the Trim tool in the toolbar.

6. Select pairs of lines to trim. The first pick is any line you want to trim. The second pick is the line you want to trim to; you'll see a preview of the result, as shown in Figure 4.55.

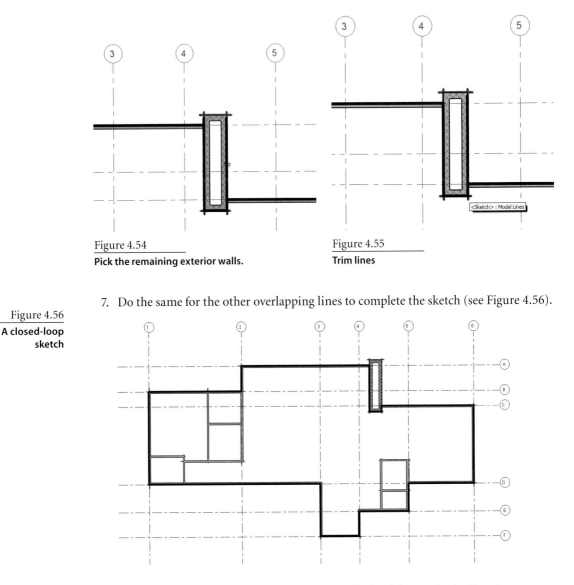

Figure 4.54

Pick the remaining exterior walls.

Figure 4.55

Trim lines

Figure 4.56

A closed-loop sketch

7. Do the same for the other overlapping lines to complete the sketch (see Figure 4.56).

8. Now that the sketch looks good, click the Finish Sketch button in the Sketch Design tab.

9. Open the 3D view and you'll see the floor. Select it by hovering the cursor over an edge of the floor and clicking when it highlights. (You can press Tab to select it if it doesn't highlight immediately.) The floor can be reedited using the Edit button on the Options bar. Figure 4.57 shows the floor in 3D.

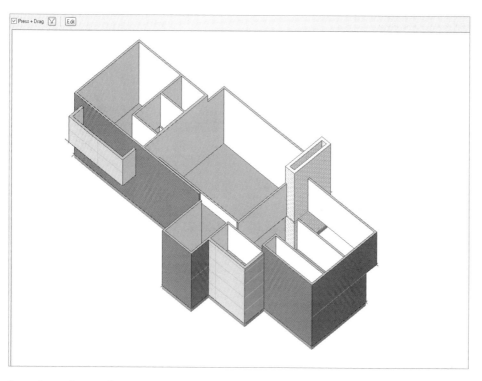

Figure 4.57

The 2D sketch generates a 3D floor.

Copying Floors from Level 1 to Level 2

Revit has some great copy and paste features that allow you to paste elements from one view into another with relative ease and also keep elements lined up in 3D space. In this section, you'll copy and paste the floor plate from Level 1 into Level 2 and then edit the sketch to match the design:

1. Select the floor in the 3D view, and copy it to the clipboard using Ctrl+C.

2. To paste the floor, choose Edit → Paste Aligned → Select Levels by Name → Level 2, and click OK (see Figure 4.58). The floor is pasted into Level 2.

3. Select the floor you just pasted, and click the Edit button in the Options bar. This will put you back in Sketch mode, where you can amend the sketch to accommodate the new shape of the floor plate on Level 2.

4. Switch the view to Level 2 plan so that it's easier to visualize the relationship of the lines to the walls (see Figure 4.59).

5. As the floor plans for each level are not the same, you'll need to adapt the sketch to meet the shape of the second floor. To do this, start by adding lines to the interior to make way for the double-height living room. Using the Pick Walls tool, select the two interior walls shown in Figure 4.59.

Figure 4.58

Pasting Level 2 in a 3D view

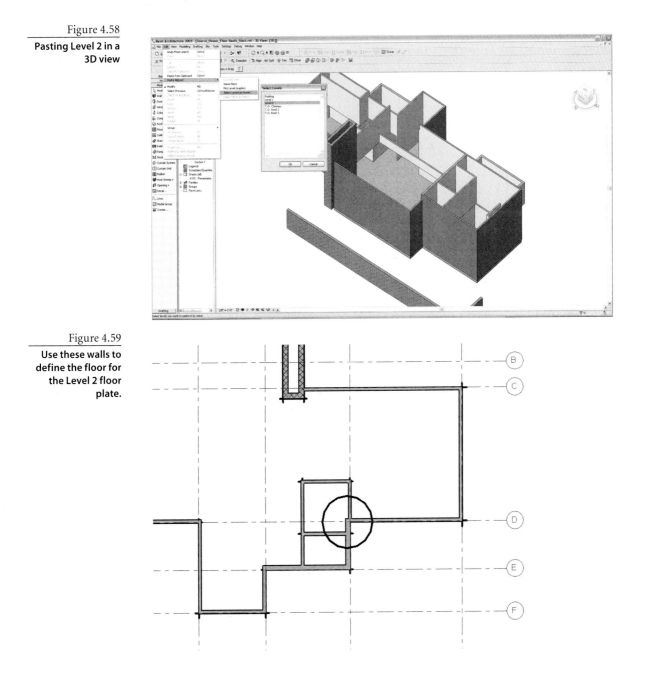

Figure 4.59

Use these walls to define the floor for the Level 2 floor plate.

6. Do the same for the walls that cantilever over Level 1. You'll get a warning about keeping elements joined when picking the cantilevered wall (see Figure 4.60). Click the Unjoin Elements button in the warning dialog box to continue.

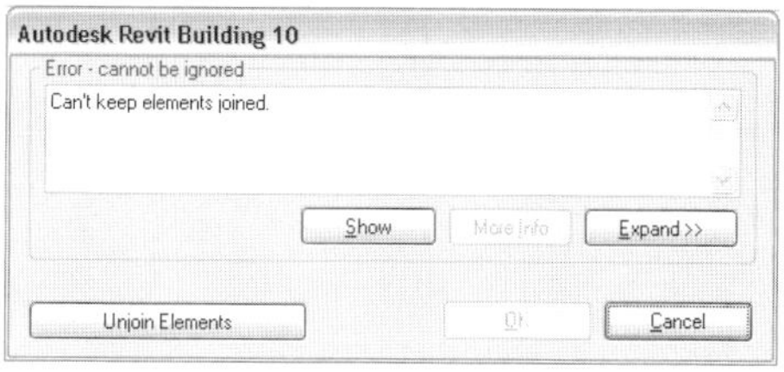

7. Using the Trim tool, clean up the sketch lines to form a continuous loop of lines. The untrimmed lines are shown in Figure 4.61. After trimming the lines, delete the leftovers.

Figure 4.60

Error message

Autodesk Revit Building 10
Error - cannot be ignored
Can't keep elements joined.

Show   More Info   Expand >>

Unjoin Elements   OK   Cancel

8. You need to continue editing the sketch to include the bump-out in the lower-left corner of the model and account for the stairwell. To do this, first pick the bump-out walls using the Pick Walls tool. If the pick puts the line on the inside of a wall, click Flip Arrows to toggle the line to the outside face. For the stairs, delete lines that you don't need.

Figure 4.61

Before the lines are trimmed

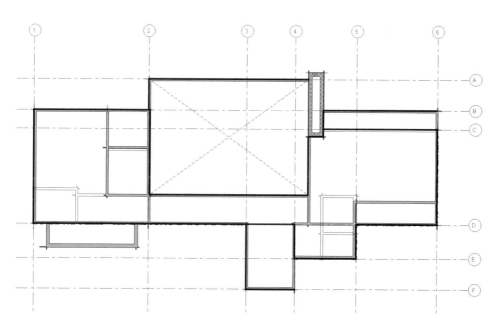

Next, you'll clean up the lines so the sketch forms a closed loop. Here are the steps:

1. Use the Split tool to split the horizontal line into two segments, as shown in Figure 4.62.

2. Complete the sketch by trimming the lines to one another.

Figure 4.62

Split the lines, and then trim.

3. Click Finish Sketch in the Sketch tab. A dialog box opens, asking if you want the walls to attach to the bottom of the floor (see Figure 4.63).

Figure 4.63

Dialog box asking if you want to attach the walls to levels

4. Click Yes. The interior walls will connect to the bottom of the floor. This ensures that section views of the model look correct. When walls are attached to floors, they dynamically adjust their height to match the bottom of the floor, even when floor thickness is changed or given an offset from a level.

5. The next dialog box asks if you want to join the floor with wall geometry (see Figure 4.64). Click Yes.

Figure 4.64

Joining floor and wall geometry

This option automatically joins walls that overlap with the floor—in this case, the exterior walls. The resulting graphics manifest in section views, producing a cleaned-up relationship between the layers in the walls and floors.

Adding the Main Roof

Now that you've created the basic floors, let's add some roofs to the house. Roofs are created in the same manner as floors: as sketches that relate to a level in the project and that define the base shape of the roof. As you'll see, roofs allow you to specify slopes for each line in the sketch, which lets you rapidly create hipped, gable, shed, and flat roof configurations. Follow these steps:

1. Open the Level 2 floor plan.

2. From the Basics tab in the Design bar, select the Roof tool ◈ Roof :. A flyout menu appears. Select the option Roof by Footprint. Just as with floors, you're placed in a sketch-editing mode where you can use existing geometry to construct the sketch boundary lines or draw the desired shape with lines. Since we are working on a flat roof, make sure the Define Slope option is unchecked before you start drawing.

3. Use the Pick Walls option. Look at the Options bar, and set the roof overhang to 1'-0″ (30cm). This offsets the sketch line from the wall to produce a parametrically associated overhang distance.

4. Hover the cursor over an exterior wall and press Tab. When the perimeter walls are highlighted, click to select them. The beginning of the sketch is created, as shown in Figure 4.65.

5. Add lines for the cutout around the fireplace.

6. Delete lines over the staircase—you'll add a separate roof over that area later. Figure 4.66 shows the lines to delete. Use Trim to form a closed loop and get the sketch to look like that in Figure 4.67.

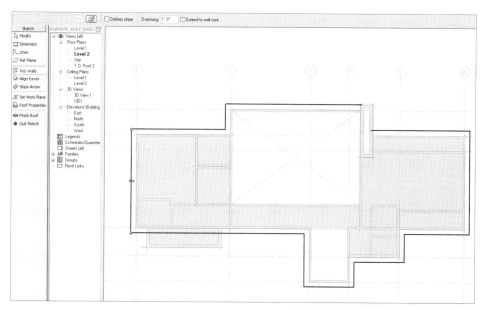

Figure 4.65

Use the Tab key to select sketch lines.

Figure 4.66

Figure 4.66

Initial lines created from a Tab-selection of the exterior walls

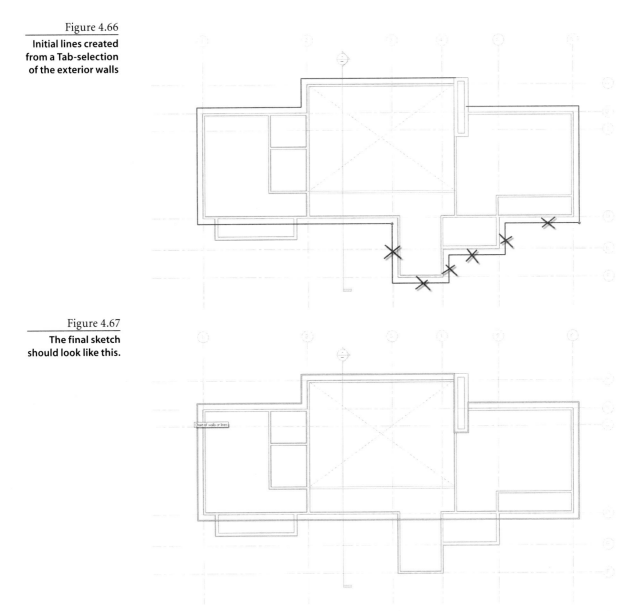

Figure 4.67

The final sketch should look like this.

7. Before finishing the sketch, set the base constraint. In the sketch Design bar, click the Roof Properties button ⬒ . Set Base Level to T.O. Roof 3 (see Figure 4.68).

8. You've just created a flat roof. However, you want the roof to have a slight slope, creating a gently sloping shed. Select the bottom horizontal sketch line. In the Options bar is a toggle ☑ Defines slope for setting lines to define slope: toggle it. An icon appears

beside the sketch line indicating that it's slope-defining. Select the line and change the slope value from 9 ½″ to 1″ (Figure 4.69). Finish the roof sketch ✅ Finish Roof . If you get an error that you have overlapping lines, check where Revit indicates the problem and clean up the lines.

Figure 4.68
Roof properties

Element Properties	
Family:	System Family: Basic Roof
Type:	Generic - 12″

Type Parameters: Control all elements of this type

Parameter	Value
Construction	
Structure	Edit...
Default Thickness	1' 0"
Graphics	
Coarse Scale Fill Pattern	

Instance Parameters - Control selected or to-be-created instance

Parameter	Value
Constraints	
Base Level	T.O. Roof 3
Room Bounding	Footing
Related to Mass	Level 1
Base Offset From Level	Level 2
Cutoff Level	T.O. Roof 2
Cutoff Offset	T.O. Roof 3
	T.O. Chimney
Construction	
Rafter Cut	Plumb Cut
Fascia Depth	0' 0"
Rafter or Truss	Truss
Maximum Ridge Height	0' 0"
Dimensions	
Rise/12"	
Thickness	1' 0"

Once you've defined a slope in a roof, this can be changed from outside of Sketch mode. Simply select the roof, open the Element Properties dialog box, and then change the Slope parameter value.

9. Look at the model in 3D.

10. Select the roof, and change its type from Basic Roof: Generic – 12″ to Basic Roof: Metal Roof. The metal roof has a pattern of lines that represents standing seam roof panels defined in the type properties of that roof type (see Figure 4.70).

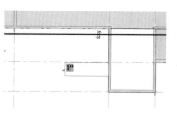

Figure 4.69
Changing the roof pitch

If you spin the model to the side, you'll notice a gap between the top of the walls and the roof. This is easily rectified using the Top/Base Attach tool in the Options bar Top/Base: Attach Detach . In Figure 4.71, you can see where the walls aren't attached to the roof.

11. Spin the model a bit, and then use the Tab-selection method to select the exterior walls.

Figure 4.70

Modifying the roof type

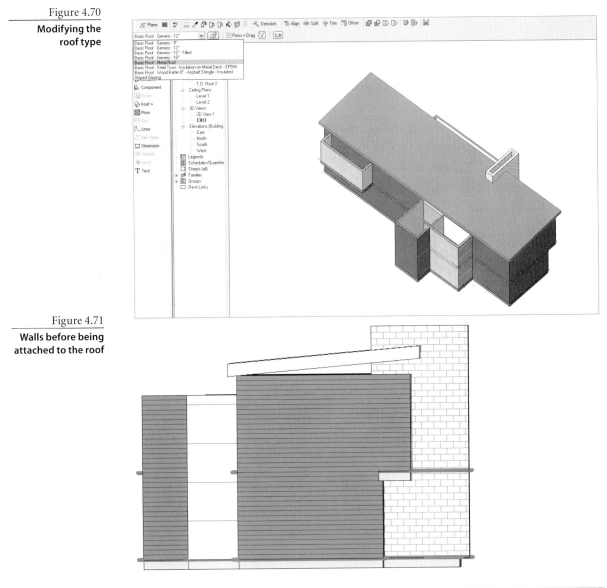

Figure 4.70

Modifying the roof type

Figure 4.71

Walls before being attached to the roof

12. Click the Top/Base Attach button in the Options bar, and then select the main roof. The walls extend up to meet the underside of the roof. When you get the warning message shown in Figure 4.72, click Detach Target(s). This detaches walls that aren't entirely below the roof (the walls in the foreground). The resulting geometry should look like Figure 4.73.

Figure 4.72

Warning message

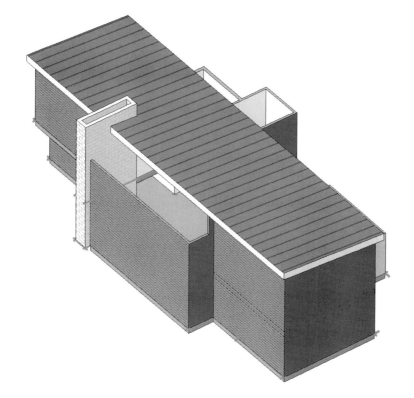

Figure 4.73

Walls are now attached to the roof.

The great thing about the Top/Base Attach tool is that if the roof pitch is changed, the walls will parametrically adapt to the new slope! To experiment with this, select the roof and open the Element Properties dialog box. Change the roof slope, and watch as the walls dynamically update.

Creating Additional Roofs

You'll now add the remaining roofs and make walls attach to them:

1. Open the plan view T.O. Roof 2 using the Project Browser.

2. Start with the roof in the lower left in Figure 4.74. Use Roof by Footprint, pick the three exterior walls, and then draw the last line to make a closed rectangle. (Switch to Draw mode by clicking the pencil icon in the Options bar.) Also using the Options bar, set the overhang to 0´-0˝, and make sure all the lines are non-slope-defining.

3. When you've got a closed loop of lines, click Finish Roof.

4. Create additional roofs over the entry and the main living space (see Figure 4.75) using the same techniques. Make one roof for each condition.

Figure 4.74

Adding a roof with no slope

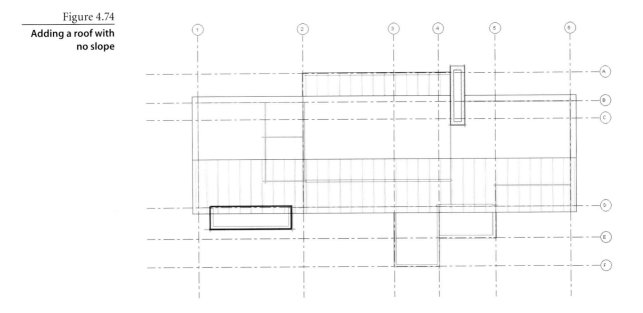

Figure 4.74

Adding a roof with no slope

Here are some best practices for roof creation. When walls are already created in your design, use the Pick Walls option. Then, switch to the Lines tool to finish drawing the sketch. Use the Trim tool to clean lines and get rid of any overlapping or unconnected lines. When no walls are present or the base geometry of the roof doesn't match the geometry that the exterior walls create, go directly to the Lines tool and draw the shape of the roof.

Modifying an Existing Roof

Go to the 3D view. If the roofs aren't already the Metal roof type, you need to change them. Using selection (picking the roofs) and the Type Selector (changing to the type you want) is a common method, but there is also a nice tool that lets you pick a type and then apply that type to other elements with a few clicks.

This tool is called Match Properties ✐, and it's located in the toolbar. To use the Match Properties tool, you first select the type of element you want to convert other elements into. You then select elements of the same category, and they will change type with each subsequent mouse click. This tool works for the majority of existing Revit elements. Try it out:

1. Select the Match Properties tool in the toolbar.

2. Select the main roof. Note that the cursor appears filled—as if you sucked that type into your dropper. With each selection, you can change types belonging to the same category (in this case, the category Roof; see Figure 4.76).

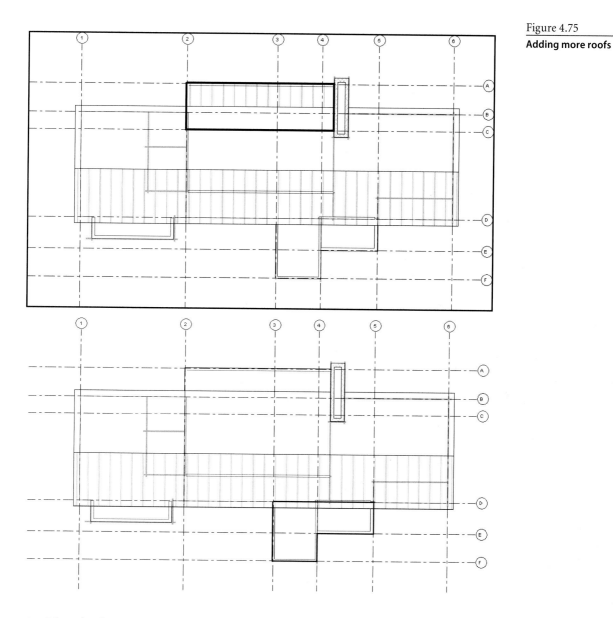

Figure 4.75

Adding more roofs

3. Select the three roofs whose type you wish to change.

   Next, you'll give these roofs a negative offset from the level to make room for some clerestory windows.

4. Select all three roofs by holding down Ctrl and selecting them. Open the roofs' Element Properties dialog box, as shown in Figure 4.77.

Figure 4.76

Select the roof with the Match Properties tool.

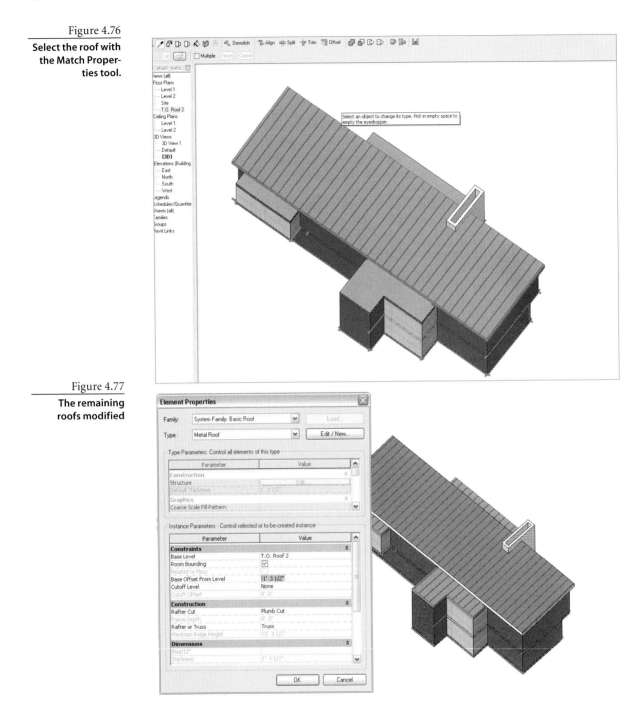

Figure 4.77

The remaining roofs modified

5. Change the Base Offset to −1′3 ½″ (40cm), the thickness of the roof.

6. Select the walls below the roofs you just created, and attach them to the roof as shown in Figure 4.78.

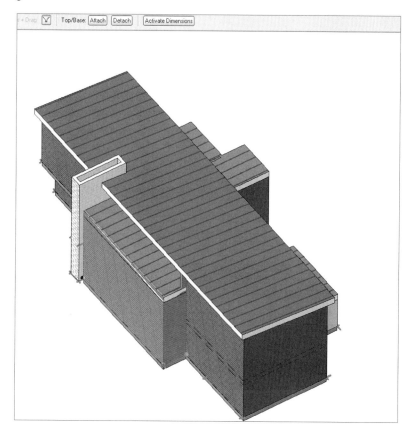

Figure 4.78

Attach the walls to the roof.

7. When you get the error message shown in Figure 4.79, click the Detach Target(s) button. This changes the attachment of the wall so that it connects with the lower roof.

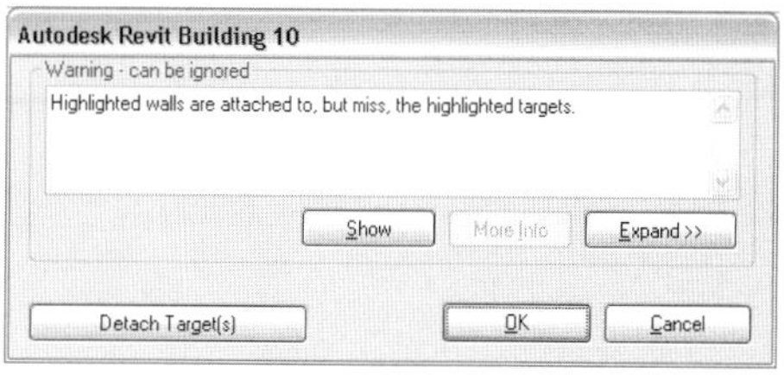

Figure 4.79

Detach Target(s) error message

Attaching Interior Walls to the Roof

To attach the tops of the interior walls to the underside of a roof, you need to be able to select them first. With the roof in the way, this might appear to be a problem. To resolve this issue, you can temporarily make the roof transparent, select the walls through the roof, and then attach the walls. When you are done, you reset the roof graphics to clear the transparency override.

1. Select the main roof, right-click, and select Override Graphics in View by Element from the context menu. Check the option to make the roof transparent, then open the Surface Patterns node and uncheck the Visible option. The roof will turn 100 percent transparent, and the surface patterns will be turned off (Figure 4.80).

Figure 4.80

Model with the roof made transparent and surface patterns turned off

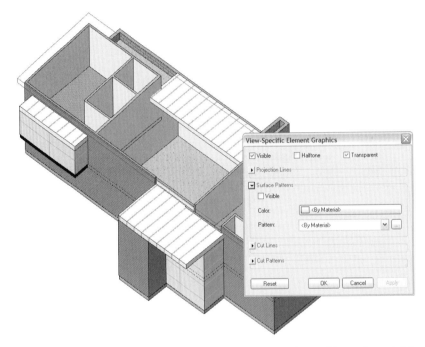

2. Select the interior walls on Level 2 by holding down the Ctrl key when picking.

3. With walls still selected, click the Top/Base: Attach button in the Options bar, then select the roof.

4. Select the roof, and open the Element Overrides dialog box again using the context menu. Click the Reset button to clear all the overrides (Figure 4.81) and click OK to finish.

To see the effect of the wall meeting the roof, you can temporarily hide the roof using the temporary hide/isolate tool in the View control ⬚. Select the roof and then choose Hide Element from the flyout menu.

A TIP ABOUT SKETCH DESIGN

With a sketch-based design, an element is created from a closed loop of lines. More than one loop is allowed. If you draw a loop of lines within the boundary of another loop, then the shape defined by the interior loop will be negative space. This makes it easy to create openings for stairs, chimneys, and so on—just draw a second loop of lines in the shape of the opening, and voilà!

Making Curtain Walls

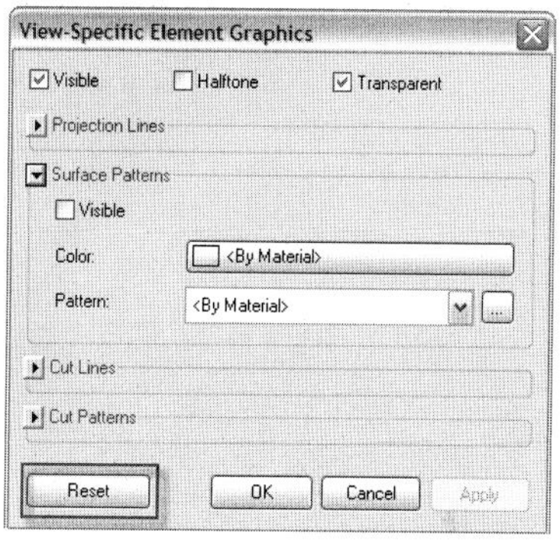

To add some clerestory windows to the design, you have two options: you can create a new window type or, even faster, you can use the Curtain Wall tool. Curtain walls are a special wall type that lets you place mullions and panels on a grid surface. Each gridline divides the wall into sections, which become panels. Mullions separate individual panels and are placed on curtain grids. For this exercise, you'll use a curtain wall where the mullions and panels are predefined in the wall type, and automat-

Figure 4.81
Resetting the Hide command

ically embed themselves into basic walls when drawn on top of a basic wall. This makes layout extremely quick and easy to manage. You can continue with the file you created so far, or open the file Source_House_CurtainWall_Start.rvt. Follow these steps:

1. In the default 3D view, hide the main roof using the Temporary Hide/Isolate control located in the View Control bar. Select the roof, and then choose the option Hide Element from the View Control bar.(see Figure 4.82).

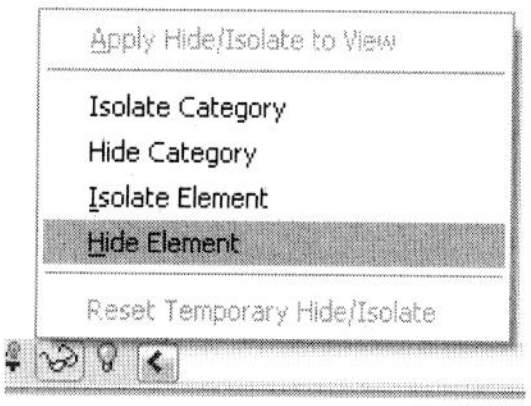

2. Once the roof is hidden, use the Wall tool in the Basics tab to set the wall type to Curtain Wall: Storefront. In the Options bar, set Level to T.O. Roof 2 and Height to T.O. Roof 3.

Figure 4.82
The Hide Element option for the roof

3. Draw the curtain wall, as shown in Figure 4.83. Use snapping to get the correct placement.

4. Add a similar curtain wall to the opposite side of the model (see Figure 4.84).

5. Choose Reset Temporary Hide/Isolate from the View Control bar so the roof reappears.

6. Select the curtain wall at the back of the house, and attach it to the roof above using the Attach button in the Options bar.

Figure 4.83

Draw the curtain wall as shown.

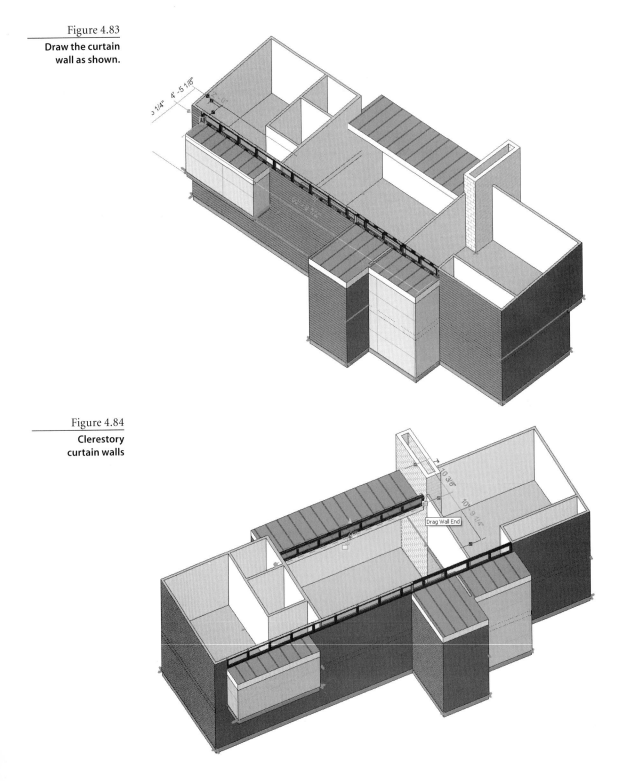

Figure 4.84

Clerestory curtain walls

7. You'll get a message about elements becoming invalid. Click the Delete Element(s) button (see Figure 4.85). This isn't a problem; Revit is just letting you know that it needs to delete the elements in order to re-create them. The mullions will be regenerated once the curtain wall is attached to the roof.

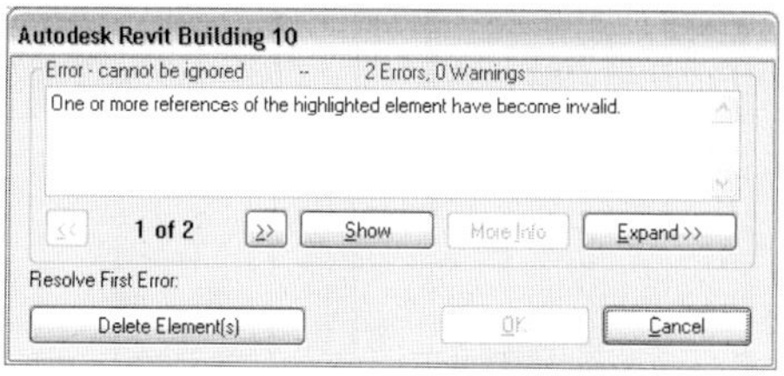

Figure 4.85

Warning dialog box with option to delete elements message

Adding Curtain Walls to the North Façade

Now that you have the clerestory windows in place, let's use the same tool to add a glass wall to the façade:

1. Open the Level 1 plan view and choose the Storefront curtain wall type again.

2. Set the Height to T.O. Roof 2 in the Options bar.

3. Draw the wall from the edge of the fireplace to the center of the wall (see Figure 4.86). A triangle snap icon appears when the wall's end hits the center.

Figure 4.86

Draw a curtain wall from the chimney to the wall midpoint.

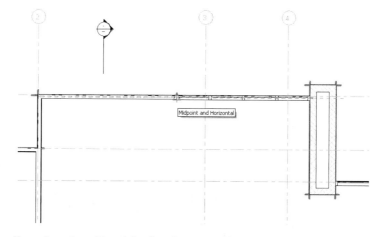

4. Add a curtain wall on the other side of the fireplace as well, as shown in Figure 4.87. Set this wall's height to Level 2.

5. Open the north elevation. In this view, you can see the effect of the curtain walls you just made, as shown in Figure 4.88.

6. Select each curtain wall, and attach each to the roof above using the Top/Base Attach tool you used for the interior and exterior walls (the button on the Options bar). To select the curtain wall, hover the cursor over an outer boundary of the curtain wall until a dashed frame appears. Note that selecting a mullion or panel doesn't select the curtain wall.

Figure 4.87

Adding the second curtain wall

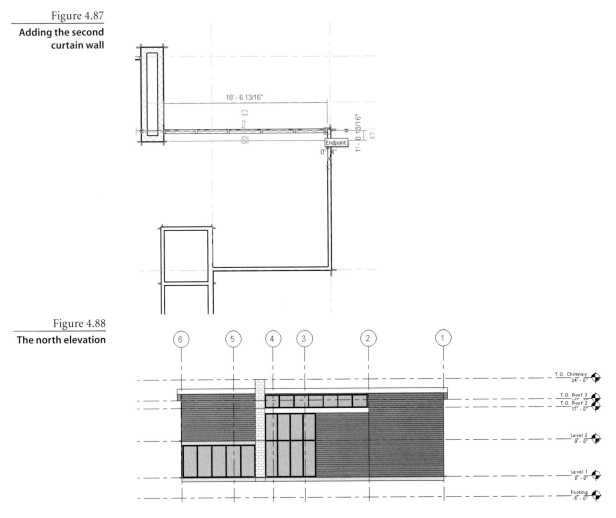

Figure 4.88

The north elevation

7. You'll get the message shown in Figure 4.89 about mullions being removed. Again, this isn't an error; it's Revit alerting you to its process. Click the Delete Element(s) button to continue.

Figure 4.89

Mullions being removed

Changing the Grid Pattern

The curtain walls you've been placing preset the spacing of grids, which in turn determines the spacing of mullions and panels. You can deviate from the pattern interactively to make patterns that are more irregular:

1. To align the curtain wall on the north façade with the clerestory windows, activate the Align tool. Select a curtain grid in the clerestory first, and then select the edge of

the curtain wall. When selecting a grid, make sure you select a grid, not a mullion (press Tab when the mouse is over a mullion until the dashed line representing the grid shows up and then click). The two curtain walls should now be aligned.

2. Remove some grid segments and mullions to give the wall more interest. To do so, hover the cursor over the vertical mullion nearest gridline 4. Press the Tab key to cycle the selection until a curtain gridline highlights (be careful—*not* the mullion, but the curtain grid). Select this grid.

3. Note that the gridline has a pin icon associated with it. This indicates that the grid is locked into place and can't be moved interactively. This is because the grid is defined in the wall type—as a spacing rule. However, the grid can be unpinned and then moved interactively if you desire. Click the pin to unlock it, and drag the grid. For now, let's leave the grid pinned and only deal with removing segments of grids. You can see the pins in Figure 4.90.

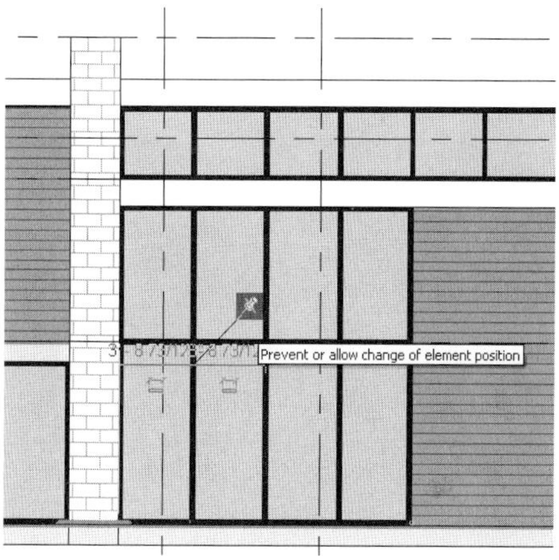

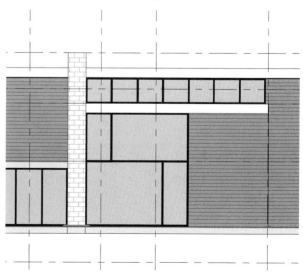

Figure 4.90

Curtain wall modifications

4. With the curtain grid selected, click the Add or Remove Segments button on the Options bar Add or Remove Segments . You can now add and remove segments of grid that span between other grids. Remove the bottom grid segment by selecting it. You'll notice that the mullions are also removed. Do the same for the adjacent grids until the picture looks like Figure 4.91 (two bottom grid segments and two top segments removed).

Figure 4.91

The completed curtain wall

5. To replace grids and mullions on the curtain wall, select a curtain gridline and use the Add/ Remove tool again. Selecting on a dashed grid segment puts back the segment as well as the mullion.

6. Open the Exterior Perspective 3D view, and look at your model in 3D (see Figure 4.92). Remember, you can use Shift+middle mouse button to orbit the model in 3D.

Figure 4.92

The completed curtain wall in the 3D model

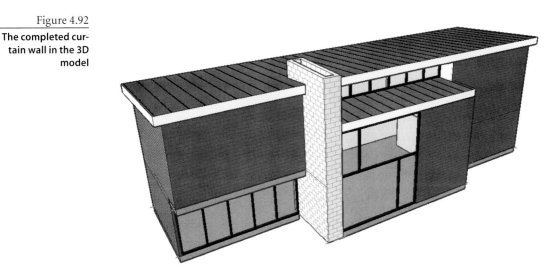

Adding Doors and Windows

Now that you've constructed the basic envelope of a small house, let's move back to the inside and place some windows and doors. Follow these steps:

1. Go to the Level 1 floor plan.

2. From the Basics or Modeling tab, select the Door tool.

3. Set the door type to Single-Flush 34″ × 84″ (85 × 210cm).

4. Move your cursor over walls in the model—note that the door previews before it's placed. If the mouse isn't over a wall, no preview appears, and the door can't be placed.

5. Place the door as shown in Figure 4.93.

Figure 4.93

Adding a door

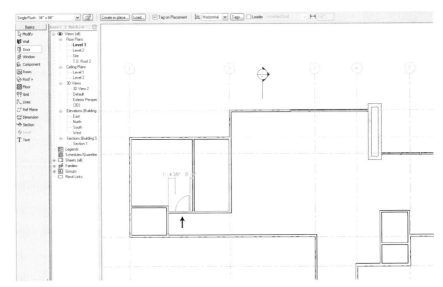

Note the helpful dimensions that appear during placement.

Temporary dimensions show up during and after placement to aid you in locating the door. Once the door has been placed, the dimensions become active controls that you can use to precisely position the door relative to nearby references, such as walls, grids, or other doors:

1. To edit a dimension value, click the numeric value, and it becomes an editable text field.

2. Clicking the blue squares of the temporary dimension cycles the dimension between centerlines and opening conditions.

   For example, after placing the door, select the blue control for the temporary dimension that snaps to the door centerline, and move it toward the door leaf. Note that the dimension jumps to a new location. Now, click the dimension value and set the distance to be 6″ (15cm). See Figure 4.94.

You'll notice that the door was given a tag when it was placed. This is an option available in the Options bar during placement. For this exercise, you don't need to see tags yet. Go ahead and delete the tag (hover the cursor over the tag; if you can't select it, use the Tab key to cycle to it), and select the Door tool again. This time, uncheck the option Tag on Placement in the Options bar. This will prevent the doors from being tagged automatically from here on out.

Let's continue to place doors. When you're placing doors, get accustomed to using the spacebar to flip the door orientation and make the door face correctly. If you don't place a door correctly, no problem—select the door and press the spacebar until the door looks right. For now, place the same door so the image looks roughly like Figure 4.95.

Figure 4.94

Locating the door

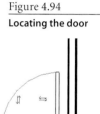
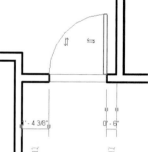

Figure 4.95

Placing more doors

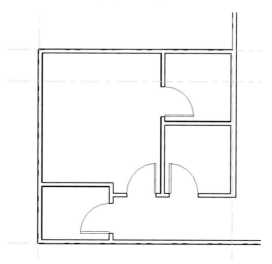

Once the doors are placed, you can create constraints between the doors and nearby walls. This is useful if you want to maintain a specific relationship between a door and a wall so that if the wall moves, the doors move with it.

To do this, you'll convert a temporary dimension into a permanent dimension and then lock the dimension to create a constraint. You'll then delete the dimension but leave the constraint in place. Here are the steps:

1. Choose Settings → Temporary Dimensions.

2. In the Walls options, select Faces of Core; in the Doors and Windows options, select Openings, as shown in Figure 4.96.

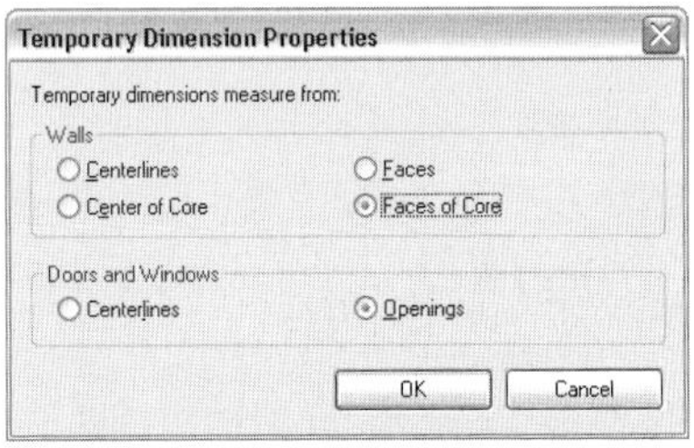

3. Go back to the view and select a door; notice that the behavior of the temporary dimensions is different—the dimensions follow your new rules when initialized. This will let you set distances between door openings and the stud faces in your walls with a few clicks.

Temporary Dimension Properties

Temporary dimensions measure from:

Walls
- Centerlines
- Center of Core
- Faces
- Faces of Core

Doors and Windows
- Centerlines
- Openings

OK   Cancel

Figure 4.96

Change the temporary dimensions for walls to Faces of Core; and for doors and windows, change them to Openings.

4. Use the temporary dimensions to get the door opening 6″ (15cm) from the stud face of the wall, as shown in Figure 4.97.

Figure 4.97

Temporary dimensions at the door

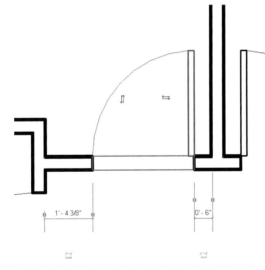

1'- 4 3/8"   0'- 6"

5. Click the icon that looks like a blue dimension string. This converts the temporary dimension into a regular dimension.

6. Select the dimension and click the lock icon. This creates a fixed constraint between the door and the wall (Figure 4.98).

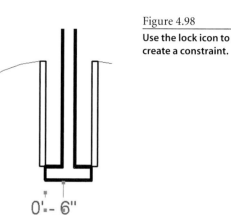

Figure 4.98

Use the lock icon to create a constraint.

7. You don't want to have that dimension when you print later—you just used it to set a rule. You'd like to delete the dimension but keep the rule you defined. When you select and delete the dimension, you'll get a warning message (see Figure 4.99); you can either unconstrain the condition or click OK and keep the constraint but still delete the dimension. Click OK.

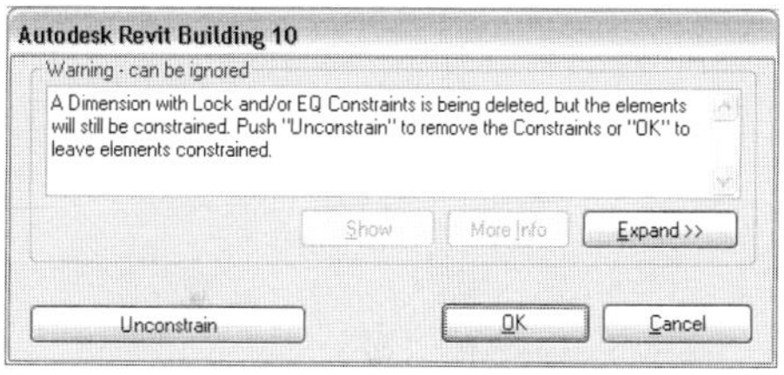

8. Do the same thing for the door on the other side of the wall.

9. Select the wall, and the locks show up again, indicating the presence of a constraint. Clicking the lock (unlocking it) deletes the constraint. Figure 4.100 shows the constraints.

Figure 4.99

Revit allows you to keep or remove your constraints.

Figure 4.100

Locks indicate a constraint.

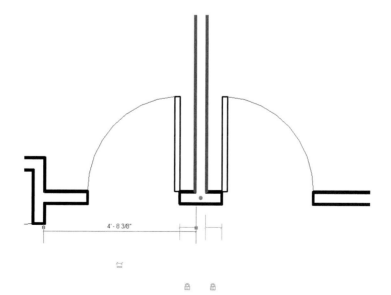

10. If you move the wall by dragging it or using the temporary dimension, the doors will also move. Go ahead and change the temporary dimension from 4′8″ to 5′0″ (130cm to 150cm) to see this work.

11. Place more doors in the project: glass doors for the exterior doors and smaller doors for the bathroom and the closet near front entry. Figure 4.101 shows additional door locations.

Figure 4.101

Additional door locations

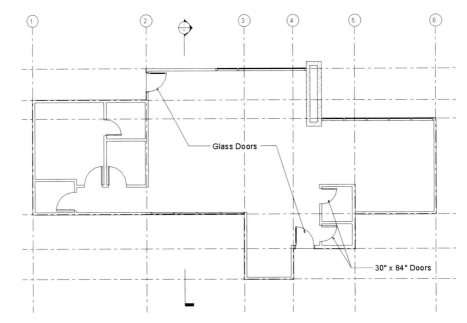

12. Changing door types is just like changing wall types. Select the door and use the Type Selector to swap the door with a different type.

    For the moment, don't worry if you don't find the exact type of door you wish to use. We'll explain later how you can find more doors or adjust existing ones to serve your needs.

Adding Doors to Level 2

Let's continue to place doors in the model:

1. Open the Level 2 plan view.

2. Place the following types of doors in Level 2, as shown in Figure 4.102:

   - By-pass sliders

   - Single flush 34″ × 84″ (85cm × 210cm)

   - A pocket door

   Use temporary dimensions to place door openings 6″ (15cm) from stud faces, as you did on Level 1.

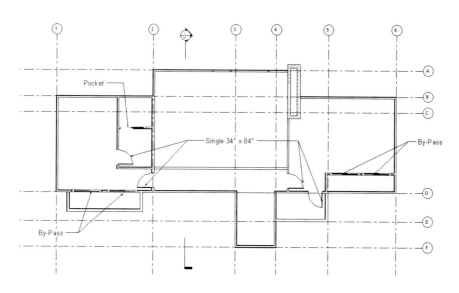

Figure 4.102

Place these second-floor doors.

Placing Windows

Placing windows is just like placing doors. Use the Window tool in either the Basics or Modeling tab of the Design bar. You'll start by placing some sliders and then some fixed openings. The sliders have a fixed-size set in the type properties, and the fixed windows have instance-based sizes. We'll explore the behavior of both type and instance families. Let's start placing windows:

1. In the Level 2 plan view, select the Window tool from the Basics tab. Choose the type Slider with Trim: 7′0″ × 4′0″ (215cm × 120cm). Uncheck the Tag on Placement option. Place windows in the walls as indicated in Figure 4.103.

2. Place windows of type Fixed – Varied Size in the locations shown in Figure 4.104.

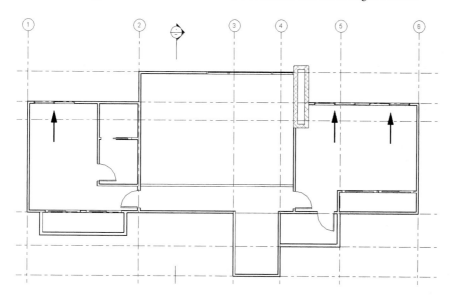

Figure 4.103

Placing slider windows

Figure 4.104

Placing the remaining windows

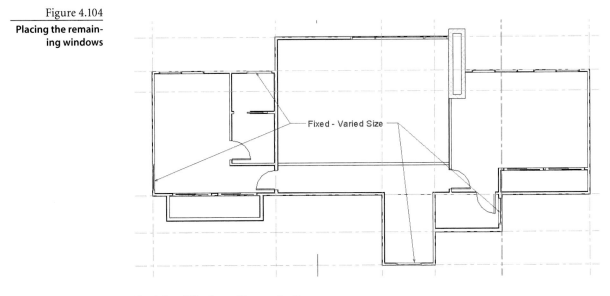

Fixed - Varied Size

Resizing Windows Dynamically

The Fixed – Varied Size window is designed so that its width and height are set to be instance parameters as opposed to the window you previously used, whose width and height were set to be type parameters. Setting the dimensions of an object to be instance parameters gives you the advantage of working with more flexible, directly editable elements; you can modify them with the blue grips that display when they're selected.

To see how to dynamically size a window using the blue grips, select the window and make it wider.

> Be aware that instance parameters, when changed, don't propagate that change throughout all similar elements in the project. The change is applicable only to that one instance of the element.

To adjust the height of the window, open the West Elevation view and select the window. Similar controls appear. Dragging the controls resizes the window dynamically.

Feel free to change the sizes of the other windows you just placed by opening each elevation and making adjustments, as shown in Figure 4.105.

Let's place one more window. Open the South Elevation, select the Window tool, and choose the Fixed – Size Varies type. Place the window in the façade and adjust its size as shown in Figure 4.106.

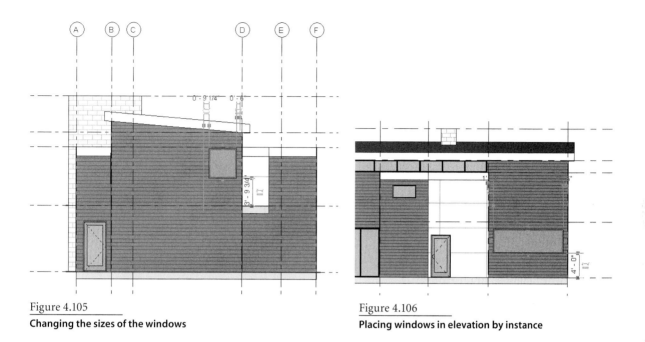

Figure 4.105

Changing the sizes of the windows

Figure 4.106

Placing windows in elevation by instance

Getting Additional Content Online

The windows you've placed are fairly generic. The beauty of Revit is that these windows can be swapped out with different window types on the fly at any stage of the project. Remember, it's never too late to do any changes in Revit. Content from the default libraries, from the Web, or your own custom-made elements can be loaded into the project and swapped. Try searching the web library for additional window and door types, and load them into the project:

1. Open an Internet browser.

2. Using Internet Explorer, Browse to `http://revit.autodesk.com/library`.

3. Browse for content and save it to disk (see Figure 4.107).

4. Once you've saved the content, select the Window tool and click the Load button in the Options bar. This will take you to a file browser. Locate the files you downloaded and click Open.

> If you create library elements on your own or download them from the Web, make sure you create a separate folder to store these in. You can then specify this location as an additional path when loading content that shows up in the left pane of the Load Family dialog box. To add a new library, use Settings → Options dialog box. Open the File Locations tab and add a new Library location.

Figure 4.107

Autodesk online families

Revit families can be dragged and dropped from Windows Explorer but not from the Web. If you have Windows Explorer open, try dragging and dropping a family (.rfa) file directly into your Revit project. You can also open a family directly using the Open option when downloading families. Doing so opens the family in the Family Editor—the tool used to design and build families. To get the family into your project, you can then use the Load Into Projects button in the Design bar.

Figure 4.108

Content in the Type Selector

Placing Components

For the next step, you're going to add furniture, plumbing fixtures, and other interior equipment in the building. You can use the file that you have created until now or open the file named Source_House_Components_Start.rvt from the book's companion web page.

Placing Furniture

Placing freestanding furniture is simple. Using the Component Placement tool in the Basics or Modeling tab populates the Type Selector with available components. The list doesn't include windows and doors, but it does have a mixture of other categories of elements. For example, furniture, plumbing fixtures, and plantings appear on the list. An example is shown in Figure 4.108.

As this list is really long (and full of elements from multiple categories), you may find it easier to drag from the Family list in the Project Browser.

If you can locate the type of family you want to place, this method works fine:

1. Open the Level 1 plan view.

2. Choose the Dining Table and Chairs family from the drop-down list.

3. Move the cursor into the view. A temporary graphic representing the table and chairs appears on the cursor (Figure 4.109).

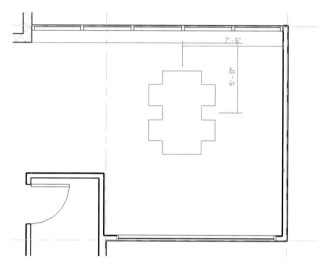

Figure 4.109

Inserting a dining-room table

4. Press the spacebar prior to placement to rotate the table by 90 degrees.

Next, continue placing more furniture components in the model: couches and tables. Follow these steps:

1. Place the Sofa Loveseat, Sofa Couch, and Coffee Table using the Component tool. Create the furniture arrangement in the living space.

2. To mirror the Loveseat across from the Coffee Table, select the Loveseat, and then select the Mirror ⊞ Mirror tool in the toolbar at the top of the interface.

3. Select the center reference of the table as the mirror axis. The Loveseat mirrors across this axis, creating a new instance (see Figure 4.110).

To place additional furniture elements, such as beds and nightstands, use the same technique. Use the Component tool, and choose appropriate families from the Type Selector. Open the Level 2 plan view, and place some beds to get familiar with this behavior.

Figure 4.110

Furniture placement

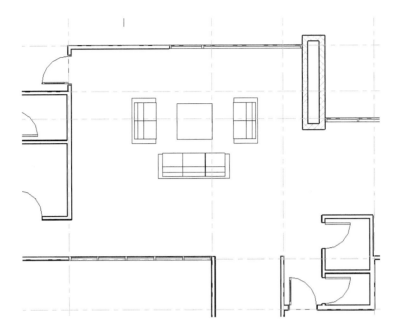

Placing Plumbing Fixtures

Placing plumbing fixtures follows the same paradigm as placing other components. However, for this exercise, you'll use the Project Browser rather than the Component tool to place your components:

1. Open the Families node in the Project Browser.

2. Open the Plumbing Fixtures node: this represents the category of element you wish to place.

3. Open the Shower Stall-2D node: this is the family name. The family types show up under this node (see Figure 4.111).

4. To place a component from the browser, drag the family type from the browser into the view. The visual feedback is exactly as if you chose the type from the Type Selector—the element appears on your cursor, ready for placement.

5. Drag the family into the view, and press the spacebar to rotate it.

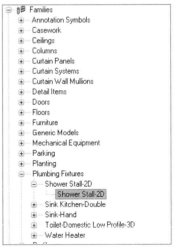

Figure 4.111

Fixtures under the Families node

6. Place it so that it snap-aligns to a wall. To see this, hover the component over a wall: the wall edge highlights.

7. Using the same method, place the sink (Sink-Hand) and toilet (Domestic-Low profile). The completed bathroom looks like Figure 4.112.

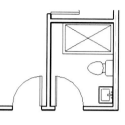

Figure 4.112

The finished bath-room layout

Remember to use the spacebar before placement, and hover the cursor near walls to orient the object correctly.

Using the same technique, you can finish the other bathrooms in the model (Figure 4.113). Be sure to take advantage of the Place Similar tool by first selecting the component you want to duplicate (such as a sink or toilet) and then clicking Place Similar. This puts the component onto your cursor, and you can bypass the need to search for content in the Type Selector or family browser.

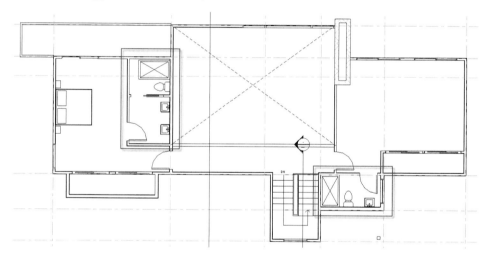

Figure 4.113

The finished bath-room layout on Level 2

Some additional families are loaded into the project, which you can experiment with. Using the furniture components in the project, attempt to create a kitchen configuration.

Stairs and Railings

Stairs in Revit are created using a Sketch mode where you can define stair boundaries, risers, and runs by drawing a 2D line sketch. Those sketches are then used to automatically generate a smart parametric 3D stair element of any complexity level. A number of stair-type variations are shown in Figure 4.113. Figure 4.114 shows a stair in Sketch mode and 3D view. Different colors are automatically assigned to risers, boundary, and runs.

Figure 4.114

**Stairs in Sketch
mode and in 3D
view**

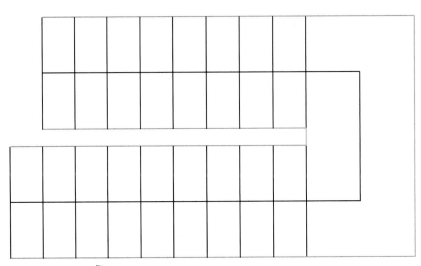

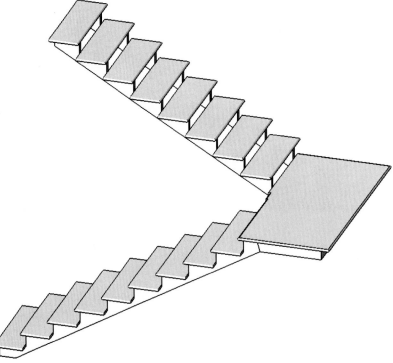

Stairs are considered complex architectural elements because their construction is dependent on local building rules defined in building codes. Revit allows you to set different rules based on your building code requirements. Just as with walls and floors, stairs are constructed using relationships to levels: all stairs have a base level and a top level that are used to calculate tread depth and height based on min–max rules.

These parameters, shown in Figure 4.115, change from stair to stair and are the most important parameters used for constructing stairs.

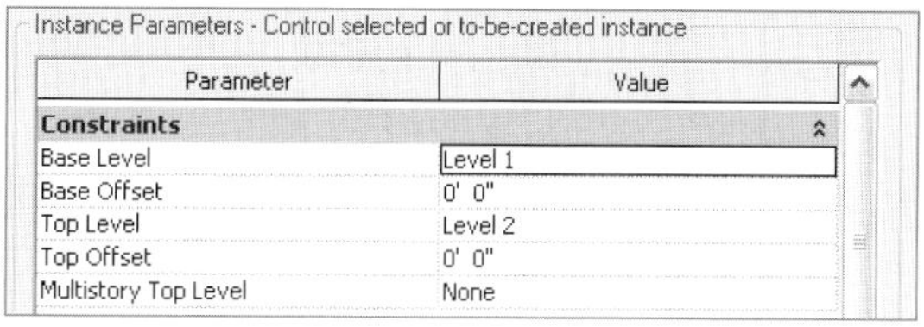

Figure 4.115
Stair levels

Instance Parameters - Control selected or to-be-created instance	
Parameter	Value
Constraints	
Base Level	Level 1
Base Offset	0' 0"
Top Level	Level 2
Top Offset	0' 0"
Multistory Top Level	None

Geometric variation of the individual elements of a stair (tread, riser, stringer, and so on) is managed with type properties that provide dimensional and material parameters. Figure 4.116 shows those type values.

The most important parameters are rules that establish minimum tread depth and maximum riser height. These values are used to automatically guarantee minimum and maximum distances to keep your stairs within the constraints of what your building codes dictate. Revit won't break these rules. Your stairs start and end where you want them, and the correct number of risers and treads are autogenerated for you when making the stair. You'll see this in the exercise later in this chapter.

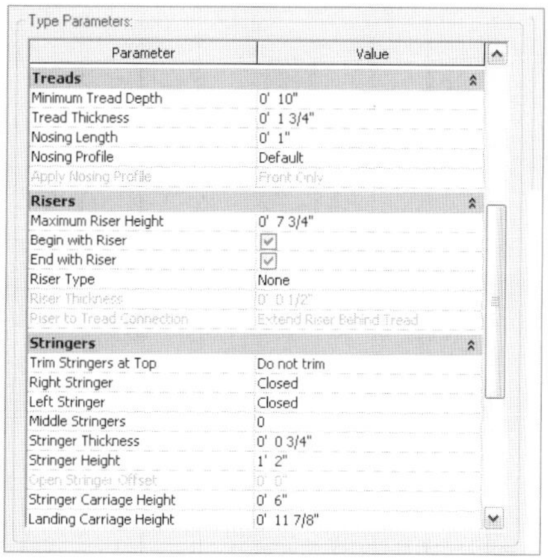

Figure 4.116

Stair properties

Type Parameters:	
Parameter	Value
Treads	
Minimum Tread Depth	0' 10"
Tread Thickness	0' 1 3/4"
Nosing Length	0' 1"
Nosing Profile	Default
Apply Nosing Profile	Front Only
Risers	
Maximum Riser Height	0' 7 3/4"
Begin with Riser	✓
End with Riser	✓
Riser Type	None
Riser Thickness	0' 0 1/2"
Riser to Tread Connection	Extend Riser Behind Tread
Stringers	
Trim Stringers at Top	Do not trim
Right Stringer	Closed
Left Stringer	Closed
Middle Stringers	0
Stringer Thickness	0' 0 3/4"
Stringer Height	1' 2"
Open Stringer Offset	0' 0"
Stringer Carriage Height	0' 6"
Landing Carriage Height	0' 11 7/8"

Creating a Stair

You need to create a stair from Level 1 to Level 2 in your model. From the Chapter 4 folder on the book's companion web page, open `Source_House_Stairs-Railings_Start.rvt`. You'll start by sketching the stair in Level 1 and making sure it's going up to Level 2. You'll then look at the stair using a 3D sectional view and change the type.

Select the Stairs tool from the Modeling tab ⌗ Stairs . You'll enter the Stair Sketch Editor. Note that the Design bar is replaced with new tools specific to stair creation (shown in Figure 4.117).

Revit puts you into the Run tool by default. This tool autocreates boundary and riser lines as you draw a run line.

Now, let's discuss something briefly. When Revit prompts you to draw a stair run, it always uses the middle of the run as a justification point. Often, however, you won't have a reference to the location of the stair centerline. So, you need to either draw help lines at the distance from the wall that represents half the stair width or draw the stair in an approximate location and then move it into place.

Figure 4.117

Stair design tools

Sketch
⌖ Modify
⌗ Dimension
⟋ Ref Plane
⌗ Boundary
⌗ Riser
⌗ Run
⌗ Set Work Plane...
⌗ Stairs Properties
⌗ Railings Type
●¦● Finish Sketch
● Quit Sketch

To make this exercise useful for teaching you about other Revit editing tools along with the Stairs tool, you won't use a help line; instead, you'll draw the stair in a position close to the correct one and then adjust it to the right location using other tools. Follow these steps:

1. Start drawing the riser line by snap-aligning to the horizontal gridline to begin the run. (The blue dashed line indicates that snap.) As mentioned, the line is drawn through the center of the stair, with boundaries shown offset. A halftone text graphic also appears as you drag the run line. The text shows how many risers have been created and how many remain to get the stair from Level 1 to Level 2.

2. Drag the line until the text shows 8 RISERS CREATED, 8 REMAINING, and click the mouse once. This is where you'll break the stair for a landing. It should look similar to Figure 4.118.

Figure 4.118

Starting the stair

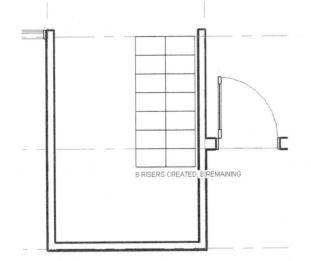

3. Begin a new run line to the left of the first stair; snap the beginning of the run to the end of the last riser.

4. Draw the run until you see 16 RISERS CREATED, 0 REMAINING. This should be a point that is aligned with where you started the stair. You've created a stair return; your drawing should appear similar to Figure 4.119.

5. By default, railings are added to stairs when created. You can preset a railing type, or choose to not autogenerate railings. In the Sketch tab of the Design bar, click the Railing Types button, and then choose None.

In order for the railings to work properly, you need to adjust the sketch a bit. Let's add a riser to the bottom of the stair and remove one from the beginning of the next run:

1. Drag the blue run line at the bottom segment of the stair until another riser appears. Revit will tell you that an additional riser is present (–1 REMAINING).

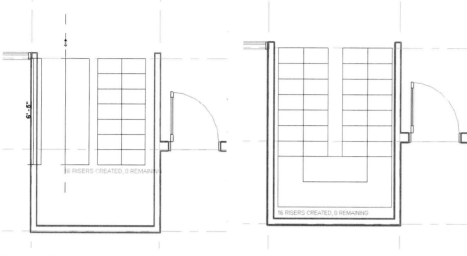

Figure 4.119

Start the return run; at right, the completed command.

2. Delete the riser at the top of the first run of stairs, as shown in Figure 4.120.

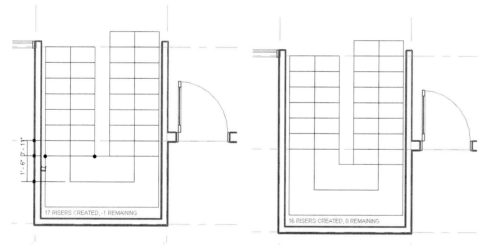

Figure 4.120

Extending the run line and the resulting lines after adjusting the risers and treads

There is a gap between the outer boundary of the stair and the bounding walls. You need to adjust the boundary lines to fit the model.

The initial width of the run is set in the stair properties. This stair is set to 3′-0″ (90cm), but you could change that to any value prior to drawing the run lines.

3. To make the stair fit between the walls, align the outer boundary lines to the bounding walls. Still in Sketch mode, align the landing by selecting the Align tool, then the interior side of the wall at the bottom of Figure 4.121, and finally the landing boundary.

Figure 4.121

Align the stair boundary to the wall.

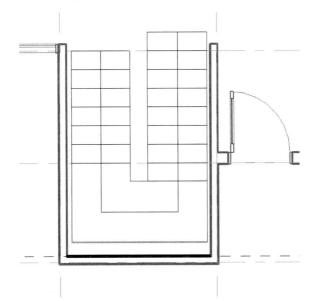

Next, you'll move the stair so it's centered in the stairwell. Using a crossing selection, select all lines in the sketch. Because you're in Sketch mode, no other model elements are selected, so you don't have to be too careful about what you select—Revit will grab only what's in the sketch. Now, follow these steps:

1. With the sketch lines of the stair selected, click the Move tool.

2. With the first pick, select the center of the stair boundary by the landing side, and then select the middle point of the wall. This should place the stair in the center between the two walls. You'll know you've found the center of the stair line and the wall when you see the triangular snap shown in Figure 4.122.

3. Use the Align tool to align the left and right boundaries to the wall. Select the Align tool, and then pick the inside edge of the wall on the right, and then the right boundary line of the stairs. Doing so aligns the right run to the wall. Repeat for the left run. Figure 4.123 shows the stairs, properly located.

4. You can also preset a railing type to be added to the stair and drawn automatically when you finish the stair sketch. Click the Railing Type button in the Design bar ▤ , and then choose Handrail – Pipe from the Railing Type dialog box.

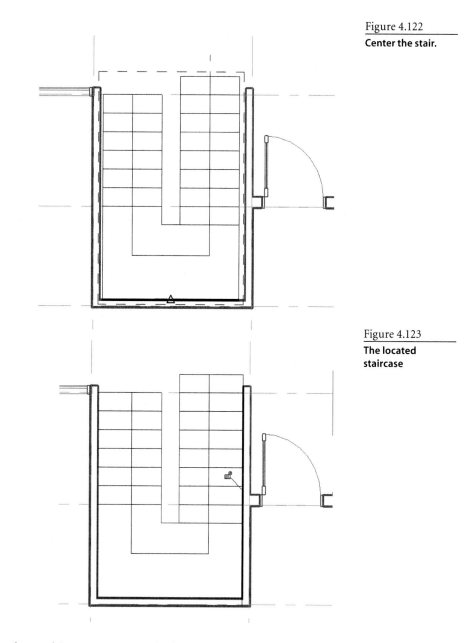

Figure 4.122
Center the stair.

Figure 4.123
The located staircase

5. Finish the sketch to see the resulting geometry. To do that, click the Finish Sketch button in the Design bar ▪▪ Finish Sketch . To visualize the stair in 3D view, go on to the next steps.

Users often forget to finish a sketch; then, they wonder why everything is grayed out and not all the tools are available. Always check on the left side to see whether the Finish Sketch button is available. If it is, click it to finish the operation.

3D Sectional View of the Stair

A great way to see the stair in an isolated 3D view is to create a section through the stair and then orient a 3D view to the section view. Here are the steps:

1. Use the Section tool in the View tab of the Design bar to draw a section, as shown in Figure 4.124.

2. Right-click the section, and choose Element Properties. Rename the view by changing the View Name property from Section 2 to **Stair Section.**

3. Open the default 3D view by clicking the 3D button.

4. Choose View → Orient → To Other View.

5. Select the section that you just created: Section: Stair Section.

   The 3D view reorients and becomes cropped to the same crop extents as the section view. The view you see looks like a section through the stair, but it's a 3D cropped portion of the entire stair. Figure 4.125 shows the finished view.

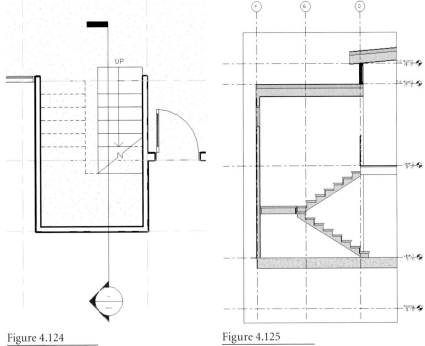

Figure 4.124

Cutting a section through the stair

Figure 4.125

The completed section view

6. To see the stair in 3D, press Shift+middle mouse button, and slowly spin the model (see Figure 4.126).

7. Right-click the view name 3D in the Project Browser and rename the view **3D Stair.**

   Saving with a new name saves the view as a unique view. The next time you click the 3D button in the toolbar, a new default 3D view that shows extents of the model will be generated for you.

Railings

Railings are also sketch-based elements that are generated from a 2D path (sketched line) and a set of design rules. Figure 4.127 shows some of the elements of a railing; the primary ones are the path, rails, and balusters. The path is made from 2D lines, the rails are made from 2D profiles, and the balusters and corner posts are made from 3D solid geometry.

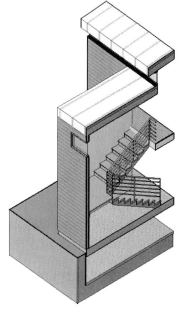

Figure 4.126
Resulting 3D image

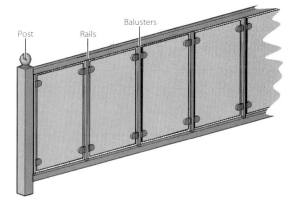

Figure 4.127
Railing elements

Rails are simply 2D profiles that sweep along the length of the railing path. There can be many horizontal rails in a railing, and they can each be given a horizontal offset from the path to accommodate handrails and other more complex scenarios.

Balusters are 3D families that get arrayed along the length of the path. Don't think of a baluster as something that has always to be vertical and rectangular. In Revit, a baluster can be any geometry you wish to repeat at a regular interval. Figure 4.128 shows a post family and repeating baluster pattern.

Figure 4.128

Baluster pattern

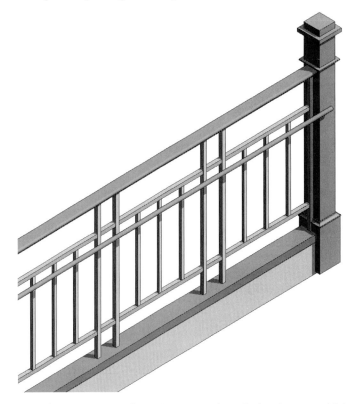

Balusters consist of a main pattern (a unit that is repeatable) and posts. Posts can be start, corner, or end posts. They can also have varying geometry.

Creating a Railing in the Model

Railings can be freestanding elements or hosted by another element such as a stair or floor. To draw a freestanding railing, use the Railing tool in the Modeling tab of the Design bar ▦ Railing . You'll be put into a Sketch mode in which the path is drawn. The path can be composed of multiple lines, and all lines must be connected. If you draw a path with lines that aren't connected, Revit will give you a warning.

You can have a single line as a railing (imagine a railing in the middle of a stair). But the moment you draw a second segment in the same sketch, Revit will expect you to connect them in a chain.

Once you've drawn the path and finished the sketch, the rail geometry is constructed and conforms to the path. An endless number of railings can be defined using the combination of custom profiles and balusters. For this exercise, you'll add a predefined rail to the project and then change the type to make a different configuration. Follow these steps:

1. Open the Level 2 plan and start the Railing tool.

2. You will be put into a Sketch mode. Using the Lines tool , draw a railing along the edges of the exterior deck, as shown in Figure 4.129.

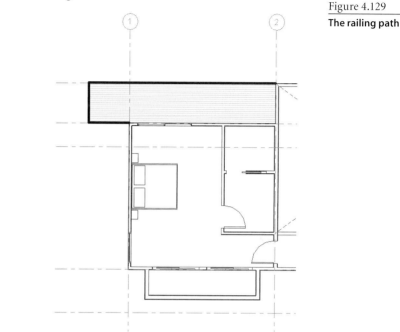

Figure 4.129

The railing path

3. Finish the sketch.

4. Open the 3D view and spin the model to see the railing.

5. Select the railing and change its type to CABLE RAIL—CABLES using the Type Selector. The railing changes to a cable-style rail and looks like the railing in Figure 4.130.

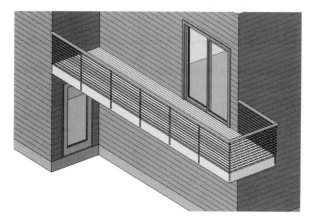

Figure 4.130

Cable railing

Modifying Existing Railings

Looking at the model, you can see the result of your sketch. Note also the presence of railings; Revit automatically places railings on stairs. The railings can then be changed or deleted as desired, independently of the stair. However, if you delete a stair with an associated railing, the railing will also be deleted. You'll also notice some modeling issues that need to be resolved. For example, the stringers are embedded in the wall, and you don't need that railing along the outside edge where you have the wall.

To fix the railing problem, select the railing in the wall and delete it (make sure you're selecting the railing, not the wall or the stair; help yourself using the almighty Tab key). Don't delete the internal railing.

To fix the stringer problem, let's change the construction a bit. Rather than have the stringers on the outside edge of the treads, you can move them under the treads—a more typical method for wood construction:

1. Select the stair, and open the Type Properties dialog box.

2. Scroll down to the Stringers parameters.

3. Change Right Stringer and Left Stringer from Closed to Open (see Figure 4.131).

Figure 4.131

Modified stair stringers

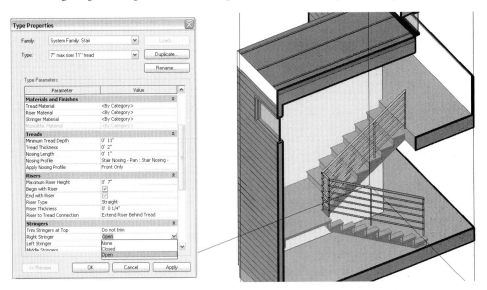

4. Click Apply to see the effect in the model. The stringer geometry changes.

Feel free to experiment with other parameters available in the stair Type Properties. It's possible to create treads with nosing profiles or that have slanted risers, and to change the materials of each sub-element in a stair or change the construction of the stair to monolithic.

Note that you're editing type properties when changing how treads, risers, and stringers are defined—meaning that other instances of that stair (if you've drawn a couple of staircases in the building) will update as a result of type changes. To avoid undesirable changes, duplicate the stair first, name the new type, and then begin your experiments.

Setting Hosts

Railings can be freestanding or hosted by floors and stairs. Often, a railing that was originally hosted by a stair needs to be deleted and later redrawn. You can become confused trying to place the railing on the stair, because it always ends up on the floor below the stairs. To re-place a rail so that it's hosted by a stair, select the Railing tool and sketch a railing path that is on top of the stair. Use the Set Host tool in the Sketch tab of the Design bar ⊕ Set Host to attach the railing to the stair. Do this before finishing the railing sketch. When you finish the sketch, the rail will wind its way up the staircase. This is also possible after drawing the railing: select the railing, click the Edit tool in the Options bar, select the Set Host tool from the Design bar, and then pick a stair to host the railing. Figure 4.132 shows what happens when you don't set the stair to host the railing.

Your Model Is Started ... Now Have Some Fun!

We just went through a series of exercises meant to get you familiar with the basic modeling tools available in Revit. Obviously, we did not get into the nuts and bolts of every tool, but with time you will begin to dig deeper and experiment with more of the features. Also, we will revisit some of these tools in Chapter 6. Now that you have a basic model started, feel free to experiment with it: change the roof, lay out a kitchen, load some additional doors and windows. Most of all, have fun, be creative, and be patient with yourself and the software.

Figure 4.132

The stair without the railing hosted

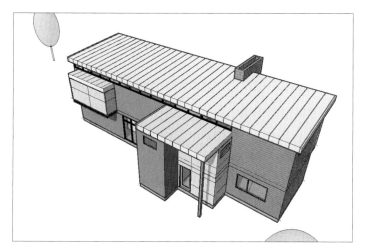

CHAPTER 5

Modifying Elements

Once you've started modeling with Revit, you'll probably need to make changes to the model as your design evolves and becomes more refined. You'll need to move, mirror, and array elements; change properties of elements; apply different graphics to various elements; and even hide and unhide elements. This is where the editing tools and graphic override features come into play. The basics of these tools will be explained in this chapter.

This chapter reviews the essential modification tools available in Revit. Topics we'll cover include:

- ▪ **Standard editing tools**
- ▪ **Additional editing tools**
- ▪ **Graphic and visual overrides**

Standard Editing Tools

This section describes some of the standard editing tools in Revit. For each of these tools, you first need to select elements, and then invoke the appropriate command:

- Copy, paste, and cut
- Move
- Copy
- Rotate
- Array
- Mirror
- Resize

Copy, Paste, and Cut

Copy, paste, and cut are familiar tools used in almost all software applications, and Revit has the basic shortcuts that you'd expect for these interactions (Ctrl+C for copy, Ctrl+V for paste, and Crtl+X for cut). It also has some surprising timesaving options when you're pasting elements that are driven by the nature of a building model.

To copy any element to the clipboard, select it and press Ctrl+C to copy or Ctrl+X to cut. Elements are now ready to be pasted. To paste, press Ctrl+V. In the majority of cases, Revit will place your selection on your cursor, with a dashed box that represents the size of the bounding box containing your to-be-pasted elements. Clicking anywhere in the model will place the elements.

In addition to the familiar copy and paste tools, Revit offers some other paste options that can be used with elements copied to the Windows clipboard.

Paste Aligned

Once elements have been copied to the clipboard, they can be pasted into other views with a variety of options. This allows you to quickly duplicate elements from one view to another (from one floor to another floor, for example) while maintaining a consistent location in the X–Y coordinate plane. After selecting elements and copying them to the clipboard using Ctrl+C, choose Edit → Paste Aligned from the Edit menu, as shown in Figure 5.1.

Five options are available. Depending on the view from which you copy and what elements you copy, the availability of these options will change. For example, if you select a model element in a plan view, you'll have all the options shown in Figure 5.1.

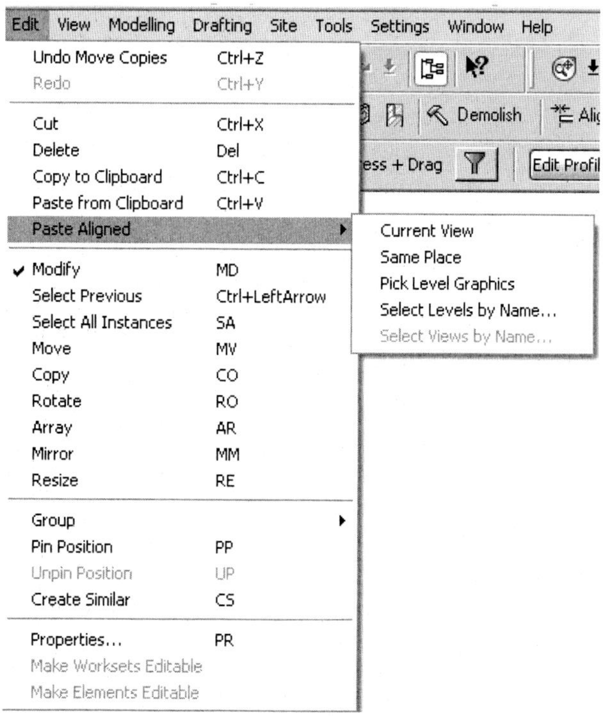

Figure 5.1

The Paste Aligned submenu

CURRENT VIEW

This option pastes the elements on the clipboard in the currently active view, in the same relative spatial location. For example, if you copy a series of walls in a view, Revit remembers the walls and their location. Using this feature, you can copy elements from one view (level 1) and then switch to another view (level 2) of the same type and paste the elements into that view. This can be particularly useful if you'd like to copy walls and other elements between different floors. Open a restroom plan on one floor, copy it to the clipboard, open the second floor, then choose Paste Aligned → Current View. This will duplicate those elements to the open floor plan in the identical location vertically.

SAME PLACE

This option places an element from the clipboard into the exact same place on the same level from which it was copied or cut. One use for this tool is copying elements into a design option (design options allow you to iterate on multiple designs in the context of one file and are covered in Chapter 12). Another example might be if you want to save portions of the design while you manipulate other sections. Using this feature, you can "remove" portions of the project, make other changes, and then restore those elements cleanly to their previous location.

PICK LEVEL GRAPHICS

You can use this option to copy and paste elements between different levels. Once you select the elements, you're placed into a pick mode, where you can select a level in section or elevation. You must be in elevation or section view to have this option available. The level you select determines the Z location of the paste and preserves the X–Y location. You might use this method to copy balconies on a façade from one floor to another in an elevation view.

SELECT LEVELS BY NAME

This method is similar to the previous one, but the selection of levels doesn't happen graphically. Instead, you choose levels from a list in a dialog box and you can paste to multiple levels at once. This is useful when you have a multistory tower; in such a case, manually selecting levels in a view can be tedious. Similar to other options, the X–Y position is maintained, and the pasted elements are copied in the vertical dimension. This is useful for pasting groups on multiple levels simultaneously.

SELECT VIEWS BY NAME

This option lets you copy elements to other views by selecting views from a dialog box. A list of parallel views is provided, and you choose which views you want to paste the element into. For example, if elements are copied from a plan view, only other plan views will be listed. Likewise, if you copy from an elevation view, only elevation views appear as possible views to paste into.

Move

Your projects will be changing constantly as the design takes shape and adapts to requirements. You will often need to move and reshuffle elements from one place to another, especially in the initial phases of a project. Thanks to parametric constraints in Revit, many objects move in relation to other objects in an automatic manner, but you also need the ability to move things manually. There are a couple of ways to accomplish this in Revit: using an explicit two-click *move* command or using the keyboard arrows to *nudge* elements.

The Move tool (⋈ Move) is located in the toolbar and becomes active when elements are selected. Once you've selected an element and activated the Move tool, you select a start point (that is often a point on the element itself for easier referencing) and end point to determine a move distance and vector. The start and end points can be anywhere in your active view; these picks establish the distance and direction of the move. For example, to move a desk to the left by 3′-0″ (1m), you select the desk, click the Move tool, pick a start point, and then drag the mouse to the left 3′-0″ (1m) using the temporary dimension as a reference. You then click to finish the command. If you know the distance you want to move, you can also type in the value—just be sure you give the move a vector by dragging the mouse in the direction you want to move—and then start typing a value. Revit automatically understands that you're telling the element to move by the distance you type and will finish the command when you press Enter on the keyboard, as shown in Figure 5.2.

When the Move command is active, several options are available in the Options bar:

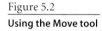

Constrain When this option is selected, it constrains movement to horizontal and vertical directions. Use this to guarantee elements don't get placed off axis.

Disjoin Hosted elements such as windows and doors can't change host (a wall, for example) and move to another host without explicitly being disjoined from their host. This tool allows that disjoin. If you need to move a door from one wall to another, select the door, select the Move tool, check the Disjoin option in the Options bar, and move the door to another host element.

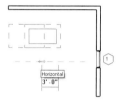

Copy This option makes a copy of the selected element and then moves that copy to the desired location. The original element stays in place.

Figure 5.2

Using the Move tool

Nudge

Use the nudge command when you need to move an element incrementally. Any time an element is selected, you can use the arrow keys on the keyboard to move the element horizontally and vertically in very small increments. Each press of an arrow key nudges the element a specific distance based on your current zoom factor. So, if you are zoomed way out, it will move elements farther than if zoomed in tight.

Copy

Copy is an interactive tool that is nearly identical to the Move tool but makes a copy of the selected element at the location of the second pick (⊞ Copy). Note that this isn't the same Copy tool as Ctrl+C (the one found in the Edit menu that copies elements to a clipboard). This tool doesn't copy anything to the clipboard; it copies an instance of an element or selection of elements in the same view exclusively. To activate this tool, first choose the elements you want to duplicate, and then select the tool.

> You can also make copies of elements by selecting them, then pressing the Ctrl key and dragging your mouse. Once you release the mouse button, a copy of selected elements will be placed in the model. With this method, you'll see a preview of the element being copied, not an empty boundary box.

Rotate

There are two ways to rotate elements in Revit: using the Rotate tool and using the spacebar.

Rotate Tool

To rotate an element, select it and click the Rotate *tool* (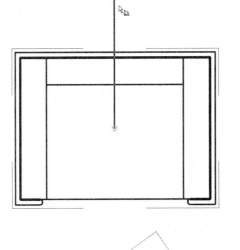 Rotate). A round rotate icon indicates the center of the rotation and appears at the center of the element's bounding box (Figure 5.3). This icon can be repositioned to set the desired center of rotation.

More often than not, the center of the element isn't the point around which you want to rotate. If this is the case, you need to reposition the center of rotation. To do this, select the icon and drag it to the point you wish before rotating the element—this temporarily relocates the origin. Once the origin is established, begin rotating the element using the temporary dimensions as a reference or typing in the angle of rotation explicitly.

Figure 5.3

The Rotate command

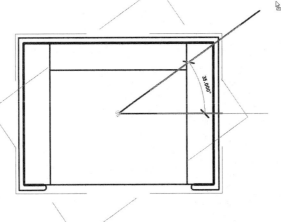

Spacebar

Many family components (furniture, casework, doors, windows, etc.) can be rotated in 90-degree increments by selecting the element, then pressing the spacebar (rotating with the spacebar also works during creation of an element). This is a quick way to lay out room configurations. If the element you are rotating is near a reference that is not horizontal or vertical (an off-axis wall under 30 degrees, for example), the spacebar will pick up that reference as you cycle through possible positions. Press the spacebar until you get the right orientation, then exit the command by either clicking the Modify button or pressing the Esc key twice. If you press the spacebar as you start to sketch a wall or after you select a wall that has already been sketched, the wall will flip with respect to its location line.

Array

An *array* is a way to make multiple instances of an element with consistent spacing between elements. Revit arrays are much more intelligent compared with array tools from other CAD or BIM packages, and can be parametrically grouped and associated so that the array spacing and number of elements in the array can be modified after you make the initial array. The Array tool (📐 Array) is one of the standard tools available for model and drafting elements.

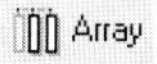

The steps to create an array depend on the settings in the Options bar (see Figure 5.4).

Figure 5.4

The array Options bar

You can create two types of array: linear and radial. Linear is set as the default. A linear array puts a series of elements on a straight segment of a line; that line can either use a set distance between elements or equally space a number of elements over a given distance. The radial array works in a similar fashion, but it revolves elements around a center point.

The Group and Associate option lets you treat the array as a group that can be modified later to adjust the number or spacing of the array. If this is unchecked, then the array is a one-off operation similar to Copy, and you have no means of adjusting the array after you create it.

In the Number field, set the number of elements to be arrayed. This option is active when Move To: 2nd is checked. For example, if you type 7 as the number and check Move To: 2nd, the element will be arrayed seven times. The distance between elements is determined by the distance between two subsequent mouse clicks in the view.

Figure 5.5 shows two arrays drawn from A to B, number 5, illustrating the difference between choosing Move To: 2nd and Move To: Last.

Figure 5.5

Top: Array by num-
ber; bottom: an
array between
two points

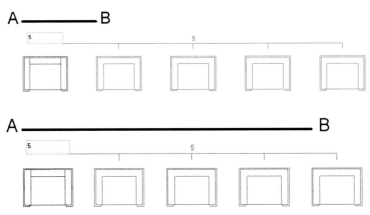

In both examples, Group and Associate were activated. When an element in the array is selected (after the array has been placed), a numeric control similar to a temporary dimension appears, indicating the number of elements in the array (shown as a 5 in the center of the array in the previous figures). This allows you to change the number of elements in the array by directly editing the number. Revit will maintain an associated array as long as all the original members of the array still exist and are equally spaced. If you wish to change the position or delete just one of the arrayed elements, you will need to select the element, select Ungroup from the Options bar to deactivate (break) the association between the arrayed elements, and only then perform individual actions with that element.

Mirror

The *Mirror* tool (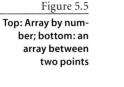) allows you to mirror elements across an axis to create a mirror image of an element, like the chairs in Figure 5.6. The tool lets you either pick an existing reference in the model (the arrow icon) or draw the axis interactively (pencil icon).

Use the pick method (⬚) when you have an existing element with a meaningful center axis. If nothing in the model exists to pick as a mirror axis, use the Draw mode (✎) and draw your own axis, as shown in Figure 5.7.

> To mirror doors and windows in a wall, it is faster and more intuitive to use the spacebar or the blue flip arrows after selecting an element. You can of course also use the Mirror command, but the methods mentioned previously are specifically designed to address this.

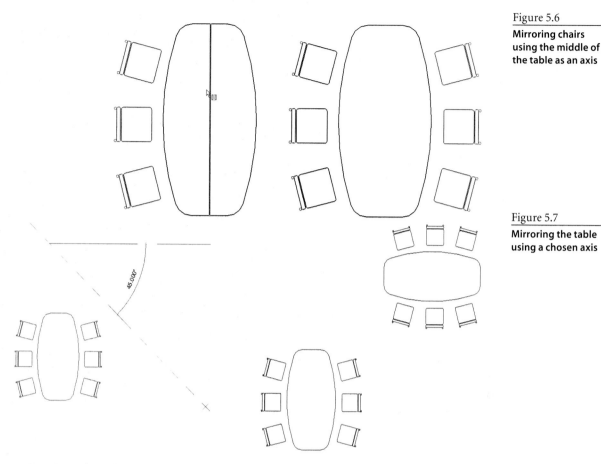

Figure 5.6

Mirroring chairs using the middle of the table as an axis

Figure 5.7

Mirroring the table using a chosen axis

Certain real-world objects are not meant to be mirrored, such as mechanical equipment, specialty equipment, and plumbing fixtures. These objects may look graphically correct when mirrored, but doing so may adversely modify the element's analytical data. For example, mirroring a piece of medical equipment may result in the mechanical engineer proposing utility connections at an inappropriate location. The same applies for doors.

Resize

The *Resize* tool is well suited for working with imported images that need to be scaled to match real-world dimensions. Say you've scanned a drawing of an existing building that you wish to convert into a model. Chances are, the image isn't at any reasonable scale when imported and needs to be scaled relative to some model element. Resize also lets you modify the relative size of a sketch created during Sketch mode, or a selection of lines or detail lines.

The Resize tool will become active once you select an imported image. After you select the Resize tool, click a point to enter an origin (say, the left corner of the image); the second point you click is the width of the image that you want to fit within a certain size; finally, the third click is the new length you want (see Figure 5.8).

Figure 5.8

Resize an image using the Resize tool

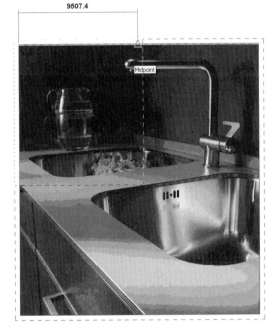

Additional Editing Tools

An additional set of editing tools is available in Revit for editing your design. You'll find them in a separate toolbar, just above the Options bar. From a workflow perspective, unlike the standard editing tools, these tools work by first selecting the tool and then selecting the elements on which you want to perform operations.

Align   Split   Trim   Offset

Aligning Elements

When placing and dragging elements, Revit autocreates temporary alignment lines to similar types of elements in the model. Use these alignment lines to place elements in relation to other elements. When you drag elements around, take note of these helpful alignment lines, and use them to line things up. This works for all categories of elements, including annotations. Figure 5.9 shows autoalignment when placing a tag.

These alignments are great for lining up annotations such as room tags. Select a tag and drag it—note how it aligns to other tags in the view, making it a snap to create organized drawings. Figure 5.10 shows autoalignment while interactively dragging.

In addition to the autoalignment graphics, the Align tool is one of the favorites among Revit users. It makes lots of common manipulations easy and precise. The Align tool matches the edge of one element precisely to another. In some cases, this will move an element more accurately than measuring the distance that an object needs to move and then moving the object that distance.

Autoalignment

Revit has embedded placement and can modify the alignment between elements of the same category. That is to say, when you drag elements around, they locate nearby similar elements, and alignment graphics are drawn to aid you when laying out the model or adding annotations. Figure 5.9 shows autoalignment during tag placement.

If you wish to put room tags in order on your drawing, and you start moving one to align with another, Revit shows an alignment line and snaps to the other tag. Figure 5.10 shows autoalignment during editing.

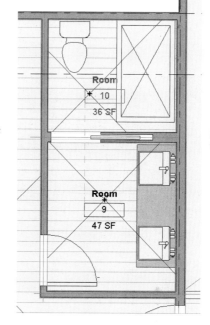

Figure 5.9

Alignment of a room tag during placement

Figure 5.10

Alignment of a room tag during editing

Manual Alignment

You can explicitly align references from one element to another using the Align tool. For example, you can align windows in a façade in an elevation view to line up their center-lines. To use the Align tool, select a target line and then select what you want to align to that first pick. The second element picked moves into alignment. Whenever an alignment is made, a blue lock icon will appear. Clicking that icon locks the alignment, creating a constraint between the two elements. Once constrained, if either element is moved, both elements will move together.

Locking elements together is a powerful part of Revit. However, locking too many elements together can overconstrain your model. Be careful when you choose to use this tool and lock objects sparingly until you have a comfortable understanding of the resulting constraints.

Figure 5.11 shows the use of the Align tool to align windows on a façade. The top window's mid-axis is selected as the alignment reference. After that, the mid-axes of the lower windows are clicked, and the lower windows automatically align to the top window.

Figure 5.11

Manual alignment

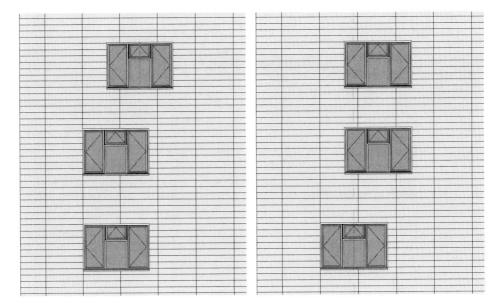

The Align tool also works for aligning geometry with surface patterns like brick or stone. Figure 5.12 shows how you can align the edge of a window to an expansion gap.

The Align tool is useful in the Family Editor environment, where you can align an element to a reference plane that will control the behavior of that element and lock it.

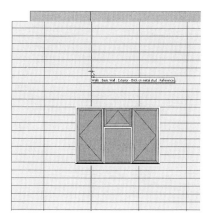 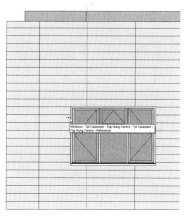 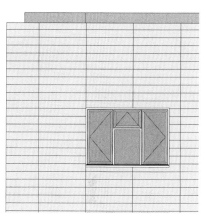

Split

The *Split* tool is used only on lines and walls and is used to split these elements into separate entities. When activated, place the mouse over a wall or line. A knife icon will appear; clicking will split the wall or line into two separate segments. If you need to make two splits, with the intention of removing the segment between the two splits, use the Options bar check box: Delete Inner Segment. See Figure 5.13.

Figure 5.12

Aligning windows and patterns

Figure 5.13

Splitting the wall where the two perpendicular walls intersect will produce the following image with just two clicks when the Delete Inner Segment option is checked.

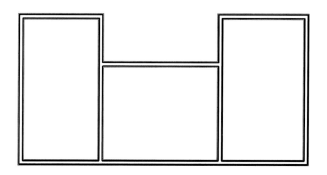

Trim and Extend

Use the *Trim* tool to trim and extend lines and walls to one another. The Trim tool has several options, which appear in the Options bar as you select the tool and then the elements.

The first option is the default, *Trim/Extend* to Corner ( ). It trims elements to one another, creating a connected end-join condition when you finish. For example, to clean up the T intersection shown in Figure 5.14, use the Trim tool.

Figure 5.14

Trim/Extend to Corner

Figure 5.15 shows two walls before and after using the Trim/Extend Single Element tool ( ).

Figure 5.15

Trimming a single element

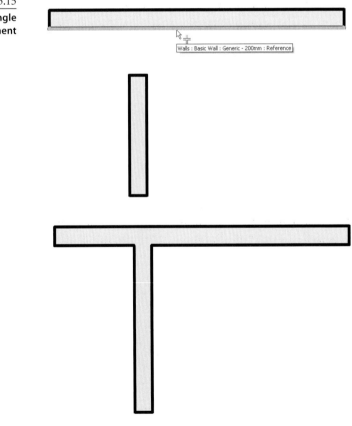

Figure 5.16 shows multiple walls before and after using the Trim/Extend Multiple Elements tool ( ).

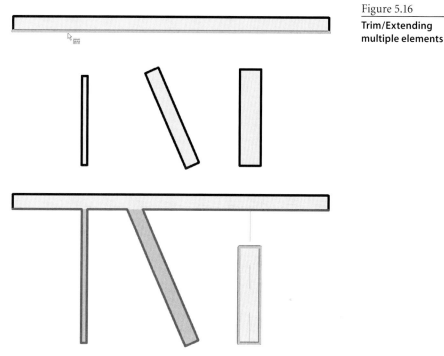

Trim/Extending multiple elements

Offset

The *Offset* tool is similar to the Move and Copy tools: it makes a copy of a selected element parallel to the edge you select as a reference for offset. You can find the Offset tool either on the Edit toolbar or on the Options bar (Figure 5.17) when you're sketching lines or walls.

Figure 5.17

The Offset tool (above) on the Edit toolbar and (below) on the Options bar

This tool is particularly useful in the Family Editor when you're making shapes that are a consistent thickness in profile, such as an extruded steel shape. Offset is also handy when you're making roof forms or soffits with known offsets from a wall. You can either offset a line and maintain the original (copy) or offset the line and remove the original. Figure 5.18 shows the offset of a loop of lines using the Copy option.

Figure 5.19 shows how you can use the Offset command to make the roof boundary wider in every direction.

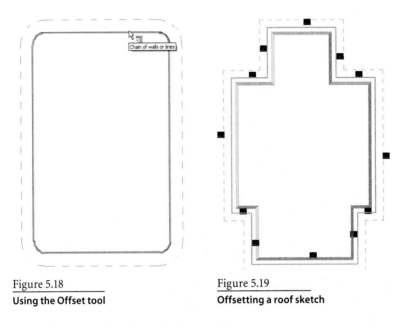

Figure 5.18

Using the Offset tool

Figure 5.19

Offsetting a roof sketch

Graphic and Visual Overrides

Revit provides a rich set of controls that allow you to change the graphic appearance of elements on a view-by-view basis. Every element belongs to a category, which provides a baseline graphic appearance for any given element. However, the category graphics may need to deviate, depending on what you're trying to convey in a drawing. For example, the furniture category uses a solid black line by default. This is set in Settings → Object Styles. Changing the default values in the Object Styles dialog box affects furniture in all views, as shown in Figure 5.20.

Figure 5.20

Object Styles dialog box

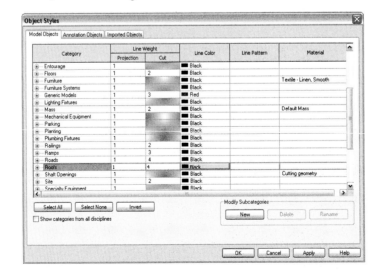

Let's say you need to create a plan view where all furniture is shown as halftone, dashed, or hatched. No problem. With Revit, this is handled with view-specific graphic overrides that can be applied to entire categories or individual elements.

Each view is a unique view of the model that can be graphically tailored to meet your needs. Graphically overriding an element or a category doesn't mean you're changing the element—you're changing its appearance. To override graphics in a view, you can use the Visibility/Graphic Overrides dialog box or the view-specific element overrides dialog box:

- To access the Visibility/Graphic Overrides dialog box, you can either go directly to the dialog box from the menu—View → Visibility/Graphics Overrides—or right-click in the view and choose View Properties from the context menu. You'll see the Visibility/Graphics Overrides parameter in this dialog box as well.

- You can also access the dialog box when an element is selected using the right-click menu. Select an element, and choose Override Graphics in View → By Category (Figure 5.21).

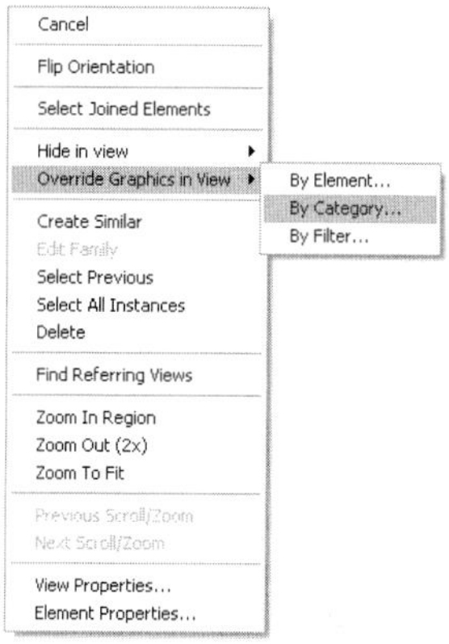

Figure 5.21

When an element is selected, you can access the Visibility/Graphics setting from the right-click menu.

Cancel
Flip Orientation
Select Joined Elements
Hide in view ▶
Override Graphics in View ▶ → By Element...
→ By Category...
→ By Filter...
Create Similar
Edit Family
Select Previous
Select All Instances
Delete
Find Referring Views
Zoom In Region
Zoom Out (2x)
Zoom To Fit
Previous Scroll/Zoom
Next Scroll/Zoom
View Properties...
Element Properties...

When you use the context menu, the dialog box preselects the category for you based on the elements you selected. For example, to override the furniture category, select a piece of furniture and use the right-click menu to access the override options.

Figure 5.22 shows a chaise longue chair in elevation: default mode and overridden with line pattern dashed.

Once you're in the Visibility/Graphic Overrides dialog box, you'll see a list of all the categories and the various ways of manipulating the graphics. To get a handle on this, we'll walk through the override options from left to right, as they appear in the dialog box.

Categories

Top-level tabs divide elements based on type: Model, Annotation, and Imported. The Filters tab is also available as a way to manipulate graphics based on parameter criteria. If a view includes imported or linked files, there will be tabs for those as well, which will allow you to change the visibility and appearance of imported layers. This dialog box is powerful and allows for total control over the graphics of anything in your view.

Visibility

The first column combines a list of categories and subcategories with a visibility toggle. To turn off the visibility of a category in the view, uncheck the box next to the category, as shown in Figure 5.23.

Figure 5.22
**Overriding
an element**

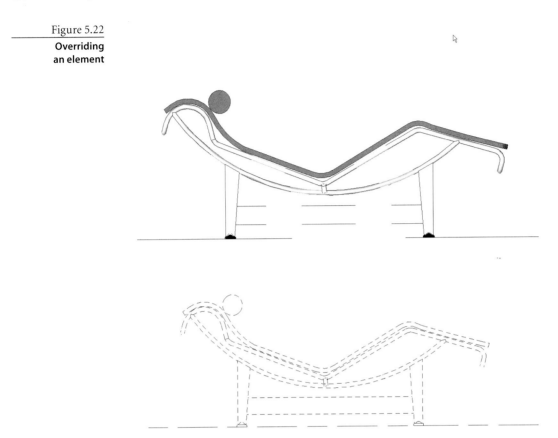

Figure 5.23
Controlling visibility

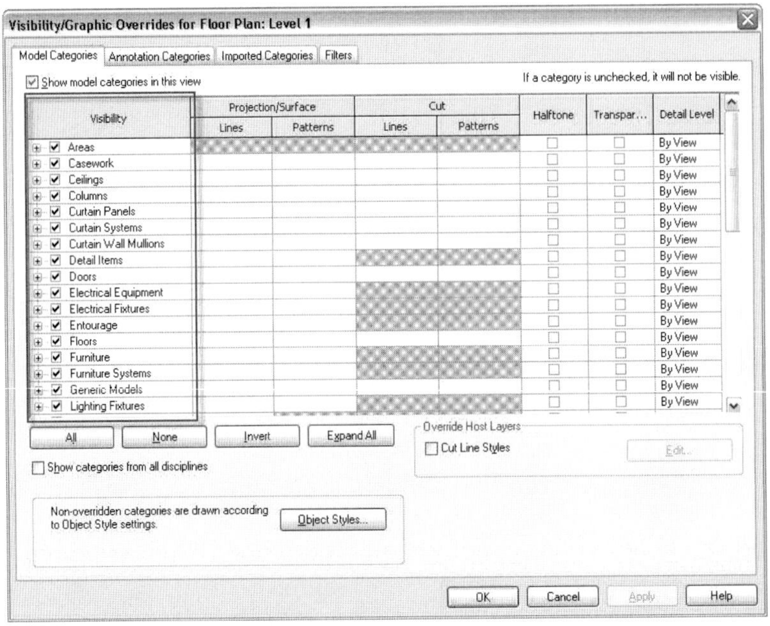

Each category has a list of subcategories; to turn off any particular subcategory, uncheck it.

Figure 5.24 shows an example of controlling visibility by unchecking subcategories from the Visibility/Graphic Overrides dialog box. The first image shows the view with the doors turned on, the second image shows what subcategory is unchecked, and the final image shows the result.

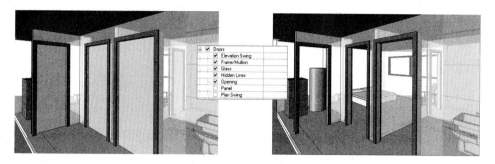

Figure 5.24

Visibility examples

The lines and surfaces of elements in projection can be overridden. With these controls, you can change the line style of any element and also apply hatches to surfaces.

Line and Pattern Overrides

For most model categories, you can apply overrides to projected and cut lines as well as surface and cut patterns (shown in Figure 5.25). Using these overrides allows you to alter line color, thickness, and pattern. You can also apply a hatch pattern override to any surface, whether projected or cut.

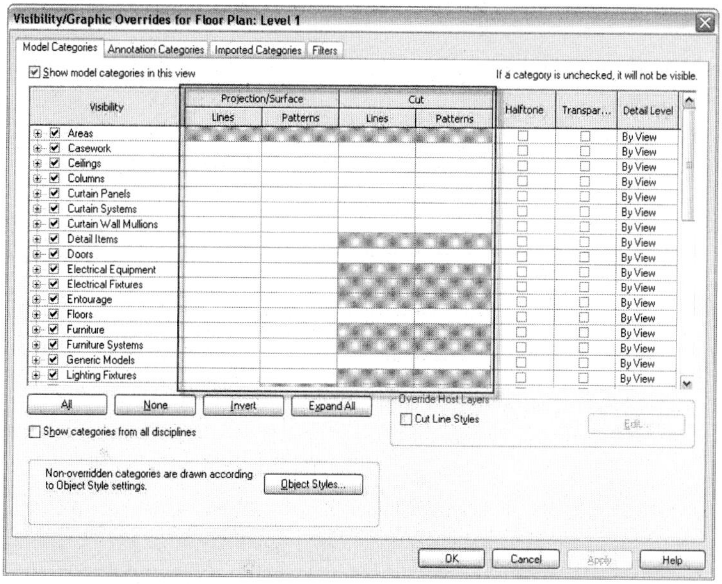

Figure 5.25

Line and pattern overrides

To add an override, click the desired override for the category you want to change. The row will then display a series of buttons, as shown in Figure 5.26.

Figure 5.26

Element choices

Clicking Override takes you to dialog boxes where graphics can be overridden. Figure 5.27 shows the Line Graphics override dialog box and the Fill Pattern Graphics override dialog box. Note that the options in the dialog boxes vary based on what you're trying to manipulate.

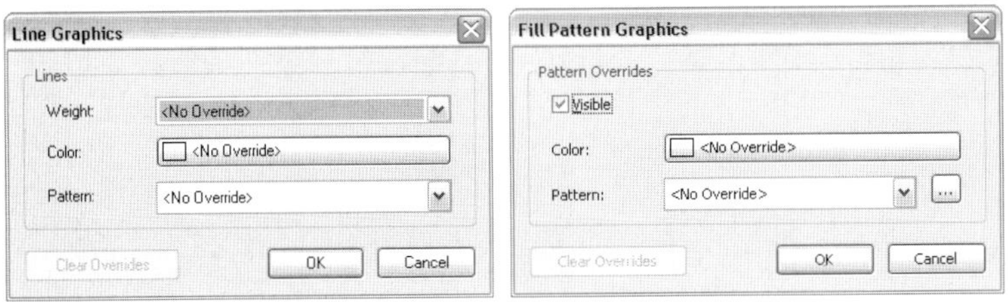

Figure 5.27

Line Graphics and
Fill Pattern over-
rides dialog boxes

The controls are fairly self-explanatory. Feel free to experiment with the behavior.

> Here's something important to note about the Fill Pattern Graphics dialog box: if you want to hide the pattern of a category, use the Visible check box in the Pattern Overrides options. Don't change the pattern color to white, because doing so can cause problems if you end up exporting the view. The lines are still there—they just don't appear, due to the screen background color.

Halftone and Transparent

These columns (shown in Figure 5.28) are check box controls that change lines and surfaces. The Halftone option takes the line color and tones it down by 50%. The Transparent check box makes all surfaces of the category 100% transparent, so that you can see through these elements in the view.

Detail Level

The last column controls the detail level appearance for categories. This allows you to show fine levels of detail for some categories, even if the view is set to coarse. Until you get into sophisticated content creation, this level of override can be safely ignored.

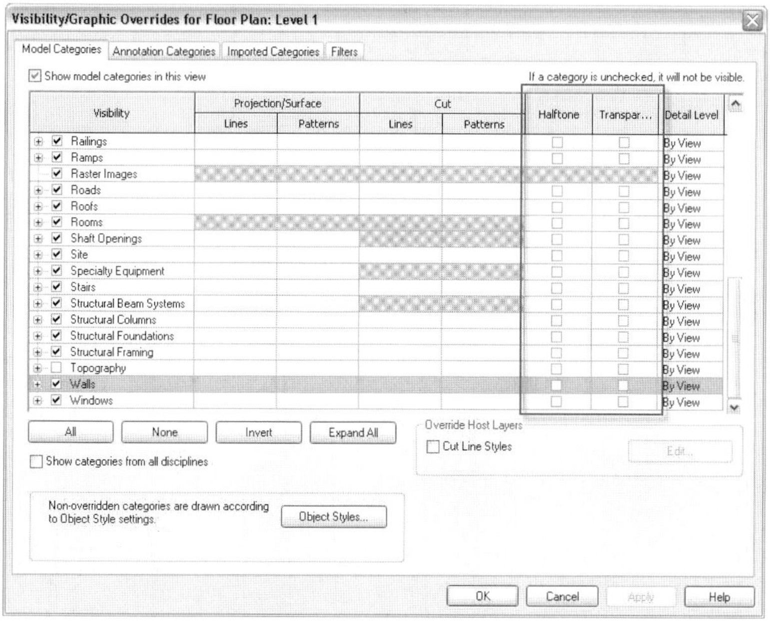

Figure 5.28
Halftone and Transparent overrides

Override Host Layers

The Visibility/Graphic Overrides dialog box contains an additional override feature specific to layers that make up walls, floors, and roofs (in Revit terms, these are considered "host" elements). You can see it at lower right: the Override Host Layers section. Using this edit control, it's possible to override individual layers within wall, floor, and roof elements. For example, this will let you make the structural stud layer of walls appear in a heavier line weight than the finish layer.

Element Overrides

When elements are selected, you can hide them in the view and also override their graphics. This allows you to change the visibility of individual elements, not just entire categories. To do so, right-click any element, and then use the context menu option Hide in View → Elements, as shown in Figure 5.29.

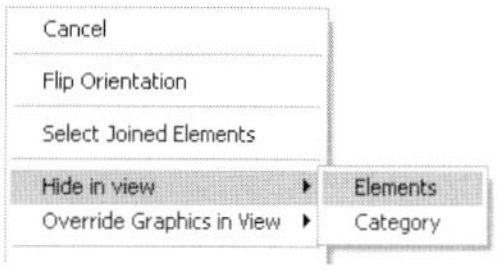

Figure 5.29
Element overrides

The selected elements are hidden in the view. Figure 5.30 shows an example of hiding only a few elements of a category in a view. In this case, the trees are obstructing the camera view, so a few of them have been overridden to improve legibility of the view.

Figure 5.30

**Hiding elements
in a view**

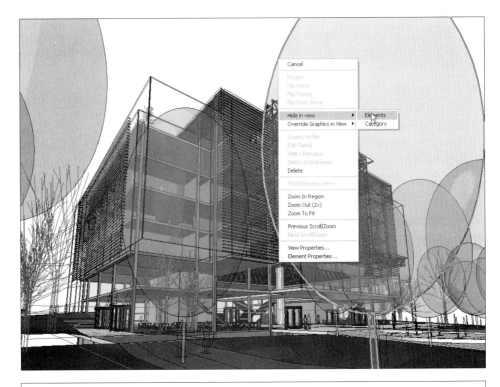

To override the graphics of a selected element, choose Override Graphics in View → By Elements from the context menu. Doing so brings up a dialog box with the same graphic overrides available in the Visibility/Graphic Overrides dialog box but in a collapsed state (see Figure 5.31).

Along the top of this dialog box are check boxes for making an element visible, halftone, or transparent. Below that are groups of controls for overriding lines and patterns. Clicking the small arrow button opens and closes groups of controls for each kind of override. Figure 5.32 shows the dialog box with Projection Lines expanded.

Figure 5.33 shows various element overrides: the bed is set to transparent, the doors to halftone, and the shower to invisible.

Figure 5.34 shows an example using a transparent override per element in a 3D view; the roof and the front wall are transparent.

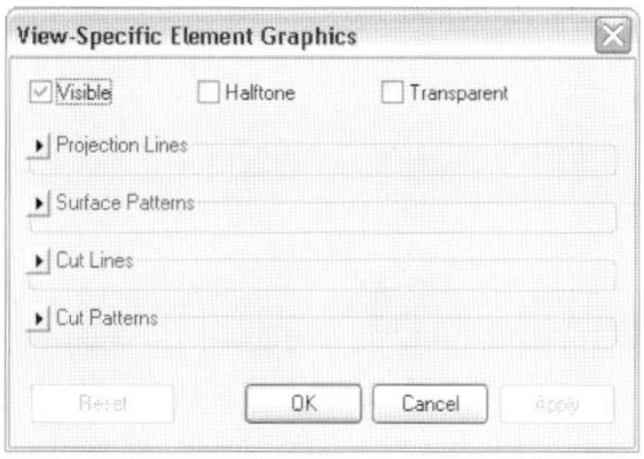

Figure 5.31
View-Specific Element Graphics

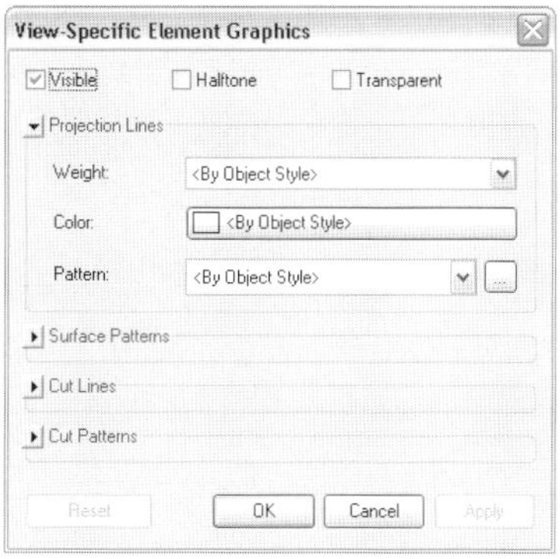

Figure 5.32
Projection Lines override group expanded

Figure 5.33
Use case for graphic overrides

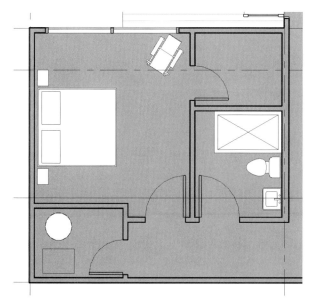
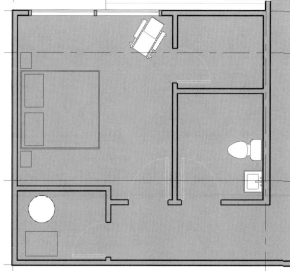

Figure 5.34

Graphic overrides using transparency

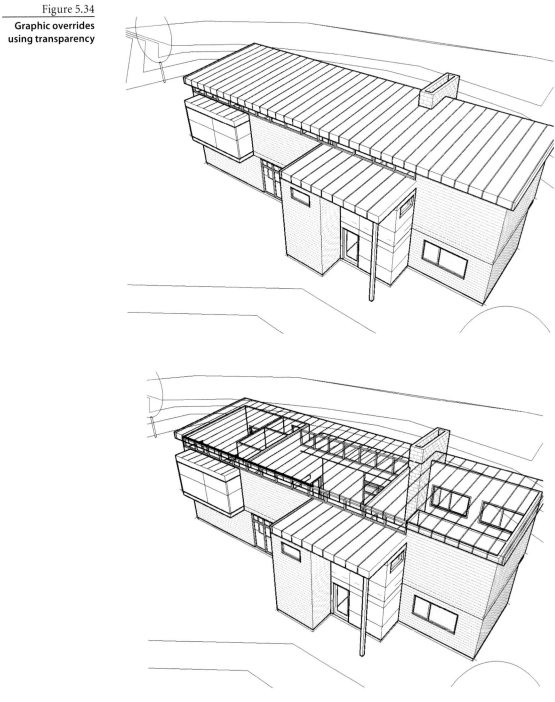

Graphic overrides applied on a per-view basis allow you to quickly turn a working drawing into a presentation drawing. For example, you can override all elements that are cut with a solid fill color with a few simple clicks, to get another style of presentation drawing. Figure 5.35 shows how you can modify the color of the wall in a plan view.

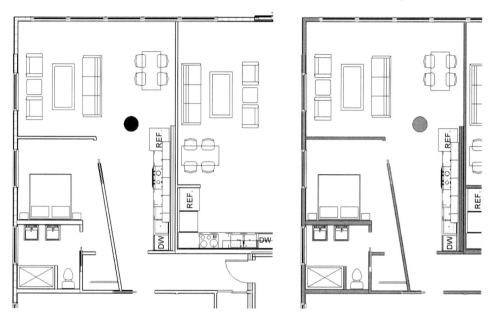

Figure 5.35

Graphic overrides for walls

Unhiding Elements and Categories

After an element or category has been hidden, you can use the *Reveal Hidden Elements* toggle to see hidden elements and then unhide them. To do this, click the light bulb icon in the View Control bar.

The view halftones all visible elements and draws hidden elements with magenta color. A magenta border is also drawn around the entire view to make it more obvious that you're in a special mode. Hovering the mouse over hidden elements displays a tooltip that explains how the element is being hidden: Hidden Category or Hidden Element. Figure 5.36 shows some examples of hidden elements and categories.

To unhide the element, use the buttons in the Options bar () or the right-click option Unhide in View → Element. To reset the view to its normal display, click the light bulb icon again.

As you can see, Revit provides a full range of tools that give you control over how your model looks and feels. Using the interactive editing tools, you can manipulate elements spatially and then make decisions about how elements should be displayed, depending on what you're trying to convey with your drawings.

Figure 5.36

Hidden elements and categories

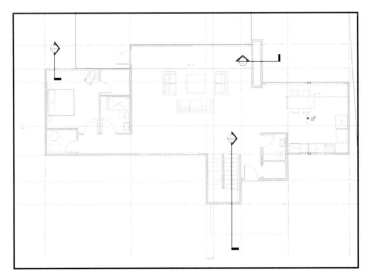

CHAPTER 6

Extended Modeling

In the previous chapters we covered basic modeling techniques to construct a simple building. We skipped over many additional features so that you can get a handle on essential workflow, the user interface, and making modifications to the model. In this chapter we'll cover more advanced features that are available any time you're modeling in Revit. As you'll see, with a little refinement and creativity, you can make almost anything using standard creation tools. Topics we'll cover include:

- Walls: advanced modeling features

- Curtain walls: advanced design techniques

- Roofs and slabs: advanced shape editing

Walls: Advanced Modeling Features

With Revit, walls are made from layers of materials that represent the construction materials used to build real walls. These layers can be assigned functions, allowing them to join and react to other similar layers in the model when walls, floors, and roofs meet. The wall *core* is one of these special layers, and understanding it will help you when you're designing your walls.

Revit has a unique ability to identify a wall core that is much more than a layer of material. The core influences the behavior of the wall and how the wall interacts with other elements in the model. Every wall type in Revit has a core material with a boundary on either side of it. These core boundaries can be dimensioned and snapped to. When other host elements (walls, floors, ceilings, roofs) are drawn, you can use wall-core boundaries to maintain critical relationships. For example, a floor sketch can be constrained to the structural stud layer of walls by using the wall-core boundary to create the sketch. If walls change size or are swapped, the floor sketch maintains its relationship to the core boundary and will adjust automatically.

Figure 6.1

Wall assembly materials

To access and edit wall-core boundaries and material layers, select a wall, open the Element Properties dialog box, click Edit/New to open Type Properties, and then click the Structure parameter. This will open a new Edit Assembly dialog box. From here you can define materials, move layers in and out of the core boundary, and assign functions to each layer (see Figure 6.1).

To get a feel for how core layers are used in relation to a floor, start a new session of Revit and follow these steps:

1. Open a new project, and draw a simple floor plan using walls. Select a multilayered wall type in order to understand the value of the exercise—the Brick on CMU wall type works well. Draw some walls in the shape shown in Figure 6.2.

2. Use the View bar to switch to fine or medium detail so you can see all wall layers. (In coarse views, wall layers are never displayed.)

3. From the Modeling tab in the Design bar, select the Floor tool, keep the default Pick Walls option, and in the Options bar (Figure 6.3) check the Extend Into Wall (To Core) option.

4. Position your mouse over an edge of the wall (do not click the mouse yet), press Tab to highlight all the walls, and then click to select. Zoom in. A sketch line indicating the shape of the floor will be created. This sketch line indicates the position of the floor relative to the wall—it's drawn at the exterior edge of the wall core. Make sure you've selected all walls as a reference to create the floor, and click Finish Sketch.

5. From the View tab of the Design bar, create a section through the wall, and open the section view. Again, make sure your view is set to medium or fine level of detail. You'll see the edge of the floor and how it aligns with the wall construction (Figure 6.4).

6. Go back to the floor plan, and select all elements in the view. Click the Filter button in the Options bar, and uncheck all but the Floor category. Click OK. In the Options bar, click the Edit command to edit the floor sketch. Revit returns you to Sketch mode.

Figure 6.2

Create brick walls in this configuration.

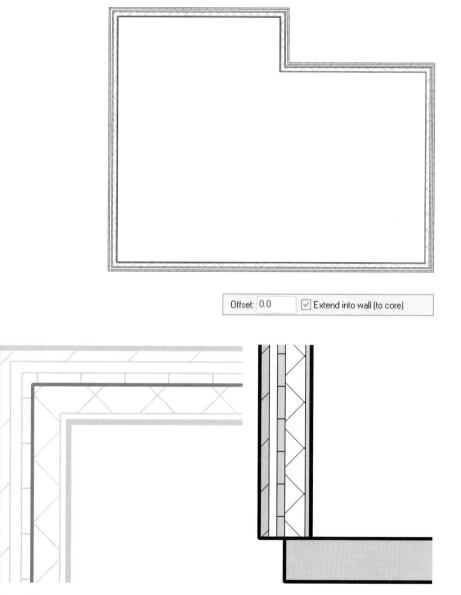

Figure 6.3

This option allows you to constrain lines to wall-core boundaries.

Figure 6.4

On the left, the floor sketch in plan view; on the right, how the floor looks in section in relation to the wall.

7. Tab-select the floor lines to pick all lines in the sketch. In the Options bar, set an off-set of 6″ (150mm).

8. Finish the sketch.

9. Switch back to the section view (Figure 6.5). The floor now extends 6″ (150mm) beyond the edge of the core.

10. You can continue by changing the wall type to another type and see that the floor always maintains its position relative to the core of the new wall. If you change your design and move your walls to make the floor plan bigger or smaller, the floor will always adjust with the change.

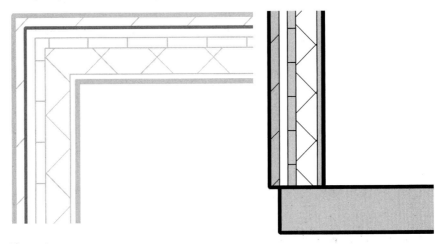

Figure 6.4
Floor with offset from the wall-core boundary

Layer Join Cleanup

Figure 6.6

Wall functions

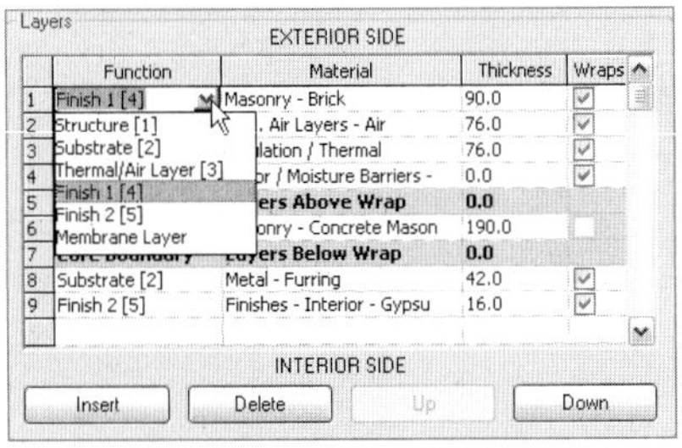

As mentioned in Chapter 4, the wall-layer priority determines the interaction and cleanup of joins between walls of different types. There are six functions (levels of prior-ity of wall layers), with Structure having the highest priority (as shown in Figure 6.6).

When you create a new wall type and begin adding material layers to the wall, you need to assign a material, thickness, and priority to the layers. When you're assigning a priority, think about the function of the layer in the wall—is it finish? Substrate? Structure? This decision will help clean up your walls down the road.

If you encounter situations where the automated wall cleanup doesn't correspond to your expectations, Revit will let you cycle through a range of possible layer configurations using the Edit Wall Joins tool, located in the Options bar.

Editing Wall Joins

The *Edit Wall Joins* tool lets you edit wall-join configurations ( ). The default wall join is set to butt join. Activate the Edit Wall Joins tool, and place your mouse over a wall join. (This can be a corner where two walls meet.) The Options bar shows some alternative configuration options: Miter and Square. A miter join is shown in Figure 6.7.

Disjoining Walls

Disallow Join is another tool designed to provide more flexibility in wall-join behavior. If you select a partition wall that cleans up with your exterior wall, but that isn't the desired behavior for that partition wall, you can right-click the blue control dot at the end of the wall and select Disallow Join from the context menu. Doing so breaks the autojoin cleanup. Figure 6.8 shows the walls intersecting in a Disallow Join condition. Note that once a join has been disallowed, a reallow

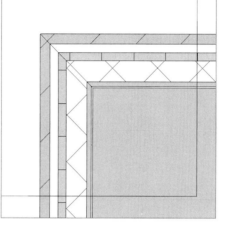

Figure 6.7

A miter join

join icon will appear when the wall that is disjoined is selected. Clicking on this icon will rejoin the two walls. This is a newly introduced help functionality in Revit 2009. Note that the controls are available at wall ends (T-join of walls) and mid-end joins (vertical lines in elevation profile in the middle of the wall or in wall opening); and they only appear when a single wall is selected.

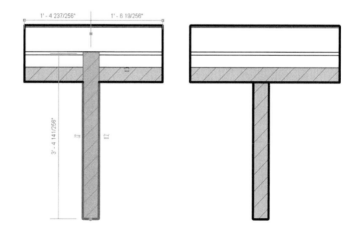

Figure 6.8

Disallow Join

Stacked Walls

Walls in a building, especially exterior walls, are often composed of different wall types that vertically stack on top of one another over the height of the façade. At the very least, most walls sit on top of a foundation wall. To guarantee that if the foundation wall moves, the walls above it also move, you can use a special wall type in Revit: Stacked Wall. (see figure 6.11)

Figure 6.9

Stacked walls

Stacked walls allow you to create a single wall entity composed of vertically stacked different wall types. The wall types need to be existing types already available in the project. Note that stacked walls may only be composed of basic walls, not curtain walls or other stacked walls.

To understand how stacked walls work and how to modify one, follow these steps:

1. Open a new session of Revit, and make sure three levels are defined (if you don't have three levels defined, go to an elevation view, add a third level, and then go back to your floor plan view).

2. Pick the Wall tool and select the Stacked Wall: Exterior – Brick Over CMU with Metal Stud (located at the bottom of the list in the type selector). Open Element Properties, click the Edit/New button, and then duplicate the wall type to create a new stacked wall (Figure 6.9).

3. Edit the Structure parameter, and click the Preview button to see the wall in section (Figure 6.10). When you're editing the stacked wall type, you'll notice that the dialog box is slightly different than when you're working with a basic wall. Rather than editing individual wall layers, this dialog box allows you to stack predefined wall types.

Figure 6.10

**Modifying a
stacked wall**

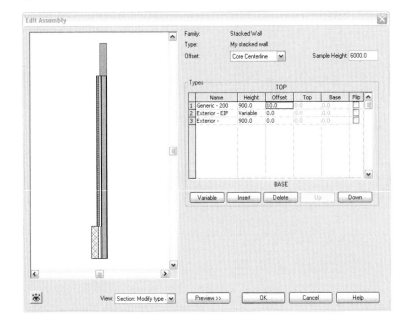

4. Click the Insert button to add a new wall. A new row appears in the list and allows you to select a new wall. Select the Generic wall type from the Name list, and set the Height value; you also may need to define an Offset value to make the three walls flush with the interior face. With a new row selected, click the Variable button. This will allow the wall to vary in height to adjust with levels.

5. Go back to your plan view and draw the new wall, setting its top constraint to Level 3. In 3D, the wall should look like similar to Figure 6.11.

6. Cut a section through the model and change the heights of Level 1 and Level 3 to see the effect this has on the wall. (Make sure the level of detail is set to medium/fine to see the wall layers.) You'll see that changing Level 2 does not change the bottom walls, as they are fixed in height. However, changing the height of Level 3 will change the height of the variable wall (see Figure 6.12).

In Revit it is never too late to add or change something. There is no need to rearrange things to accommodate late changes to the project, because that is exactly where Revit excels—it revises instantly when you apply a change to one place.

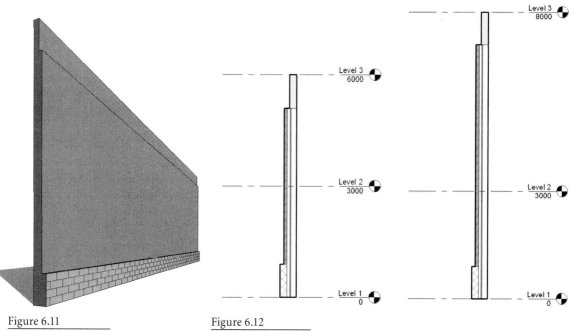

Figure 6.11

A finished stacked wall

Figure 6.12

Variable instance in a stacked wall

Walls with Integrated Sweeps and Reveals

Walls are often complex, highly articulated compositions. Cornices, reveals, corrugated metal finish, and other projections are used all the time to give texture and delineate space. Revit can accommodate any of these types of design elements. Some examples of compound walls are shown in Figure 6.13.

Figure 6.13

Compound wall types

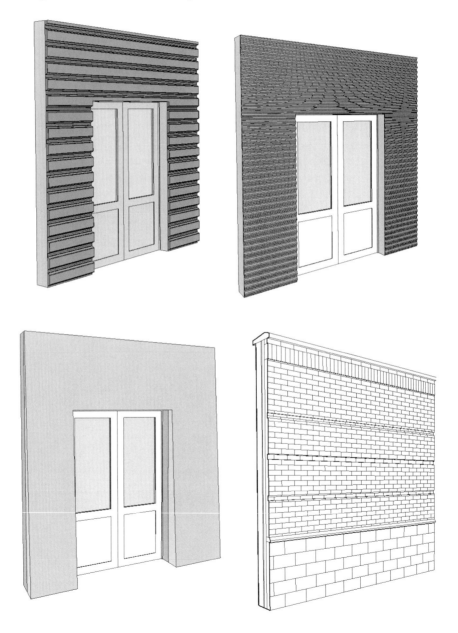

From the type properties of any basic wall, you can enable a preview of the wall. This preview allows you to view the wall in either plan or section. When the section preview is active, additional tools also become active and allow you to place geometric sweep and reveal components on the wall (see Figure 6.14).

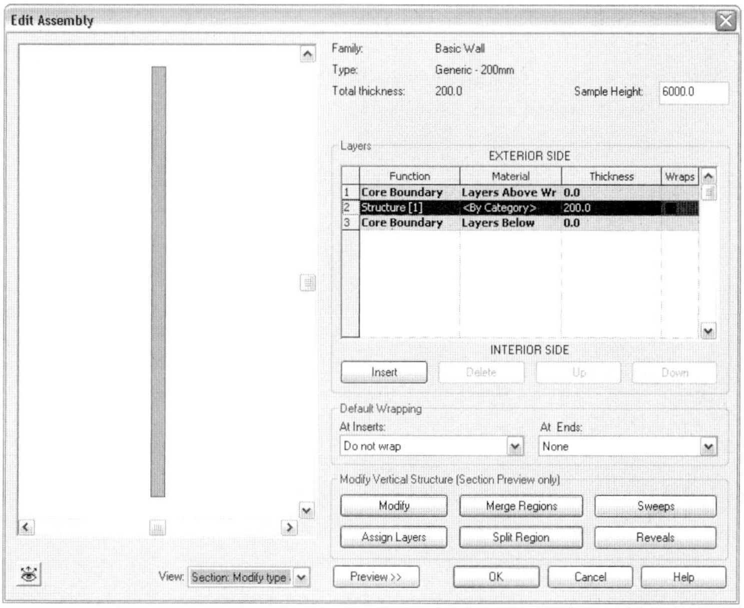

Figure 6.14

Wall-section preview

Sweeps and Reveals

Clicking the Sweeps or Reveals button in the Edit Assembly dialog box opens a new dialog box where you can define profile families to use as sweeps or reveals. These profiles, which are no more than 2D shapes made out of simple lines, are then swept along the length of the wall at a specified height. Many profiles representing cornices, skirting, and chair rails ship with Revit; but if you need to create a custom profile, you can use the Profile Family template. Choose File → New Family → Profile to access the Revit Family Editor. From here, you draw one closed loop of lines at the desired real-world scale, save the family, and then load the profile back into your project. Note that you cannot have more than one closed loop of lines when creating profiles. To place an integrated wall sweep onto a wall type, follow these steps:

1. Click the Wall tool and select Generic Wall.

2. Open the Element Properties dialog box, Click Edit/New, and click Duplicate. Give the wall a new name.

3. Using the Insert button, add new layers as shown in Figure 6.15. Use the Up and Down buttons to move layers in the assembly.

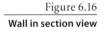

Figure 6.15

Layers in the wall

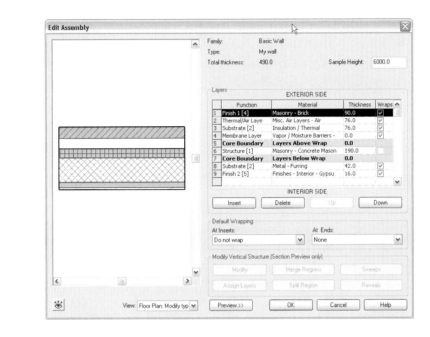

4. In the preview view, switch to section view. The six Modify Vertical Structure options become active at the bottom of the dialog box, as shown in Figure 6.16.

5. Click the Sweeps tool to open the dialog box shown in Figure 6.17. At present, no sweeps are defined in your wall, so let's add some.

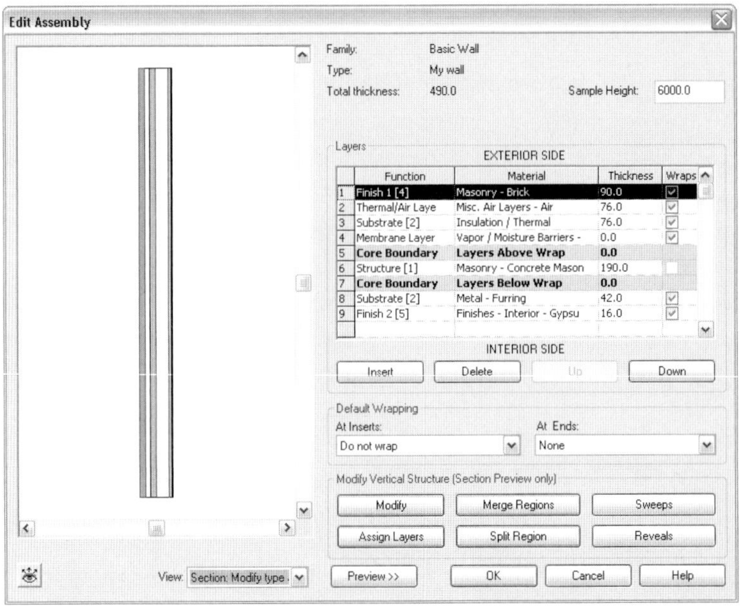

Figure 6.16

Wall in section view

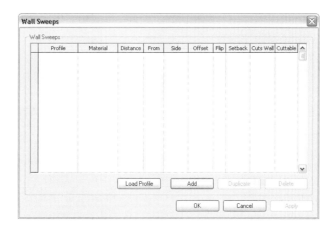

Figure 6.17

Wall sweeps

6. Click the Load Profile button, browse to the Profiles folder, and load these two pro-files, as shown in Figure 6.18:

    *   Cornice profile: Traditional (1)

    *   Skirting profile: (Base 2, Ogee, or similar)

7. Click the Add button. This adds a row in the dialog box that lets you select one of the loaded profiles and set its position relative to the wall geometry. Figure 6.19 shows the profiles loaded in the wall.

8. Add both profiles. Set the Traditional profile's From value to Top and the Ogee pro-file's From value to Base. Doing so attaches the profiles to the top and bottom of your wall. Figure 6.20 shows the profiles attached to the top and bottom of the wall.

9. Click OK. Draw a segment of this wall in the drawing area. Check out the wall in section and 3D views to see the resulting wall. Figure 6.21 shows the final result of the wall.

Figure 6.18

Load these wall profiles.

Cornice profile: Traditional (1)

Skirting profile: Ogee

	Profile	Material	Distance	From	Side	Offset	Flip	Setback	Cuts Wall	Cuttable
1	Traditional	<By Categor	0.0	Top	Interio	0.0	☐	0.0	☑	☐
2	Ogee : 18m	<By Categor	0.0	Base	Interio	0.0	☐	0.0	☑	☐

Figure 6.19

Adding the profiles to the wall

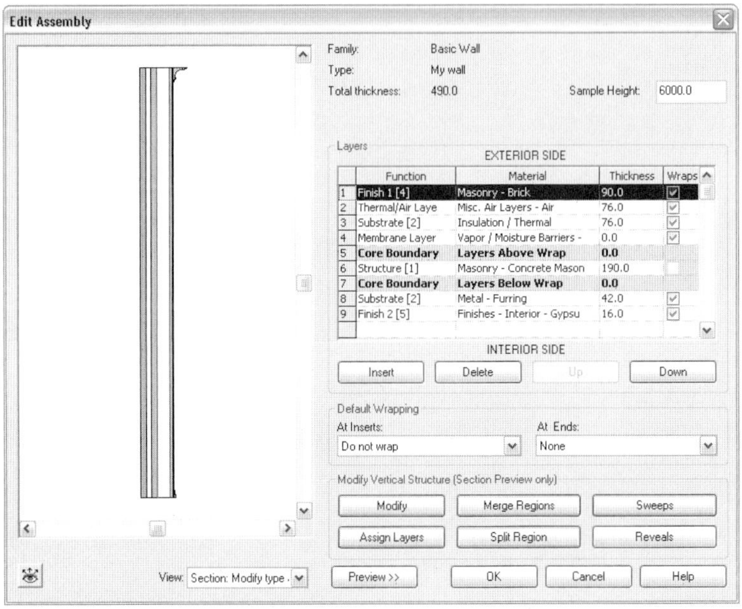

Figure 6.20

**The profiles
on the wall**

Often layers in a single wall do not extend all the way throughout its height: in a bathroom the tiles sometimes only go up to 5′-0″ (1.50m) or a façade starts at 50cm off the ground. To make it possible to have wall components finish earlier or start later within the height of the wall, there is another useful feature that enables you to unlock wall layers and manipulate their heights. To do this, switch to the Section preview in the Edit Assembly dialog box, click Modify, and zoom in to the bottom of the wall. Hover the mouse over the bottom edges of the layers in the preview, and they will highlight. With the help of the Tab key, select one of the bottom edges and a lock icon will appear. By default, all top and bottom edges of layers are locked into place; however, if you unlock this edge it becomes free to move up and down. Note that this editing can't be done in the Assembly dialog box—only within the project environment. You can then manipulate individual layers dynamically or with parameters. When you unlock layers, the instance parameters for Base and Top Extension Distance become enabled. Figure 6.22 shows the lock and the ability to unlock the material and extend it farther than the wall base.

Using the same principles outlined for adding traditional-looking elements, you can get creative and add any type or profile you want. Figure 6.23 shows a wall with a corrugated siding added as an integrated wall sweep.

Reveals

Reveals can be added to a wall using the same workflow as with sweeps, the only difference being that the profile is subtractive rather than additive. Note that the profile must overlap the geometry of the wall when used to create a wall reveal.

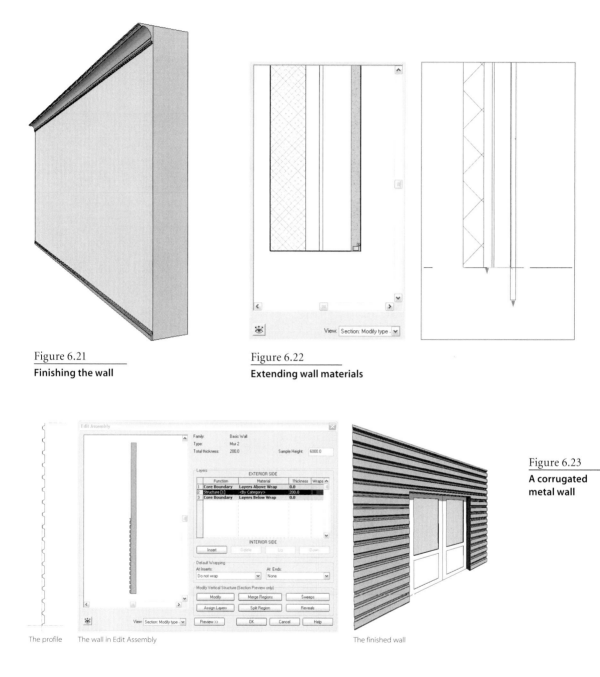

Figure 6.21
Finishing the wall

Figure 6.22
Extending wall materials

Figure 6.23
A corrugated metal wall

The profile   The wall in Edit Assembly

The finished wall

Wall Sweep Returns

When you're working on traditional architectural projects, the wall sweeps usually wrap around door openings in thick walls. Revit can accommodate that using the Change Sweep Return command.

To understand this feature, follow this simple exercise:

1. Open a new session of Revit and place a generic wall.

2. Rather than placing a sweep in the wall type, we can use another method for placing sweeps: the Host Sweep tool in the Modeling tab of the Design bar (shown in Figure 6.24). Choose Wall Sweep, and then select a wall sweep from the Type Selector. These sweeps can be placed either vertically or horizontally using options in the Options bar.

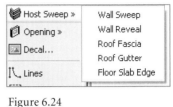

Figure 6.24

Host Sweep

3. Add a horizontal sweep to the middle the wall. Use the temporary dimensions to place the sweep at the desired height.

4. Using the Opening tool, also located in the Modeling tab, draw an opening that intersects the sweep, as shown in Figure 6.25.

5. Select the sweep—it will display a blue grip at the end (the edge of the opening). Click the *Change Sweep Return* command on the Options bar; the cursor turns into a knife symbol, and when you click somewhere on the profile, it creates a new segment that wraps around the edge of the opening. Press Esc or use the Modify tool to exit the command. You will need to zoom in close to the end of the sweep to really see the effect. If you zoom very closely, the lines might become very thick and ugly—in that case, click the Thin Line Mode button that was explained earlier in the book (🖫).

6. Select the sweep again, and drag the control to adjust the length of the sweep. Figure 6.26 shows some examples of modifying an instance of a host sweep.

Figure 6.25

Wall with a sweep and opening, prior to applying the Change Sweep Return functionality

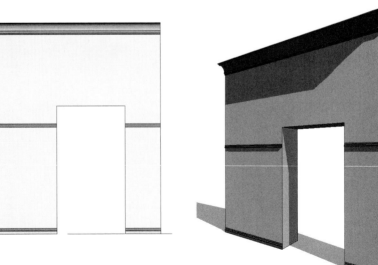

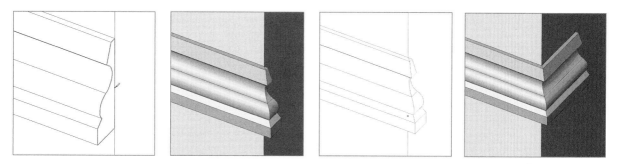

Figure 6.26
**Modifying a
sweep return**

Wall sweeps created using the Host Sweep tool from the Modeling tab of the Design bar can
be scheduled. Integral wall sweeps created from within the wall properties cannot be scheduled in Revit at present. That is the main difference between these two types of sweeps.

Creating Special Walls Using the Create Tool (In-Place Walls)

When you're working on traditional architecture or restoration of historic buildings,
you'll often need to create walls that are irregular in shape. The Create tool, found in
the Modeling tab of the Design bar, lets you address such wall styles; Figure 6.27 shows
an example.

Figure 6.27
**Create in Place
showing a series of
connected blends**

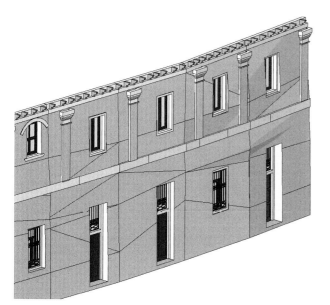

The finished wall

The two wall blends combined
to make the wall

This tool allows you to create a family using solid geometry that can be made from extrusions, sweeps, revolves, and blends. Each in-place family can be assigned a specific category that is later used to control visibility and behavior in the model. For example, assigning the family to the category Wall allows the wall to host inserts such as windows and doors as well as schedule as a wall.

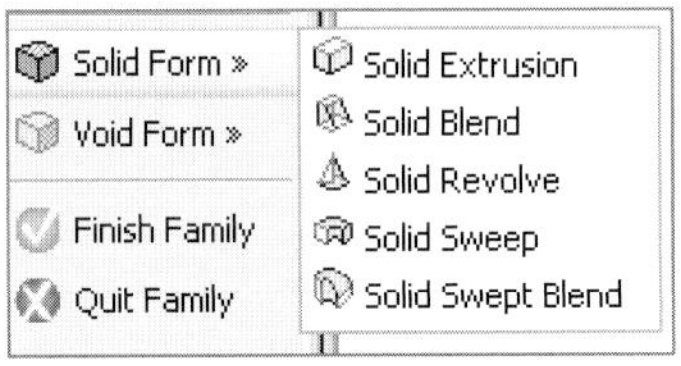

Figure 6.28

The Solid Form toolbar showing the new Solid Swept Blend tool

New to Revit 2009 is the introduction of an additional modeling technique: a Swept Blend tool. This tool combines features of blends and sweeps into one tool. This is similar to the existing blend functionality, but it allows you to define the path as either linear or curved. The new tool can be accessed when making families or massing components from the Solid and Void pullout menus, shown in Figure 6.28. Figure 6.29 shows an example of the type of forms you can create using this new tool. In previous versions of Revit, shapes of this type would need to be created using a combination of masses and voids.

The wall in Figure 6.30 is created using a series of blends assigned to the wall category. It still behaves as a wall: you can make doors and windows, and they cut through the geometry of the wall as with standard walls. Various wall types can be created using this method.

The beauty of Revit modeling tools is that you can always go back to the sketch and change your idea (the sketch), and all related drawings will update. You do not need to redraw the profile. The same applies for the sweep path—if you used the sweep technique, you can at any point edit the path while keeping the profile.

Figure 6.29

An example of a solid swept blend

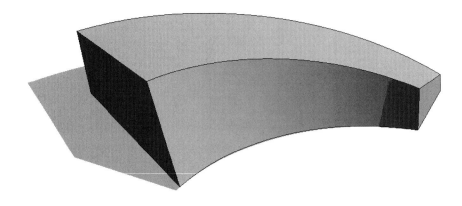

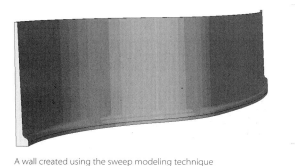

A wall created using the sweep modeling technique

A twisted wall created using the blend technique—drawing the base and the top shape, and setting a distance between them

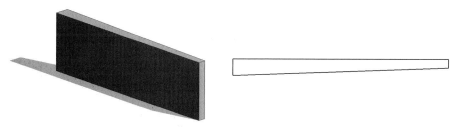

A wall with various thicknesses created using the extrusion method

Curtain Walls: Advanced Design Techniques

The Curtain Wall tool is designed with flexibility in mind. You can use it to generate anything from simple storefronts to highly articulated structural glass façades. In this section, we'll look at the basic principles and how to extend these principles to create a range of designs.

As we mentioned in Chapter 4, the composition of a curtain wall is divided into four primary elements, shown in Figure 6.31:

- The wall and its geometric extents
- Curtain grids
- Mullions
- Curtain panels

The wall A curtain wall is drawn like a basic wall and is available in the Type Selector when the Wall tool is active. It has top and bottom constraints, can be attached to roofs, can have its elevation profile sketch edited, and schedules as a wall type.

Curtain grids The curtain grid is the layout grid that defines the divisions of the curtain wall facade, which is used to set panel sizes and mullion placement. The layout grid can be designed freely as a combination of horizontal and vertical segments or can be a type with embedded rules that specify regular divisions. Figure 6.32 shows two dramatically different types of curtain wall systems.

Mullions The mullions represent the metal or PVC profiles on a glass façade, and in Revit they follow the geometry of the grid. They can have any shape that is based on a mullion profile family.

Figure 6.31

Taxonomy of a curtain wall

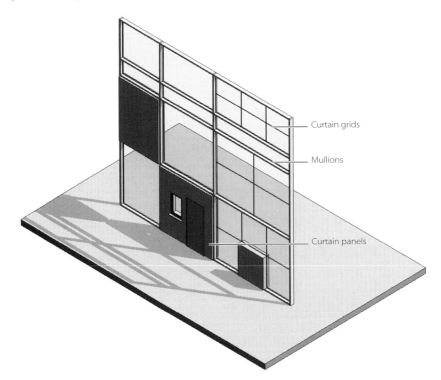

Curtain panels The curtain panels fill in the space between gridlines and are always one of the following:

> **Empty panels** No panel is placed in the mullions.

> **Glazed panels** Can be made out of different types of glass that can have any color or transparency.

> **Solid panels and panels with wall types** Can take on any geometry you wish and thus create most interesting structures, like the one shown in Figure 6.33.

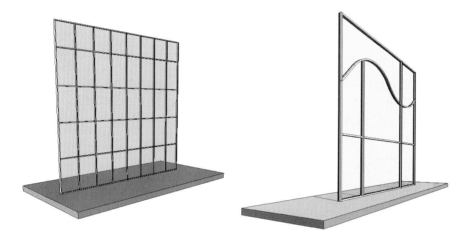

Figure 6.32

Curtain wall examples

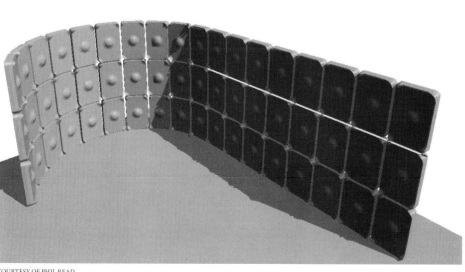

Figure 6.33

A curtain wall system with formed panels

Selecting the Elements within the Curtain Waall

Revit provides specially tailored selection options in the context menu to aid with workflow and interaction when working with curtain walls. When you hover over or select an element in a curtain wall, take note of the status bar in the lower-left of the screen: it tells you exactly the type of element you're about to select or have already selected. Depending on what the mouse is hovering over, various selection options are available. The elements you can select include the following:

- The entire curtain-wall entity (this selection is indicated by a green dashed line surrounding the curtain wall)
- A gridline
- A mullion
- A curtain panel

To select the element you want, use the Tab key until the element of choice is highlighted.

Designing a Curtain Wall

In this exercise, we'll walk through the creation of a simple curtain wall. To draw a curtain wall, you can either draw a standard wall and then change its type to Curtain Wall or select a Curtain Wall type from the Wall Type Selector first. Follow these steps:

1. Select the Wall tool.

2. From the Type Selector, select Curtain Wall.

3. In the Level 1 plan view, draw a curtain wall. Use the wall type Curtain Wall 1.

4. Toggle the view to see the result in 3D.

5. To divide the wall into panels, use the Curtain Grid tool on the Modeling tab. Mouse over the edges of the wall to get a preview of where the grid will be placed. Revit has some intelligent snapping built into grid placement that looks for midpoints and points that will divide the panel into thirds.

6. You can then start placing mullions using the Mullion tool in the Modeling tab. Place one mullion at a time by selecting separate segments; or, if you want to apply the same mullion on all segments, hold the Ctrl key and click a gridline to select all segments and apply the mullions. The series of images in Figure 6.34 shows the approximate results you should get.

7. Let's say you want to add more mullions, but this time you don't want them to extend the entire height of the curtain wall. Select the Curtain Grid Line tool, and place new grids as shown in Figure 6.35.

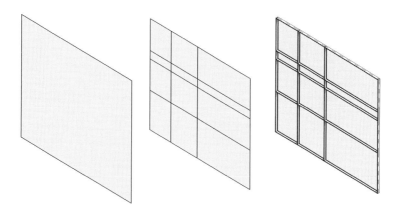

Figure 6.34

Making the curtain wall and adding mullions

8. Before applying a mullion to the new gridline, delete the segments of the gridline where you don't wish the mullion to occur. Exit the grid-placement tool, and select the newly created gridline. Click the Add/Remove Segments button in the Options bar, and click the segment you want removed. Remove the top and bottom segments; you should have an image similar to Figure 6.36. Place mullions on the gridline to finish.

9. To change mullion types—in this case, the border mullions—use the context menu to isolate mullions for selection. Hover the cursor over a mullion, right-click, and select Mullions → Border Mullions to select all border mullions.

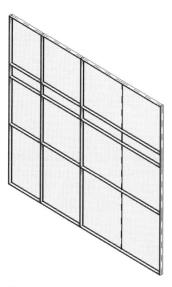

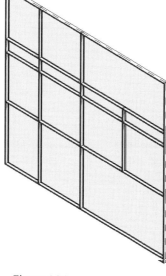

Figure 6.35

Adding another grid

Figure 6.36

Removing portions of the grid and applying mullion

10. Swap them for another type using the Type Selector. If you don't find a mullion type with the dimensions you need, no worries—it's easy to create a new one on the fly:

A. Open the mullion properties.

B. Select Edit → New, and then click Duplicate.

C. Name the mullion type. In the Type Properties, change the thickness to the new value to 8″ (200mm) and the two parameters for width (this represents half the width of the mullion) to 1.25″ (35mm). Figure 6.37 shows the finished exterior mullions.

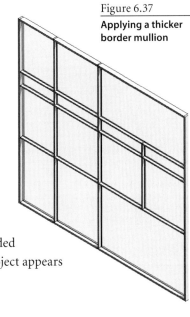

Figure 6.37

Applying a thicker border mullion

The result shows thicker mullions on the border of your curtain wall.

Curtain mullions are usually rectangular, and you can make new types of different sizes on the fly, as shown in the previous exercise. However, not all mullions are simple rectangles. With Revit, you can use complex profile shapes as extruded mullions. Mullion profile families can be made with the Family Editor.

The default library provides some mullions that use custom profiles. To use these, load them into your project, duplicate an existing mullion type, and set the type parameter profile to one of the newly loaded profiles. A list of available profiles loaded into the project appears in the field shown in Figure 6.38.

Figure 6.38

Modifying the mullion profile

Construction		
Profile	Default	
Position	Default	
Corner Mullion	System Mullion Profile: Circular	
Thickness	System Mullion Profile: Rectangular	

In reality, curtain-wall mullions can have complex internal details from a manufacturing perspective. Many curtain-wall manufacturers provide DWG details showing the actual manufactured look of the mullions. You'll probably want to show more of those details when you do detailed drawings.

Curtain Panels

Curtain panels fill the space between the curtain grids and mullions. These elements are created in the Family Editor using the Curtain Panels family template. They can be found under File → New Family → Curtain Wall Panel.rft. The Revit default template has a couple of curtain panels preloaded: System Panel Glazed and System Panel Solid.

You can duplicate different types of these families and change the material, thickness, and offset to customize the appearance.

By default, Revit applies glazed curtain panels as panels for the curtain wall. Using the method explained earlier, select one of the curtain panels and use the Type Selector to change it to System Panel Solid. It will look like Figure 6.39.

Doors and Windows

Curtain walls can host specially designed doors and windows. Keep in mind that standard doors and windows cannot be hosted by a curtain wall. These specially designed elements are recognizable by their name, indicating that they are curtain wall doors or windows and that they schedule as doors and windows, but that their behavior is dependent on the curtain wall. Curtain-wall doors and windows adapt their width and height to fill in grid cells. Essentially, they behave exactly like panels—they've just been made to appear and schedule as doors or windows.

To insert a door within a curtain wall, choose File → Load from Library → Load Family. Navigate to the Doors folder, and select a Curtain Wall Door (Single or Double). A door is added to the curtain wall, as shown in Figure 6.40.

> Be sure you make the distance between gridlines or between mullions reflect a standard door size. You can do this before or after the placement of the door. The curtain wall is highly parametric, so changes are allowed at any time during the design process.

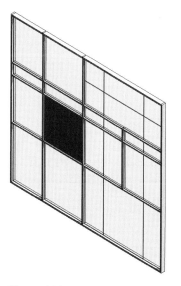

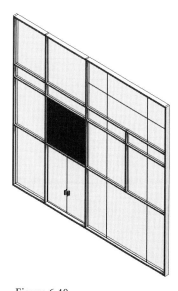

Figure 6.39
Changing a panel within the curtain wall

Figure 6.40
A curtain wall with an inserted door

Parametric Behavior

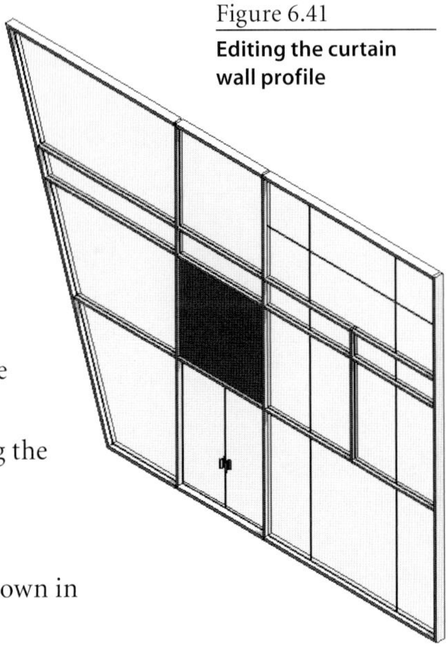

You can edit the profile shape of a curtain wall, just like a basic wall. Select the curtain wall and click the *Edit Elevation Profile* button in the Options bar to start editing the sketch outline of the wall. Follow these steps:

Figure 6.41

Editing the curtain wall profile

1. Draw four walls on Level 1 in shape of a rectangle.

2. Add a Roof by Footprint on Level 2, picking all four walls with the Tab key (be sure to select the outside face of walls, and go ahead and give the roof an overhang using the Options bar).

3. Switch to 3D view.

4. The resulting curtain wall should be as shown in Figure 6.41.

   For the sake of the next exercise, undo this last profile edit.

Attaching the Curtain Wall to a Roof

Curtain walls have a highly parametric relationship with other modeling elements. Like a basic wall, when a curtain wall is attached to a roof, it maintains its connection to the roof as the roof shape adjusts. To see how this works, start a new session of Revit and follow these steps:

1. Draw four walls on Level 1.

2. Add a Roof by Footprint on Level 2, picking all four walls with the Tab key.

3. Switch to 3D view.

4. Toggle two ends of the sketch to be on-slope defining, using the Options bar. This will generate a gable roof when the sketch is finished.

5. Change one wall to the Curtain Wall: Storefront type.

6. Select all the walls, and attach them to the roof using the Attach/Detach button located in the Options bar.

7. Select the roof and drag the blue arrow on the top to make the roof pitch higher. The curtain wall automatically readjusts its size and shape to accommodate the change, as shown in Figure 6.42.

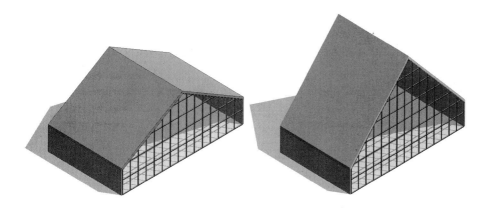

Figure 6.42

Curtain wall conforming to roof changes

Curtain walls can also use standard wall types in lieu of panels. Using the same method described previously, select a curtain panel and exchange it with a basic wall using the Type Selector.

Complex Curtain-Wall Panel Possibilities

Look at the complex-shaped curtain panels in Figure 6.43. You may think, "Oh, I can *never* do that!" Well, Revit can help you do it—and do it easily. To be fair, you'll need to have some mileage in using Revit before you can create such a curtain wall. But isn't it inspiring to look at all the possibilities that you'll be able to master one day?

Figure 6.43

A complex curtain wall designed in Revit

The creation principle behind any of these types of curtain walls is the same as we just reviewed. All that differs is the geometry of the curtain panel.

The curtain walls in Figure 6.44 were created with curtain panels that—instead of a standard rectangular solid shape—are made of a solid extrusion that is perforated with four corner openings. An additional solid geometry represents one quarter of the spider clamp.

Figure 6.44

A spider-clamp curtain wall

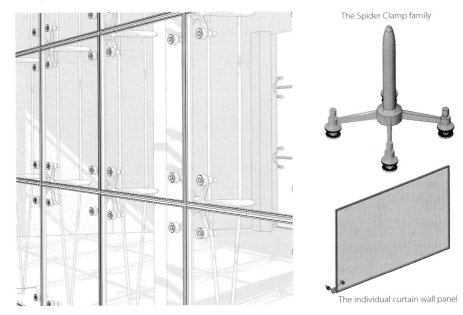

The Spider Clamp family

The individual curtain wall panel

Roofs and Slabs: Advanced Shape Editing

No flat roof is ever really flat! Creating roofs with tapered insulation over flat roof (Figure 6.45) is easily accomplished. This powerful tool is a modifier that is applicable to roofs or floors and offers the ability to model concrete slabs with multiple slopes, often referred to as warped slabs.

Figure 6.45

Flat roof with sloped insulation

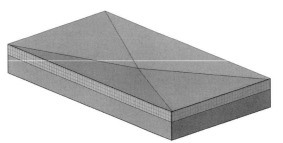

Inspirational Revit Projects

This gallery of projects comes from architects all around the globe who have embraced the move to a smarter way of working on projects and who use BIM as their main methodology. They have different approaches to how they start a project, from a conceptual massing or legacy CAD files to hand-sketching and importing from other modeling applications. All have different skill levels with Revit, but what ties them together is that they managed to produce beautiful architectural examples using BIM. They have all adapted their workflows and are able to offer a competitive advantage as a result.

All projects shown have been modeled in Revit, using many of the concepts, principles, and techniques explained throughout this book. The renderings vary: some are done within Revit, using Accurender, the rendering engine that was embedded in Revit up to release 2008; the majority, however, have been rendered using 3ds Max and VRay, producing some stunning visuals.

BIM is not a myth. These are real people, real projects, and real sources of inspiration. And don't forget: it's technology; it's digital; but still, what really matters is that it's good architecture.

We would like to express our sincerest gratitude to all of the architects who generously shared their work.

Enjoy!

KUBIK+NEMETH+VLKOVIC, SLOVAKIA

Hotel and wellness center

Andrea Torre

Residential design

ARCHITECT: ANDREA TORRE, ITALY

Andrea Sader and Ines Magri

Residential design

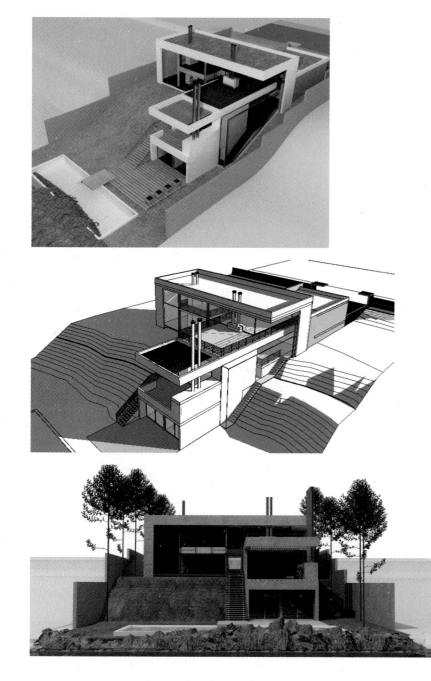

ARCHITECTS: ANDREA SADER, INES MAGRI, URUGUAY

Felipe Manrique Diaz

Student project, Universidad de las Americas, Cancer patient center

RMJM Hillier

Addition to St. Louis Public Library

Kubik+Nemeth+Vlkovic

Housing project

Gensler

American University of Beirut, School of Engineering

Gensler

Government office building

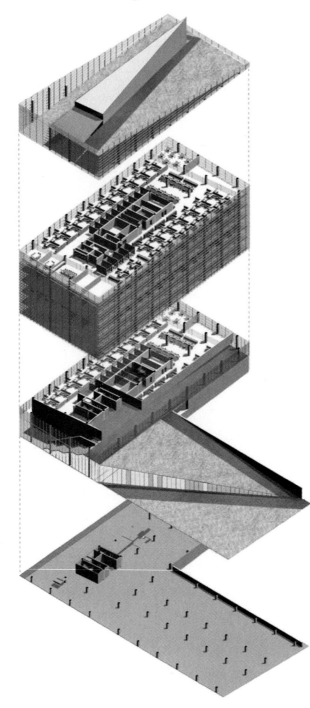

HOK

School design, Kazakhstan

ARCHITECT: HOK, UK

HOK

Tower designs

Siggi Pfundt

Single-family house

abstellraum
bad wc
galerie
steg
technik
wf
wohnen
kochen
zimmer

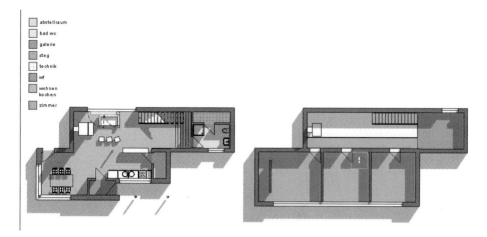

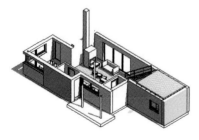

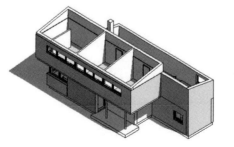

ARCHITECT: SIGGI PFUNDT, GERMANY

SPBR Architects

Library

Simone Cappochin

Unbuilt Kahn student project

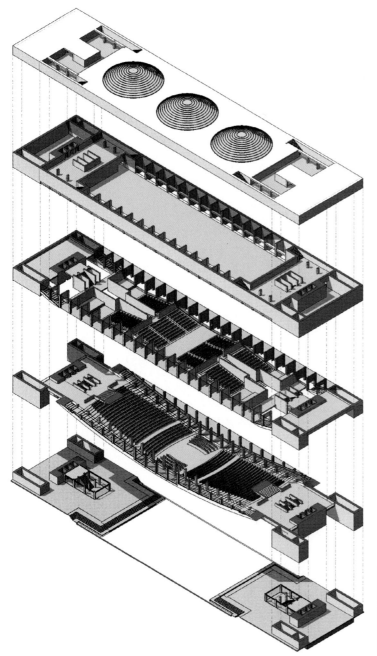

Simone Cappochin

Loggia del Capitano, Palladio

Philippe Drouant

Custom families

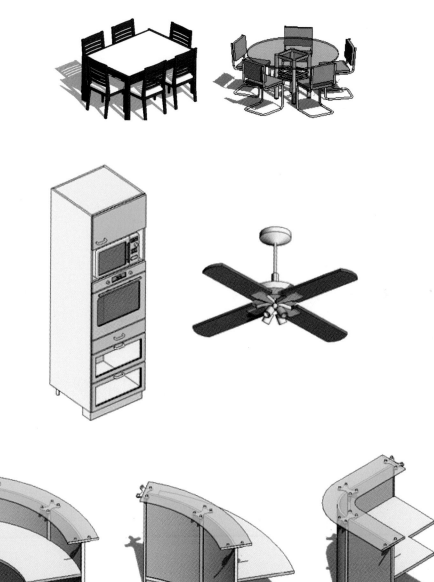

Philippe Drouant

Custom families

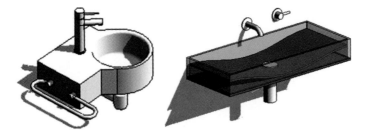

Shape Modification Tools

The modification tools appear in the Options bar when a roof or floor is selected (Figure 6.46).

Here is what each tool is for (left to right):

Direct Editing tool   Edits element geometry using selection and modification of points (vertices) and edges.

Draw Points tool   Adds points on the top face of a roof or floor. Points can be added on edges or surfaces.

Draw Split Line tool   Allows sketching directly on the top face of the element, which adds split lines to the floor and roof so that hips and valleys can be created.

Pick Supports tool   Allows picking linear beams and walls to create new split edges at the correct elevation automatically.

As you can see, there is also a Reset Shape button. This button will remove all modifiers applied to the floor or roof that is selected.

Let's do a short exercise that shows how to make a sloped roof as shown in Figure 6.47.

1. Open the file Modifying roof shape start.rvt.

2. Select the roof that has been already prepared for you.

3. Activate the Draw Split Line tool (note that the color of the rest of the model grays out while the roof is highlighted with a dashed green color).

4. Sketch ridge lines to divide the roof into areas that will be independently drained.

5. Using the same tool, draw diagonal lines within those areas to create the valleys. Note: when drawing the diagonals you will need to snap to the existing edge points—if you fail to do so, no worries, you can always Tab select an end point of the diagonals and move it to the intersection point.

What you have done is split the roof surfaces in many sub-slabs, but they are still all at the same height and inclination. You should have a roof that looks like Figure 6.48.

Figure 6.46

The Shape Edit modifying tools

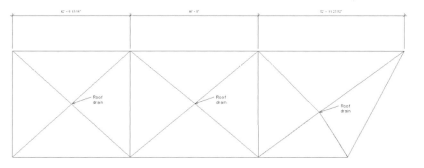

Figure 6.47

A roof plan showing a roof divided in segments with drainage points

Figure 6.48

Using the Draw Split tool, you create ridges and valleys.

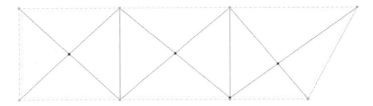

6. Switch to a 3D view.

7. To add a slope (height of the drainage points), Tab-select the crossing point of the diagonals. New controls that allow you to edit the text appear, and you can either move the arrows up and down or type in a value for the point height. Type in **0′-5″ (13cm)** as shown in Figure 6.49.

8. Repeat the same for the other three drainage points.

9. If needed (as often happens to accommodate what's happening in the room below the roof), move the point to another position, which is easily done by selecting, then dragging and dropping of the point. See Figure 6.50.

10. Switch to Level 2 and make a section through the roof—if possible somewhere through the drainage point. Open the section; change the detail level to Fine to see all layers and change the Roof type from Generic Roof to Basic Roof – Steel Truss on Metal Deck – EPDM. You will see that the entire roof structure is sloped toward the drainage point. See Figure 6.51.

Figure 6.49

Edit points to change the height.

Figure 6.50

Drainage point moved to a new position

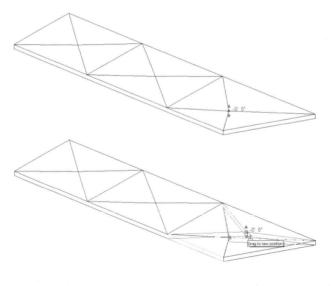

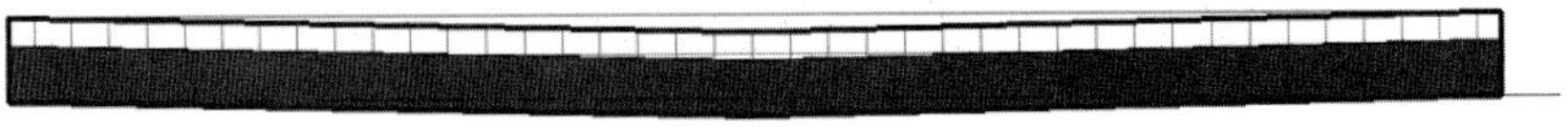

Figure 6.51

Section through roof showing the slope

Now, what if you wanted just the insulation to be tapered but not the structure? For that, you can edit a property of individual layers to make the thickness variable.

11. Select the roof and open the Element Properties dialog box. Click Edit/New, and then edit the roof's structure.

12. Activate the preview. You'll notice that in the roof-structure preview you do not see any slopes. That is correct and will not change: this preview is just a theoretical preview of the structure and will not show the exact sloping. Look back to the roof layers: you'll see a Variable column under Layers. This allows layers of the roof to vary in thickness when slopes are present. Check the insulation material to be variable (Figure 6.52).

13. Go back to the section view and take a look at the difference that this change provoked: as you will see, only the insulation is tapered now, while the structure remains flat. See Figure 6.53.

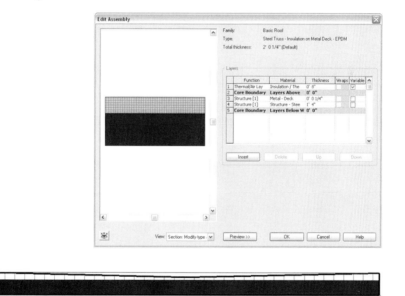

Figure 6.52

Editing the Roof assembly

Figure 6.53

Section of the roof with variable thickness

You can find a final state of this exercise on the book's companion web page as `Modifying Roof Shape End.rvt`.

If you want to see what the Reset Shape functionality does, select the roof and click the Reset Shape button in the Options bar.

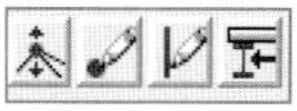

Figure 6.54

Roofs with curved sketches are not a problem in Revit 2009.

New to Revit 2009 is that these modifiers can now be applied to a floor or roof of any shape—there is no restriction that the sketch be made entirely of straight lines as it was in Revit 2008 (see Figure 6.54).

You could achieve similar results without using the Draw Split Line tool by adding points in the middle of the flat roof. Try it out to see how that simplifies the process.

Warped Surfaces

Warped surfaces can also be created using this tool. Draw a flat roof (no slopes) and then select the roof. Using the Modify tool in the Options bar, you can start moving edge points up and down (Figure 6.55). When edges or points are selected, use the temporary dimension field to accurately change the height of the subelement. Boundary edges are shown as green dashed lines and internal split lines show as solid blue lines. Points on the edge are green squares, and internal points are blue squares. Select a blue edge control and drag it up or down to warp the surface (Figure 6.56). You will get an ignorable warning when doing this: "Thickness of this Roof may be slightly inaccurate due to extreme Shape Editing. Dimensions to this element in sections and details may not accurately indicate the Thickness shown in Type Properties."

Rotate the 3D view to understand what you have just created. See the final result in Figure 6.56.

Figure 6.55

Edit the edge point to warp a flat roof.

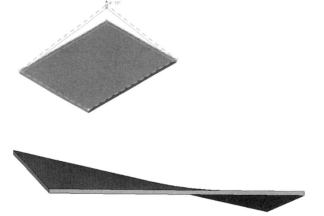

Figure 6.56

Axonometric view of a warped roof

CHAPTER 7

Working with Other Applications

Now that we have developed a language for working within Revit, let's look at how you can use it to work and communicate with others. The building industry is a complex organism with many moving parts and participants. Partners, consultants, contractors, subcontractors, and owners are all involved in the process and need the ability to exchange vital design information. Because of the robustness of information within the Revit model, it's possible to do things with data that weren't possible with basic 2D drafting. Even so, data exchange with other applications is still a requirement. Revit provides tools to import and export a wide range of information.

In this chapter, you'll learn how to export your Revit model in forms that others can read and how to import information that is relevant to your project from other sources. We'll first review all the possible export and import file formats, and then dig into more detailed use cases. Topics we'll cover include:

- **Exporting your data**

- **Exporting DWG drawings**

- **Importing and linking**

- **Working with imported files**

- **Working with civil engineering DWG files**

- **Converting 2D drawings into a 3D model**

- **Starting a model from a scanned drawing**

Exporting Your Data

You can find the export options under File → Export. Revit offers several export formats depending on the format and type of data you want to export.

Here's a list of the types of files that Revit can export using information from the Revit model:

- CAD formats
- Animations, including walkthroughs and animated solar studies
- Open Database Connectivity (ODBC) database tables
- Images
- Schedules
- Green Building XML Schema (gbXML)
- Room/area reports
- 3ds Max (FBX)

CAD Formats

CAD formats lets you export a view or sheet of the model into a 2D or 3D CAD format. The following CAD file formats can be exported directly from Revit: `.dwg`, `.dxf`, `.dgn`, and `.sat`.

DWG

DWG refers to the original patented Autodesk exchange format, RealDWG. DWG has been the established standard for exchange of digital data in the construction industry for the last 20-plus years. Revit can export an entire project, collections of sheets and views, or any individual sheet or view to the DWG format.

Revit exports views to DWG in two different manners: it exports a 2D DWG drafting format (from a majority of the views) and 3D DWGs (from the 3D views). The 3D DWG exports can be viewed in a 3D environment in AutoCAD or any other application that reads DWG. When exporting to DWG, some of the metadata (property information) of elements is also exported and can be read within AutoCAD.

Exporting DWG files is discussed in more detail later in this chapter (see "Exporting DWG Drawings").

DXF

Data Exchange Format (DXF) is a format for storing vector data. DXF is regarded as a legacy standard and is almost out of use in the industry. However, in some parts of the world or with some strongly established practices, it still finds its use, and for those reasons Revit supports exchange with DXF. If you haven't used DXF files in the past, be careful exporting 3D data to DXF. A file can get very large very quickly!

DGN

DGN is the name used for CAD file formats supported by Bentley Systems' MicroStation and Intergraph's Interactive Graphics Design System (IGDS) CAD programs. Note that Revit supports export to DGN file formats only up to MicroStation V7.

SAT

SAT stands for Standard ACIS Text. ACIS can store modeling information in external files called save files. These files have an open format so that external applications, even those not based on ACIS, can have access to the ACIS geometric model. Revit exports to version 7 of SAT.

Exporting Animations: Walkthroughs and Solar Studies

You can create walkthrough animations in Revit and save them as .avi files. To export a walkthrough, choose File → Export → Walkthrough. You'll find the Walkthrough tool on the View tab of the Design bar.

Revit lets you make animated solar studies, and those can also be exported as .avi files. To export an animated solar study, choose File → Export → Animated Solar Study. Creation of solar studies is covered in Chapter 8.

ODBC Database Tables

You can export almost all the information embedded in your Revit model to an ODBC table. Doing so creates a link between your Revit file and another external database such as Excel, Access, FileMaker Pro, or SQL Server. ODBC gives you the opportunity to download data from any of the tables in Revit directly to a database using the Microsoft ODBC connector. An example of this functionality is a cost-estimating software add-on package that gets material quantity take-offs directly from the model.

ODBC is an advanced topic that won't be covered in depth in this book. However, if you do need to export to a database, here's how to use the Microsoft ODBC connector:

1. Open the file Station.rvt at the book's companion web page, www.wiley.com/go/ introducingrevit2009.

2. Select File → Export → ODBC Database.

3. Click New to create a new data source name (DSN).

4. Select a driver. This driver will normally be associated with the software program you export to: for example, Microsoft Access, dBASE, or Paradox.

5. Click Next.

6. Type a DSN name, and, if necessary, navigate to the directory where you wish to save it. Click Next. A confirmation dialog box appears. If any information is incorrect, click Back and correct it.

7. Click Finish.

Next, create the database file:

1. Click Create in the ODBC Microsoft Setup dialog box.

2. Navigate to the directory where you're saving the database, type the database name, and click OK.

3. Click OK in the confirmation dialog box.

4. Click OK in the ODBC Microsoft Access Setup dialog box.

Schedules

Revit will let you export schedule tables, view lists, material take-offs, key legends, and note blocks as a tab-delimited text (`.txt` format) file that can then be read by Excel or any other spreadsheet/database application. Note that none of the formatting created within a Revit schedule, such as column spacing or font style, will be maintained. To export to `.txt`, open the schedule you want to export, then choose File → Export → Schedules. To make an `.xls` out of it, open Excel and open the .txt file.

gbXML

Green Building XML (gbXML) is an XML data type that was created to support the growing trend of sustainability and green building design. gbXML is an export function within Revit and other BIM applications that allows you to export specific data about a model for the purpose of performing energy analysis and evaluating building perfor-mance. A number of different applications are available that can read gbXML-formatted files. These applications are primarily designed around performing energy analysis using the Revit model as a basis. This allows a tremendous time savings, allowing you to reuse your model geometry instead of re-creating it in another analysis application. Some of these energy analysis applications are Green Building Studio (`www.greenbuildingstudio .com`) and IES <VE> (`www.iesve.com`). You can find more information on them at `www.gbxml.org`.

Room/Area Reports

Room/Area Report is a tool that creates a graphical and mathematical HTML report as a proof of the digital calculation of rooms in your project. Some authorities in Europe require these area reports as a part of permit documentation. Each room surface is divided into basic geometrical shapes (triangles, rectangles, arc segments), and each shape is described with a name that, in the table, has the geometrical formula used to calculate area.

You have the option to report the window area as a percentage of the room area. To comply with certain standards in different countries, you can choose to exclude columns from the total room area calculations by making your columns non-room-bounding. This is done through the Element Properties of individual columns.

To create such reports, select File → Export → Room Area Report, select the view or project, and define your graphic settings. You'll receive an HTML page of the report. A sample report is shown in Figure 7.1. These reports are not parametrically connected with the Revit model. If you make changes in the model, you will need to re-export the report.

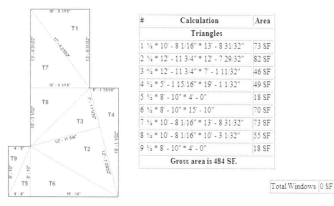

Figure 7.1

Room area report example

Industry Foundation Class (IFC)

Industry foundation classes (IFCs) allow for exchange of intelligent data between architectural and downstream applications, based on STEP application protocol. IFC is a nonproprietary file format that has been recently resurrected as a possible BIM interoperability standard. The goal is to allow the transfer of information between models that have been created using different BIM authoring packages. More information on IFCs and their current and future uses can be found at www.iai-international.org.

Revit Architecture 2009 supports first-stage IFC 2x-3 certification import and export. Revit also has full (second-stage) IFC Singapore Code Checking (BCA) certification, which is export only. IFC can be imported into any other BIM or CAD application that accepts IFC class files.

> If you decide to use the IFC for import or export of data, there are a few items to keep in mind. Although multiple industries have made great advances with the IFC 2x-2 data exchange standards, no IFC file will be as robust as the parent file from which it was created. There will always be some data loss as you migrate your data to a more uniform data type.

3ds Max (FBX)

The FBX export is a way to export a 3D model and all the material definitions so you can open the file in 3ds Max and do more advanced renderings and animations. All the materials assigned in the Revit model will translate 100 percent into 3ds Max.

Exporting DWG Drawings

DWG is the industry standard and is used by the majority of applications as a data exchange method. We'll review some of the specific options and use cases for DWG exports.

In the majority of cases, you'll need to export 2D DWG drawings for owners and consultants or other engineers who are still not on a BIM platform and are not using Revit and will work with the file directly or use it as an underlay. Let's review all the options you should be aware of when exporting to DWG.

Select CAD Formats from the export options and you'll see a dialog box like that shown in Figure 7.2.

Figure 7.2

The Export CAD Formats dialog box

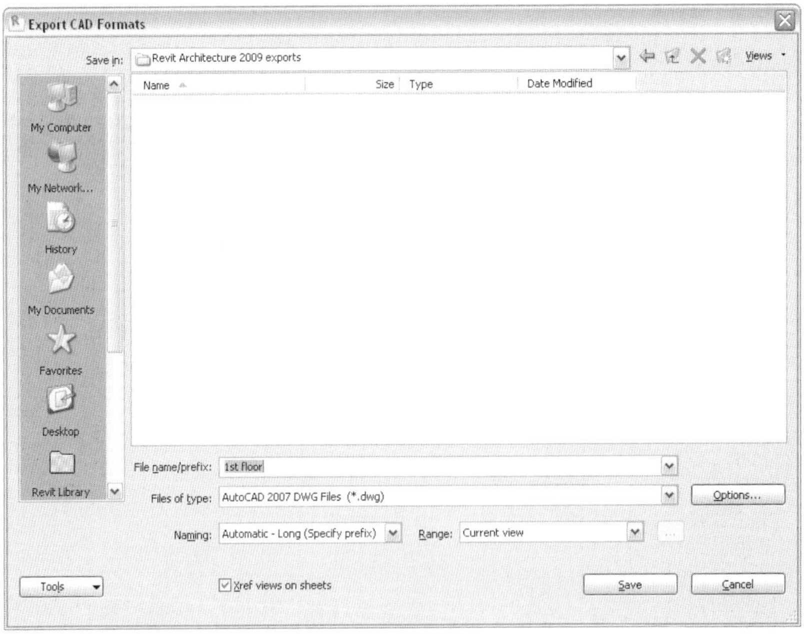

Under the Files of Type menu, you have the option to select to export to the following CAD file types: .dwg, .dxf, .dgn, and .sat. For a DWG export, you can choose to export to an AutoCAD 2000, 2004, or 2007 file format (Figure 7.3). After you select an export file type, you have a few additional options.

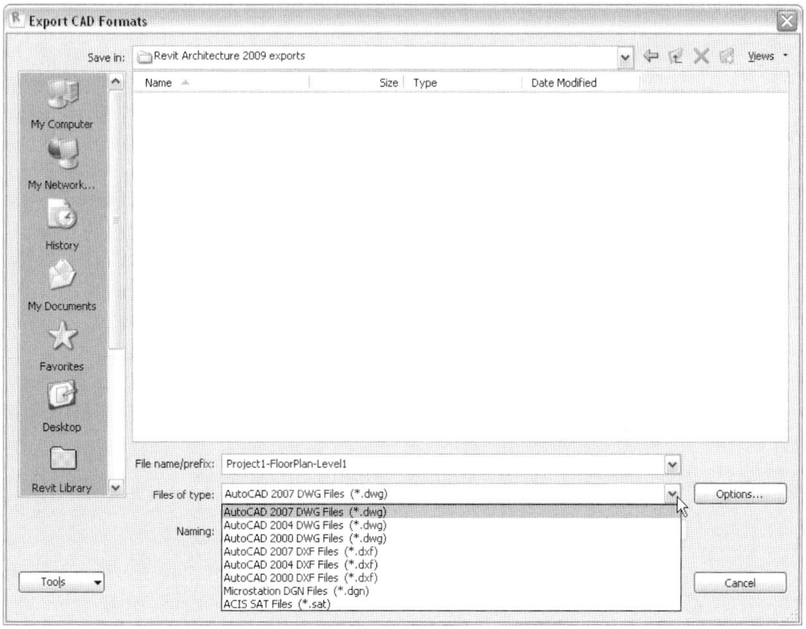

Figure 7.3

Export options

Naming This section allows you to have Revit name the file for you in a short or long format. Alternatively, you can name it yourself with the Manual option:

Automatic (Long Specify Prefix) If you choose the Automatic (Long Specify Prefix) option, the Short format grays out the File Name text box and applies the view name or sheet name (depending on what you're exporting) to each of the exported views. This option activates the File Name text box and allows you to put in a prefix for all the files you export. You can enter a project name, a date, or something else as a prefix.

Automatic (Short) With the Automatic (Short) option, you can choose to add a short system-defined prefix or a long user-defined prefix to the export file.

Manual (Specify Name) If you choose this option, you must name the exported file—the Name field will be empty upon selection of this option.

XREF Views on Sheets When you deselect this option, Revit combines each view on the sheet into a single file. This option is automatically deselected for DXF files; it isn't available for DGN or SAT files.

With this box checked, Revit exports each view on a sheet into a separate file and creates a cross-reference (XREF) to the files. If you're exporting a single view, using this feature won't make much difference, but if you're exporting a series of sheets with a number of views on each sheet, this feature will have a very different effect. In this case, with the box checked Revit exports each sheet as separate file as 2D vector-type views, and then those separate files are combined via XREF within a parent file. For example, if you start with a sheet with four views on it, five DWGs will be exported. With this option unchecked, the views and parent sheet will be a single file with all of the views in the drawing as blocks.

Range The Range box in the Export dialog box allows you to select either your current view or a range of selected views and sheets. If you chose the latter, Revit opens a dialog box showing all of the views and sheets currently in the model. After you select the views or sheets you want to export, you have the option to name and save that selection so you can quickly export those same sheets again later on in the design process.

Export Options

The Export Options dialog box, shown in Figure 7.4, gives you some advanced options for exporting to CAD formats:

Figure 7.4

**Export Options
dialog box**

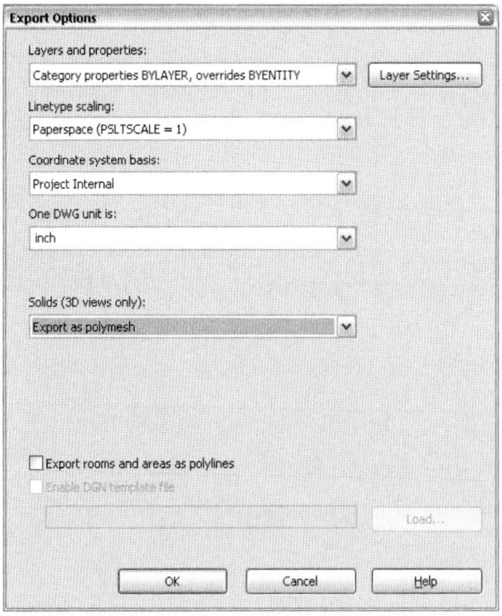

Layers and Properties The Layers and Properties setting determines what happens to a Revit element if it has attributes that differ from those defined for its object style category. In AutoCAD 2009 and in Revit Architecture 2009, view-specific element graphics are referred to as overrides. This option allows you to control how categories are exported and to specify their layer controls. The override options depend on the overrides you've set in the individual views you're exporting. If no view overrides are defined in your exported views, this menu won't change your export.

Layer Settings Revit automatically maps categories and subcategories to preconfigured layer names for export to DWG. Clicking Layer Settings ( ) lets you view or define the layers to which each object or component will be exported.

By default, the U.S. version of Revit shows an export list linked to the standard AIA layering schema. If you scroll down this list (see Figure 7.5), you'll notice that you can define the layer name and color for each of the categories and some subcategories of the elements in your model. It's important to point out that this list is dynamic. As you add elements and entities to the Revit model, this list will grow to include them as well as linked and imported CAD and Revit files. This list is also available directly from the File menu under Import/Export Settings.

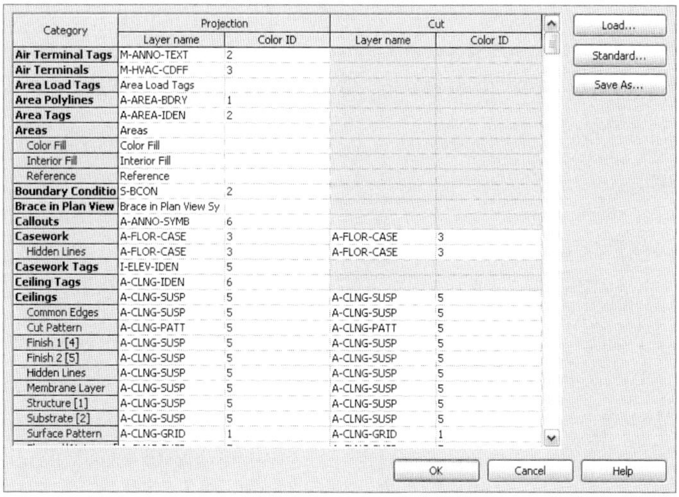

Category	Projection		Cut	
	Layer name	Color ID	Layer name	Color ID
Air Terminal Tags	M-ANNO-TEXT	2		
Air Terminals	M-HVAC-CDFF	3		
Area Load Tags	Area Load Tags			
Area Polylines	A-AREA-BDRY	1		
Area Tags	A-AREA-IDEN	2		
Areas	Areas			
Color Fill	Color Fill			
Interior Fill	Interior Fill			
Reference	Reference			
Boundary Conditio	S-BCON	2		
Brace in Plan View	Brace in Plan View Sy			
Callouts	A-ANNO-SYMB	6		
Casework	A-FLOR-CASE	3	A-FLOR-CASE	3
Hidden Lines	A-FLOR-CASE	3	A-FLOR-CASE	3
Casework Tags	I-ELEV-IDEN	5		
Ceiling Tags	A-CLNG-IDEN	6		
Ceilings	A-CLNG-SUSP	5	A-CLNG-SUSP	5
Common Edges	A-CLNG-SUSP	5	A-CLNG-SUSP	5
Cut Pattern	A-CLNG-PATT	5	A-CLNG-PATT	5
Finish 1 [4]	A-CLNG-SUSP	5	A-CLNG-SUSP	5
Finish 2 [5]	A-CLNG-SUSP	5	A-CLNG-SUSP	5
Hidden Lines	A-CLNG-SUSP	5	A-CLNG-SUSP	5
Membrane Layer	A-CLNG-SUSP	5	A-CLNG-SUSP	5
Structure [1]	A-CLNG-SUSP	5	A-CLNG-SUSP	5
Substrate [2]	A-CLNG-SUSP	5	A-CLNG-SUSP	5
Surface Pattern	A-CLNG-GRID	1	A-CLNG-GRID	1

Figure 7.5
Export Layers

You can access a few preset export layer standards by clicking the Standard button. The predefined standards options are shown in Figure 7.6. Once you've gone through this list and specified the layers to which you want your Revit file to export, you can save the list to a separate `.txt` file to be used in other projects. Alternatively, you can load other `.txt` files into your project that have been exported from other projects.

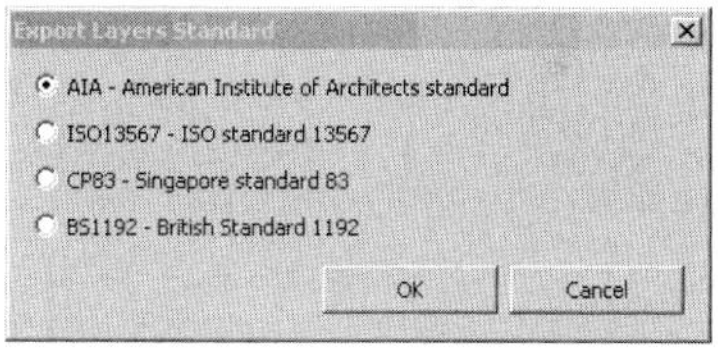

Figure 7.6
Export Layer Standards

In a default template file, go through the export list and modify it to suit your standard layer settings. Then, perform a Save As to a `.txt` file, and keep that as an export template for other projects.

Linetype Scaling This control sets your paper space line type setting in AutoCAD (psltscale) to either 1 or 0 or scales the line types by definition. This setting ensures visual fidelity between the line type scales used in Revit and those in the exported DWG file.

Coordinate System Basis This option lets you choose between a project-internal or shared coordinate system. It ultimately sets a 0,0,0 point for your CAD file based on the selected coordinate system (either by the internal project 0,0,0 point or by the shared coordinates between multiple project files).

The Shared option isn't available for MicroStation files; only the Project Internal option is available for SAT files.

One DWG Unit Is CAD packages typically deal with measurements in units, unlike Revit, which builds the model in real dimensions. This menu allows you to correlate export units with Revit data. You can specify the export units: inches, feet, millimeters, centimeters, or meters.

Solids (3D Views Only) To export 3D solids, you need to have a 3D view active. Revit provides two types of solid exports: as Polymesh or as ACIS solids.

Export Rooms and Areas as Polylines If you're exporting area or room plans, checking this option means that in AutoCAD, the room and area bounding lines will be polylines rather than normal lines (the default option).

Enable DGN Template File This option is available only when you're exporting to a .dgn format. This means you can include a .dgn template file in the exported .dgn. Thus you can export to a MicroStation template file to control the levels at which objects and components export.

Exporting Images

It's possible to export any of the views within Revit to an image file. To export a Revit view to an image file, open the desired view and choose File → Export → Image.

In the Export Image dialog box (Figure 7.7), many of the options are similar to the other export and printing functions. Export Range, for example, gives you the option to export either the current view or a series of views, similar to the Print dialog box.

Figure 7.7

Export Image dialog box

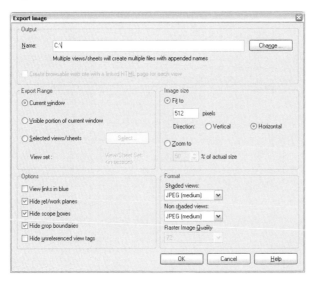

The Name group allows you to browse to a path in any of your folder directories to place the image. By default, the image name is the same as the view name. Similar to the options available when printing, you can choose to exclude elements such as crop boundaries, scope boxes, and work planes. This will give you nice results without having to worry about turning categories on and off every time you want to print or export an image.

Revit can export any view or sheet in several image file formats: `.bmp`, `.tif`, `.tga`, `.png`, or `.jpg`. However, you should keep in mind that while you can export to these image types, Revit can only import `.jpg`, `.bmp`, and `.png` files.

Creating a Browsable Website from the Revit Model

When more than one view is selected for export to image, pick Selected views/Sheets under the Export range, and an option becomes active in the Output section of the Export Image dialog box that lets you create a browsable website with a linked HTML page for each view, as shown in Figure 7.8.

Revit exports every view as an image and links to them with an HTML file, all packaged neatly into a folder. This allows you (or someone else) to scroll through the project views quickly and easily.

> This technique is practical when you create PowerPoint slides for a project presentation and need all views exported in image formats.

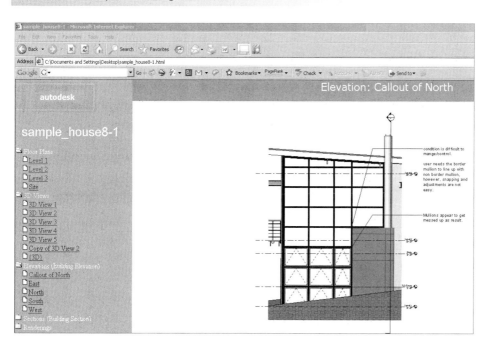

Figure 7.8

Browsable website page

Image Size

This section in the Export Image dialog box allows you to set the size of the exported image. You can either fit it to specific pixel dimensions or zoom the image to a proportion of its actual size. Keep in mind that this is a proportion of the view size, not the model. So, if your view dimensions are 10″ × 10″ (25 × 25cm), and you're zooming to 50 percent, your exported image will be at 72 pixels per inch (ppi) and 5″ × 5″ (10 × 10cm), not at 1:2 scale.

Format

This section in the Export Image dialog box allows you to choose your export file type from the list shown in Figure 7.7 earlier. It also gives you the option to raise the ppi exported from 72 ppi to a higher density. The more ppi, the longer the export time will be, and the larger the final image file. As a general rule of thumb, use 72 ppi for images that will only be viewed on a monitor or screen. Use 150 ppi for images that will be sent to a laser printer and 300 ppi for any image printed by an offset press or when there's a need for high-resolution imagery. Figure 7.9 shows an example of an exported image.

Figure 7.9

Exported Image

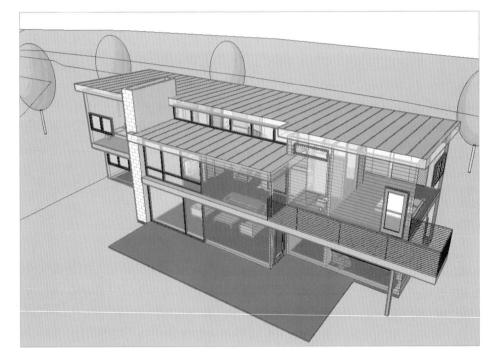

Importing and Linking

Now that you know what you can export from the Revit model, let's discuss the types of files you can import into Revit.

Choose File → Import/Link (Figure 7.10). The resulting submenu contains all the file types you can import into Revit, many of which we've already discussed in this chapter in the export context:

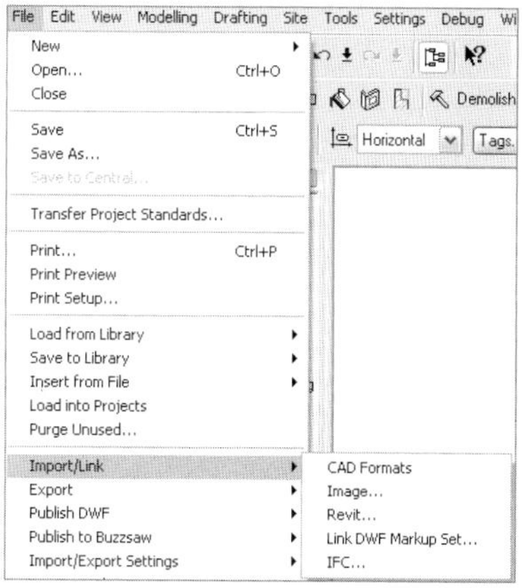

Figure 7.10

Import/Link

- CAD formats: .dwg, .dxf, .dgn, .sat, and .skp files

- Image: .jpg, .bmp, and .pgn files

- Revit: .rvt files

- Link DWF Markup Set: Single- or multipaged .dwf files

- IFC: .ifc files

We'll explore the uses of each of these options. Before drilling into details, we want to make clear the distinction between importing and linking.

Linking

Linking creates a live connection to another file. This allows you to work on the linked file, and then have the Revit model update to reflect the changes in the link. This behavior is similar to an XREF in AutoCAD.

Linking CAD Formats

The ability to link one file into another can be helpful in a collaborative environment. Perhaps someone on your team—a person working on details within your office or an external consultant—is working in an AutoCAD environment while you build up the project in Revit. Linking lets you have her latest work updated in your Revit model. If you import without linking, you get a static file that will not update. When you link, however, it's possible to always get the latest state of the DWG by updating the link within Revit.

From File → Manage Links (Figure 7.11), you can reload, unload, import, or remove a CAD link or see what is already loaded.

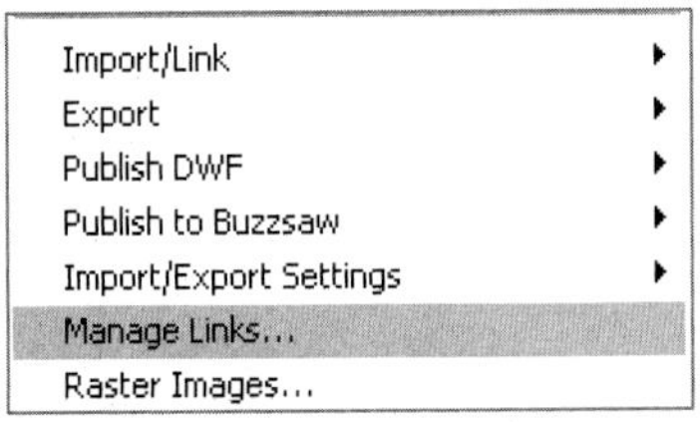

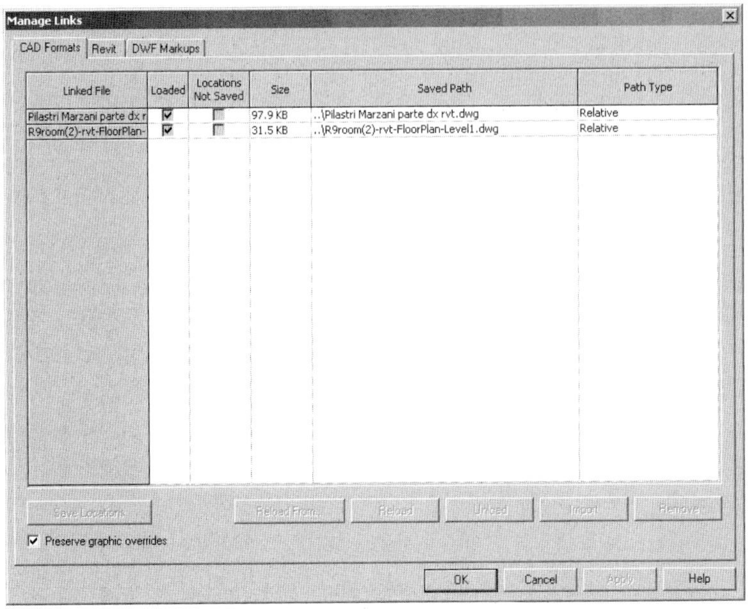

Figure 7.11

Managing links

Linking Other Revit Models

Linking other Revit files in your Revit project can be used either for a large campus project where buildings are distributed among separate project teams, or for one project that is being worked on by multiple teams in the same office.

When you're working on a campus-style project that contains more than one building, consider making separate models for each building and later connecting them in one file via the linking method. Doing so gives you some flexibility to model individual buildings in individual files and without the burden of the rest of the buildings, while still having the versatility to see the campus or building groupings in a file that combines all linked buildings. You can also cut sections or make elevations in which you can see all the buildings or schedule elements across all linked files.

> When you're doing campus-style projects, linking optimizes system performance. Working on several smaller files for individual buildings is less memory-intensive than working on one large file with many buildings.

Another use of linking is for collaboration in a full BIM project team where the structural engineer is using Revit Structure and the mechanical, engineering, and plumbing (MEP) engineer is using Revit MEP. Using the linking methodology, you can view their models within yours. You can even select and read the properties of the structural or MEP elements from your model, although you can't modify them.

Additionally, these three discipline specific BIM products—Revit Architecture, Revit Structure, and Revit MEP—incorporate tools that let you copy and monitor changes among linked models. This, however, is an advanced topic not covered in this book.

When you link two or more Revit models together, you're linking more than just the model geometry. Linking Revit models allows you to do the following:

- View the content of a Revit file that comes from another discipline (the structural engineer who made the structure with Revit Structure or a piping system made with Revit Systems).

- Combine scheduled elements of your building in a single schedule, regardless of whether they come from the parent file or from linked files.

- Control the visibility of what is displayed from the linked file or imported DWG files in the linked file.

- Schedule elements by link instance name so that if an element appears in multiple instances of identical buildings, Revit can identify which instance comes from which link.

- Dimension to or from elements and objects in the linked or parent file and establish user-defined relationships and constraints between the two (example: distance between a property line that is in the main file and the edge of the building that is linked).

- Copy and paste elements from the linked to the parent file.

- Control and change the visibility properties not only of the linked file but of the nested links as well, without modifying the primary file.

- Display nested links (a linked file in a Revit file that is linked into another Revit file) in the host file in two different states—attach or overlay.

- Bind a Revit link within the parent model (this is similar functionality to the Bind option in AutoCAD: when using the Bind option, the Revit link turns into a Group and becomes fully integrated in the host model).

- Copy Revit links across documents.

- Display areas and area boundaries in linked files and schedule them and apply color fill to rooms.

- See linked as well as nested links in the Project Browser from where you can unload, reload, open and unload, copy to another level by drag and drop, and access the linking manager.

EDITING A LINKED FILE

If you've linked a Revit file into your model, you cannot open that link file and start working on it in the same session of Revit. However, if you launch another session of Revit, you can open and edit the linked files. Each session of Revit will show up as a separate application running on your machine.

How to Link Files in Revit

To link an RVT file, choose File → Import/Link → Revit. The resulting dialog box looks like Figure 7.12. This dialog box is a standard file open format, with a few options specific to Revit: Open Worksets and Positioning. We'll look at each option and explain what it means.

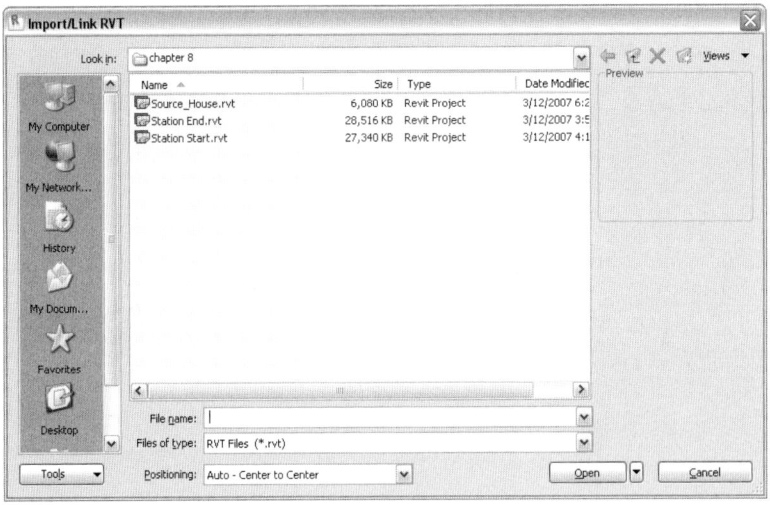

Figure 7.12

Import/Link Revit Files dialog box

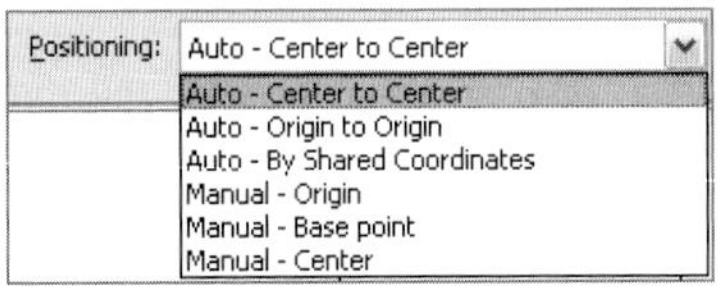

Figure 7.13

Positioning options

Positioning

The Positioning drop-down list provides options for linking the model. You can choose Auto or Manual placement methods, as shown in Figure 7.13.

The Auto placement options will do the following:

Center-to-Center Aligns the 3D center points of both models.

Origin-to-Origin Places the world origin of the linked file at the model's origin point. If the linked model was created far from the origin point, linking with this option may put the linked file far away from the main model.

By Shared Coordinates Places the linked file geometry according to the shared coordinate system created between the two files. If no shared coordinate file has been created, Revit will alert you.

WHAT ARE SHARED COORDINATES?

Every Revit project has an internal origin that can be related to other projects. When a project location is moved or rotated, this information is used to create relative positioning between files. Basically, a shared parameter is a user-defined origin.

Acquire Coordinates Allows you to take the coordinates of the linked file into the host model. There is no change to the host model's internal coordinates; however, the host model acquires the true north of the linked model and its origin point.

Publish Coordinates Allows you to publish the origin and true north settings to your linked model. Revit understands that there may be other things in your linked file and you may not want this to be a global change to the linked file. An additional dialog box appears that gives you the option to name separate locations for each set of coordinates.

Specify Coordinates at a Point Allows you to manually key in X, Y, and Z coordinates relative to the origin point or define where you want your 0,0,0 point to be.

Report Shared Coordinates Shows the E/W (east–west, or *X*), N/S (north–south, or Y), and Elevation (Z) coordinates of any point in the model (see Figure 7.14).

Figure 7.14

Reported coordinates

| E/W: | 34' 9 75/128" | N/S: | -16' 5 73/256" | Elevation: | 19' 0" |

The Manual placement options for links do the following:

Cursor at Origin Puts the origin point of the linked model at your cursor location.

Cursor at Base Point Puts the base point of the document at your cursor location. This is primarily used for files that have a base point, such as CAD files.

Cursor at Center Puts the 3D center of the building at your cursor location.

Open Worksets

Worksets are used to divide a model into user-defined groups so that a team of collaborators can simultaneously work on the same Revit project. Worksets can be used to cluster chunks of a building together, and the Open Worksets option lets you choose which worksets to link in. This technique is practical when you're working on big projects where performance may be an issue. By only linking in a subset of a linked file, you ensure that the graphical and memory resources are not taxed as much.

Importing or Linking CAD Formats

Site plans, consultant files, and details or drawings done with CAD technologies on prior projects all are examples of information you may want to link or import into Revit from a CAD format. This isn't limited to 2D data; you can link in 3D files and data as well.

The data you import or link into your model can be view specific (this means that it will be imported and visible in one view only, as opposed to all views), so start by opening the view into which you want to bring data. Choose File → Import/Link → CAD Formats. The CAD Formats dialog box includes additional options.

As discussed previously in this chapter, you can link or import five types of CAD files in 2D or 3D in Revit:

.dwg Files made from AutoCAD or other applications that can export to this standard format

.dxf Drawing Exchange Format files (most software packages write to a .dxf format)

.dgn MicroStation native files

.sat Standard ACIS text files (many modeling and fabrication applications can write to this file type)

.skp SketchUp native files

Here are the most common use cases for importing CAD files:

- To import a context of the surrounding with streets and buildings
- To import a civil engineering file with your topography
- To use CAD detail previously created for another project or directly dragged and dropped from the manufacturer's web catalog
- To use Revit to continue a previous stage of the project that you did in CAD, building a 3D model based on the 2D imported CAD file
- To work with colleagues who deal with certain aspects of the project in another environment (CAD drafters working on details, principals working on massing studies with SketchUp, Rhino, or some other modeling tool)

Import or Link

In Figure 7.14, the Import or Link section of the CAD Formats dialog box gives you the option to import your file or link it. As explained earlier, there are some pros and cons to each option:

Linking If you link a file, any changes made in that original file will be apparent in the Revit file in which it was linked. If your office or team workflow has personnel who are dedicated to working solely on details, they can continue creating and changing the details in AutoCAD, for example, and you can update the link to reflect the changes automatically. You can also manipulate the linked file through the Manage Links dialog box (choose File → Manage Links).

Importing An import is not tied to the imported external file, which will allow you to explode the file and modify the CAD drawing directly in Revit. You cannot explode or modify lines of a linked import. Once an import has been exploded, the import ceases to exist as a recognizable file but is reduced to lines and becomes a part of the main file. These lines are just that—lines, with no inherent intelligence. You can change their line type, thus changing their graphic appearance.

Regardless of whether you link or import a CAD file, you can always control the visibility of the lines in any view through the Visibility/Graphic Overrides dialog box. For linked files or CAD files that have been imported but not exploded, the lines appear in their own tab under Imported Categories. If the file has been exploded, the CAD lines are integrated into the model (in the case of files not linked with Current View Only) and appear on the Model Categories tab, under the Lines subcategory. If the CAD file was linked Current View Only, the linework will become detail lines.

> One of the primary uses for importing CAD files is to use them as details in the Revit model. If possible, eliminate all the unneeded linework from your CAD file before you import it into Revit. We suggest cleaning up your CAD details in the native format first, then importing— rather than exploding your details in Revit and then cleaning up lines.

In Figure 7.15, the Link check box gives you the option to import your file or link it. Again, there are some pros and cons to each option.

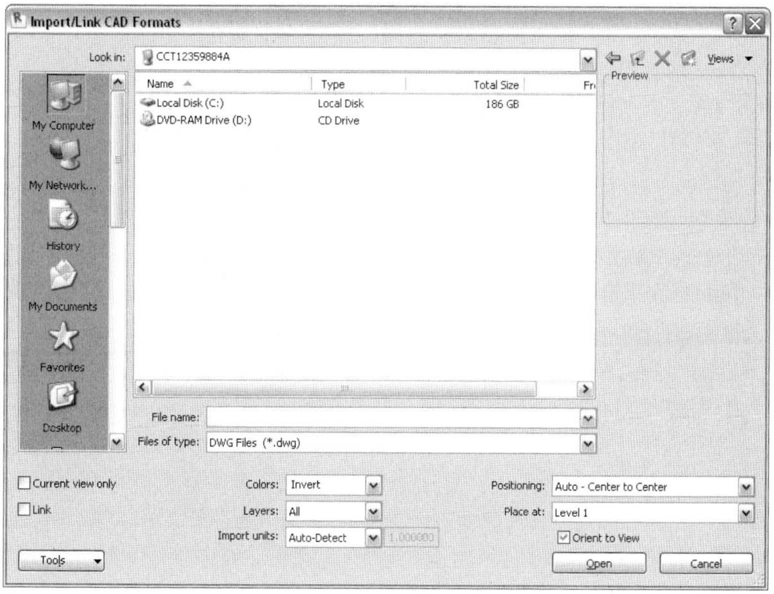

Figure 7.15

Import/Link dialog box

CURRENT VIEW ONLY

Selecting the Current View Only check box brings the linked or imported file *only* into the view that is currently active. It's not always desirable to see your CAD files in all the views in your model. More often than not, you'll want to select this check box. Remember, if you import with this unchecked, the file will be visible in all of your views, and you'll need to manage its visibility via the Visibility/Graphic Overrides dialog box, or with view templates.

> If you're importing a CAD file you want to use as a site, make sure you're importing it into all views; otherwise, you won't be able to convert it into a toposurface. It's now possible to convert any solid geometry created in other software packages into a toposurface.

LAYERS

The Layers drop-down menu gives you the option to import or link in all the layers, only the layers that were visible at the time the CAD file was last saved, or a selected group of layers. (Layers are a DWG-based naming convention. Revit allows the same functionality with layers from DGN drawings.)

LAYER/LEVEL COLORS

The default view background in AutoCAD is usually black. So, the colors used in Auto-CAD are easily visible on a black background. When you import a DWG file in Revit, which has a white background, many of the colors usually used in AutoCAD (yellow, light green, magenta, cyan) are difficult to read. Revit recognizes this issue, and in the Layer/Level Colors section of the Import/Link dialog box, it gives you the option to invert these colors into colors that are easier to read on a white background. It also gives you the option not to change the colors, if you prefer, or to convert them to black and white, which is Revit's default approach.

IMPORT UNITS

The Import units drop-down menu will let Revit autodetect the scale at which the imported or linked drawing was created and convert accordingly. Or, you can apply your own custom scale factor and type it in manually.

POSITIONING

This drop-down list is the same as the Revit Link dialog box, but with the option to choose what level to place the link at in the Revit model and the option to orient the link relative to the view.

Importing Images

In every project, you'll need to import an image—be it a photograph of the site and its surroundings; background information, such as scanned hand drawings of a historic building; or images that can represent advertising or marketing material (see Figure 7.16).

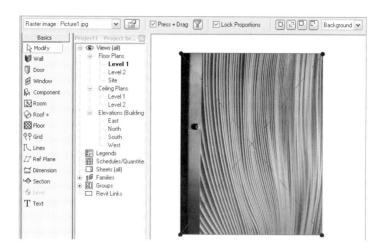

Figure 7.16

Inserted image

To import an image into Revit, use File → Import → Image. Navigate to the appropriate folder, and choose your image file. You can also drag and drop an image file directly from Windows Explorer into a Revit view. Imported images are specific to the particular view you've imported them into.

Once you've inserted the image, you have a few options to edit its size and proportion. Selecting the image highlights the corner grips and lets you resize the image dynamically. Doing so also highlights the Options bar and the Type Selector. The Options bar allows you to push the image forward or backward, or bring it all the way to the front or back. The Background/Foreground selection tells the image that you want it above or below the model geometry. You can also change the shape of the image by deselecting the Lock Proportions check box.

The Type Selector allows you to toggle between different imported images just as you would any component family.

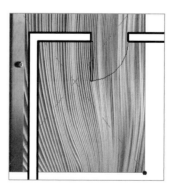

Figure 7.17

Image properties, and the image placed in the background

The Element Properties dialog box shown in Figure 7.17 controls the same element parameters that appear in the Options bar (in Figure 7.16) when an image is selected, but provides a bit more precision. From here you can set the exact size of the image in project units. Figure 7.16 shows how the image looks when the Draw Order property is set to Background.

Working with Imported Files

Now that you've learned how to import and export drawings with Revit, what do you do with them? In this section, we'll explore the use of the various tools used to manage CAD files when they're in Revit.

As we've discussed a number of times, Revit doesn't build the model based on layers like other CAD packages do. Although layers offer an easy way to control the visibility of objects, they're also the reason other software packages can't guarantee quantities. Layers make it possible for an object to be duplicated on many layers and therefore appear more than once in the database. In Revit, every object can exist once and only once. As mentioned previously, Revit uses categories and subcategories for objects that exist in real life and uses annotation elements that describe them to control the visibility of what is presented where.

That may be good, but you work with—and need to exchange digital files with—people who give you information in a DWG layers structure. Therefore, you need to give them layer-structured drawings. Revit can understand imported drawings with layer structures and can also export drawings with a customized layer structure. When you import a file in DWG or other CAD formats in Revit, you can do the following:

- Turn layers on or off in imported CAD files
- Change the default color of a layer
- Delete a layer
- Explode a DWG file so you can modify or delete elements from the imported file

Managing Layers

Once your CAD file is imported into Revit, either as a link or as an insertion, you can begin to manage the layers and colors of the CAD objects as they appear in Revit. To do this, you need to use the Visibility/Graphic Overrides dialog box. You can access this dialog box in three ways: by pressing VG on the keyboard, by selecting The View menu: View → Visibility/Graphics Overrides, or by using the context menu when right-clicking in a View Properties → Visibility/Graphics Overrides → Edit. If you import a CAD file into your view, Revit adds an Imported Categories tab. Selecting that tab, shown in Figure 7.18, gives you a list of all the CAD files imported into this particular view. Remember, this list is view specific; Revit changes the list as you add or remove CAD files from the model and from this view.

Selecting the check box next to the name of your CAD file displays a list of every layer present in the file. Use the check box in front of the layer name to control its visibility. Here you can also override the line color and pattern of the layer or turn it to halftone.

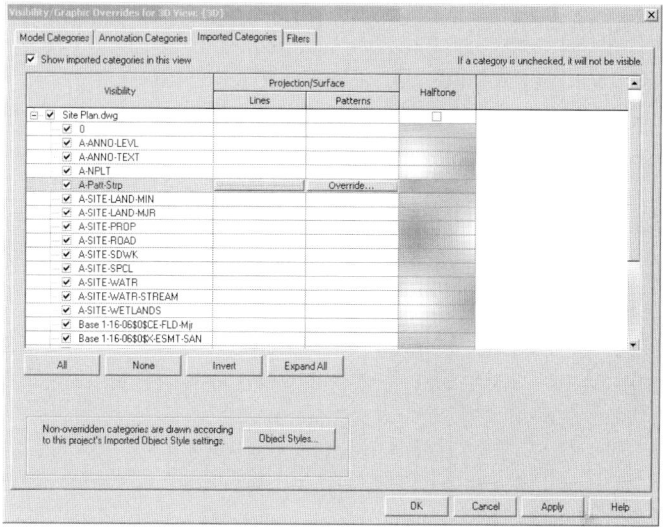

Figure 7.18

Visibility/Graphic Overrides dialog box

Modifying a CAD File

Often, you'll need to modify or delete some of the geometry in a CAD file that has been imported into Revit. Let's review how this works and all the options available.

Open the view your DWG is imported into, and click the DWG to select it. Let's take a look at the tools offered on the Options bar (shown in Figure 7.19).

Figure 7.19

DWG Options bar

Delete Layers

This tool lets you delete an entire layer from the imported file. With the DWG selected, click Delete Layer, and select from the list of displayed layers those you wish to delete. A sample dialog box with its associated layers is shown in Figure 7.20. As with most Revit dialog box lists, you have the option to select all or to select none as well as to invert the order of choices.

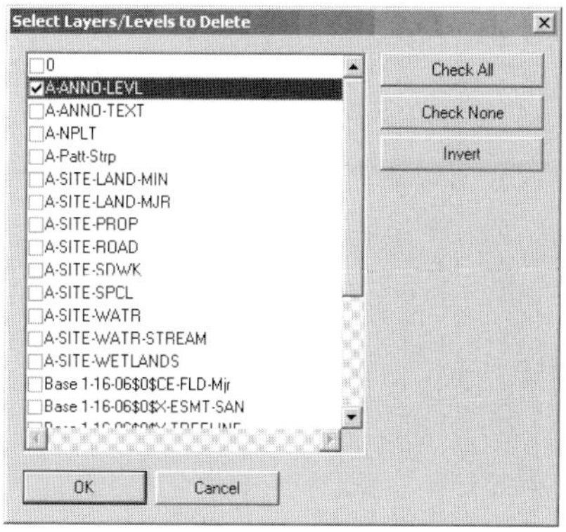

Figure 7.20

Select layers/levels to delete.

Full Explode

An imported DWG behaves as one entity when brought into Revit. If you want to modify any of the imported geometry in Revit, you need to perform an *explode*. Depending on what you wish to modify, you might choose to do a partial or full explode. The Full Explode option disassembles the entity as well as any blocks or attributes and simplifies it down to the lowest level of lines, arcs, texts, and hatch (filled regions). Also note that Revit doesn't allow linework or other elements smaller than 1/32″ in length (0.8mm). If you explode a CAD file with line elements shorter than these lengths, they will be deleted.

Partial Explode

The Partial Explode option disassembles the imported file to the first and highest level of entities: blocks, attributes, unassociated lines, arcs, and circles. Blocks remain as blocks and aren't converted to individual lines. In cases where you have blocks within blocks in your inserted CAD file, a first partial explode explodes the drawing, leaving the nested blocks combined. A second partial explode explodes the nested block, leaving the block within that block intact. A third partial explode turns everything into lines.

> Given the fact that exploding DWGs can produce a multitude of elements that pollute the database and may affect the performance of the overall application, it's strongly recommended that you consider exploding only when you need to modify the imported DWG. As an alternative, consider using Partial Explode, which may be sufficient to achieve the desired modifications.

Query

The purpose of the Query tool (Query...) is to find the attributes of individual blocks and layers without having to explode the DWG. After you import a drawing into a project, you can query the inserted object for information about entities contained in the drawing. After you click Query and click an entity, Revit first highlights the lowest-level entities.

To select a block within the CAD file, use the Tab key to cycle through your selection options (see Figure 7.21).

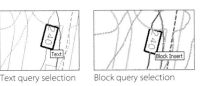

Figure 7.21

Query selection

Text query selection   Block query selection

Selecting an entity causes the following information about that block or line to be displayed:

Type Information about the type of the entity selected (line, text)

Block Name The name of the block that contains the entity, if applicable (N/A means "isn't available"; the entity doesn't belong to any block)

Layer The name of the layer containing the entity

Style By Indicates whether the entity style comes from the layer or is defined by color

These results are reflected in an Import Instance Query dialog box (Figure 7.22).

To find out the property information of the layer or instance, select the DWG, click the Query tool, and click the object or geometry that you want additional information about.

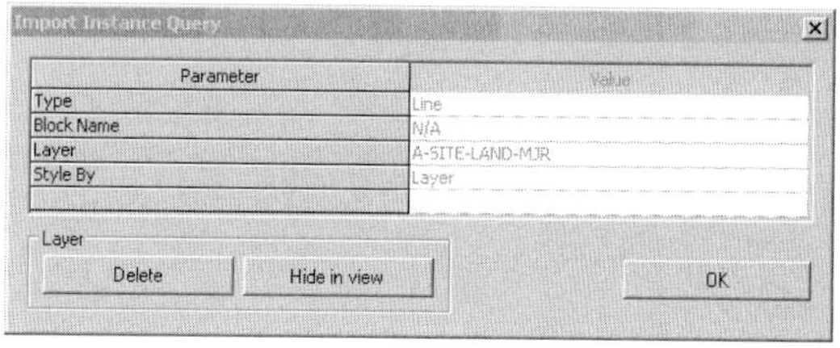

Figure 7.22

Import Instance Query dialog box

Once you have this information, you can do two things:

- Delete the layer on which that instance belongs

> Once you delete a layer, you can't recover it from anywhere unless you use the Undo function or reimport the DWG.

- Hide the layer in that particular view

> To turn the visibility of a layer back on after using the Hide in View command, choose Visibility/Graphics → DWG/DXF/DGN Categories.

Working with Civil Engineering DWG Files

Civil engineering plans are usually rich in data and information, not all of which is needed by architects. Architects constantly need to clean up civil engineering drawings, retaining only the data that is of importance to the architect for display in their drawings. Revit has a great way to import site information created by civil engineers in DWG file format and turning it smoothly into Revit topography.

Cleanup is one of the challenges when you import civil engineering data. DWGs have numerous layers on which different data is placed (roads, utilities, vegetation, and topographic information). You need to know which layers contain the topographic information and select only those when creating the topography.

Another challenge is that the coordinate worlds of civil engineers and architects often differ. Creating a link between the two coordinate systems is important for a seamless workflow. Engineers typically have their maps facing north, whereas architects either orient them in whatever way is the most practical to work with or lay them out horizontally.

Transforming DWG Site Info into Topography

In this exercise, you'll transfer an imported DWG data into Revit and make it into a Revit toposurface:

1. Start a new drawing (File → New).

2. Activate the site view by selecting Site in the Project Browser.

Figure 7.23

Importing the site DWG

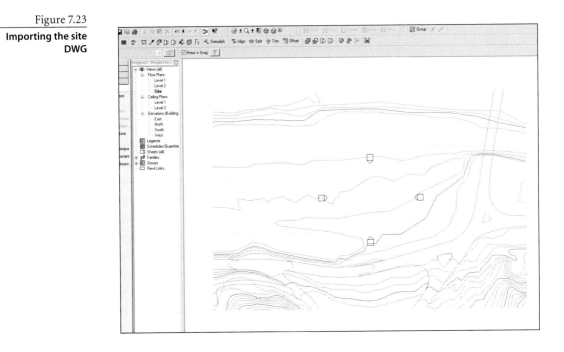

3. To import the DWG, begin by choosing File → Import → CAD Formats. Select the file provided on the book's companion web page named Site.dwg. Make sure you *do not* select Current View Only, and click OK (see Figure 7.23).

4. From the Site tab in the Design bar, select Toposurface (Toposurface).

5. Select Use Imported → Import Instance (Import Instance Points File).

6. Remember that you need to import topography information into the site view. If you forget to switch to site view and are still in a floor plan when you import the site DWG, you may get the message displayed in Figure 7.24. To correct this, do what

Figure 7.24

Error message: file imported into the wrong view

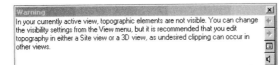

the message says: interrupt the import by pressing the Esc key, and then switch to site view to repeat the import.

In Revit versions 9.1 and later versions of Revit (2008, 2009), you have to import the site in all views. If you select the option Current View Only, you won't be able to convert the DWG into a site plan.

7. Open the Site design tab, and select the Toposurface tool. Click somewhere over the DWG in your drawing area to highlight the site DWG (it will become red). A dialog

box (Figure 7.25) will open, and you'll see a list of all the layers included in the DWG. You need to know the layers on which the topography information is stored and select only those layers. In this case, click Check None (Check None), and select the layers called 3D contours. Click OK. A toposurface will be generated from the imported geometry. Click Finish Surface to complete the task.

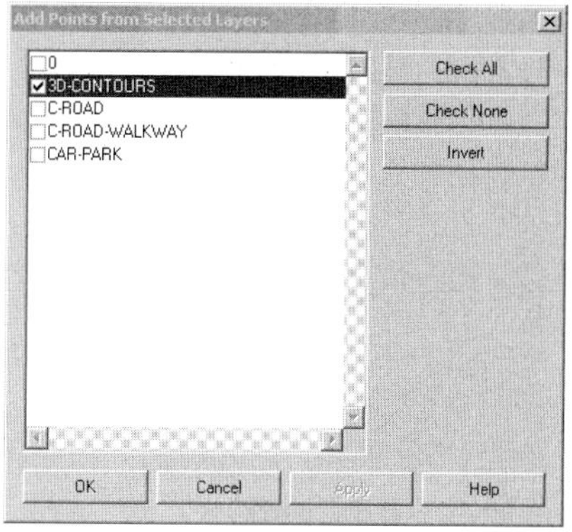

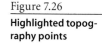

Figure 7.25

Select only the layers with contours when converting DWG to toposurface.

Should you fail to do this and select all layers, Revit will probably fail to create a toposurface.

If you don't have a convention of layer naming with your civil engineer, and you're unsure which layer your contour lines lie on, you can find out by toggling various layers on and off using the Visibility/Graphics dialog box.

After you select the correct layers, Revit will highlight the points on the contours, and your drawing will appear as shown in Figure 7.26.

8. Select Finish Surface (Finish Surface) from the Design bar. You'll see the image shown in Figure 7.27.

Figure 7.26

Highlighted topography points

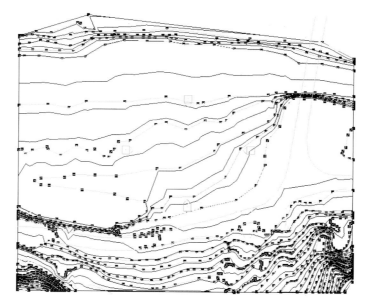

Figure 7.27

**Finished
toposurface**

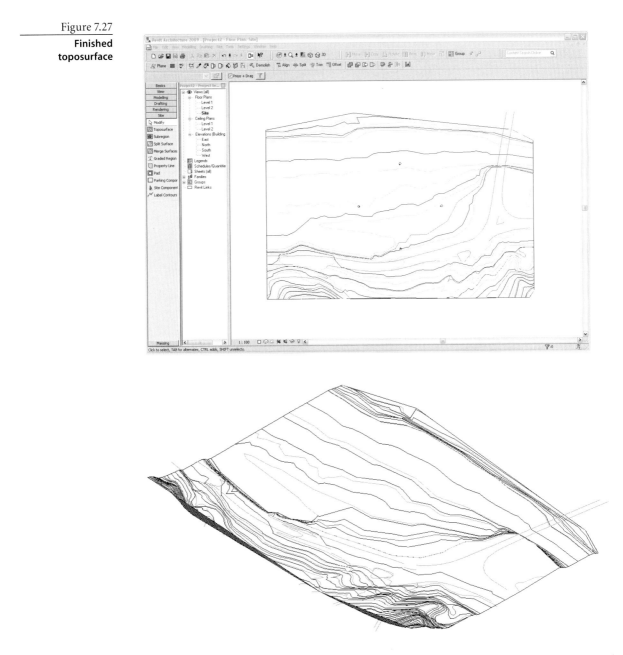

How anticlimactic: Figure 7.27 doesn't look much different from the DWG you started with. Now, switch to a 3D view, and activate the shaded view. Here you can see the topography you've created (see Figure 7.28).

The default material for the topography is Earth, as defined in the Object Styles dialog box shown in Figure 7.29.

Figure 7.28

Shaded toposurface

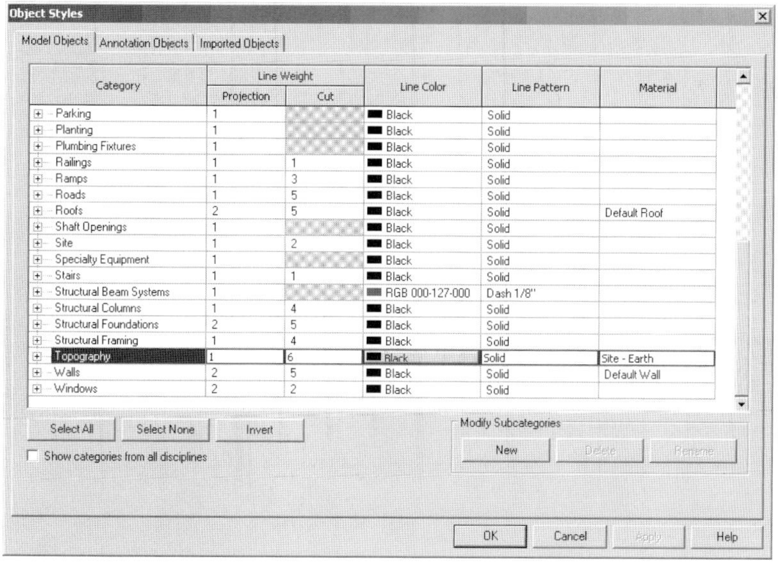

Figure 7.29

Object styles for topography

If you want to change the material of the topography, select the toposurface in the Settings → Object Styles dialog box and open its properties. Here you can choose another material (try Site – Grass). The topography will turn green.

All the site-related materials are listed under Site in the materials table found at Settings → Materials. In that list, Earth is labeled as Site – Earth, grass as Site – Grass, and so on.

You'll notice that there are many 2D lines you don't need. Those come either from the contour lines from the imported DWG or from the Revit toposurface primary and secondary contours. Revit allows you to control the visibility of those separately using the Visibility/Graphics Overrides dialog box.

Open the dialog box, scroll to the Topography Model category node, and uncheck all subcategories of topography, as shown in Figure 7.30.

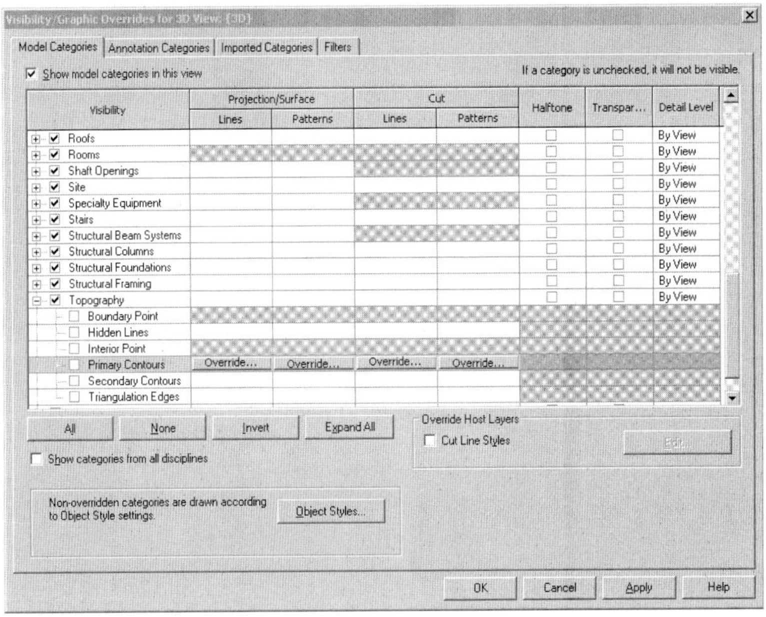

Figure 7.30

Visibility/Graphic Overrides for topography

Now, switch to the Imported Categories tab, and uncheck the entire imported site. To uncheck all the subcategories at once, you can deselect the parent heading, as shown in Figure 7.31. Click OK. This should look much better: You can see a nice, smooth topography covered with grass.

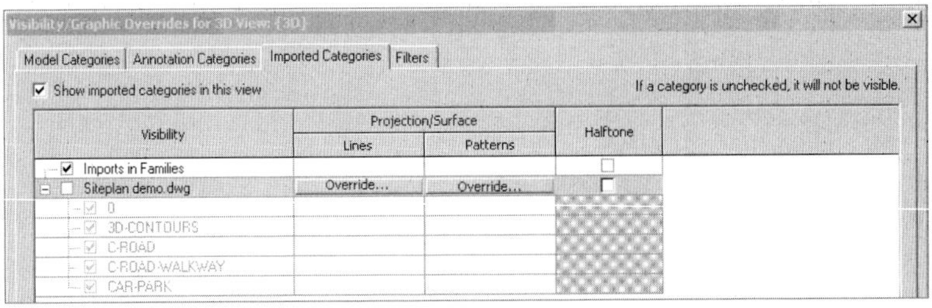

Figure 7.31

Visibility/Graphic Overrides for imported files

Other Ways to Create Topography

There are two other ways to create topography in Revit besides using an imported DWG:

- You can create a toposurface using an imported points file.
- You can create a toposurface from scratch.

Importing a Points File

You can automatically generate a toposurface based on a points file. A *points file* is a list of points described with their X, Y, and Z coordinates. It must contain X, Y, and Z coordinate numbers and be in a comma-delimited file format (.csv or .txt). If you receive a points file from a civil engineer, you can view it in Notepad or Microsoft Excel. Here is a sample of a points file:

T-1	0	0	0.055
T-2	0	59.916	5.179
T-3	45.181	64.991	1.974
T-4	45.181	59.916	5.599
T-5	22.539	62.454	4.522
T-6	50.061	29.857	1.738
T-7	40.106	10.142	0.221
T-8	24.881	-0.008	0.06
T-9	44.986	42.739	2.917
T-10	24.296	45.862	2.665
T-11	8.875	62.844	4.462
T-12	1.848	26.538	1.815
T-13	24.686	16.974	0.459
T-14	32.494	12.289	0.962
T-15	8.095	15.607	0.686
T-16	33.274	29.661	1.146
T-17	51.037	28.1	0.981
T-18	46.743	56.598	5.875

To create a toposurface from a point file, follow these steps:

1. Click the Site tab in the Design bar.
2. Select the Toposurface tool.
3. Using the Use Imported/Points File drop-down, select the file Points.csv from the book's companion web page under Chapter 7.

4. Open the points file in your Windows browser. (Note that only .csv or .txt file formats are recognized.)

5. On the Format tab, set the units in which the points file needs to be imported (see Figure 7.32).

6. Click the Finish Toposurface button. Figure 7.33 represents an editable toposurface in Revit and the completed toposurface.

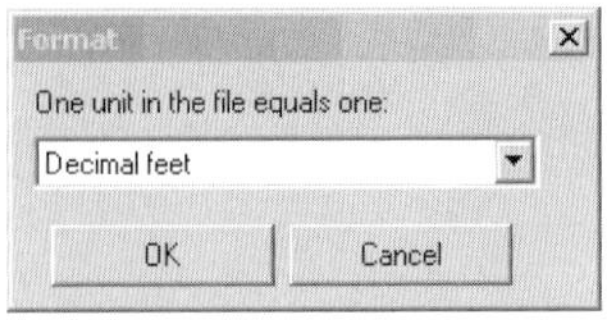

Figure 7.32

Setting the unit format

Figure 7.33

Left, an editable toposurface; right, the finished toposurface

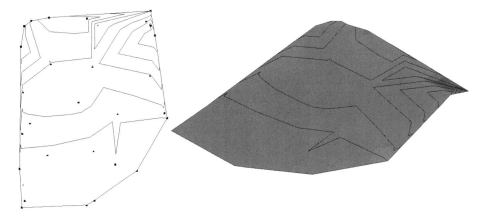

Depending on the file you import, after the import you may not see anything on the screen. This means your site is outside of the crop region predefined for the site. To find your site, deactivate the crop region and choose Zoom to Fit All to find the site.

Creating Topography from Scratch: Drawing Points

When you don't have any civil engineering data to import and convert to topography but you do have a paper drawing with points information, you can create your toposurface by drawing points and defining their heights. Revit will create a smooth toposurface out of them.

1. On the Site tab in the Design bar, click the Topo-surface button.

2. Select the option Point.

3. Start drawing points that define your site contour. (Try it with four points to start with, as shown in Figure 7.34.)

4. Revit closes the points into a loop.

Figure 7.34

Creating your own toposurface from points

Figure 7.35

Adding contours to a toposurface

If you don't change anything and just draw four points, all points have the same elevation of zero (Z coordinate = 0). You can give them a height coordinate during the drawing by typing elevations in the Options bar (Elevation: 0' 0").

Alternatively, after you've defined the shape in plan view, you can start reselecting and defining elevation coordinates. For the moment, leave the four initial points at 0.

5. Without finishing the toposurface, draw an additional four points, select them all, and change their elevation to 20″ in the Options bar (see Figure 7.35).

Figure 7.36

The graded toposurface

6. In the Design bar, select Finish Toposurface. Revit will grade the distance between the elevations with contour lines, as shown in Figure 7.36. You'll notice that some lines are stronger and some are lighter. Those that appear stronger are the primary contours. The lighter ones are the secondary contours.

7. Switch to 3D view, and activate the shaded view (Figure 7.37).

Figure 7.37

Completed toposurface

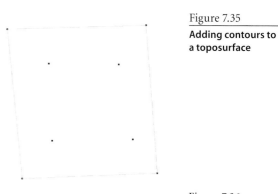

As with any other preset, you define the distance at which the secondary contours are placed under Settings → Site Settings, shown in Figure 7.38. In this dialog box, you can define or change the material that appears in section when the toposurface is cut. It's also where you can control the height in elevation where the base of the toposurface begins to show in section view (see Figure 7.39).

The default settings place the primary contour lines at 10′ (3m) intervals. If you change that to 5′ (1.5m), you'll see a site similar to that shown in Figure 7.40.

Figure 7.38

Site settings

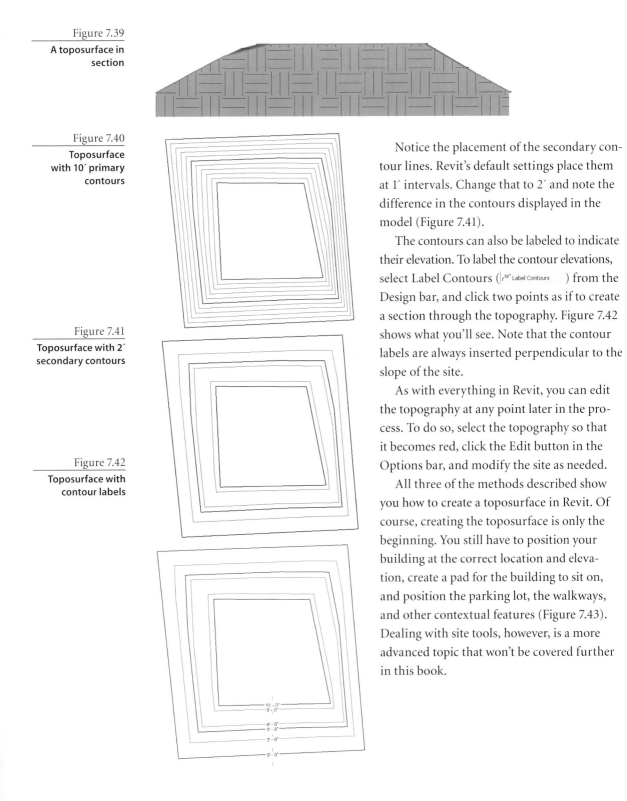

Figure 7.39

A toposurface in section

Figure 7.40

Toposurface with 10′ primary contours

Figure 7.41

Toposurface with 2′ secondary contours

Figure 7.42

Toposurface with contour labels

Notice the placement of the secondary contour lines. Revit's default settings place them at 1′ intervals. Change that to 2′ and note the difference in the contours displayed in the model (Figure 7.41).

The contours can also be labeled to indicate their elevation. To label the contour elevations, select Label Contours ( ) from the Design bar, and click two points as if to create a section through the topography. Figure 7.42 shows what you'll see. Note that the contour labels are always inserted perpendicular to the slope of the site.

As with everything in Revit, you can edit the topography at any point later in the process. To do so, select the topography so that it becomes red, click the Edit button in the Options bar, and modify the site as needed.

All three of the methods described show you how to create a toposurface in Revit. Of course, creating the toposurface is only the beginning. You still have to position your building at the correct location and elevation, create a pad for the building to sit on, and position the parking lot, the walkways, and other contextual features (Figure 7.43). Dealing with site tools, however, is a more advanced topic that won't be covered further in this book.

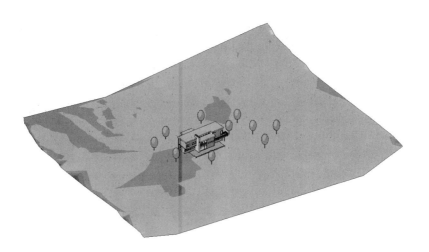

Figure 7.43

There's a long way
to go from topo-
surface creation to
finished site.

Converting 2D Drawings into a 3D Model

Here's a common situation: you have 2D plans, sections, and elevations, and you wish to
transform them into a 3D building information model. When you first start to work on a
project, you may have previously created DWGs. Maybe your firm has just started using
Revit, so the project was begun in AutoCAD; or maybe you're working with an existing
building created by another architect. Revit offers you the flexibility to incorporate legacy
material in your model.

The development and adoption of intelligent software means that someday redrawing
will no longer be a necessary option. Revit offers ways to maximize the reuse and referencing of existing data. Converting existing DWGs so they can be used in a Revit model
isn't terribly complicated and avoids the need to retrace entire drawings.

You can create Revit objects three ways:

- Drawing (   )
- Picking references out of which the object can be created (   )
- Picking a face (this is an advanced topic not covered in this book) (   )

These buttons appear in the Options bar when you select any of the host element tools,
such as the Wall tool. Let's analyze the first two approaches.

The pencil tool (   ), activated, indicates that you're in Draw mode. You can draw
the shape of the object that will be created using standard drawing options. This is the
default mode for all Revit tools that require you to draw something.

The second option, denoted with the arrow symbol, is Pick Lines (   ). Instead of
manually drawing, this option gives you the ability to create elements by picking references. This means you can pick (and thus convert) any line of an imported drawing
into an object. Note that the original line remains available.

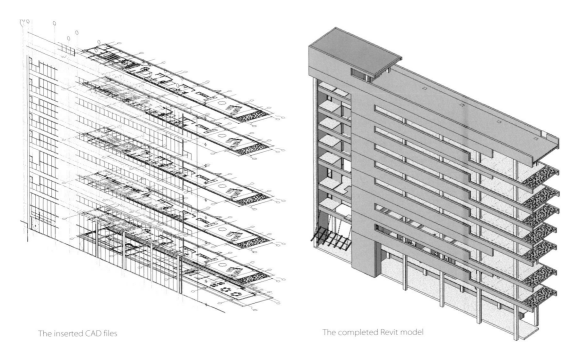

The inserted CAD files · The completed Revit model

Figure 7.44

Converting 2D CAD files to a Revit model

Using a 2D DWG floor plan as starting point for generating a 3D BIM model is best explained using a concrete example, so let's do an exercise. Figure 7.44 shows a series of 2D AutoCAD files set on their corresponding levels in a Revit model and the 3D BIM model created from those plans and elevations.

Here's our strategy for this approach. Import the DWG of each floor into the corresponding level in Revit. In the Import/Link CAD Formats dialog box, select the Current View Only option (see Figure 7.45). Note that if you forget to select this option, your ground floor DWG will appear in every level. This will be confusing, to say the least.

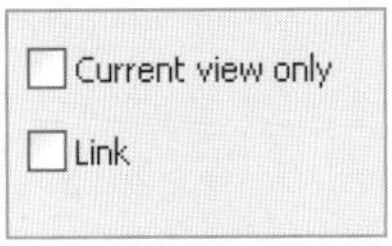

Figure 7.45

Using Current View Only

☐ Current view only

☐ Link

A tip before you start: AutoCAD drawings can be busy, containing information that isn't relevant or creates visual clutter. When you want to quickly convert them to a 3D model, it helps to turn off the visibility of some of the DWG layers using Visibility Graphics/Imported Categories. Uncheck the layers you don't need, such as dimensions, text, hatches, and so on. Doing so will speed up object selection and facilitate the conversion process.

Starting a New Project

Start by defining the number of stories (levels) that your building will have and giving the levels floor-to-floor heights. To do this, open a new project, go to any elevation view (let's say south), and modify the project so it has three levels (if you're opening the default Revit template, you'll need to add one level). As we previously discussed, you do that by selecting the Level tool, drawing three levels, and placing them 10′ (3m) apart.

You are now ready to import some DWGs into the corresponding levels. Follow these steps:

1. Activate Level 1, and import the DWG Level 1.dwg file found at the book's companion web page in the Imports folder.

2. On Level 2, import the DWG Level 2 file.

3. Open a south elevation, and import the DWG Elevation South file.

4. After the import, you may get a notification that none of the imported elements is visible in this view. As previously mentioned, this means the import is somewhere outside the boundaries of the crop region. To remedy this situation, turn off the crop region. Zoom all, and you'll find your DWG.

5. Reposition the DWG as needed using the Move command.

6. In the south elevation view, you will need to reposition the levels so that they match the level lines in the DWG import. (Level 1 matches with Level 1-A from the DWG, etc. If needed, rename the levels to match the naming of the levels in the DWG drawing).

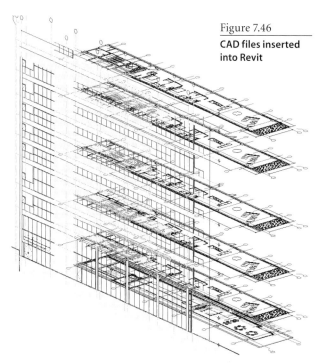

Figure 7.46
CAD files inserted into Revit

Figure 7.46 shows approximately what the resulting drawing should look like.

Converting DWG Gridlines into Smart Revit Gridlines

Most of the floor plan that you have imported as a reference drawing will have gridlines in it. Generating Revit gridlines from imported lines is simple: select the Grid tool and set the creation method to Pick in the Options bar. Next, pick any gridline in the import. Revit will create a gridline on top of the DWG gridline and number it. Revit usually starts with the number 1, but if the DWG grid uses lettered coordinates, you can change the Revit gridline on the first one you create. The remainder will number (or letter) in sequence, so they should append correctly. Otherwise, you can renumber them later.

Figure 7.47 shows an imported DWG image. In the second image, the gridlines have been converted to Revit grids using the pick method. Note that the grid bubbles in Revit change dynamically with the view scale. If the bubble sizes don't match, don't panic—just check your scale factor.

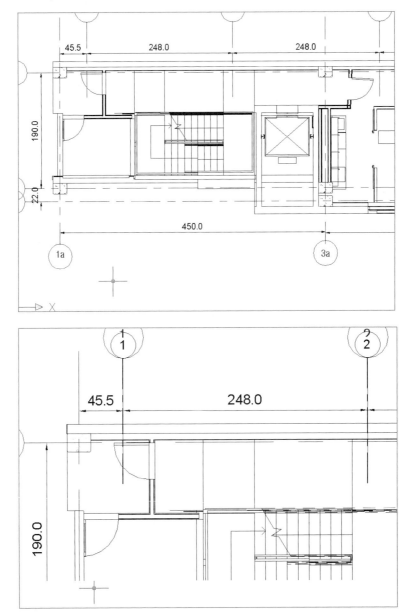

You need to convert CAD gridlines to Revit gridlines in one level only. Gridlines in Revit span the entire building because they're datums that show up in every level. This is practical when the grid system is the same for each level.

Working with Scope Boxes

If you have multiple floor plans where the gridlines aren't the same for all levels, you need to use the Scope Box tool (⬚). This tool limits the range in which datums (grids, levels, and reference lines) appear. Imagine that you have a building with a shopping center on the first three floors and a hotel tower above. Obviously, the grid systems for the lower and upper parts of the building will be different. You need to create two scope boxes, assign the grids from the first three levels to one scope box and the rest to the other, and control the area covered by each scope box so they show up correctly. Figure 7.48 shows how scope boxes work in a 3D view.

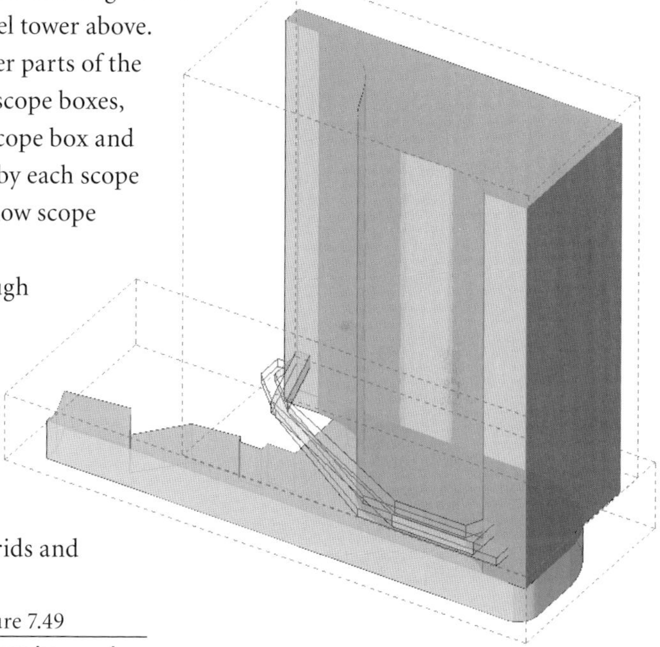

Scope boxes are also visible in 3D views (although not in perspective views), and you can easily manipulate their extent directly using the grips. Assigning grids or other datums to a scope box is easy: select the grids, choose Element Properties → Scope Box, and then select the scope box where the datums should belong. Figure 7.49 shows the Element Properties dialog box for the grids and the associated scope box.

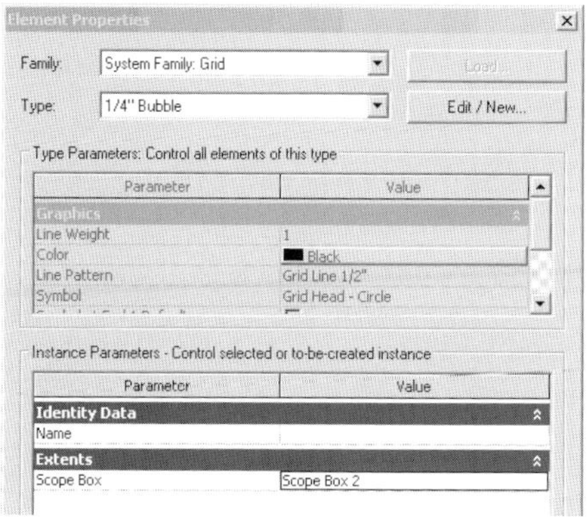

Figure 7.48

Scope box can be seen in 3D.

Figure 7.49

A scope box can be assigned to grids using Element Properties.

Using DWG Lines to Create Revit Walls

In a 2D CAD application, walls are represented with two parallel lines. You can use one of these two lines as your reference line for creating Revit walls. Create a wall type that is the same thickness as the one used in the DWG. Then use the Pick option when placing new walls, and pick on lines in the import. Be sure to set the Wall Location line to a meaningful value (Exterior Core or Center Line, for example) to get correct alignment.

A rule of thumb when following this creation approach is to set your exterior and shaft walls' top constraint to the top of the building, and set your interior partitions to only go up to the next level. If you have repetitive floors with identical or similar floor plans, create the walls once, then leverage the copy and paste functionality to repeat the walls.

Figure 7.50 shows the beginning of a Revit model created using DWG floor plans as a base. DWG wall lines were used as a reference to create the walls with the pick method, and the wall location line was set to the exterior face.

Figure 7.50

Beginning the conversion process

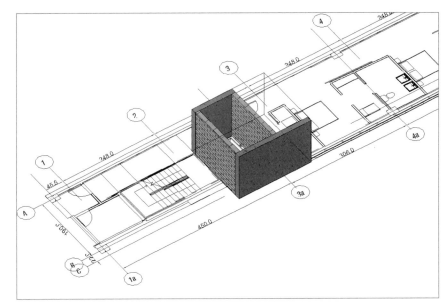

Using DWG Lines as a Reference to Create Revit Floors

After you create the walls, the next step is to create floors. To create floors, select Floor from the Basic or Modeling tab in the Design bar, and again, select the Pick option in the Options bar. Hover your cursor over the outer edge of the floor or walls and press the Tab key until the DWG floor lines are highlighted. Click to generate sketch lines. If the shape of the floor isn't the shape you want, make corrections using edit tools. Remember, a sketch is a line drawing that has to form a closed loop so Revit can create an object out of it.

In Figure 7.51, the lines in the DWG that represented the outer wall faces have been selected, the magenta lines have been adjusted to a rectangular shape (using trim lines), and the floor has been created.

Figure 7.51

Adding floors

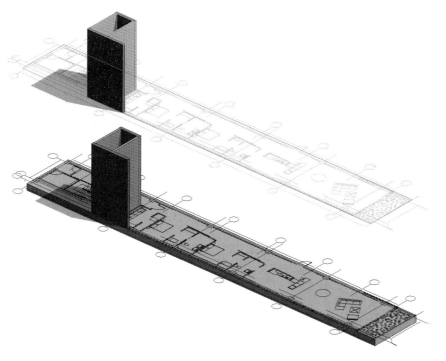

If your workflow permits, draw interior walls before you create the floors so that when you create a floor, it will be attached to the walls and have a relationship with them.

Once you have your wall and floor structure, it's easy to starting adding windows, doors, and other elements.

Working with Imported Library Components in DWG Format

Autodesk's i-drop technology allows you to drag and drop content (drawings) from the Web directly into a Revit drawing. This corresponds to the DWG import process and utilizes Revit's default import settings. From a workflow perspective, it's practical. As you work on your project, you can quickly go to the Web and search for a detail or piece of content in DWG format. Once you find what you need, you can drag and drop it into your Revit file.

Many manufacturers now have their content in i-droppable 2D or 3D DWG format. Figure 7.52 shows some sample i-drop content.

Figure 7.52

i-drop examples

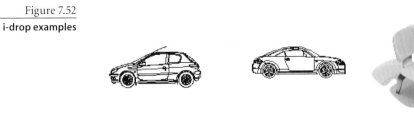

Importing Library Components in SketchUp (.skp) Format

Another recently introduced source of downloadable library components that can be useful in Revit is Google's 3D Warehouse, which offers files in SketchUp (.skp) format. Revit can read SKP files, and you can import SKP files into an RFA (Revit family file) to create content. These families aren't always parametric—many families don't need to be parametric—because certain manufacturer content exists only in single dimensions and shapes. Figure 7.53 shows some samples of SketchUp content.

The best way to utilize this 3D content is to create a new family (File → New → Family) and select a family type, such as furniture or plumbing fixtures. You then can import a 3D SketchUp model into this family. If needed, you can quickly create simplified orthographic projections using the linework tool instead of using a 3D object to generate those projections. This is useful if you need to show simplified versions of the 3D object in plan, elevation, or another orthogonal view. More details about family generation are covered later in this book.

You can learn more about 3D Warehouse at `http://sketchup.google.com/3dwarehouse`.

Figure 7.53

Sample SketchUp content

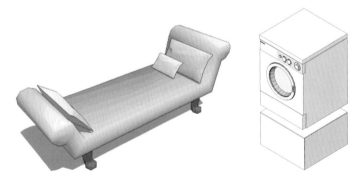

Starting a Model from a Scanned Drawing

There are various ways for an architect to start a project. We have reviewed two of them: starting from scratch, and starting from an already available 2D digital document (CAD file). However, you may have old paper documents of the building that you need to work on.

This happens a lot on smaller projects, usually restorations or additions. Architects may get few floor plans and elevations that they need to redraw before starting a new project. Let's review how you can use them as a basis to begin a new project.

You start by scanning the floor plan and importing it in Revit as an image in the floor relevant to the drawing. Any of the image types we discussed earlier will work fine for your scanned image. An example of a scanned floor plan is shown in Figure 7.54. Follow these steps:

1. Import and position the scanned image into the appropriate level or view. So, if you have a first floor plan, insert it into your Level 1 view.

2. Scanned images are usually never perfectly orthogonal, so you need to rotate the image to square the lines of the walls. Use the Rotation tool, and try to rotate the image as close to orthogonal as possible. To do that, select the image, click the Rotate button, and rotate the image. The rotated image is shown in Figure 7.55.

Figure 7.54

An example of a scanned plan

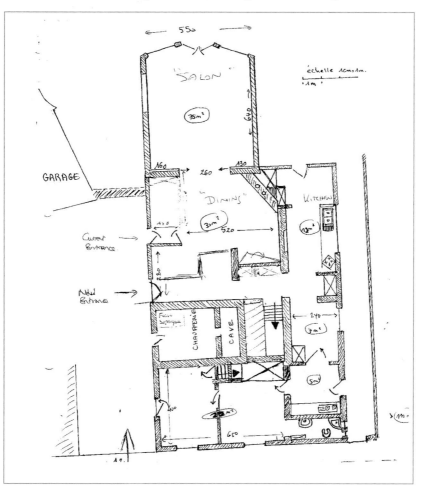

Figure 7.55

The rotated image

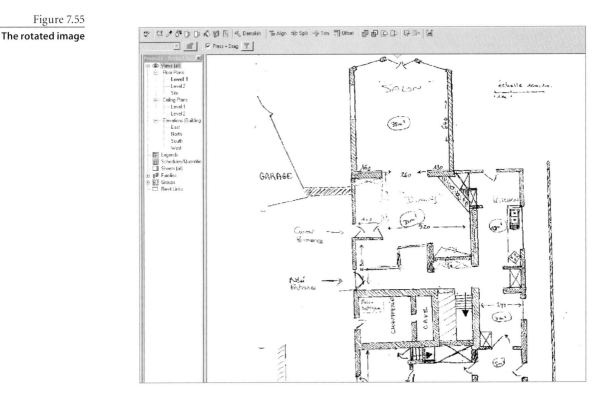

3. You need to verify the drawing scale or adjust the scan to fit the scale you're working in. To do so, zoom in on the image, and find at least one wall that has a dimensioned length. In this example, the original drawing was done in metric units.

4. Using the Resize tool ( ), measure the length of the wall. The tool prompts you to choose two points, and a temporary dimension will show up indicating the length (see Figure 7.56). Make your first two picks correspond to the length of the wall in the image, and then select a third point to resize the image. Use the temporary dimensions to help visualize the change.

5. Click the wall and then across to the right to the end of the wall. The wall length in the scan is 160cm and measures 3200cm in the drawing. Bring your mouse back to the left, and watch the temporary dimension numbers get smaller (as shown in Figure 7.57). When they reach 160cm, click again, and your image will be resized.

You can now start tracing over the imported image and create the framework for your project. Obviously, scanned drawings can never result in total accuracy, so you'll probably want to field-verify your dimensions. However, this is a good way to get started. Figure 7.58 shows the project with all of the new walls located over the scanned image.

You just scaled the drawing. If you dimension the piece of wall, it should show 160cm.

Once you've finished referencing the scanned image, you can delete it or hide it in the view.

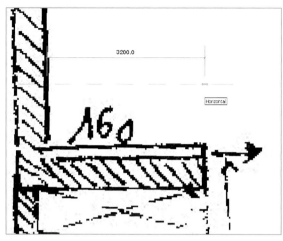

Figure 7.56

Resizing the scanned image

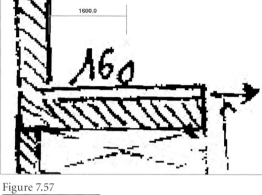

Figure 7.57

Finishing the image edits

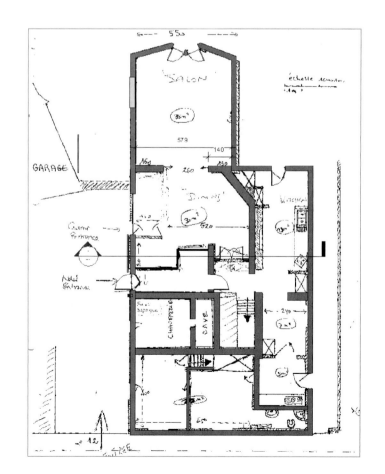

Figure 7.58

The scanned image with Revit walls

CHAPTER 8

Preparing Documents for Clients

There are many points in the design process where it's necessary to convey your ideas to others. As architects, we use a wide range of representational techniques ranging from the loose napkin sketch to the photorealistic rendering. We use 2D diagrams to convey plans and sections, and perspective views to convey a more human-scaled expression. This chapter will focus on a few techniques that you can use directly with Revit. We'll look specifically at creating color-coded area plans, presentation techniques for plans and sections, animated sun studies, and simple renderings that let you explore materials and lighting. Topics we'll cover include:

- Color-coded drawings

- Creating presentation graphics

- Shadows and solar studies

- Rendering a perspective

Color-Coded Drawings

In this section, we'll discuss some common types of graphical documents: color-filled plans and sections. These types of views take advantage of a feature called *color fill schemes*, which allow you to assign colors to room and area parameter values and display them in the view.

Figure 8.1

Area plans branch in the Project Browser

Color fill *plans* and *sections* are basically standard views that are color-coded to represent room properties such as department, name, and usage. *Area plans* are used to convey building usage that extends beyond the shape and size of individual rooms, such as rentable area, office space, and circulation. While plans that are color-coded will appear under the Plans or Sections branch in the Project Browser, area plans have their own branch in the Project Browser, shown in Figure 8.1.

A color fill scheme is a fast, easy, and smart method for generating color-coded plans. It lets you apply color to room and area parameter values to help graphically illustrate spatial organization. For example, you may want to create a colored plan that represents units in an apartment complex, or show various departments with different colors (Figure 8.2) to distinguish space usage such as office, storage, and corridor. You may want to show the same information in a section view to see how your program is distributed vertically.

Figure 8.2

Color-fill plan

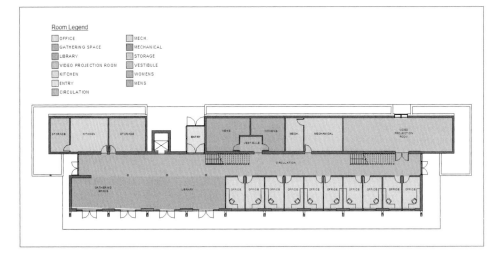

One of the benefits of using color schemes in Revit is that the colors dynamically adjust as changes are made in the model. If a new department is added, a new color is automatically assigned, and the plan view updates immediately to reflect the change.

Revit also makes it easy to change colors to match your aesthetic requirements if the autocolor isn't what you want. You can apply color fills to plan views using the View Properties dialog box. Right-click in a plan view, and select View Properties from the context menu. In the View Properties dialog box you will see a parameter for Color Scheme, with the option to edit it. Click the Edit button, and the Color Fill Schemes dialog box opens, where you can assign an existing scheme to the view or create a new one. You can also color a plan and section view when placing a Color Scheme Legend from the Drafting tab in the Design bar (⊞ Color Scheme Legend).

Defining a Color Scheme

A color scheme is defined once, and can then be applied to multiple views in a project. Using the Transfer Project Standards feature, you can also transfer color schemes from project to project to maintain a consistent color palette across projects.

To define and edit color schemes, choose Settings → Color Fill Schemes. The Edit Color Scheme dialog box, shown in Figure 8.3, has a number of options to help you format your color scheme. The right pane of this dialog box, labeled Scheme Definition, allows you to specify what information you want to color-code:

Title This text box lets you name your color-fill legend. You will probably use the same name that you gave the scheme. The title appears in color-fill legends.

Color This drop-down list allows you to choose the criteria by which you'll color-code the plan from a list of all the room properties. By default this goes to Department, but you will probably not have Department defined in your rooms, so change it to Name to see the effect.

Figure 8.3

Edit Color Scheme dialog box

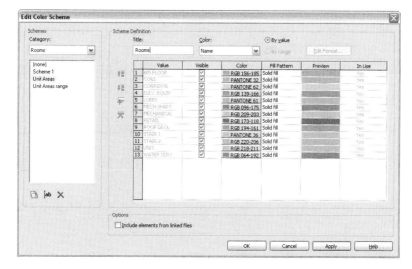

By Value This option is checked by default and uses the value defined in the Color field to list and sort the rooms. For example, if you color by Name, it will list all names used in the project alphabetically and assign a color to each unique name.

By Range This is a second option (see Figure 8.4) for sorting a scheme definition and is *only* active when the color criteria are set to Area or Perimeter. In that case, this option sorts all the areas by size range (from–to), ranging from smallest to largest. This is practical when you need to see how well your project matches a program with specific area goals.

Figure 8.4

Color by Range

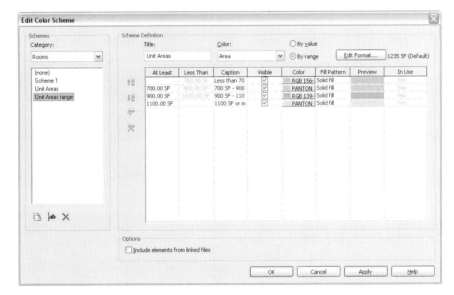

Let's review some of the fields available when the option By Value is selected, as that will be what you will most often need:

Value This is a noneditable field that displays a list of all the parameter values that will appear in your color-fill legend. By default, this column fills up with in-use values based on what is in the model. You can add values to this list by clicking the Add button. This allows you to set some values and colors that can be used by rooms later in the design process. For example, if you have a common list of room names, you could fill out this table before starting to model anything, and then use the list when assigning names to rooms. When a row is selected, you can adjust the order of the values using the up and down arrow buttons. The order established in this dialog box will be reflected in the color-fill legend.

Visible Although all the names are reported in this dialog box, you may not want the legend to show them all. This check box allows you to turn off individual values. This is likewise reflected in the color-fill legend.

Color These colors are customizable and can be changed by clicking the Color button. You have the option to define CMYK, RGB, or Pantone values or to choose from the standard Microsoft color picker.

Fill Pattern This option allows you select the fill pattern from any of the drafting patterns available. By default, Revit chooses the Solid Fill pattern. To add or modify the fill patterns, choose Settings → Fill Patterns.

Preview This field gives you a visual preview of the color as it will appear on the screen in the view.

In Use This field tells you if the particular value is being used in the model. For example, if you add a value to the Value column but don't add it to a room in the model, Revit returns No in this column. This comes into play if you add rooms to a room schedule but don't add those rooms in the model. The color fill knows if rooms exist or not in the model. Note that only values that aren't in use can be deleted.

When the By Range option is selected, one more field is available:

At Least In the At Least column, you can change the minimum area to 1,000 square feet or whatever value you want to show. Revit automatically adjusts the colors in the view to reflect the changes for the color scheme.

In the lower portion of the right pane of the Edit Color Scheme dialog box (labeled Scheme Definition), are the fields shown in Figure 8.5 and described here:

Figure 8.5

Color scheme definition

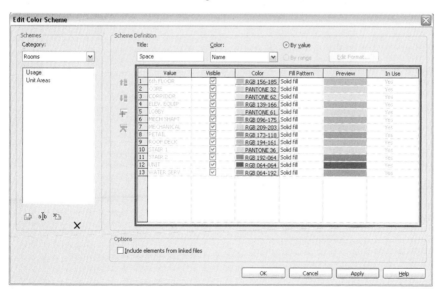

Display Options At the bottom of the Scheme Definition pane are some additional options for color display. You can choose to include linked room area information from other Revit models.

Color Fill Placement In the view properties, you have the option to display the color fill in the foreground or the background of the view. Displaying color in the background puts color beneath all model objects, whereas the Foreground option colors all model objects. The effect is illustrated in Figure 8.6.

Figure 8.6

Displaying color fill

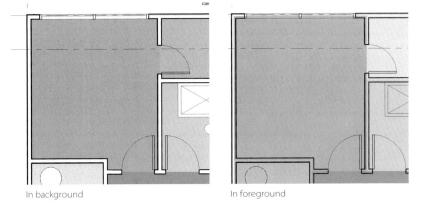

In background   In foreground

Adding a Color Scheme to a View

In this exercise, you'll create a color-coded plan and add it to a view:

1. Open the Station_Start.rvt model found in the Chapter 8 folder on the book's companion web page, www.wiley.com/go/introducingrevit2009, and open the plan view called Level 3 Pres.

2. Define a new scheme in which you'll color the rooms and areas by name. To do that, choose Settings → Color Schemes.

3. In the Schemes portion of the dialog box, click the Duplicate button located at the top. Name the new scheme **Room Name.**

4. In the Scheme Definitions section, give the scheme a title by typing **Room Legend,** then choose Name in the Color drop-down list.

5. The result will be a list of rooms sorted alphabetically by name. If you wish to change the order to be nonalphabetical, use the Move Rows Up or Down buttons on the left of the list. These buttons become active when you click on any of the names. If you don't like the automatically assigned colors, change the colors by clicking on the color field.

6. Click OK.

7. You are back in the view—select the Drafting tab in the Design bar and choose Color Scheme Legend.

8. The legend shows up on your cursor. Position the color-fill legend somewhere close to the plan. You will be prompted to choose a color scheme: choose the scheme you just created, named Room Name. The plan is automatically colored based on the names of the rooms in the plan view.

> The Color Fill tool assigns colors to various properties of rooms and thus they will show only if you have created rooms in your project. If you work on a new project but have not yet defined rooms, and you place a color-fill legend, it will report that no colors are defined. What that message means is that there are no rooms defined for the color scheme you are trying to assign to referencing. Select the Room tool from the Room and Area tab in the Design bar, and start placing rooms in your spaces; you'll see the new rooms are colored in as you place each one and give it a unique name.

The Color Scheme Legend can display the colors used in the current view or all the colors used in the project. To toggle between the two, select the legend, open its Element Properties dialog box, and in the Type properties set the Values Displayed parameters By View or All. The usual case is that you will need to set it By View. The All option can be helpful when you make an overview legend for the entire project.

Try a short exercise for color-coding a plan using the Area/By Range option:

1. Open Level 3 Pres and duplicate the view, giving it a new name.

2. Click Settings → Color Schemes.

3. In the Schemes portion of the dialog box, click the Duplicate button located at bottom of the schemes list. Name the new scheme **Unit Areas**, and change the title to Unit Area Legend.

4. Choose to color Area and click By Range.

5. By default, the At Least column reads 20 SF. Highlight that value, and change it to **700 SF.**

6. While the At Least column is still highlighted, click the Add button to add a row to the column.

7. The new value defaults to 1400. Change it to **900**, and click OK. Add one more row using the same method, and set the At Least range to 1100 SF. Your settings should be similar to the ones shown in Figure 8.7.

8. Close the dialog box. In the View Properties dialog box, set the Color Scheme Location to Foreground (see Figure 8.8).

As the Color Fill Legend is a property of a view, you can at any point change the color fill from one type to another or set it to None. To access the color fill from the view, choose View Properties → Color Scheme.

Figure 8.7

Color scheme settings

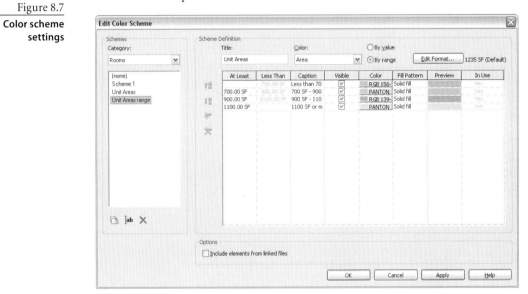

Figure 8.8

Finished color-fill view

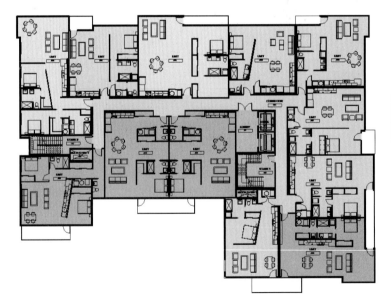

Area Plans

Area plans are views of the model used to calculate the areas of rooms according to various calculation standards. Some of the standards for area calculations are as follows:

Gross area This is the overall area of a floor or footprint of the building.

Rentable area Different developers and leasing companies have different standards for rentable areas. One example may include all the spaces in a building except egress corridors, vertical transportation, and mechanical spaces. However, this includes the floor area taken up by columns and some walls.

Usable area This area defines only the usable space in a plan. It doesn't count areas taken up by columns, walls, mechanical rooms, shafts, and other non-usable space.

BOMA area BOMA is the Building Owners and Managers Association standard. Widely used in the United States, it was created to help standardize office-building development. BOMA has its own set of standards used to calculate areas. More information on BOMA standards can be found at www.boma.org.

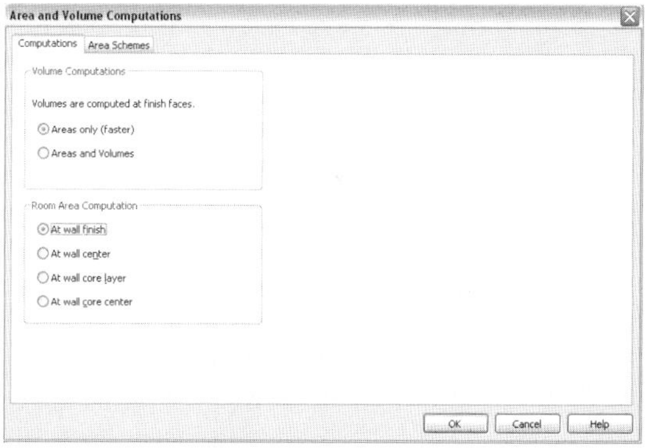

Revit allows you to choose among several predefined area schemes or to create your own scheme based on standard calculation variables. To add or modify the area settings, choose Settings → Area and Volume Computations. Some of those settings, shown in Figure 8.9, include boundary locations such as wall finish and wall center, and the heights at which to calculate area.

Figure 8.9

Area and Volume Computations dialog box

> The Room and Area Settings dialog box gives you the option of calculating room volumes. This tool is useful in a number of applications, but you should use it only when needed, because the additional calculations can create performance issues based on project complexity.

The Room Calculations tab allows you to change how the areas are calculated for each area scheme. You can set a height and boundary type that Revit uses to autogenerate room areas.

The Area Schemes tab, shown in Figure 8.10, lets you add different schemes to calculate room areas, allowing you to calculate multiple area types in Revit.

Figure 8.10

Area Schemes tab

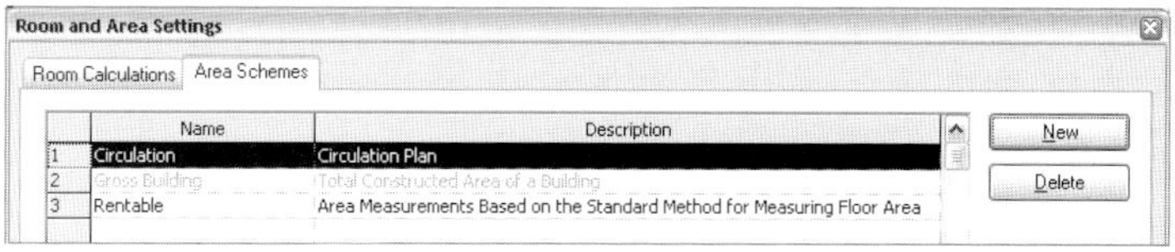

To add an area plan to your model, open the Room and Area tab in the Design bar, and click the Area Plan button (Area Plan...). Doing so opens the New Area Plan dialog box (Figure 8.11), where you select area scheme, level, and drawing scale.

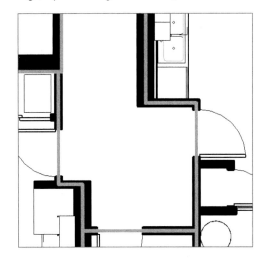

When you click OK, Revit automatically adds a new node to the Project Browser called Area Plans and adds area plans for each level you choose. In your view, you'll see a duplicate plan view of the level you selected, with purple lines defining the area boundaries. These lines are placed on the walls according to the type of area plan you selected (such as gross area or rentable area). You can move or delete the lines if they don't appear where you want them to be. To add area boundary lines, use the Area Boundary tool available in the Room and Areas tab of the Design bar (Area Boundary).

Area boundaries must be closed loops of lines (see Figure 8.12) in order for Revit to be able to calculate the area. Any breaks or gaps in the area lines, or lines that don't intersect, will result in Revit returning a Not Enclosed value for the area. (Should you get that error message, try trimming the corners.)

Figure 8.12

**Area boundary with
closed loops**

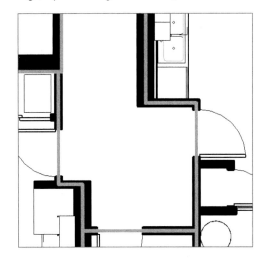

Color-Coded Section Views

The ability to color-code section views is new to the Color Fill tool, introduced in Revit 2009. The same parameters for Color Fill are available in section views. Once a room has been placed in the model, it can be tagged in both plan and section, and likewise colored. By default, rooms will be shown as rectangles, spanning from level to level.

For nonrectangular situations—where the room has a barrel vault slanted ceiling, for example, you first have to change the rule for how Revit calculates rooms so that volumes are calculated and thus room sections are able to be colored.

To enable room volume calculations and thus have colors appear in sections as well, go to Settings → Room and Area Settings. Select Areas and Volumes in the Volume Computations section (Figure 8.13).

You can then place rooms and open a section view to see results.

Make sure that room visibility is set to On when adding a color fill to section views.

New to Revit 2009, the height of a room can be dragged interactively in the view (Figure 8.14).

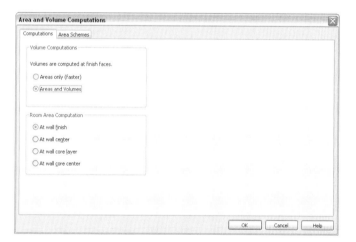

Figure 8.13

To color-fill sections accurately, you need to compute room volumes.

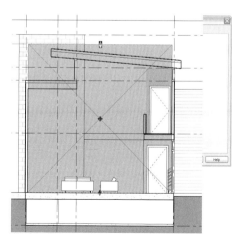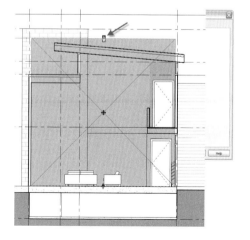

Figure 8.14

The height of rooms can be dragged interactively in section view.

You can see in Figure 8.14 that the room did not respond to the roof angle—this is what you will get with default room settings. To clean up that image, change the room and area setting so that volumes are calculated to get the right image (Figure 8.15).

Figure 8.15

The completed color fill

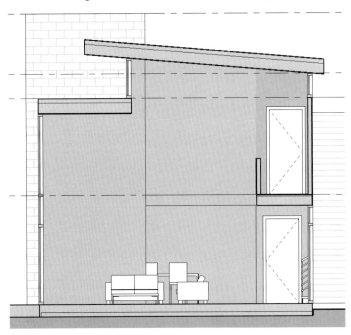

Creating Presentation Graphics

Creating compelling visual representations of your design is an important device for conveying design intent and telling the story of your project. As you've seen, Revit lets you create standard forms of representation, ranging from floor plans and sections to perspectives. Using some simple techniques, you can bring these typically flat drawings to life. In this section we'll explore methods to help you make some great-looking drawings. We'll also touch on how to create photorealistic renderings using the brand-new rendering engine and interface added to the 2009 version of Revit.

Floor Plans: Accentuating Walls

Making clean, easy-to-read floor plans requires only a few steps. A typical plan view in Revit can become cluttered with lots of annotations and doesn't create striking figure–ground images. Figure 8.16 shows a typical floor plan in Revit.

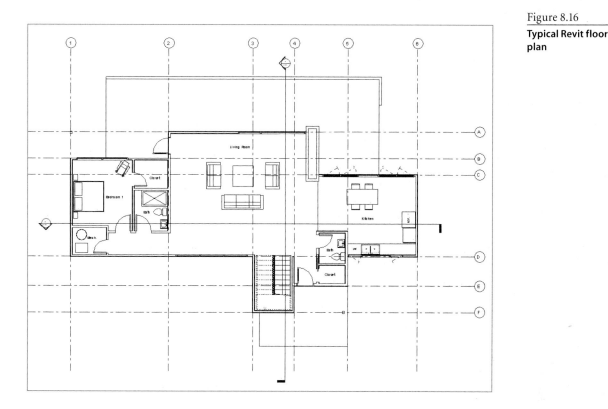

Figure 8.16

Typical Revit floor plan

To clean up this image, you can hide the annotations and override the cut for all the walls with a solid color. To do so, follow these steps:

1. Open the Visibility/Graphic Overrides dialog box, click the Annotations tab, and deselect the check box Show Annotation Categories in This View (see Figure 8.17). This hides all annotations with a single click.

    Visibility/Graphic Overrides for Floor Plan: Level 1

    Model Categories | Annotation Categories | Imported Categories | Filters

    ☐ Show annotation categories in this view

    Figure 8.17

    Uncheck this box to hide all annotations in the view.

2. Go back to the Model Categories tab, and scroll down to the Walls category.

3. Select the row, and override the Cut Patterns column by clicking the Override button. In the resulting Fill Pattern Graphics dialog box (shown in Figure 8.18), you're given options to select pattern and color overrides. Set Color to Black and Pattern to Solid Fill.

4. If you have columns in your project, you may want to do the same for them as well. When you've finished, click OK to close both dialog boxes.

The effect on the plan view is immediately obvious, as shown in Figure 8.19. The same technique can be applied in section views. Be sure to override other categories relevant to section view, such as Floor, Roof, and Topography. Figure 8.20 shows a section with the same graphic overrides. Try these techniques in any of the sample files provided on the book's companion web page to get a feel for the interaction.

Figure 8.18

Fill Pattern overrides

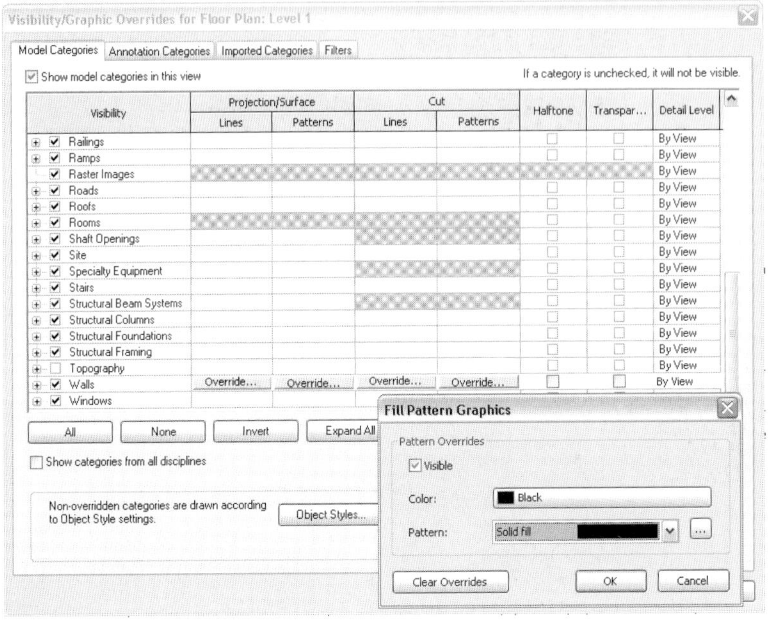

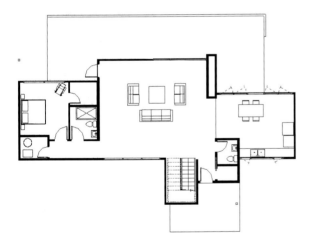

Figure 8.19

Plan view after applying graphic overrides

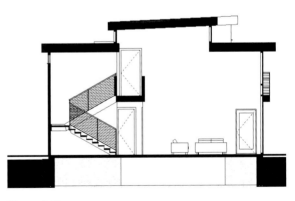

Figure 8.20

Section view with cut pattern overrides

Making Elevation Graphics

Colored elevation views are a nice way to convey materiality, even if in the abstract. Change your elevation views to Shaded with Edges, using the view controls at the bottom of the view, to get a feel for this mode. A sample of this view style is shown in Figure 8.21.

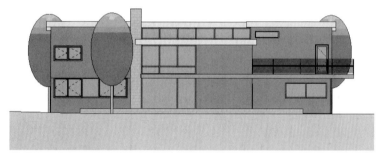

Figure 8.21
**The default
shaded view**

Every material used in Revit refers back to an RGB value in shaded view; however, many users have noticed that color is rarely matched in the view, and will even look very different from view to view. To overcome this effect, and approximate the same colors set up in materials in the view, you can use Sun and Shadows Settings to control precisely where light is coming from and thus improve the visual fidelity. A sample of this modified view style is shown in Figure 8.22 (the image in black and white is subtle, but will become readily obvious if you do this in Revit).

Figure 8.22
**The same elevation
with the sun
repositioned**

To edit and adjust material colors and patterns, choose Settings → Materials. You can also access this dialog box from element properties directly if the Material parameter is present. For example, if you aren't sure what material is on the exterior of a wall, select the wall in question, then open the wall's Element Properties dialog box, next access the Type Properties button, then the Structure options. From here, you can select the Finish Layers Material, and you'll be taken directly to the Materials dialog box.

Figure 8.23
**Shadow options in
the View Control bar**

To get this effect, open the Advanced Model Graphics dialog box from the View Control bar located at the bottom of your view (shown in Figure 8.23). Access to the command to open this dialog box is located with shadow controls.

Advanced Model Graphics…

0 Shadows Off

⌐ Shadows On

In the Advanced Model Graphics dialog box, click the ellipsis button ([...]) next to the Sun and Shadow Settings drop-down box to open the Sun and Shadows Settings dialog box. Then, do the following:

1. Create a new entry by clicking the Duplicate button, and name it **True Color.**

2. Set Sun to Directly, Azimuth to 0, and Altitude to 90.

3. Make sure the Relative to View check box is selected (see Figure 8.24).

4. Click OK to return to the Advanced Model Graphics dialog box.

5. Be sure shadows are enabled. Using the Sun slider in the Intensity section, change the setting to 80, and turn Shadow down to 0. This way, no shadows will be cast, and the light source will always be directly above the model. The effect is that light won't cause unpredictable effects on material colors.

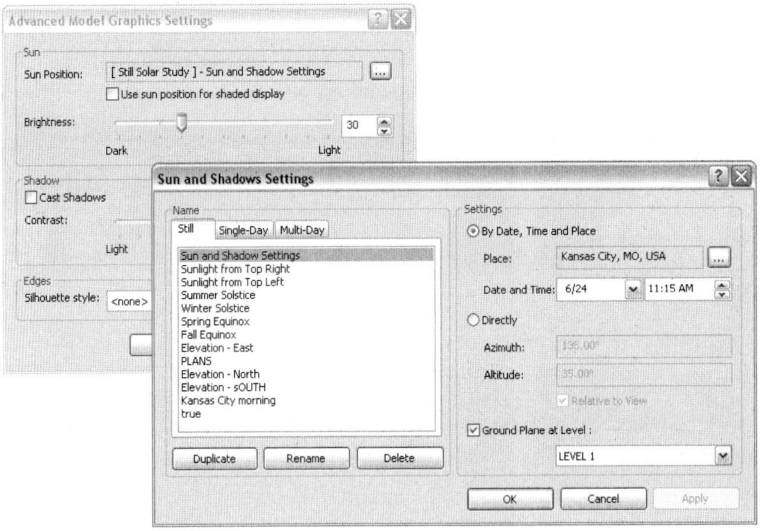

Figure 8.24

Set the sun angles using the Sun and Shadows Settings dialog box.

Using Images in Elevation Views

Using images in elevation views is a great way to add some visual character to your drawings. Two useful techniques involve taking advantage of the draw order options for images when placed in a view. When you select an image, the Options bar gives you the ability to push the image to the foreground or background (Figures 8.25 and 8.26). By making a color-gradient image, then importing it into your elevation, you can then send the image to the background and produce high-quality images right in Revit.

Figure 8.25

When the image is selected, send it to the background using the Options bar.

Figure 8.26

This PNG image is set to Foreground.

Another great technique is to use the transparency channel available in the PNG format. By making the background layer transparent in Photoshop and pushing images to the foreground in Revit, you can add trees, people, and cars, and the background will not mask the model.

Shadows and Solar Studies

Using shadows can help articulate depth in your façade. You can toggle shadows on and off in any view using the view controls. A nice feature in Revit is the ability to orient shadows consistently from view to view.

Turn on shadows (using the View Controls at the bottom of the view). From the same flyout menu, open the Advanced Model Graphics dialog box. Open the Sun and Shadows Settings dialog box and choose Sunlight from Top Right. Close the dialog boxes to get a feel for the behavior. Change your view display to Hidden Line, and note that shadows are still cast. Return to the Advanced Model Graphics dialog box and experiment with the Sun and Shadow Intensity settings. Increasing Shadow to 100 yields high-contrast images and dropping the value to 0 essentially turns off the shadow. A hidden-line view of the default sun settings is shown in Figure 8.27.

Figure 8.27

Hidden-line view with shadows enabled

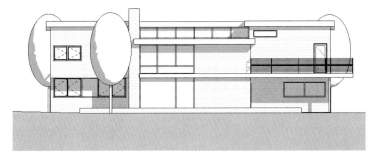

Creating a Solar Study

Understanding the effect your building will have on its environment is an important part of a design. Often, architects are required to show how a new building will cast shadows on its neighboring buildings and open space. For these purposes, Revit provides a tool that lets you generate an animated solar study that can show the effect of shadows over time, throughout the year.

To access the feature, you'll first need to enable shadows in your view, and then set up some information about time and location of the project. The steps to create a solar study are described next. For the purpose of this exercise, any view can be used, but we suggest using a site plan, as it's a great view to use when visualizing shadows.

1. Open the Advanced Model Graphics dialog box, and click the ellipsis button to open the Sun and Shadows Settings dialog box.

2. Choose the Multi-Day tab, shown in Figure 8.28.

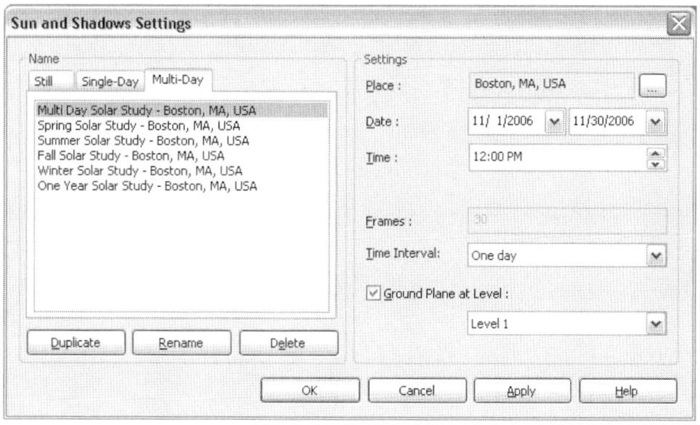

Figure 8.28

Click the Multi-Day tab to access these settings.

3. The predefined options on this tab are good starting points. You choose your project's location from a drop-down list of cities; a start date; an end date; and a time of day. Choose a time interval as well. Use the default settings for a Multi Day Solar Study, and change Place to a city near where you are right now.

4. Click OK, and go back to your view.

5. Once you've set up a multiday study, new options appear on the View Control bar (see Figure 8.29). Click Preview Solar Study to activate animation controls in the Options bar.

Figure 8.29

Previewing the solar study provides these animation controls.

Clicking the Play button starts the animation. In the view, you'll see a live animation of the shadows as the days of the month go by.

Once you're happy with the results, you can export the view as an animated movie. To do so, choose File → Export → Animated Solar Study. From here, you can choose a location to save the file, change the model graphic styles, and choose the size of the image in pixels. To make smaller files, try using the Microsoft Video 1 codec and lower the quality settings. The resulting file can be played with a standard digital video player such as Windows Media Player.

3D Views

A great way to visualize the model is to use a perspective camera and enable the section box. This allows you to create 3D sectional views that slice through the model, providing stunning graphics that can help better explain plan, section, and 3D in one view.

To take advantage of this form of representation, open a perspective view (or make a new one using the Camera tool in the View tab of the Design bar), and open its View Properties dialog box using the right-click menu. Enable the Section Box parameter in the Extents parameter group, as shown in Figure 8.30.

A new 3D box appears in the view: this is the section box. Select the section box, and controls appear that you can use to clip the view from all six directions of the box. To experiment, drag the top arrows down until the box cuts through the model.

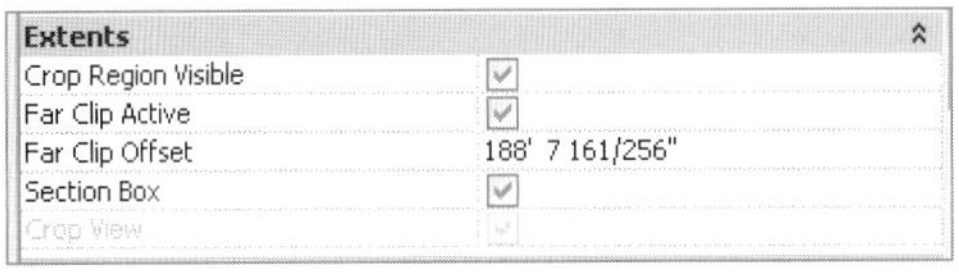

Figure 8.30

Enabling the Section Box option

Extents		
Crop Region Visible	☑	
Far Clip Active	☑	
Far Clip Offset	188' 7 161/256"	
Section Box	☑	
Crop View	☐	

To hide the 3D cropping box, select it, and hide it by choosing Hide in View → By Element from the right-click menu. The same thing works with 3D axonometric views, but the camera views give different dynamics to the graphic presentation. A sample view of a 3D floor plan is shown in Figure 8.31.

Figure 8.31

Perspective view with the section box enabled

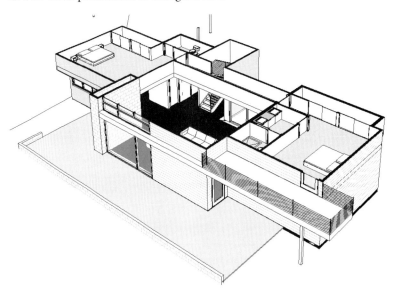

You can apply the same graphic overrides to a 3D view as we outlined for plan and section views. This way, you can graphically override the color of everything that has been cut (walls, columns, roofs, etc.) and assign a solid fill color. Take advantage of these techniques to produce some really slick presentations!

Rendering a Perspective

Revit has an integrated rendering engine that lets you visualize the model with material texture maps and more realistic lighting effects. New to the 2009 release, the rendering engine has been changed from AccuRender to a much more powerful mental ray rendering engine. A brand-new material library has also been included that was designed specifically for architectural renderings. Now you can generate great-looking images with relatively minimal time investment, and you don't need to be highly skilled in visualization techniques and complicated shaders.

> If you're familiar with Autodesk 3ds Max or Autodesk VIZ, you will know about FBX: you can now export a 3D view of a Revit model to FBX and open that file directly in 3ds Max 2009. What this means is that there is no need of translating the Revit file into DWG to be able to render it. FBX is very powerful exchange format that will allow for all geometry, materials, lights, and your active camera to make it to 3ds Max for further refinement. From the main menu, choose File → Export → 3ds Max (FBX).

Let's walk through how to render an exterior view.

The following exercise will take you through a simplified rendering workflow. Many of the materials in the model have been predefined for you.

1. Open the file `Source_House_Complete.rvt` from the Chapter 8 folder on the companion web page.

2. We've provided some custom materials for use with this file. In order for the rendering to process the files we've provided, you need to copy the folder named `Materials` from the web page to your `My Documents` folder. Be sure to copy the files there, or some materials will not render.

3. To render a view, open or create a new perspective view of the exterior of the building. Any 3D view can be rendered, but you'll get the best results from perspective (camera) views.

4. 3D View 1 has already been created, so you can open it.

5. Enable the Rendering dialog box by clicking the Rendering icon (teapot) in the View Control bar at bottom of the view (⬚ Perspective ⬚ 🔲 🔵 🔲 🔲 🔲 🔲 ⬚). This opens the dialog box in Figure 8.32.

6. The Rendering dialog box is where you set up quality settings, lighting, and backgrounds for the rendering. You can also save and export renderings with this dialog box. To render the view, click the Render button.

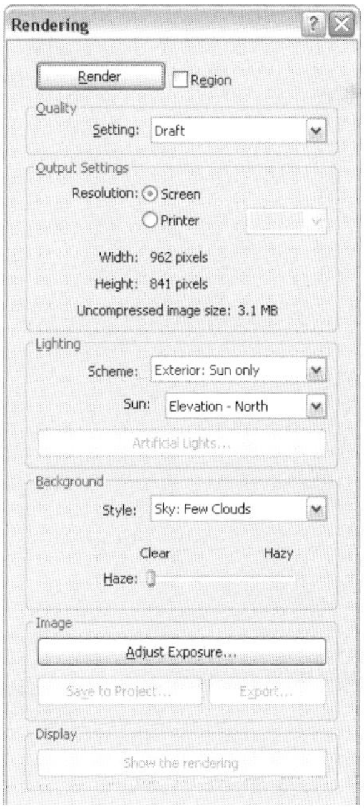

Figure 8.32
The new Rendering dialog box

> If you check the Region option next to the Render button, a rectangle appears in the view that can be resized. When you render the view, only the area within this region is rendered. Use this to render smaller areas of view to speed up iterations.

7. The view will start to render. You'll see an image begin to appear in your view. You can cancel the rendering at any time by clicking the Cancel button at the bottom of the screen near the progress meter. When the render is finished, the image should look like Figure 8.33.

Figure 8.33

The finished view

This rendering, although exceedingly simple, illustrates some of the critical aspects of rendering: the camera, lighting, materials, background, and foreground. We'll step through each of these to give you an idea of where you can find these features in the user interface and how to make adjustments.

The Camera

The Revit camera is easy to manipulate. When you're in a perspective view, clicking the SteeringWheel button (👁) in the toolbar brings up the SteeringWheel (Figure 8.43).

Figure 8.34

The SteeringWheel for perspective views

Use the Walkthrough options to move the camera in space. The Pan option moves the camera in the vertical plane, and Walk will move the camera forward and backward. Use Look to swing the camera from side to side. Use the submenu in the SteeringWheel to change the focal length of the camera and slide the crop boundary around. When you're changing focal length, the camera doesn't move; the zoom factor changes.

Quality Settings

At the top of the Rendering dialog box is where you set the image quality. Quality settings (Figure 8.35) allow you to create quick renderings for early iterations, and then dial up the quality when you're ready to generate a high-quality photorealistic rendering.

Increasing quality always has an impact on time, so run high-quality renderings only if you have time, and you've got your entire model built and all the materials assigned. Use the available presets to start. If you want to experiment, click the Edit Custom option in the dialog box to open the Render Settings dialog box.

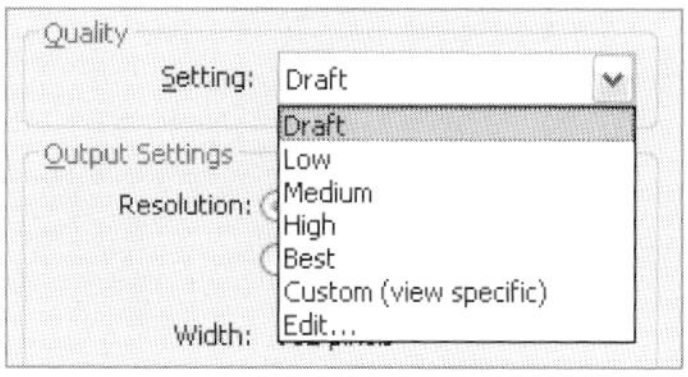

Figure 8.35
Quality options

Output Size

When rendering, you can choose what your target output is. When iterating through a rendering, keep Device set to Screen—this renders the view relative to your screen size and goes much faster. When you are ready to send a rendering at high resolution out of Revit for printing, or for touch-up in a program like Photoshop, change Device to Printer and set your desired dpi (Figure 8.36). You will see a rough estimate of how large the file will be if uncompressed— basically the size of the file if saved as a `.tiff`.

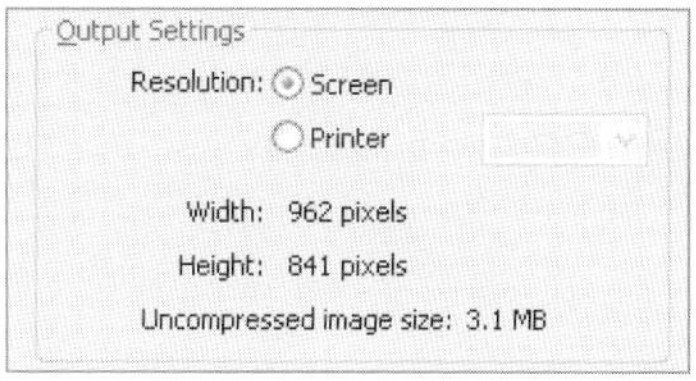

Figure 8.36
Output options

Lighting

It's possible to set highly specific date, time, and place information for your rendering. This allows you to generate accurate sun studies. All views have a default sun location that is stored in the Sun and Shadows Settings dialog box, accessible via the Advanced Model Graphics Settings dialog box. To open this dialog box, use the Shadow menu in the View Control bar, or open the View Properties dialog box and click the Advanced Model Graphics button (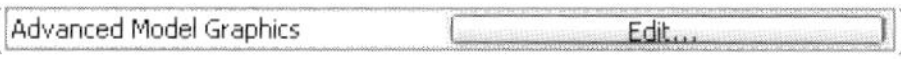 Advanced Model Graphics   Edit...). When you're rendering exterior or interior views with natural lighting, the rendering will use information from the Sun and Shadows Settings dialog box. When you're rendering interior scenes with only artificial lights, only light from lighting fixtures will be used (Figures 8.37 and 8.38).

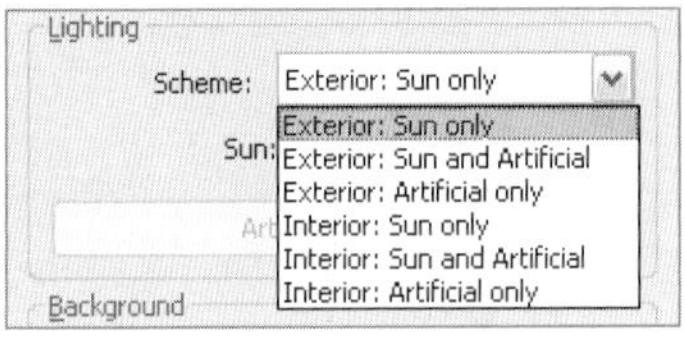

Figure 8.37

Scheme options

In the Rendering dialog box, you can choose the type of lighting scheme for your scene from the list. For both exterior and interior you have several options to choose from. For our rendering of the exterior, the Sun Only option will work fine. When rendering, you essentially need to choose whether or not you want to see the effect of sunlight in the view.

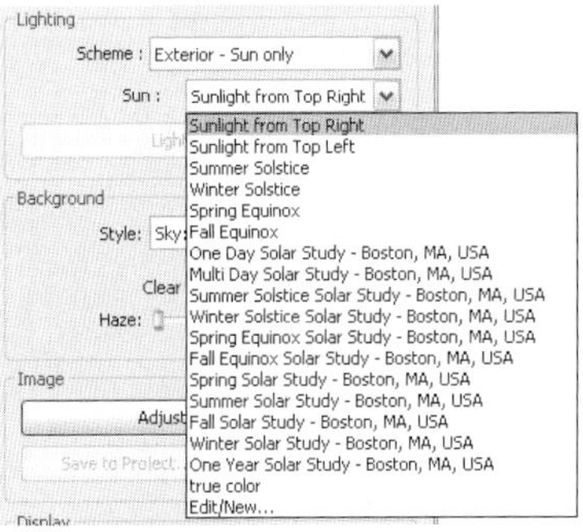

Figure 8.38

Sun position options

Depending on the type of scene you are rendering, you can make adjustments to the light sources. For the sun, choose from the list of sun settings in your project. If you are going for accurate sun angles, be sure to set the project place, using the Manage Place and Locations dialog box (Figure 8.39). For artificial lights, you can use the Light Groups dialog box to group lights and turn lights on and off.

Lights have been upgraded significantly in the 2009 release but do not automatically upgrade with new features until you open the light in the Family Editor, then reload the light. Alternatively, you can reload the family from

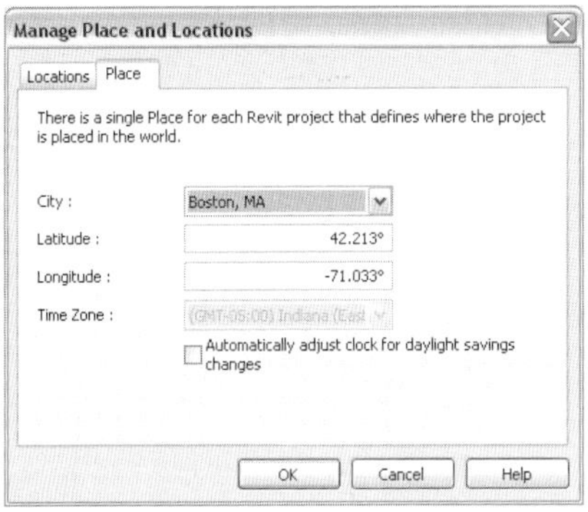

Figure 8.39

Manage Place and Locations dialog box

2009 family directories. The new features create more realistic lighting effects, and light source can be based on an Integrated Environmental Solutions, LTD (IES) definition (Figure 8.40).

To access the Sun and Shadows Settings dialog box from the Rendering dialog box, choose the Edit/New option from the drop-down list. You can then make adjustments or make new settings for your scene.

Foreground and Background

Foreground and background are used to help give your model some context by premade sky and clouds, or by using a solid color. Placing trees and bushes and other site entourage such as cars and people helps fill in the foreground. Plants, trees, people, and cars in Revit render as photorealistic images when associated with an ArchVision RPC (Rich Photorealistic Content) file. These files contain intelligent images that orient correctly relative to your camera, and they can add some realism and scale to your renderings.

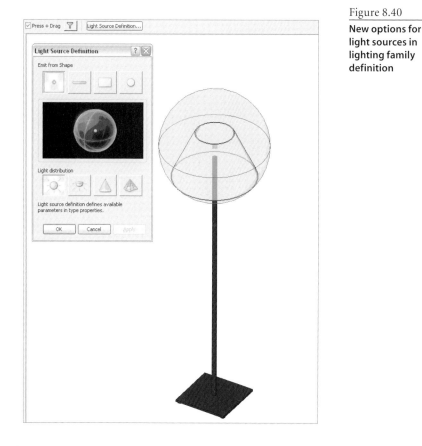

Figure 8.40

New options for light sources in lighting family definition

Be careful when working with your camera so your model doesn't look like it's floating in an abstract, empty plane. Tighten the shot using the field of view, or crop the view to reduce the amount of ground taking up space. To do this, select the crop boundary and drag the blue controls. You can also access the exact size of the crop boundary from the Options bar by clicking the Size button when the crop boundary is selected. The button reports the actual size. Clicking the button will bring up options to resize the boundary.

To set up a background for the rendered image (Figure 8.41), use the background options in the Rendering dialog box. You can use some sky and cloud settings or a solid color. If your building is without a context of other buildings or site, try to add elements that will obscure the horizon. Add building masses that represent your site conditions, and add trees and topography to make the image more realistic.

Figure 8.41

The Background options

The sky options for rendering are based on actual colors that are physically accurate. If your scene is near dusk, the sky will change color to accurately reflect sky conditions at that time of day.

Saving Your Image

Once you render a view and like it, save the image to your project, export it, or both. When saving to your project, be wary of saving huge renderings, as this will bulk up the size of your file. The renderings are stored in their own branch of the Project Browser.

When exporting a PNG, the background saves as transparent, making it easy to replace with new images or custom backgrounds in Photoshop. In Figure 8.42, you create a new Layer 1 and put it behind the default Layer 0. You can then copy and paste a background image into Layer 1, and voilà!

On the left of Figure 8.42 is a PNG from Revit; on the right is a custom background image. Using layers, you can easily position any image you want behind your model.

Figure 8.42

Positioning a sky

Materials

Perhaps the most critical aspect of producing a convincing rendering is assigning good rendering appearances to your materials. Good materials convey characteristics of texture, color, reflectivity, and transparency that you expect to see in reality.

All elements in Revit have a material, but some materials may have a generic gray render appearance assigned. To assign a specific rendering appearance, open the Materials dialog box (Settings → Materials) and select a material from the list on the left. On the right, you'll see a tab called Render Appearance. Open that tab, then click on the Replace button to open the Render Appearance Library. From here you can choose a new Render Appearance, as shown in Figure 8.43. Follow these steps:

1. Select an exterior wood siding wall and open its Type Properties dialog box. Select to edit its structure, to change the material for the exterior siding, click on the material name then click the small button next to the name. This will open the Materials dialog box (see Figure 8.44).

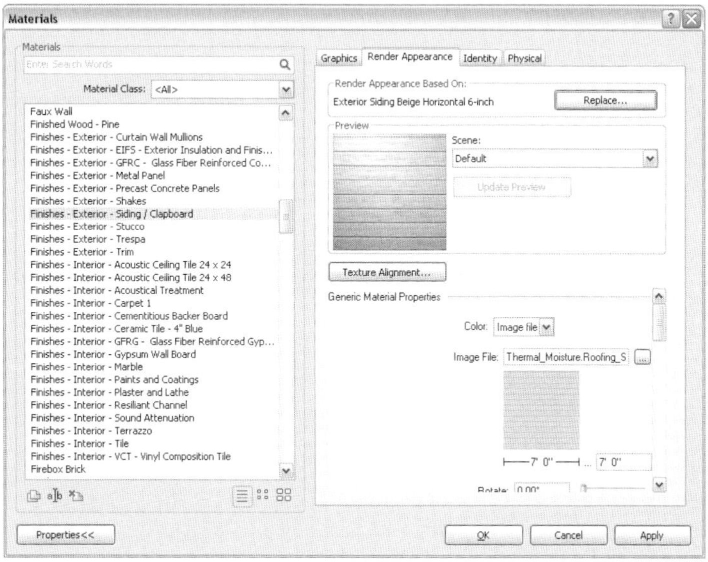

Figure 8.43

Click the New Render Appearance tab in the Materials dialog box.

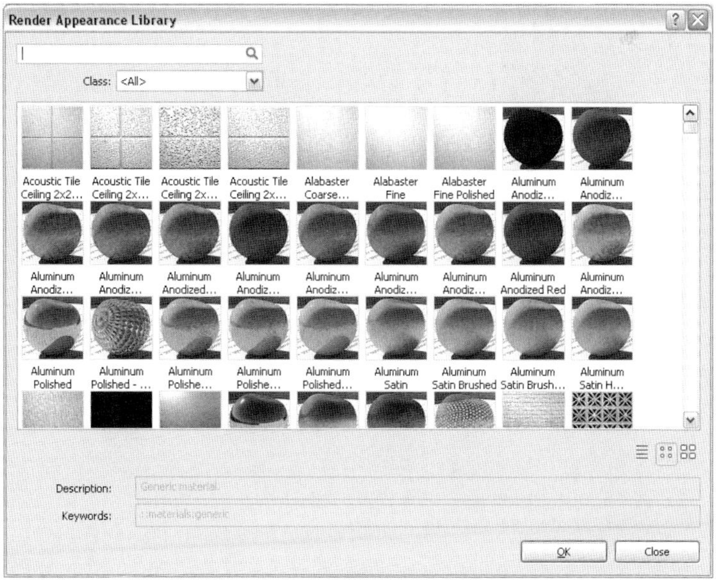

Figure 8.44

Asset Browser

2. With the Materials dialog box now open, click the Render Appearance tab. This tab has all the information used to render the material. Here you will see the custom texture and path leading to it. Note the Scale parameter—this is what scales the image map to the right size. To change the scale, type in the Sample Size field.

3. If you want to replace the render appearance and browse the asset library for additional options, click the Replace button. This takes you to the Asset Browser, where you can

search for and select new render materials for use in your project. Use the search field to find materials. You can also use the dropdown list of presets to cull the list.

4. Change the texture map you are using by clicking the small browse button next to the path to the image file. It should look like this: ⬚

    Browse to C:\My Documents\Materials, choose the file named WOOD SIDING.jpg, and click OK.

5. The scaling looks fine, so click OK through the various dialog boxes to commit to the change. This is the basic process for setting up materials.

6. Re-render the view to see the effect—all the exterior walls should now render with the new image map you chose.

7. Experiment and iterate—get used to browsing for materials and running quick renderings at low- or medium-quality settings.

8. When you're ready to crank out a great image, increase the quality and click the Render button again.

To recap: create a new Revit material by duplicating an existing material. Then use the Render Appearance tab to edit or replace rendering appearances. All the materials that are included in the materials library are properly scaled to real-world sizes, so you should not need to make many edits to those (Figure 8.45). If you choose to use your own texture maps, be sure to set the scale so that the image looks right when rendered.

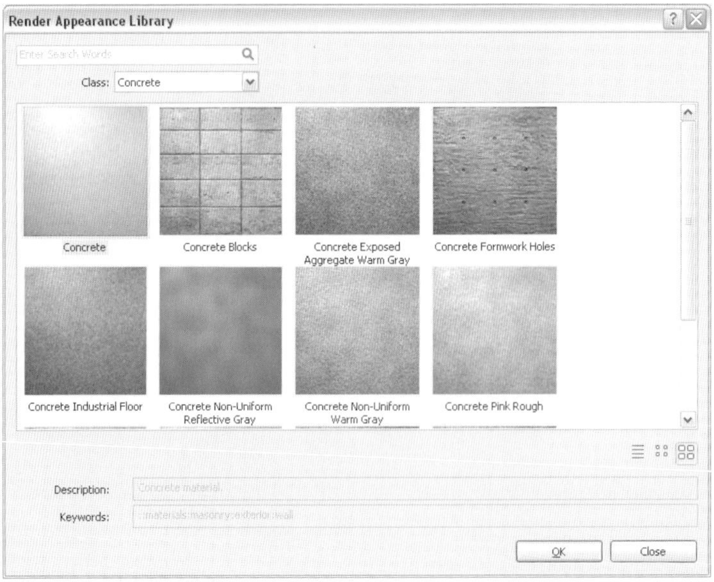

Figure 8.45

First look to the Render Appearance Library for a wide selection of great materials.

For materials such as glass, where an image isn't needed, choose from the default materials libraries that ship with Revit. Browse through the Render Appearance Library, and you'll find a set of glass options as well as a host of other materials to choose from (see Figure 8.46). For windows, use the Glazing types, as these will work great for exterior panes of glass. The glazing materials even allow you to specify how many sheets of glass are in the pane!

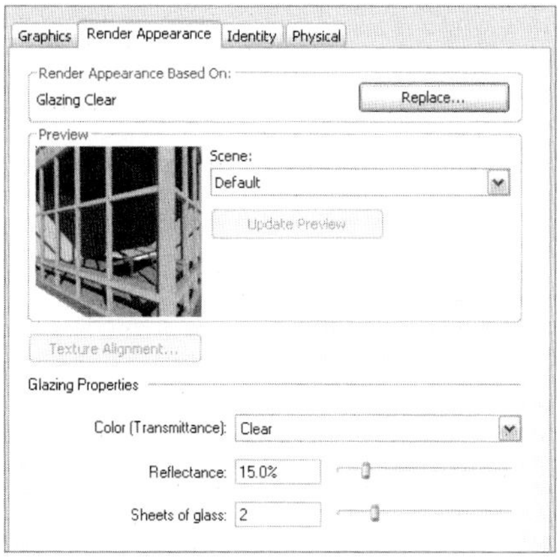

Figure 8.46

Glass material options include color, reflectance, and sheets of glass.

CHAPTER 9

Sheets

In previous chapters, we discussed how to create a model in Revit and how to make standard views to represent the model. We've explored how to create plans, sections, callouts, elevations, and 3D views of a BIM model. This chapter starts by looking at the properties of views and what these all mean. We then move on to sheets, and explore how to get your views onto sheets. In Revit, getting your views onto sheets is extremely easy: you simply drag and drop views from the Project Browser onto sheet views. Because every view has a scale, you see the effect immediately, and if you have to change scale or crop the view, you can do so in the context of the sheet. You can then print, export, or publish these sheets for use.

Topics we'll cover include:

- **Documentation trends**
- **Preparing views**
- **The sheet**

Documentation Trends

Historically, the creation and delivery of document sets has been divided into three phases: schematic design, design development, and construction documents. The final CD set becomes the legal documents of record and is used by the contractor to physically build the building. With the advent of BIM, a discussion in the industry around this traditional division of documents is taking place, and new questions are being raised. Is this a viable and sustainable practice in the context of a BIM workflow? Can a BIM model redefine the types of documents that are created throughout the life of a project? Do we even need paper documents to build the building, or could a live, up-to-date BIM model actually be the deliverable? The divisions in BIM aren't as rigid as they have been in a legacy 2D workflow. An example of BIM deliverable packages might include:

- Conceptual model and documents, where the basic geometric forms of the building are created

- Design-development model and documents, where the building geometry and major building elements are completely modeled

- Construction model and documents, where the design-development model is embellished with annotations and dimensions and the construction document set is created

This is more than just an elimination of schematic design. It amounts to a restructuring of project deliverables and, more specifically, the deliverable timetable. The traditional percentages of time per phase also no longer apply. This is an important point to remember as you move forward in documentation, because you'll need to adjust your expectations and timeframe to a different delivery methodology. You'll find additional information in the Integrated Practice and Technology in Practice sections of the American Institute of Architects (AIA) website (www.aia.org/IP and www.aia.org/TAP, respectively.). Recently AIA has produced a guide: Integrated Project Delivery Guide, www.aia.org/ipdg.

We are confident that this is a trend that will be followed worldwide.

Preparing Views

Now that we've covered most types of views you can create with Revit, let's discuss how to place those views on sheets (Figure 9.1). But before you start placing views onto sheets, it's important to know about some critical properties of views that affect how they behave when placed on sheets. Preparing views so they look correct can be done at any time in the process, either before or after placing a view onto a sheet. The way a view looks is largely based on properties of the view, which we will dig into.

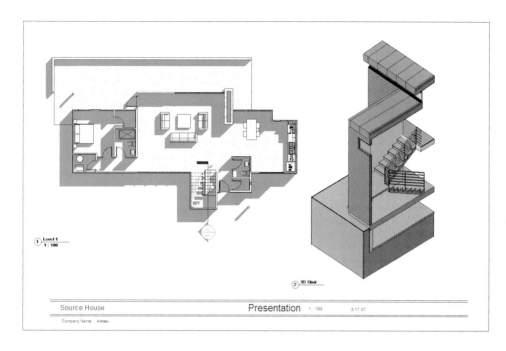

Figure 9.1

A presentation sheet with plan and 3D stair

There are several ways to access view properties. You can get to the View Properties dialog box in any of the following ways:

- Right-click any view in the Project Browser, and choose Properties from the context menu.

- Right-click in the active view window, and choose View Properties from the context menu.

- Right-click any view once it's placed on a sheet, and choose Element Properties from the context menu.

- Select View on the sheet and use the Properties button in the toolbar to open the properties.

- Select a view (click it with the mouse) in the Project Browser, and click the Properties button next to the Type Selector.

- Activate a view on the sheet using Activate View, and then use the keyboard shortcut (VP) to go to the View Properties dialog box.

View Properties

Like any other element in Revit, views have their own properties. Many of these properties can be displayed as parametric information about the view when views are placed on sheets. This is how Revit handles intelligent view titles. Other parameters control how the model is displayed graphically. Here is a list of common properties (Figure 9.2) and how they affect the view:

View Scale This sets the view scale of the drawing. You can similarly set the view scale in the View Control bar in the view window.

Scale Value This sets the drawing scale of the view that will be represented on the sheet.

Scale Value 1 This field is noneditable for the view properties. It shows what your scale value would be if it were translated to an AutoCAD paper space view. This field dynamically changes as you change the View Scale value above it.

Display Model This determines how to show (or not show) all model elements of the view. There are three settings for this field: Normal, As Underlay, and Do Not Display. In Normal, the view is unchanged from its normal graphics. As Underlay grays out all the model contents in the view—it doesn't gray out 2D information like annotations, text, or dimensions. Do Not Display turns off all the model data and shows only the 2D information in the view. This would be used in detail callouts where all the lines are 2D, and not from the model.

Detail Level This offers three choices: Coarse, Medium, and Fine. Choose one depending on the level of detail you're trying to show in your model.

Figure 9.2

Element Properties for views

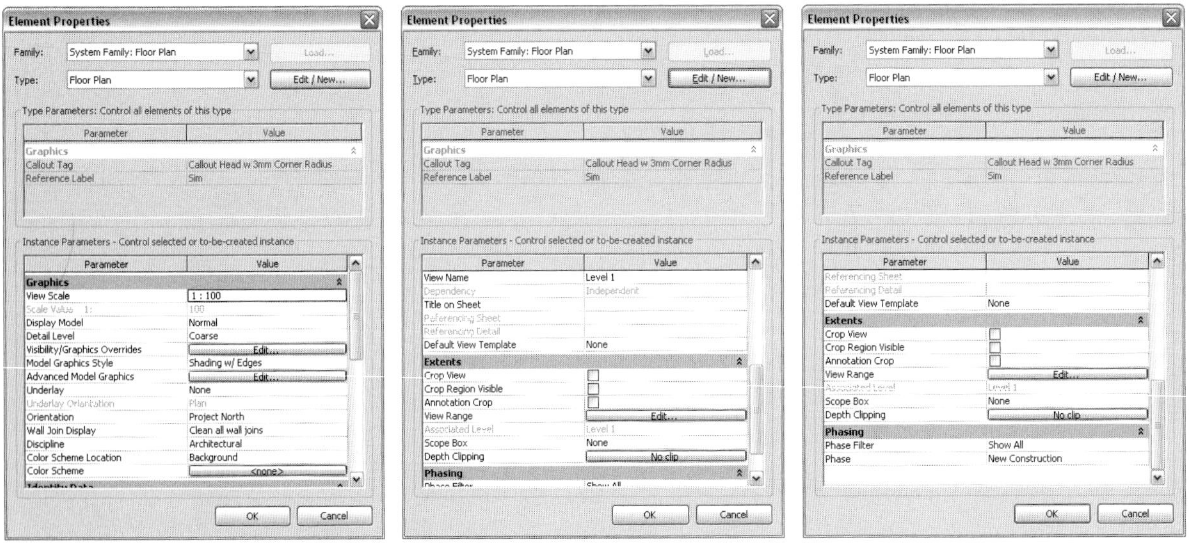

At larger scales, such as ¼″ = 1′-0″ (1:50), set the detail level to Coarse. Typically, plans or sections printed at medium or fine, but at this scale lines are so close together that they can't be differentiated on the sheet. Also, a medium or fine setting on a complex model can drastically affect load time or print time of that view.

Detail Number This sets the detail number (such as A1) on the sheet. This number must be unique to each sheet.

Rotation on Sheet This setting gives you the option to rotate the view and view tag to read from the right side of the sheet rather than from the bottom. You might use this preference if you had a tall building and wall sections didn't fit in a traditional orientation. Note that you're rotating the view, not the model. Once a view is on a sheet, it can be rotated using the Options bar when the view is selected.

Visibility/Graphics Overrides This is an alternate way to access the Visibility/Graphics Overrides dialog box for this view. This dialog box controls which elements appear in the view.

Model Graphics Style This controls how your model displays on the screen. By default, it's set to Hidden Line. Other choices are Wireframe, Shaded, and Shaded with Edges. These options are discussed in Chapter 3.

Advanced Model Graphics This option brings up the Advanced Model Graphics dialog box, which controls shadows and shading. You can also access this dialog box through the View Control bar at the bottom of the view window.

Underlay This option lets you choose another level of the building to be shown in a light gray tone as an underlay to this view. This is useful if you're trying to align walls with a floor below or when you want to make a reference to a roof from the level above.

Underlay Orientation This option is available only if you've chosen to put an underlay into your current view. You can set whether you want to see the floor plan or the ceiling plan of your underlay.

> Underlays are thought of in the 2D drafting world as a layer of trace under your current drawing. This view is useful for seeing what is happening in another view while working in your active view. In a 3D modeling world, this underlay is a live look at the model—if you delete something shown as underlay, you're deleting the element, not an abstraction.

Orientation The model is typically shown orthogonal to the view you are working in, and this extends to how the view will appear when placed on a sheet. However, in many conditions a building doesn't align with the cardinal directions of your screen and printed page. Orientation lets you align your view with either the project north (screen and sheet north) or with true north (how the building is located relative to the earth).

Wall Join Display This property is only available in plan views and offers two options: to clean up all wall joins or to clean up the same types of wall joins.

Discipline This sets the discipline (architecture, structure, mechanical, electrical, or coordination) of the view in the document set. This is useful for sorting views in the Project Browser.

Color Scheme Location This puts color fill in either the foreground (in front of model elements) or background (behind model elements).

Color Scheme This adds a color scheme to the view, and allows you to edit an existing color scheme. Use this to create color-coded plan views. This parameter is only available for plan views.

Dependency Views that are made as dependent views report which view they depend on. A dependent view displays the annotations of the parent view. If a view is not dependent, it's listed as independent.

Title on Sheet This field allows you to override the name of a view as it appears on the sheet. By default, or if this field is left blank, Revit will make the name on the sheet identical to the name of the view.

Annotation Crop This enables a second crop region that only hides and unhides annotations that are outside of it or intersecting it.

Sheet information The following four fields in the view properties are noneditable in this dialog box:

- Sheet Number
- Sheet Name
- Referencing Sheet
- Referencing Detail

These values are reported from other views in Revit. Sheet Number and Sheet Name can be modified from the sheet they reference and tell you what sheet this view has been placed on. Referencing Sheet and Referencing Detail report which views this sheet references from. In the case of our example plan, we're referencing an elevation on sheet A200.

> If multiple references depend on one view, the first reference created is reported in the View Properties dialog box.

Default View Template This sets the default view template for this view. Creating and editing view templates is covered later in this chapter.

Crop Region This option activates the crop region for a view, which limits the extent of what is visible in the view.

Crop Region Visible This setting makes the crop region visible or invisible for the view. Under some circumstances, it can be a good idea to keep the crop region visible to ensure the size of the view doesn't change. The crop region can be hidden in the print dialog box, so you don't have to worry about printing boxes around all your views.

Annotation Crop This shows the crop boundary of a parent view when views are linked.

View Range This opens the View Range dialog box discussed in Chapter 3.

Associated Level If the view is associated with a particular level (in the case of a floor plan or enlarged plan), it's reported here. This isn't an editable field.

Scope Box A scope box limits the extents of level and grids. If you have scope boxes defined, you can apply them to this view.

Depth Clipping This controls the depth of the Plan clipping and offers the options to not clip, to clip without a line, or to clip with a line.

Phase Filter This option lets you control which of the defined phase filters (basically, phase combinations) are implemented in this view. You can set the phase filters by choosing Settings → Phases.

Phase If you have phases set up in your project, you can change the phase visibility properties for the view here and set a specific phase, such as New Construction.

View Templates

View templates are powerful time-savers when you're working on a project. The purpose of a view template is to capture view settings and then apply these settings to many views with the same graphical requirements. They are a great way to ensure graphical consistency between views. You can find view templates by choosing Settings → View Templates.

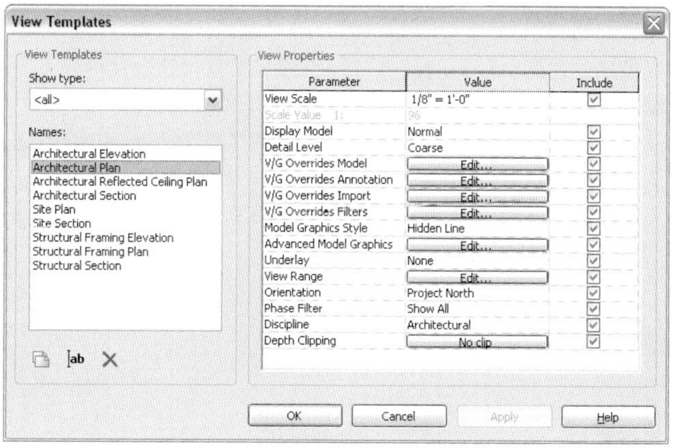

Different view templates tend to be used for plans, sections, elevations, and details. The View Templates dialog box (Figure 9.3) allows you to create a new view template, delete, or modify existing ones. You'll notice that view templates are a subset of view properties. By

Figure 9.3
View Templates dialog box

setting these values, you can create standard view characteristics and push them into other views. In the View
Template dialog box, you can preset the following view properties:

- View Scale

- Display Mode

- Detail Level

- Individual visibility and graphic overrides for model categories, annotation categories, imports, filters, and model graphics style

- Advanced Model Graphics

- Underlay

- View Range

- Orientation

- Phase Filter

- Discipline

- Depth Clipping

New in Revit 2009 is the ability to choose which parameters to include in the view template. For example, you may not want to apply a view template and have it change view scale, or detail level, but still make changes to graphic style. To exclude a parameter, uncheck the desired parameter in the Include column.

Figure 9.4

Create View Template context menu

| Open |
| Close |
| Find Referring Views |
| Make Workset Editable |
| Apply View Template... |
| Create View Template From View... |
| Duplicate View ▸ |

Although it's possible to preset all your view settings through this dialog box, you may find it easier to select the settings interactively in a view. This way, you can see the effects of settings immediately. When you like what you've set up, you can then create a new view template from your active view. Right-clicking any of the views in the Project Browser gives you an option, Create View Template from View (see Figure 9.4). You can then apply this new view template to any other view. Applying a view template to a view is a single instance event. If you apply a template to a view and then modify the template, the view will not update to match those changes. You will need to reapply the view template to that view.

To apply a view template to another view, select one or more views (not sheets) from the Project Browser and right-click. Then, choose Apply View Template from the context menu. Choose the template you want to apply to the views and Revit will update them all to use the same view properties established in the template.

Creating and Applying a View Template

In this exercise, you'll create a new view template and apply it to a view:

1. Open the `Station.rvt` model at the book's companion web page, `www.wiley.com/go/introducingrevit2009`, and open the view called Level 3 Pres. Note that there is already a Level 3 view, but this view has been set up to be a presentation-styled view. You want to create a similar view for Level 4.

2. In the Project Browser, right-click the view Level 3 Pres, and choose Create View Template from View.

3. Name the view **Plan Presentation.** Click OK. The View Templates dialog box will open (Figure 9.5)and the new template will appear in the list of view templates. From here you can make adjustments to the settings if need be. (Figure 9.5).

4. Right-click the Level 4 view, and choose Duplicate with Detailing. Doing so creates a new view called Copy of Level 4.

5. Right-click the view called Copy of Level 4, and rename it **Level 4 Pres.** It resorts itself alphabetically in the Project Browser so it appears below the Level 4 view.

6. Right-click the new view, Level 4 Pres, and choose Apply View Template. Choose the new Plan Presentation view template from the list, and click OK.

Revit allows you to apply templates to schedule views as well. The workflow is the same as with any other view, allowing automatic propagation of graphic definitions from one schedule to other schedules in the project.

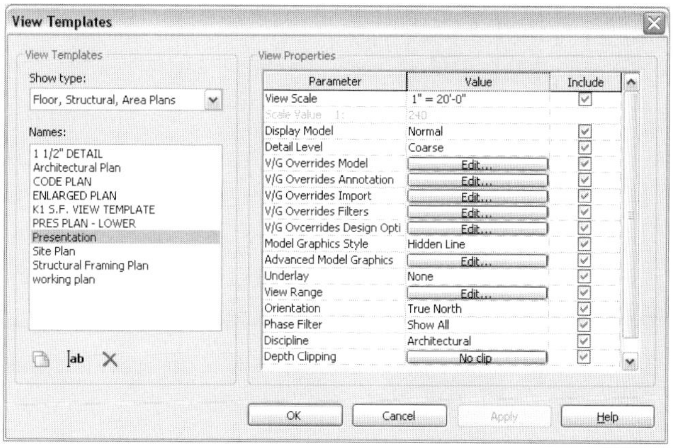

Figure 9.5

View Template dialog box

The Sheet

Construction documents are how architects convey their ideas and designs on paper to the contractor or builder so that they can build the building. The information conveyed must be sufficient and organized well enough for the builder to understand the design intent of the documents. Conflicts, errors, omissions, and coordination issues can and will occur on any document prepared by human hands. These discrepancies are magnified on the job site as cost overruns, RFIs, or lost schedule time. The goal of a good set of documents is to minimize the number of errors and convey the design clearly. Revit excels in this process by automatically managing your views and references and thereby eliminating many common errors found in traditional document sets.

Perhaps the mostly widely used type of architectural sheet system is the ConDoc system supported by the AIA. This system has identifiers for sheet name and numbering formats. If you're new to creating architectural sheets, or you're looking for additional information about construction document standards, the AIA's "Best Practices" white paper for construction documents is a good starting point:

```
http://www.aia.org/SiteObjects/files/bp%2018_05_02.pdf
```

Most firms have a defined graphic standard for sheet layout. If you're responsible for creating office-standard content, such as sheets, you should take a bit of time to create Revit sheets that mirror your firm's standards *before* you get started on a project. Not only will you then have them when you're ready to go forward into production, but you'll gain experience working with Revit families.

Before you load a sheet into your project, notice the sheet border. In the title block exercise in this section, the border is an invisible line that traces the extents of the sheet. If you move your mouse over the outside border of the sheet, the invisible lines highlight. Invisible lines are a line type that is similar to a nonplot line; they don't graphically interfere with the view on the screen.

Adding a Title Block to a Sheet

Title blocks in Revit are similar to any other family. You can create and edit them with the Family Editor. Like tags, title blocks use intelligent labels built into the family to pull data from the Revit model and apply it to the title block. This can be in the form of the view scale, project name, project address, or any parameter you see fit to use in your title blocks. To get an idea of how these labels work, let's add one to an existing sheet. This exercise presents a basic description of how to add labels and other data to your sheets:

1. Open the `Presentation - 11 x 17.rfa` file found on the book's companion web page. The file automatically opens in the Family Editor.

    This is a simple 11″ × 17″ title block. As with any sheet, you can add as much or as little detail as you want. In this sheet, you'll add a graphic scale.

2. Click the Label button () on the Family tab of the Design bar, and choose As the Type.

3. Click to drop the text in the desired location on the sheet.

4. The Edit Label dialog box (Figure 9.6) opens and asks what kind of label you'd like to add. Choose a category parameter from the list, then click the Add button (🔽) to add it to the label.

   With this dialog box you can also add prefix and suffix values to the label, and even add more than one parameter to the label.

5. Add the prefix scale, and add a space after the word. Click OK.

6. To load the title block into your project, click the Load into Projects button (🔼 Load into Projects) in the Design bar.

This process adds a label to the sheet and shows its default value (in this example, $\frac{1}{8}"= 1'-0"$). As you bring views onto the sheet, this value parametrically changes to reflect the scale of the views on the sheets.

Your sheet border may fluctuate depending on your printer type. For instance, an 11″×17″ printer typically has a print range of 10.5″× 16.5″, or ¼″ margins around the edges. On some printers, printing at paper size can lead to minor distortion of the scale of the printed views. Depending on your printer type, you may need to set your sheet size to fit within the printer margins rather than set it to the actual paper size. Once the sheet has been created, you can load it into your project by clicking the Load into Projects button on the Family tab; or, in your project, you can use the options under File → Load from Library → Load Family.

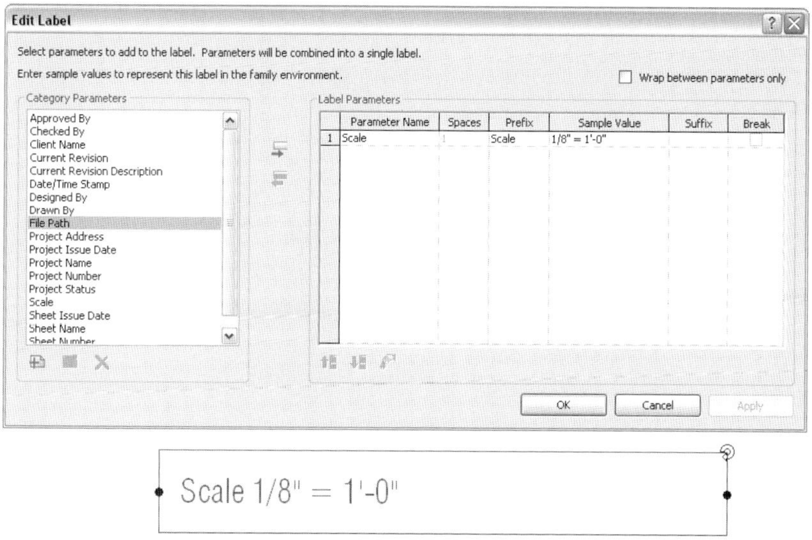

Figure 9.6

The Edit Label dialog box and resulting label

Adding a Revision Schedule to a Title Block

Revit allows you to add revision clouds and tags to sheets for tracking changes in the document set. These can be automatically tracked and displayed in a revision schedule on your title block. To place a revision schedule into a title block, follow these steps:

1. Open an existing title block family, or choose to make a new one.

2. From the View menu, choose new → Revision Schedule. Click OK to accept the defaults, then close the view.

3. From the Project Browser, open the Schedules node. You will see a Revision Schedule view. Drag and drop this view into your title block.

4. To modify the graphics and fields used in the revision schedule, right-click on the revision schedule in the Project Browser and click Properties. In the Fields parameter, you can use common fields such as Revision Number, Description, Date, and Issued To (Figure 9.7).

5. When the title block is loaded into your project and you begin to add revisions to your project, the table will automatically fill up (Figure 9.8).

Figure 9.7

Fields available for use in a revision schedule

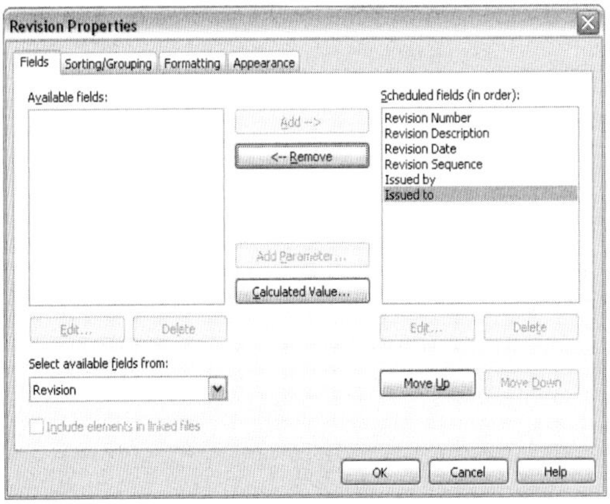

Figure 9.8

The revision schedule will fill up as you add revisions to the project.

No.	Description	Date
1	Revision 1	3/11/07
2	Revision 2	4/12/07

New in Revit 2009, you can now have revision tables that build from the bottom up. This is set in the Appearance tab of the Revision Properties dialog box (Figure 9.9). You can also set the schedule height manually, using the user-defined option. This allows you to graphically set up a blank table for your revisions (see Figure 9.10).

To add revisions to your project, select Settings → Revisions. In this dialog box, you can add revision information that will then show up in the revision schedule on your sheets. You can have revisions enumerate on a per-sheet basis, or on a projectwide basis. When you add revision clouds to your sheets (using the Drafting tab of the Design bar), set which revision it belongs to, and you'll be good to go.

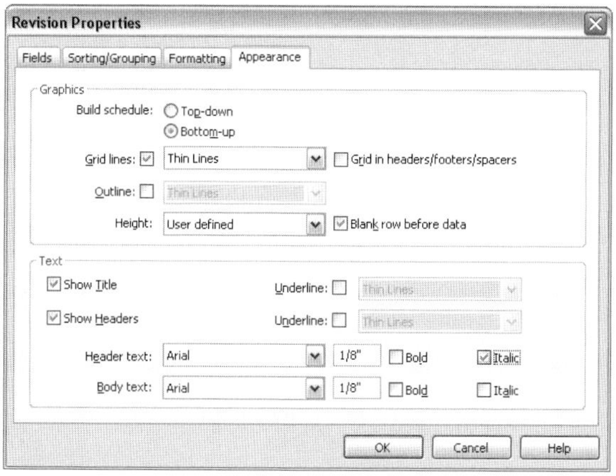

Figure 9.9
New parameters for revision schedules: Bottom-up and Schedule height

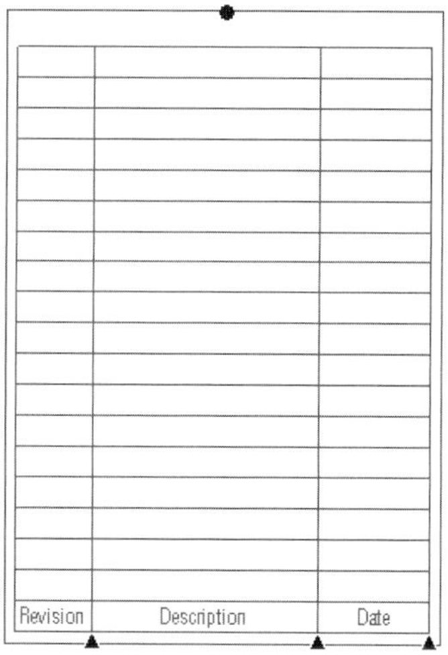

Figure 9.10
A bottom-up schedule for revisions

View Titles

A key component of a view placed on a sheet is the view title. These elements are tags that live on the sheet (see Figure 9.11) and display information about the view. Common information includes view name, scale, and detail number.

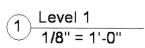

Figure 9.11
Sample view title

View titles are families like every other element in Revit, but they have a slightly different access point for editing the graphics. You can edit most families in Revit on the fly by selecting the family and clicking the Edit Family button on the Options bar. However, some families don't show this button when selected. These include view titles, level tags, callout heads, and section heads. To edit one of these types of families, locate it in the Project Browser under Families → Annotations. Right-click the family, and select the Edit option from the context menu. Doing so opens the family in the Family Editor. Editing options are similar to those available for sheets (explained earlier in this chapter) and other tags.

The view title appears automatically when you place a view on a sheet. When you place the view, the labels are automatically populated with the correct information about the view. The detail number (in Figure 9.11, it's 1) automatically increases by 1 for each view placed on the sheet. (You can change this number to a letter, or a number–letter sequence, like A1.) If the view placed on a sheet is referenced from an elevation, a section, or a callout, the detail number is automatically propagated into the view markers in the other views. If you change the detail number, it updates the tags in the other views. Basically, this means that your references are always correct on any sheet and in any view. It's impossible for views to be out of sync.

Detail numbers must be unique on each sheet. Revit doesn't allow for duplicates.

View titles are tags that report information about a view. If you select a view title on the sheet and open its properties, you'll see information about the view it is tagging. The element is called the viewport. From the type properties of the viewport, you can edit some graphic parameters for the view title such as color, whether to show the view title, and if the view title has an extension line.

If you don't want a view title to display on a sheet (as in a presentation drawing), duplicate the view title from the Type Selector, and set the view title properties to show no title and no extension line (see Figure 9.12). You don't need to create a new view title family for this purpose.

Figure 9.12

Turning off the title

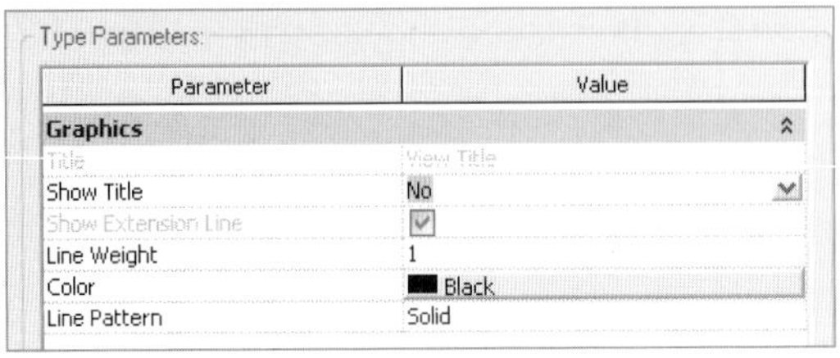

Type Parameters:	
Parameter	**Value**
Graphics	
Title	View Title
Show Title	No
Show Extension Line	☑
Line Weight	1
Color	■ Black
Line Pattern	Solid

Take care when you modify the properties of a view title. Changing a view title type changes *all* the views on all the sheets of that type. That may not necessarily be the desired effect.

Placing Views on Sheets

Placing a view onto a sheet requires a drag and drop from the Project Browser. You can drag views from the Project Browser onto a sheet name in the Project Browser, which will open the sheet view and let you place the view; or you can first open the sheet view, and then drag views onto the sheet from the Project Browser. If you don't have a sheet view set up, create a new sheet view by choosing View Tab → Sheet. Doing so opens a dialog box where you choose what type of sheet to make. Choose a sheet, and a new sheet view is created and opened. You can then start dragging and dropping any view name from the Project Browser onto the sheet (so long as the view has not already been placed on a sheet). You can place the view anywhere on the sheet, and it will be tagged with a view title.

With the exception of legend views, it's important to point out that you can't put a view onto more than one sheet. Each view is a unique, living picture of the model. Although this may not seem intuitive at first, it makes sense given that all views are guaranteed to report correct information about what sheet they're on. Every view placed on a sheet has a unique reference describing name and position on sheet.

But what do you do when you still need to place the same view on two sheets? For this purpose there is a special type of a view in Revit called a *dependent* view. This lets you create a duplicate of the view that can then be placed on another sheet. Note that this dependent view will follow any change of the original view and the two will be identical. For more details, see the section "Splitting Views across Multiple Sheets," in this chapter.

If views placed on a sheet don't fit in the space you have available, there are a couple of ways to mitigate the situation. The size of the view relative to the sheet is based on two things:

- View scale
- View extents

The view scale determines the architectural scale and can be modified, as discussed earlier. In most cases, the scale is correct, but the overall size of the view may be too large. If this is the case, there are two ways to solve this problem.

First, you can move annotations and symbols closer to the model, and tighten up the graphics to reduce the amount of empty white space. This approach buys you some precious sheet real estate. See Figure 9.13 for an example.

Moving a view marker is different from moving the view itself. For example, you can move an elevation symbol by grabbing the

Figure 9.13

Tightening up a view

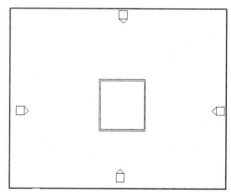
View before optimizing sheet usage

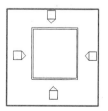
View after optimizing sheet usage

view tag without moving the front clipping plane of the elevation. In Figure 9.14, the physical extent and location of the elevation remain the same, but the tag has been repositioned.

Figure 9.14

Clipping plane location in the elevation tag

Section marks behave in similar fashion. The blue controls at the base of the head and tail graphics let you make the graphic footprint of the symbol smaller or larger without affecting the extent of the view it's referencing (shown as dashed lines in Figure 9.15).

Figure 9.15

Clipping plane location in the section tag

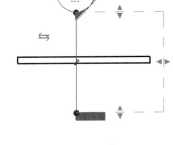

The second option to make your views fit on the sheet is to modify the view's crop region. Turning the crop region on and off was discussed in detail in Chapter 2. Modifying the crop region changes the actual size of the view and can also hide areas you don't want to show on a particular sheet. In Figure 9.16, the crop region is described by the lines bordering the view. Although there is much more to see of the model at this floor, the crop region has been minimized to show only this unit. By drawing in the crop boundaries, you can make the view smaller to display only the information necessary for that view.

Figure 9.16

Crop region

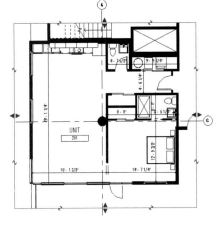

From the sheet view, you can edit views directly in order to make changes to the view in the context of the sheet layout. Select any view on a sheet, and right-click to bring up the context menu. Selecting Activate View grays out the sheet and other views placed on the sheet and lets you directly edit the view as if you had opened the view normally. You can then manipulate annotations, model data, and the crop region. When you're done editing the view, right-click in the view to bring up the context menu, and choose Deactivate View. This drops you back into sheet view.

While you're creating documents, you may decide to move a view to a different sheet than the one it's on. To do so, grab it from the sheet list in the Project Browser, and drag and drop it to the new sheet name in the list.

Splitting Views across Multiple Sheets

Revit has a specifically designed tool to let you split a view that is too large to fit on a single sheet, across a few sheets. Using the duplication method Duplicate as Dependent, available when you right-click a view title in the Project Browser, you will be able to make duplicated views that relate to one another so that you can work in one primary view and have your work appear in other, dependent views.

To understand this, let's review in more detail the three methods of duplicating a view that we touched on in Chapter 3. Right-clicking on the view names of a view in the Project Browser will give you three duplication options:

Duplicate Makes an exact copy of the model elements in a view and ignores any annotations and view-specific detail work existing in the original view. The resulting duplicated view will have no annotations or details in it. It will, however, show 3D annotations such as levels, grids, and reference planes (Figure 9.17). You will select this method of duplication when you need to make a presentation drawing of a plan in which you do not wish to see any dimensions, tags, or text existing in the original view. This method is applicable when you need to produce nice images of a project for publication purposes or marketing material ordered by your client.

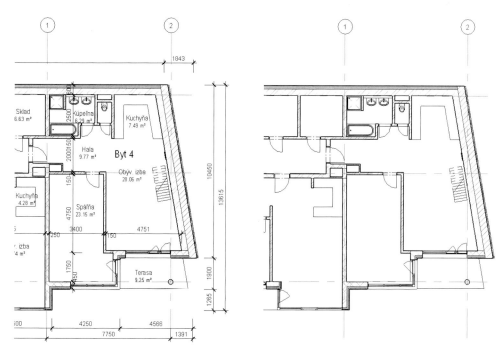

Figure 9.17
Duplicate View. The resulting duplicate view has no annotations—only the model and grids are duplicated in the view.

Model changes that happen in either the original view or in the duplicated view will propagate to the other. Annotations added in either of the two will *not* propagate to the other view.

Duplicate with Detailing Makes an exact copy of the model, annotations, and detail elements. The new view will look exactly like the original. You use this method when you wish to continue developing a plan to a different level of detail than the original. Examples for this would be when you need to make a detailed plan of a typical hotel room from a hotel floor or a technical detail of a how a column penetrates a wall, and so on.

Model changes that happen in either the original view or in the duplicated view will propagate to the other. Annotations added in either of the two will *not* propagate to the other view.

Duplicate as Dependent Makes an exact copy of the model, annotations, and detail elements. This type of duplication also maintains a dependency between the view that is duplicated and the original view. If an annotation is deleted in either view, it is deleted from both views. Any changes that happen in *either* of the two views (the original or the duplicated view) will propagate.

Use this method when you work on very large projects when the plans you want to print in a certain scale do not fit the maximum sheet or plot sizes. In this case you'll split the plan in many portions, but they'll maintain the dependencies with the other parts so they are all coordinated in both model and annotation aspect. Another scenario is when you need to place the same view on different sheets. Note that when we say *same*, we really mean *same*: you cannot change scale or any other view properties of a dependent view and not have these propagate. The only allowed and possible differences between dependent views are per view visual and graphical overrides (hiding an element or category or graphically overriding an element or category).

Use Case Scenario

You have a large project and you wish to create a sheet with your floor plan. You open a sheet view and drag the floor plan on the sheet. You realize that the plan is too big for that sheet and that splitting it into separate pieces will be necessary.

You choose the Duplicate as Dependent option on the original floor plan. If you need to split the view in order to fit the plans onto more than one sheet, then duplicate as many views as you think you need. In Figure 9.18, two dependent views will be needed but as you can imagine, in bigger projects this could range from to six to eight dependent views. Figure 9.19 clearly shows that the entire plan will not fit on the sheet size of choice for the scale selected by the user.

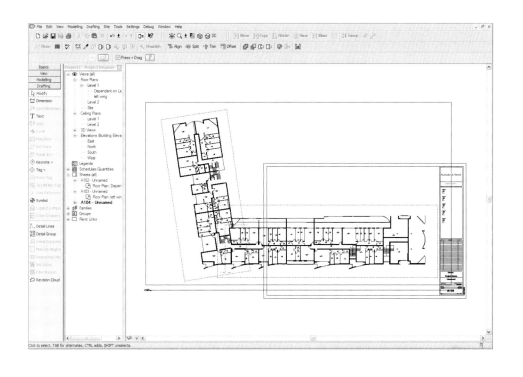

Figure 9.18
The Dependent view functionality allows you to split views and place them on separate sheets.

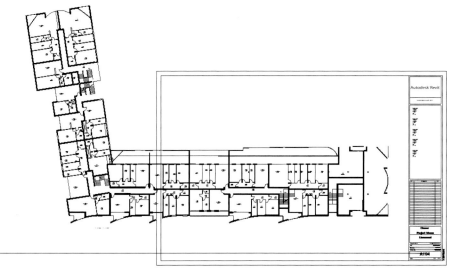

Figure 9.19
The plan does not fit on one sheet.

After creating duplicate views as dependent views, each view is cropped so that it will fit the sheet. You will notice with dependent views that the annotation crop is enabled by default. This is to keep annotations from other parts of the parent view from showing up in your cropped view. After manipulating the crop region of both views, you will end

Figure 9.20

**The two
dependent views**

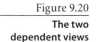

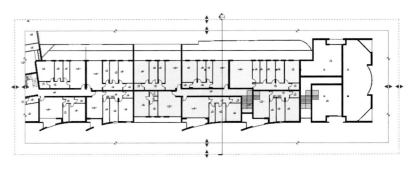

up with two dependent views, each focusing on one section of the building, as shown in Figure 9.20.

Note the double crop region: the outer boundary is the annotation crop; the inner is the model crop. When you drag the blue grips of the model crop, the annotation will follow along at a preset offset distance. Manipulating just the annotation crop has no effect on the model crop, and you cannot drag the annotation crop inside of the model crop.

If you go back to the original view and click the Show Crop toggle (![icon]) in the View Control bar, you will see both the crop regions of the dependent views and thus see how they relate to one another (Figure 9.21).

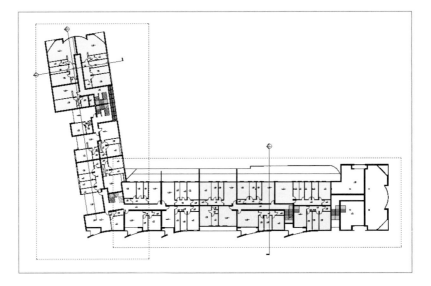

Figure 9.21

**Original view with
crop region visibil-
ity turned on**

In our example, and this can be quite typical, one wing of the building (see Figure 9.22) may be at an oblique angle relative to the screen, and by extension, the sheet. Revit provides a way to orient each dependent view so that it can better fit a sheet.

To accomplish this task, in sheet view activate the dependent view, select the crop region of the dependent view, and rotate it. Figure 9.23 shows the process of rotation of the wing. During the rotation, you will notice a green help line that finds angles of reference and can help you rotate the view parallel to the main axis of the wing. Figure 9.24 shows the rotated wing.

Figure 9.22

This wing of the building needs to be oriented to better fit the sheet.

Figure 9.23

The crop region can be rotated so that the view is rotated parallel with the model.

Figure 9.24

**The plan now fits
the sheet.**

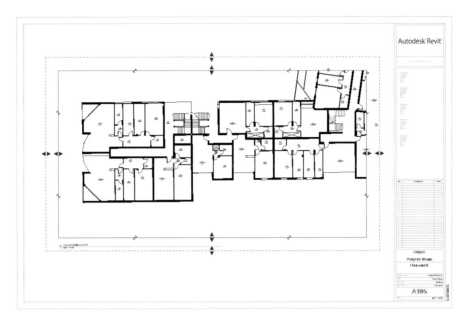

You can accomplish the same rotation by opening the dependent view itself and then rotating the crop region. Do not attempt to rotate dependent view crop regions from the original (parent) view.

You will also notice that rotating a dependent view reorients the tags in the view so they remain readable on the sheet (see Figure 9.25).

Figure 9.25

**Tags have been
smartly rotated to
be legible.**

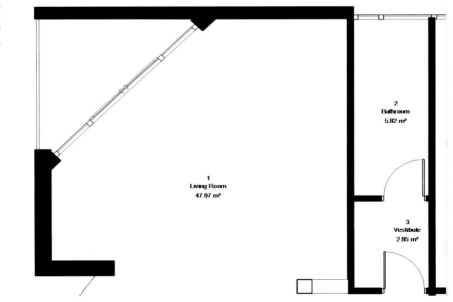

Whenever you are in any of the dependent views, you can see the other view by selecting the Crop/Do Not Crop view option in the View Control bar ( ). This will turn off the cropping and the other views will show up displaying the crop boundaries that are inactive.

As you continue working with a project divided between multiple dependent views, you will notice that any addition or change to annotation as well as model elements will appear in all views associated with the original parent view.

One very neat detail: imagine your project has 20-plus floors and the size was such that you needed to divide it into four dependent views. After you have spent time dividing the first four on Level 1, you need to do the same thing for the remaining floors. Revit streamlines this process for you. In the right-click menu of the original view that you made the dependent views from, there is an option called Apply Dependent Views that will open a dialog box where you select all the views you want to apply the same dependent view division to. With one click, this will create many dependent views.

Match Lines and View Tags

Match lines are graphic indicators in plan views that depict a split in the drawing because the whole building could not fit on a sheet (Figure 9.26). In Revit, the match line is a 3D line that extends (as grid lines do) through the entire project.

The Matchline tool (🗇) can be found in the Drafting tab of the Design bar and is drawn as you would any other line in Revit. In the properties of a match line you can define the top and the bottom constraints. This is needed when the building does not have the same floor plan through all floors, and the break line for dependent views might not be applicable to all views in the same way.

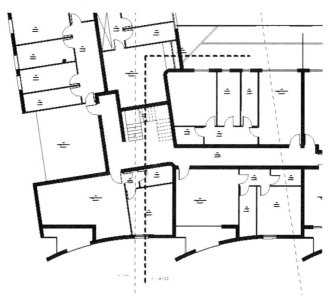

Figure 9.26

The match line indicates a break in the view.

View References

View references are a special type of annotation applicable to views only. They reference other dependent views and hyperlink to them.

You will find the View Reference tool (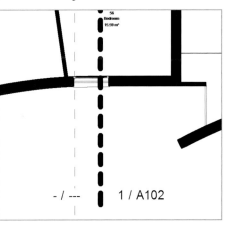) in the Drafting tab of the Design bar. If you are in a dependent view and select a view reference, it will instantly recognize the other dependent view and create a reference and hyperlink to it. If you are in the original view when more dependent views are present, you can select the View Reference tool, hover the cursor over a crop region of a view you want to reference, and place the view reference.

Note that the view reference will be empty if the dependent view is not placed on a sheet. The moment you place it on a sheet, it will fill in the number of the reference (Figure 9.27).

Figure 9.27

View reference tags for two dependent views: one placed on a sheet and another one not

A few more tips about dependent views:

- When you select Duplicate as Dependent View, the dependent view will appear as a node under the original view in the Project Browser.

- A dependent view can at any point be converted to an independent view. You can do that in two different ways:

    - Right-click on the dependent view and select Duplicate with Detailing. This will keep the dependent view *and* create a new independent view.

    - Right-click on the dependent view and select Convert to Independent View.

CHAPTER 10

Annotations

No set of documents is complete without annotations that add textual or numeric descriptions to the drawings. The need to add dimensions, tags, and text notes to aid in the communicating design intent is still very much a part of the BIM workflow; and Revit is designed to support that workflow with some very intelligent, bidirectional annotation tools.

Topics we'll cover include:

- ▦ **Annotating your project**
- ▦ **Understanding and adding tags**
- ▦ **Dimensions**
- ▦ **Adding text and keynotes**

Annotating Your Project

In any set of documents, showing geometry alone isn't sufficient to communicate all the information a builder or fabricator needs to construct the building. Tags, keynotes, text, and dimensions all need to be added to the drawing in order to clearly and concisely guide construction. They assist you in taking your model data and clearly documenting it for others to read and understand.

Starting where you left off, with some views placed on sheets, you'll continue to build out your set of drawings by adding annotations to the views.

In Revit, annotations, dimensions, and tags are placed in the views themselves, *not on the sheet.* This might be different from the way you are used to working in AutoCAD, so remember this well. This allows you to annotate a view at any point in the process, before or after views have been placed on a sheet.

Tags

Figure 10.1

The default wall tag in Revit

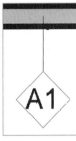

Tags are textual labels for architectural elements such as doors, walls, windows, rooms, and many other objects that architects typically need to reference in a set of drawings. In Revit, tags are intelligent bidirectional symbols that report information stored in the properties of an element. A value can be directly edited from the tag; likewise, editing an element's properties affects the tag. For example, selecting a wall tag (Figure 10.1) returns the wall type that is set in the properties of the wall itself. This is a simple, standard-looking wall tag. The tag, however, can display richer information, such as the wall's fire rating or manufacturer, or any other value of the wall's properties. You can design it to suit any graphical and informational requirements that you have.

Loading Tags

Revit comes with a variety of predefined generic tags. All of these can be customized to meet your office's graphic requirements. The set of tags preloaded into the default template covers many common requirements but is by no means exhaustive. Many firms have created their own tags and added them to their project templates so they are available during project development.

Most categories of elements in Revit can be tagged, and you can load multiple types of tags for each category. Tags are loaded like any other family or component in Revit. Choose File → Load from Library → Load Family, and navigate to the tag you want to add to the project.

Placing Tags

You can insert tags from the Tag button on the Drafting tab of the Design bar (see Figure 10.2).

Figure 10.2

The Drafting tab

The Tag button allows you to load additional tags without having to cancel the command and go back to the Load Families tool. This button is only available in certain types of views (the Tag button is deactivated in 3D views, schedule views, etc.). If you click this button but don't have a tag loaded, you're prompted to do so. During tag placement, the Options bar lets you position a tag in several ways. Figure 10.3 shows how the Options bar appears in this circumstance.

Tags can have a horizontal or vertical orientation and may or may not have a leader line. In the case of a wall tag, you typically have a leader coming from the wall, whereas you don't typically use a leader with a door or window tag.

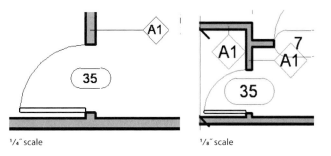

Figure 10.3

The Options bar when a tag is inserted

Tags will also dynamically adjust to the scale of the drawing. If the text of a tag is set to read at ⅛″ (3mm), it appears in the view at such a size to always print in that absolute size regardless of the scale (see Figure 10.4). This means that once a tag is placed in a view, the view can be resized and the tags will remain the same printing size. Depending on the scale of the drawing, you might need to adjust the position or location of the tags for better visibility, but once a tag is inserted, you will never have to reinsert a tag simply to change scale.

Figure 10.04

Tags change with the view scale.

¼″ scale   ⅛″ scale

Tags can be added to your project after the design phase or during the actual creation of the elements. It really depends on the workflow you follow. A majority of firms first design and then document and annotate later in the process. At the same time, small practices sometimes tend to annotate during the design phase. In this case, for some elements such as doors and windows, you have the option to tag during placement, which will annotate your drawings right from the start.

The Tag (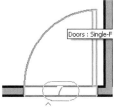) button presents three options for inserting tags:

By Category This option allows you to tag elements in the model by category or type. Examples are doors, walls, windows, and other commonly tagged elements. After you choose By Category, the elements you can tag highlight as you mouse over them in your view. Revit also displays a ghosted preview image of the tag you're inserting and the value in that tag, as shown in Figure 10.5.

Multi-Category Use the Multi-Category tag when you want to tag an element across different family types—for instance, when you're using a similar glazing type in your windows and exterior doors and you want to be able to tag the glazing consistently. The Multi-Category tag allows you to have the same tag and tag value for the glazing in both families. (Fire rating is another common application of this tag.)

Figure 10.05

Tagging by category

Material The Material tag lets you tag the materials in a given family. For example, tagging a wall by material exposes materials used in the wall construction such as gypsum board or metal studs. This allows you to tag these elements separately.

Changing a Tag Value

There are two ways to modify the value text in a tag. Selecting the tag makes the value text an active control and turns the text blue; just click the blue text and begin typing. You are not only changing the value displayed in the tag but also changing the type property of that element (the Type Mark parameter). The second option is to open the properties of the element being tagged. Using a wall example again, if you select the wall, open its type properties, and change the Type Mark field to a new value, the wall tag updates instantly and reflects this change. See Figure 10.6 for examples of each location.

Figure 10.6

Changing the wall type

Whichever way you choose, it is important to know that you will be changing the symbol text for every instance of that element type and thus of its tags. Therefore, if you change the wall type mark from A1 to A2, it will change every instance of that wall that was previously tagged A1 and all wall tags will thus display A2. If 10 walls were tagged A1, all 10 are now A2.

Only if you use the first method to modify text—changing it directly in the tag—are you notified that you're making a global change (see Figure 10.7). If you choose to change the value within the Properties dialog box, Revit assumes you understand this will change that property for each of the elements of this type within the model.

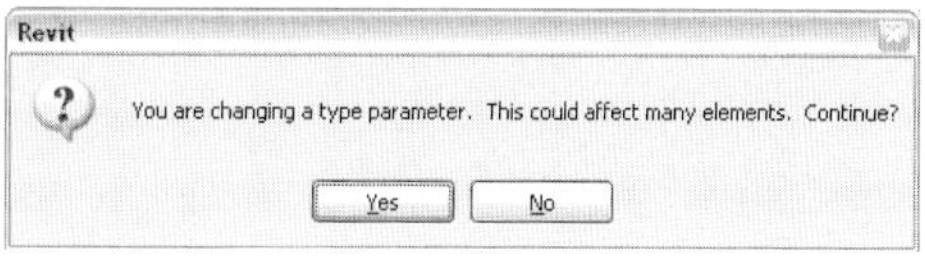

Figure 10.07

Warning when changing the wall type from a tag

Some tags only report instance values—values that are unique to the individual element. A room tag or door tag is a common example. In that case, changing the property of the room or the tag will have an effect only on that one room. The room tag graphics are consistent, but the room name varies from room to room. Doors are often tagged like this, with a unique numeric value for each door. With these types of tags, Revit will detect if you enter duplicate values and warn you when that happens.

> When you create elements that you plan to tag, you can add the tag text directly into the properties of the family or element. To do this, open the Properties dialog box and modify the Type Mark field.

The Tag All Not Tagged Tool

Instead of manually tagging each and every element one by one, in Revit you can tag many elements at once using the Tag All Not Tagged tool on the Drafting tab of the Design bar. This timesaving feature lets you tag all the elements in a view with a single click. During early phases of design, you often aren't concerned with tags and annotations but are more focused on the model. Tags can become graphic clutter that obscures the design at times.

Later in the process, when you're happy with the design, you may want to annotate the drawing quickly. This is where the Tag All Not Tagged tool is helpful. When you select this tool, the dialog box shown in Figure 10.8 opens. You can orient your tag or add a leader to it before tagging all the listed elements in your current view.

If you have some elements selected, you can choose to tag only those selected elements.

Figure 10.8

Tag All Not Tagged dialog box

In the Source_House_Begining_Detailing.rvt file at the book's companion web page, www.wiley.com/go/introducingrevit2009, open the view called First Floor Plan. In this view, using the tools mentioned, let's add tags for the doors and walls:

1. From the Drafting tab in the Design bar, select Tag → By Category.

2. Mover your cursor over a door, and click when it highlights. Make sure your leaders are turned off in the Options bar for door tags.

3. Highlight and select the interior walls. For wall tags, use the Options bar to turn on leaders and adjust the leader length from ½″ to ¼″. The finished floor plan looks like Figure 10.9.

Figure 10.9

Finished floor plan

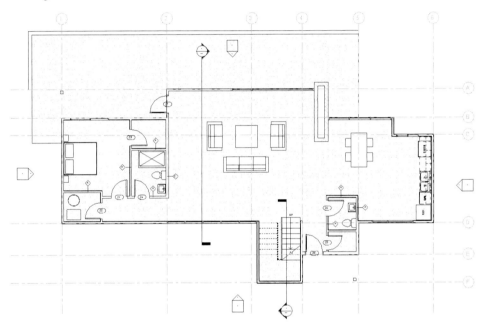

If you have forgotten to activate leaders when creating the tags, don't despair—you can always add them by selecting the tags, individually or with multiselect, and checking the Leader check box in the Options bar. The same applies if you decide you don't want tags to have leaders.

Dimensions

Dimensions are used to convey the distance or angle between elements or parts of elements. In Revit, a dimension is a bidirectional annotation that essentially tags distance or size. The word *bidirectional* means that you can edit the distance directly when elements are drawn or selected; likewise, the dimension updates automatically as the distance between elements changes (Figure 10.10). Dimensions are annotations, making them view-specific elements that appear only in the view where they're drawn. If you need to repeat the same dimensions from view to view, you can copy and paste dimensions; they will locate the same model elements. Use the paste-aligned method described in Chapter 5.

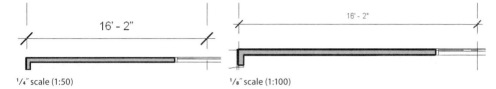

¹/₄″ scale (1:50)   ¹/₈″ scale (1:100)

Figure 10.10

Dimensions dynamically change by scale.

   The parametric nature of dimensions in Revit means that dimensions can't be overridden or cheated numerically as they can be in CAD. This preserves the integrity of the model and the design. If you hear that Revit "won't let you cheat," it's true. And trust us, this is for your own good! Dimensions in Revit report the actual value of the distance they span. If the distance is 4′-0″ (120cm), the dimension reads 4′-0″ (120cm). You can't change the numeric value of a dimension without changing the model. For example, if the distance between two elements is supposed to be 3′-6″ (106cm), you would need to modify the distance between the two elements to get the dimension to report your intent.

   Like all annotations in Revit, dimensions adjust to the scale of the drawing. They will always appear at the proper scale in the view. If you change the view scale, the dimensions automatically resize. In Figure 10.10, the first image shows the dimensions at ¼″ (1:50) scale, and the second image shows the same dimension string after the scale was changed to ⅛″ (1:100) in the View Control bar.

   By default, a linear string of dimensions only dimensions parallel entities. Non-parallel elements by their very nature have a dynamic dimensional relationship. The dimension between non-parallel elements will vary based on where the dimension falls between them. Because of this, Revit defaults to only allowing parallel objects to be dimensioned. Dimensions in Revit always read from the bottom or the right. This follows standard architectural sheet layout conventions. Dimensions autosnap horizontally or vertically to align with another dimension string if they're close to being in line with each other.

   We mentioned that you cannot override the numeric value of a dimension, but this is not to say you cannot override the value with text. New in this release of Revit 2009 is the ability to add text to multiple parts of the dimension string, including replacing the value with text. Figure 10.11 shows some examples of dimensions with text integrated.

Figure 10.11

Examples of dimensions with text

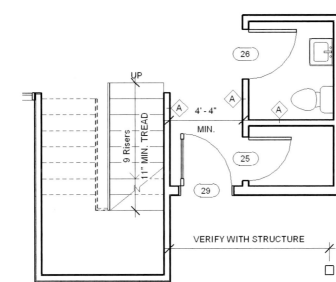

To add text to a dimension string, select the dimension, then click on the blue dimension text. A dialog box will open allowing you to add text above, below, as prefix, as suffix, or even replace the value with text (Figure 10.12).

By default, the dimension string will use the actual numeric value, shown in the upper portion of the dialog box. You can then add text by typing into the various text fields for above, below, prefix, and suffix.

To replace the value with text, choose the Replace with Text option. This will disable the prefix and suffix fields and allow you to type any text you want. Figure 10.13 shows the dialog box, with the text V.I.F written in.

Figure 10.12

The Dimension Text dialog box

Figure 10.13

Use the Replace with Text option to write in a text value for the dimension string.

If you try to add a number in this text field and click OK, you'll get a warning and will not be allowed to make that kind of edit. Figure 10.14 shows the result when trying to replace 7′-8″ with 8′.

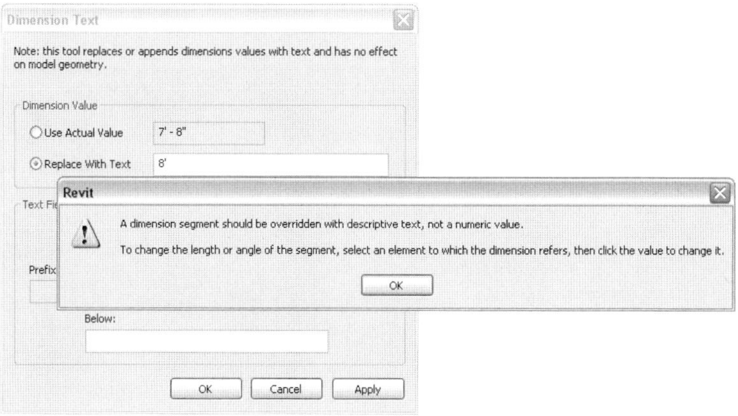

Figure 10.14

Replacing a dimension value with numeric values is not allowed.

Dimensioning Your Model

You can find the Dimension tool (⌐ Dimension) on both the Basics and Drafting tabs of the Design bar.

To create dimensions, select the Dimension tool, and begin picking elements in the model to dimension. Parallel edges (references) of elements will highlight as the mouse moves over them, indicating a valid dimension candidate. After two references are selected, a preview graphic of the dimension line appears and moves with the mouse. When you've finished selecting references, move the dimension string to the desired location, and click empty screen space to finish the string.

When you add dimensions in Revit, use the Tab key to cycle through the selection options.

Once the Dimension tool is activated, buttons on the Options bar (see Figure 10.15) allow you choose the type of dimension to create; they preset some behaviors to aid in placement. Here are the buttons in the order in which they're listed (from left to right) on the Options bar:

Aligned Aligned dimensions (✎) are the default dimension style. It places dimensions to elements parallel to the element itself. In the case of an angled wall, the dimension reads parallel to the angled wall (the top dimension in Figure 10.16).

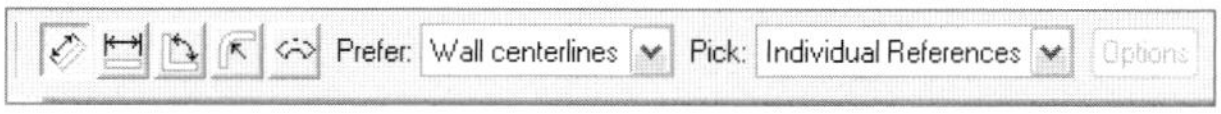

Figure 10.15

Dimensions Options bar

Linear Linear dimensions ( ) are parallel to the sheet edges. In the case of your angled wall, the dimension is parallel to the bottom of the sheet, as shown in the bottom dimension of Figure 10.16.

Angular Angular dimensions ( ) show the angle between two elements.

Radial Radial dimensions ( ) are used to dimension to the radius of an arc or circle.

Arc Length Arc length dimensions ( ) show the length of an arc.

The other choices on the Options bar allow you to choose your preferred pick points:

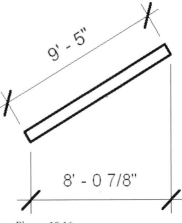

Figure 10.16

Aligned and linear dimensions

Prefer This gives you the option to choose what references in walls you want the dimension to prefer during placement. You can change what a dimension prefers during placement by using the Tab key to cycle through nearby references. The options shown in Figure 10.17 are Wall Centerlines, Wall Faces, Center of Core, and Face of Core.

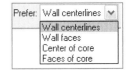

Figure 10.17

Prefer wall dimension locations

Pick This gives you the option to either choose individual references in sequence using the Individual References option or use the Entire Wall option, in which case you click walls and Revit automatically finds the ends of the walls and puts a dimension there. The Entire Wall selection has additional options—click the Options button in the Option bar—that can be further refined so door and window openings or even intersecting walls and gridlines can be automatically generated. The autodimensioning options are shown in Figure 10.18.

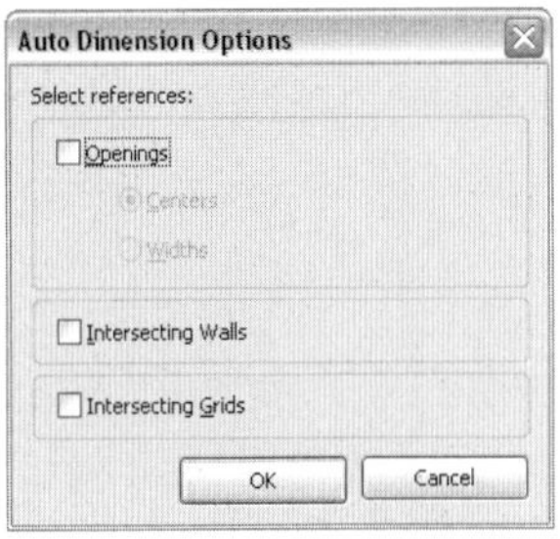

Figure 10.18

Autodimensioning options when using the Pick Wall method

To dimension non-coplanar entities, such as two walls, select the first element. Then, before selecting the second element, use the Tab key to cycle through the selection options until you highlight a *point,* as shown in the enlarged door jamb in Figure 10.19.

The finished dimension appears in Figure 10.20.

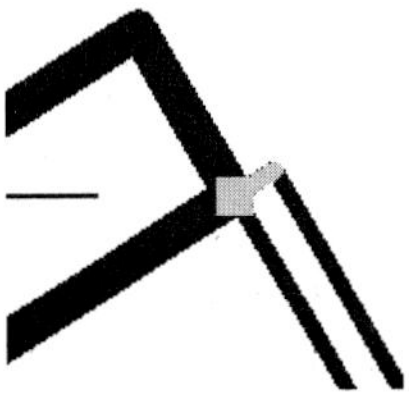

Figure 10.19

Points can be dimensioned to, as shown in this enlarged door jamb.

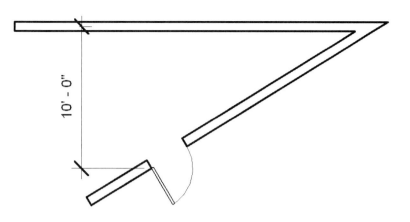

Figure 10.20
The finished dimension

Baseline and Ordinate Dimensions

New to Revit 2009 are some additional type parameters for linear and aligned dimensions that will allow you to create *baseline* and *ordinate* dimension string formats. These tend to be used by structural engineers and construction firms, but we'll explain the behavior for you.

Baseline Dimensions

Baseline dimensions are multiple dimensions measured from the same baseline (see Figure 10.21). Some construction firms practice this type of dimensioning, especially when nonorthogonal references need to be documented for clearer construction.

The way baseline dimensions work is such that the first reference selected will be the baseline for the dimension. The second reference selected will determine the direction of the dimension string. All next clicks will follow that direction.

Figure 10.21
Baseline dimensions

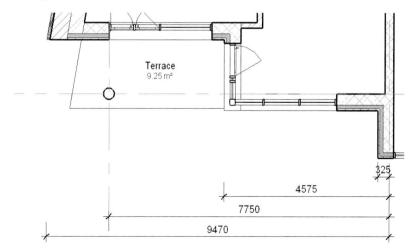

If during placement of the dimension string at some point you select a reference on the opposite side of the baseline reference, that new reference will become the new baseline reference, the dimension string will restack, and all strings will reference that new baseline reference.

Creating a Baseline or Ordinate Dimension Style

You will find examples of baseline dimensions in the default template delivered with Revit 2009, but you will most probably have your own office template and will need to create your own types. To create your own baseline dimension type:

1. Select any of your existing linear dimension types, open the Element Properties dialog box, and then select Edit/New.

2. Duplicate the type and give it a unique name (we suggest using the word *baseline* in the name).

3. Select the Dimension String Type property and change it from Continuous to Baseline (Figure 10.22).

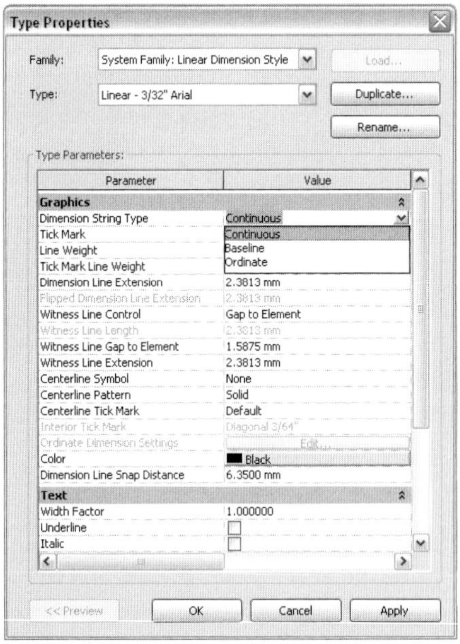

Figure 10.22

Changing the Dimension String Type property

You will notice that once a baseline dimension is created, a flip control symbol shows up: this control is located at the origin witness line and lets you flip the dimension baseline from end to end (Figure 10.23). You can access the same behavior by right-clicking and selecting Flip Dimension Direction from the context menu.

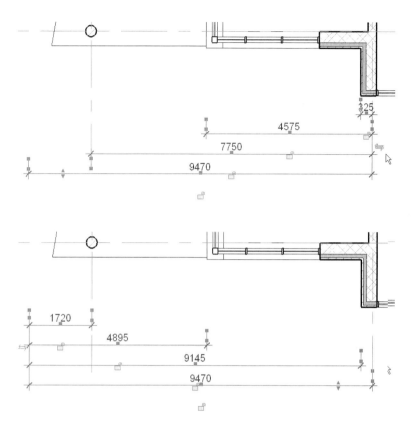

Figure 10.23

Flipping baseline dimensions

Also notice that when selecting a baseline dimension a drag control appears on the screen (Figure 10.24)—this will let you drag the entire set of dimensions to modify the baseline offset and thus adjust the position of the baseline dimension.

You can change a baseline dimension back to linear dimension using the Type Selector in the Options bar. All the dimension strings will collapse back into one string.

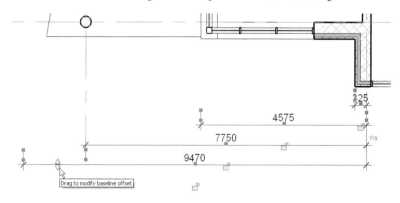

Figure 10.24

Drag control for baseline dimension

Ordinate Dimensions

Ordinate dimensions measure the perpendicular distance from an origin point called the datum to a dimensioned element. These types of dimensions are more typically used by mechanical and structural engineers. Using the same example, Figure 10.25 shows how that same dimension looks when converted to an ordinate dimension type.

Figure 10.25

Ordinate dimension type

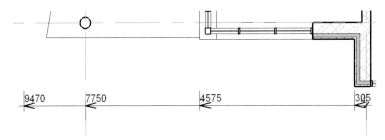

Creating your ordinate dimension type is the same as creating the baseline type, as previously explained. The difference is that you will select Ordinate as a Dimension String Type when creating the new dimension type.

New to Revit 2009 is a better recognition of intersection points of reference planes, grids, levels, walls, and lines. This allows for much more effective dimensioning, which was challenging in previous releases.

In this release, any intersection between the above-mentioned elements is recognized and can be dimensioned to or from. When you dimension to an intersection, a green dot will appear, indicating the crossing point as a reference. When dimensioning from an intersection point, you'll need to use the Tab key to get to the intersection point.

Figure 10.26

The Type Properties dialog box for a dimension

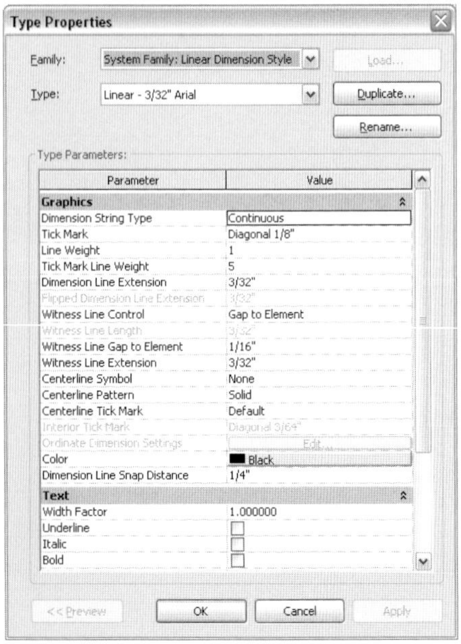

Modifying Dimension Appearance

By selecting a dimension and opening its properties, you uncover a host of options, as shown in Figure 10.26. You can also access this dialog box by choosing Settings → Annotations → Dimensions → Linear.

First, we'll discuss the parameters for which you can set values. These are listed in the upper pane of the dialog box:

Dimension String Type   This allows you to change dimensions from continuous, baseline, or ordinate dimensions, as we just covered.

Tick Mark   This option allows you to select the style and size of the tick marks in Revit. The *tick mark* is the angled line crossing the intersection of the witness and dimension lines (shown in Figure 10.27).

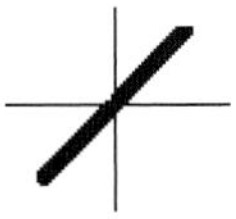

Figure 10.27

Tick mark

Tick Mark Line Weight This option controls the line thickness for the tick mark only.

Dimension Line Extension This option controls the length of the extension to the dimension line after the tick mark (shown in Figure 10.28). The *dimension line* is the line the dimension text sits on or over.

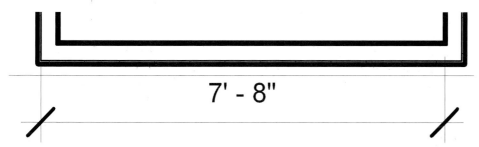

Figure 10.28
Dimension line extension

Flipped Dimension Line Extension This option is available only if Tick Mark is set to Arrow. It controls the extent of the dimension line beyond the flipped arrow if the arrow flips on the ends of the dimension string.

Witness Line Control A *witness line* is the line parallel to the elements dimensioned and perpendicular to the dimension line. This option toggles the setting to show or not show the second witness line. To have both witness lines show, use the Gap to Element setting.

Witness Line Length This field becomes active only if the Witness Line Control is set to Fixed Dimension Line. You can set the length of all the witness lines in the dimensions.

Witness Line Gap to Element This option controls the distance between the witness line and the element dimensioned.

Witness Line Extension This option controls the length of the witness line after a tick mark.

Centerline Symbol This option shows a symbol if you've dimensioned to the centerline of an element (see Figure 10.29).

Centerline Pattern This field changes the line style of a centerline.

Center Tick Mark This field by default is blank. It allows you to add a tick mark on the inside of the witness lines.

Interior Tick Mark This option is available only when Tick Mark is set to Arrow. It designates the tick-mark display for inner witness lines when adjacent segments of a dimension line are too small for arrows to fit.

Color This field changes the color of the dimension strings.

Dimension Line Snap Distance This option aids in the use of stacked dimension strings.

Figure 10.29
Centerline symbol

Next, let's look at the options in the Text pane, which occupies the lower half of the Type Properties dialog box:

Text Style Options You can make the text bold, italic, or underlined.

Text Size This field changes the size of the dimension text.

Text Offset This option changes the distance the text is placed from the dimension line.

Read Convention This option shows you the default values of the dimension text position. In Up, then Left (the default value), the dimension text reads from the bottom of the sheet and then from the right of the sheet, appearing above the dimension string depending on whether it's horizontal or vertical.

Text Font This field controls the font of the dimension string. It's possible in Revit to have a font for dimensions that's separate from notes or other text.

Text Background The options for this value are Opaque and Transparent. It changes the appearance of the box surrounding the text.

Units Format This option controls the dimension string tolerance and unit displays.

Show Opening Height This option returns the height of an opening below the dimension string. In the dimensioned window shown in Figure 10.30, the width is shown as 3′-0″ and the height as 4′-0″.

Note that while the position of the dimension text is defined in the properties of the dimension type, you can still manually change the position to avoid a clash of information and move the text to a more appropriate place in the project. To do that, use the blue dot displayed right below the dimension text when a dimension chain is selected, and move it around. Notice that when you do that, if you used the new functionality and have added text to the dimension text, all prefixes, suffixes, the text above, and the text below will also move, as they behave like one group of elements. Figure 10.31 shows a dimension value moved away from the string. Notice that the automatic leader and all dimension text values are preserved.

Figure 10.30

Show opening height

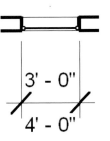

Figure 10.31

You can move dimension values interactively.

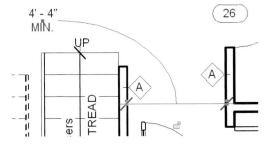

Dimensioning a Floor Plan

Now that we have covered the basics of dimensioning, let's try it on the first floor plan view you've been working on in the Source_House_End_Detailing.rvt file. Using the default dimension settings and the linear dimension style, you'll add dimension strings to the walls in the floor plan.

For interior walls, choose the Dimension tool. In the Options bar, select Wall Faces from the Prefer menu.

For the gridlines, choose the Entire Walls option from the Pick drop-down. Before placing the dimensions, click the Options button, and then select Intersecting Gridlines. Pick parallel walls that are perpendicular to the grids, and you'll see the ease with which a string of dimensions can be generated (Figure 10.32).

The finished floor plan should look similar to Figure 10.33.

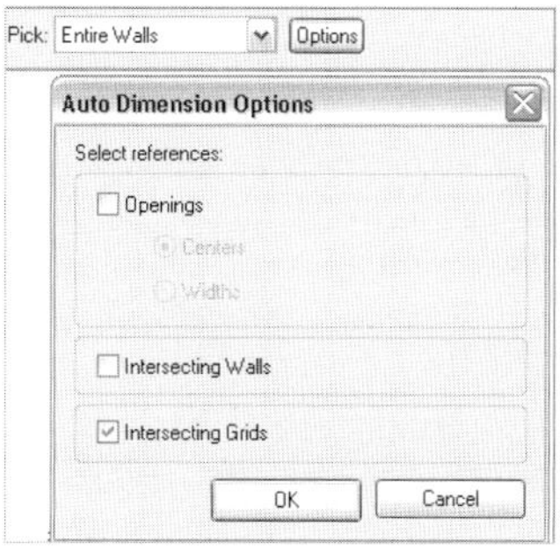

Figure 10.32

The Options bar for a dimension

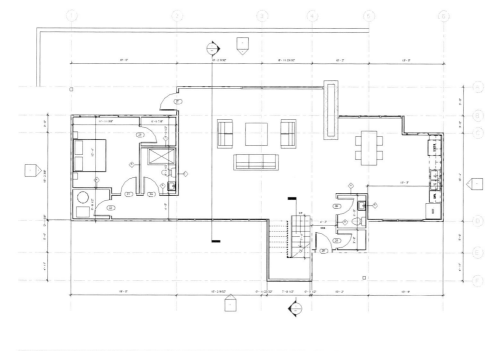

Figure 10.33

The dimensioned first-floor plan

This shows you how to use automated dimensioning. Of course, if you don't change the Pick option to Entire Walls but to Individual References, you could make individual dimensions wherever needed.

Text and Keynotes

Notes are a critical part of communicating design and construction intent to contractors, subs, and owners. No drawing set would be complete without textual definitions and instructions on how to assemble the building. Revit has two primary ways of adding this information to the sheets: text and keynotes. Text in Revit consists of words arranged in paragraphs with or without a leader. Text can be used for specialized annotations, sheet notes, legends, and similar applications. Keynotes, the other tool for annotating a drawing, are element specific and can be scheduled and standardized in the Revit database. We'll explore the use and function of both tools in this section.

Text

Text is easy to add to your view. You can access the Text tool (|T Text|) from both the Basics and Drafting tabs in the Design bar.

Text can be added to any view, including a 3D view. To begin adding text, click the Text button after you've opened the view of your choice, select where in the view you wish to place text, and begin typing. To edit text you've already placed, click the text to highlight it, and then click it again to activate the text box. To move text once you've located it, select it and drag it, or use the Move command.

When you use the Move command, you move both the text and the leader. When you move text by dragging the arrow icon, you move only the text box, leaving the leader anchored in its original position.

To drag an entire textnote, select the note and drag it.

As with all the tools in Revit, there are ways to change the look and feel of your text during creation. Once you've selected the Text tool, the Type Selector and Options bar highlight, giving you some formatting choices. Figure 10.34 shows the options available with the Text command.

Figure 10.34

Text format tools

The Type Selector allows you to choose a style for the text you're using. Each text style is managed through the familiar Properties dialog box box, where you can modify parameters such as font and size. To create a new text style from an existing one, click the Properties button in the Type Selector, and choose Edit/New in the Properties dialog box. From there, choose Duplicate, give the style a new name, and make your adjustments to the properties. This process is identical to adding a new type to any existing Revit family.

Justification options are displayed as icons, allowing for left-, center-, or right-justified text.

After selecting a note, click the blue letters to edit the text. When you're editing the text, you're given additional formatting in the Options bar for bold, italic, and underline  . These apply to whatever text you've selected in the note.

Text Properties

Most text parameters are located in the Type Properties dialog box for text. It's here that you define font, style, and size. Figure 10.35 shows the properties available for text. The following list discusses these properties and how you can modify those values to customize your text within your project:

Color This is where you can choose the font color.

Line Weight This option allows you to choose the line weight for the elements associated with this text type. This includes the line weights of any leaders or arrowheads. Note that line weight options for the leader are found under Object Styles.

Background This gives you the option to have a background for your text box that is either opaque or transparent. Opaque creates a white box (blotting out the model behind it, as shown in Figure 10.36). Transparent leaves the text box clear and lets you see the model data behind the text (Figure 10.37).

Tab Size This option sets the distance your cursor offsets when you use the Tab key in a text box.

Bold, Italic, Underline These options mirror the commands available on the Options bar, allowing you to bold, italicize, or underline your text.

Width Factor This value lets you control the width of your text. A value less than one reduces the width of the text by a factor, and a value greater than one makes the text wider.

Figure 10.35

The Type Properties dialog box for text

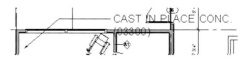

Figure 10.36

Opaque text box

Figure 10.37

Transparent text box

After you've placed a text box in the drawing, you have the option to go back and change some of the parameters. When text is selected, check the Options bar: you can add and remove leaders and change the text justification (see Figure 10.38).

Figure 10.38

Adding leaders using the Options bar

The leader buttons allow you to choose a leader style for your text before you add it to the view. From left to right in Figure 10.38, you can choose none, one segment, two segments, or an arc for a leader line. You can add any number of additional leaders to the left or right of the text box. The first two leader options are for leaders with lines, whereas the second two are for leaders with arcs. (You can't have a text box with both linear and arc leaders.) You also have the option to remove leaders you've added. Note that leaders will be removed in the opposite order in which they were added.

Model Text

Model text is 3D text that appears as a model element in your project. The properties of model text are similar to the properties of other model elements, rather than those of text. Model text can have thickness, material, keynote, and other common model properties.

A classic use for model text is signage for a building entrance (Figure 10.39).

Model text height dimensions are given relative to the model. If you want the text to be 3′ tall in the model, it stays 3′ tall but becomes larger or smaller in the view depending on the view scale.

Figure 10.39

Model text

The Model Text command (M Model Text...) is located on the Modeling tab of the Design bar. Choosing Modeling → Model Text also activates the Type Selector, allowing you to choose or add as many types of 3D text as you'd like.

To add model text to your drawing, click the Model Text button. You'll see a dialog box asking you for your text entry. Type your text, and click OK when you've finished. At this point, you're asked to place the text in the view you currently have active. If you're in a 3D view, Revit chooses a work plane based on the location of your cursor over model faces. Click to place the model text. After you've placed the text, you can select it and use the tools in the Options bar shown in Figure 10.40 to edit the text or reposition it:

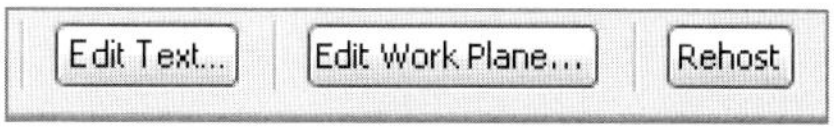

Figure 10.40

The Options bar for model text

Edit Text This button lets you change the text you typed. You can also edit the work plane on which the text was created.

Edit Work Plane This button opens another dialog box (Figure 10.41) where you can select a new work plane from an existing one or choose a plane of an existing Revit element.

Rehost This button allows you to move text from the element you've selected to another host element in the model. (We discussed this feature earlier, in the context of windows and doors.)

Figure 10.41

Selecting a work plane

Keynotes

Keynotes and *textnotes* are textual annotations that relate text strings in an external file to specific elements in the model. You can format font style, size, and justification in the same manner as for standard text, but keynotes and textnotes behave like a Revit family. This means you can insert different family types of text in Revit, just as you would door or window families. Changing one instance of the family type changes all the instances in the project. Because keynotes and textnotes act as families in Revit, they can also be scheduled. It is important to understand the difference between a keynote and a textnote.

Keynotes are a way to annotate elements with references that refer back to another table of data. These are typically shown as a number followed by a letter. An example would be "03300.AA" and it might refer to a cast-in-place concrete wall. For example, the "03300" portion of the note refers to the specification section the note is generated from, and the "AA" portion of the note is a sorting mechanism used to differentiate cast-in-place concrete from another note in Division 3 of MasterSpec. All of the notes on a given sheet are keyed back to a legend that is typically placed on the right side of a sheet. This reference is an aid to add more detail and understanding to the keynote without having to directly reference the specifications. Textnotes are similar to keynotes, but combine the text and the key into one note. This saves you from having to coordinate the legend on the sheet and puts the note right next to the item you are pointing to. See Figure 10.42 for examples of textnotes.

No matter which style you prefer, both the keynote and the textnote can be created with the same command within Revit. Since the command is called Keynote within Revit, we will refer to the process from here on out as *keynoting* regardless of the style of keynote (or textnote) you choose to use.

Figure 10.42

Keynotes

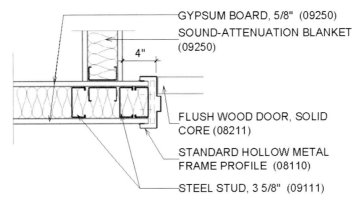

The Keynote command (◇ Keynote ») is located on the Drafting tab of the Design bar. Adding keynotes in Revit gives you three options for how to keynote an element:

Element Allows you to note an element in the model, such as a wall or a floor. This type of note is typically used if you want to note an entire assembly, such as a wall assembly. You can find this value in the family properties of that element.

Material Allows you to note a specific material in Revit. For example, this will let you annotate materials such as concrete, gypsum board, or acoustical tile.

User Allows you to select any model-based component in Revit and define a custom keynote for it. Notes defined this way differ from those defined under Element or Material because they're unique to the particular object selected. They can be used in conjunction with Element and Material notes.

Keynote Behavior and Editing

A core concept of keynoting is how the notes react in the model. Keynotes are integrated into Revit just like any model element. Keynoting an object in Revit lets you associate a text value to that family's keynote parameter. This value is consistent for every identical element in the model. For example, all doors have a type parameter that lets you set the keynote value. If you keynote that door—anywhere in the model—the keynote will show that value. Likewise, if you ever changed the value of the keynote for the door type, all keynotes would update automatically.

Keynotes are special in that *you cannot edit the text of a keynote directly in Revit*. All the keynotes in Revit are tied to an external text file, which is the only location they can be edited. This file can be modified at any point to add or remove values and notes. A sample portion of the Revit keynote file, RevitKeynotes_Imperial.txt, is shown here. This external .txt file is designed to keep annotations consistent by storing all of them in one repository. Every time you add or change the text of an annotation and reload the text file, it dynamically updates all the keynotes of that type used in the project.

03100	Concrete Forms and Accessories	03000
03200	Concrete Reinforcement	03000
03300	Cast-in-Place Concrete	03000
03400	Precast Concrete	03000
03500	Cementitious Decks and Underlayment	03000

You can edit a keynote text file (.txt) or add one to a project at any time. You can have multiple text files for various projects, but you can have only one text file per project at a time. All the notes are parametric, so changing a note in the text file will change all of the notes in the project when the text file is updated.

> A powerful way to ensure consistent use of notes throughout your office is to create a master .txt file for your various project types. These master note lists can be prelinked to materials or assemblies within your project template, allowing you to immediately begin inserting common notes into any project. Prelink these settings by choosing Settings → Materials and clicking the Identity tab. In the Keynote field, a predefined note can be added to any material.

Since the keynote .txt file is separate from the Revit file, if you send a project file to someone and don't send the keynote.txt file, that person will be able to see all the keynotes you've added to the views but won't be able to add or edit the notes without the .txt file.

Keynote File-Naming Conventions

The default .txt file in Revit resides in C:\Documents and Settings\All Users\Application Data\Autodesk\RAC 2008\Imperial Library (or Metric). To edit this file, open it in Notepad or Excel, and follow the format already established in the file. Let's look at that format to get a better understanding of how to customize keynotes.

The first few rows designate the groupings. They consist of a label (in this case, a number) followed by a tab and then a description. An example grouping looks like this:

03000   Division 03 - Concrete

Below the groupings, with no empty lines in the file, are the contents of the groupings. These are shown with a minor heading, a tab, a description, a tab, and the original grouping header. Here's an example:

03200   Concrete Reinforcement   03000

Here, 03200 is the subheading, Concrete Reinforcement is the description, and it all falls under the 03000 grouping from the previous example.

Using this method, you can add or edit notes and groups of notes to the keynote file. It might seem horribly inefficient at the beginning of the process to have to constantly go to the keynote text file to edit or add notes. Although this might seem like a burden, it can be a blessing as well.

Accessing this file ensures a level of consistency within the keynotes globally on the project that is unattainable in most 2D methods of drafting. If you are feeling frustrated with having to access this file to make changes, think about all of the time you are saving *not* having to check your set sheet by sheet to verify all of the notes pointing to a material are consistent with each other.

Keynote Settings

Once you change a keynote text file, you must reload the file into Revit to update the keynotes. Access the dialog box to change or update the text file by selecting Settings → Keynoting Settings (Figure 10.43).

The Keynote Table group lets you define the path to the .txt file used for keynoting:

Path Type Defines how Revit looks for your .txt file using one of three methods:

Absolute This option follows the UNC naming conventions and searches across your network or workstation for a specified location.

Figure 10.43

The Keynoting Settings dialog box

Relative This option locates the .txt file relative to the Revit project file. If you move the Revit file and the .txt file, and they maintain the same folder structure, Revit knows where to look for them.

At Library Location This option lets you put the .txt file in the default library location defined in the File Locations tab of the Settings → Options dialog box.

Numbering Method Defines how the keynotes are numbered:

> **By Keynote** Allows you to number keynotes as they come from the associated .txt file.

> **By Sheet** Numbers the keynotes sequentially on a per-sheet basis.

Adding Keynotes to a View

To add keynotes to a Revit model, choose one of the three Keynote Types from the Drafting tab in the Design bar. In your view, hover the cursor over the various model objects until you find the one you wish to note, and click to add the keynote to the element. Once you've placed the note, the Keynote dialog box will open (Figure 10.44), asking you to identify the element you're trying to annotate.

Expand the plus signs until you find your desired keynote, and double-click it. Doing so associates that particular note with the element or material in the model. As mentioned previously, you only need to make this association once. For example, if you keynote a material called Concrete, then every time you hover over that material anywhere else in the model with a keynote tag, you'll see the preview graphic of the tag showing Concrete (Figure 10.45). This way, you can define the materials and assemblies in the model and begin your documentation process.

With the exception of detail components (covered later in this chapter), you can't keynote lines or other 2D information.

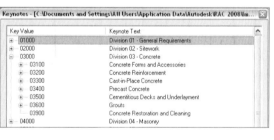

Figure 10.44

Selecting a keynote

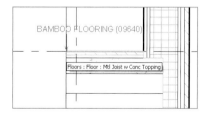

Figure 10.45

Keynotes preview prior to placement

Keynote Legends

Depending on your workflow and style of annotation, you may want to create a legend for your keynotes that appears on each sheet so that the legend only shows the keynotes used on that sheet. Or you may want to have one legend for the entire project and show all keynotes used in that project in one legend. These legends allow the builder to reference the note number with the text quickly and easily (Figure 10.46). These lists usually reside on the side of sheets near the title block information and can take on one of two forms: inclusive or exclusive.

Figure 10.46

A keynote legend

```
                      KEYNOTE LEGEND
        Key Value                 Keynote Text

      03300.AO       CIP CONC FLOOR SLAB  (03300)
      04810.BF       STONE CLADDING  (04810)
      05120.AC       STEEL BEAM  (05120)
      05310.AH       COMPOSITE FLOOR DECK  (05310)
      05500.BB       STEEL COLUMN  (05500)
      05500.BU       STEEL ANGLE  (05500)
      06105.AB       WOOD FURRING  (06105)
      06105.AC       PLYWOOD  (06105)
      06105.AD       1X IPE WOOD SUNSCREEN  (06105)
      07210.AB       RIGID INSULATION  (07210)
      08411.AA       EXTERIOR ALUMINUM-FRAMED STOREFRONT
                       (08411)
      09111.AO       HAT-SHAPED, RIGID FURRING CHANNEL  (09111)
      09250.AC       GYPSUM BOARD, TYPE X  (09250)
      09640.AA       BAMBOO FLOORING  (09640)
```

The first type is all inclusive and will show every note used in the project. This style has the benefit of being totally consistent from sheet to sheet. The same note will always be in the same location in the list. The other type of keynote list shortens the list to only contain notes present on a the specific sheet. This has the advantage of supplying a list of notes customized for each sheet without extraneous information. As you can imagine, this second list can be labor intensive and fraught with opportunities for human error. One of the beauties of Revit is its ability to accurately manage this kind of information for you. We will review how to create both styles of lists.

Creating a legend in Revit is simple: choose View → New → Keynote Legend. You'll be prompted to name the legend; enter a name, and click OK.

Only two fields are available in a keynote legend, and by default, they are both loaded into the scheduled fields side of the Fields tab:

Key Value The numeric value of the keynote

Keynote Text The text value for the keynote

Figure 10.47

Filter options for keynote legends

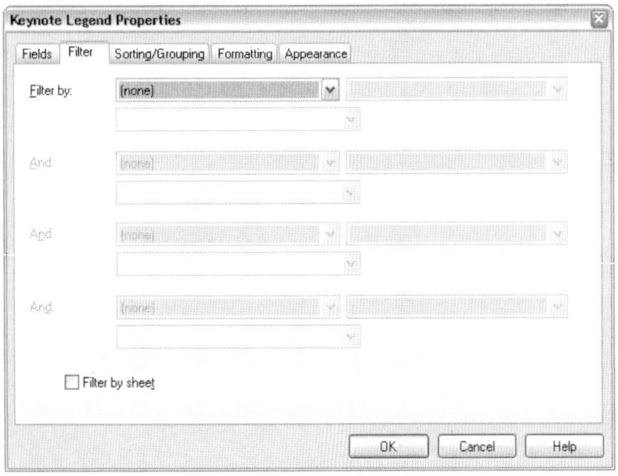

This legend works very much like any other schedule as far as formatting and appearance are concerned. By default, the sorting and grouping is already established by using the key value to sort. The one special item to note is located on the Filter tab. At the bottom of this tab is a feature unique to this type of schedule: a Filter by Sheet check box (Figure 10.47) is available. Checking this box will give you the ability to filter the list specifically for each sheet.

Both styles of legend can be placed again and again on every sheet in the project. With the filtered legend style, it will dynamically modify the note list based on each sheet and the contents on each sheet. As views are added or removed from a sheet or notes are added to the project, the keynote legend will update accordingly. So, if the keynote is not used in the view placed on the sheet, it will not show up in the legend.

New in Revit 2009, you will see all keynote legends listed in the project browser under the Legends node (Figure 10.48).

Figure 10.48

Keynote legends can be accessed from the Project Browser.

The Keynote Family

Revit comes with a keynote family that allows you to produce both keynotes and textnotes. If it is not loaded into your project, you can find it under the Annotations folder of the Imperial or Metric libraries. The family name is Keynote Tag.rfa. This family has three family types that allow you to change note styles within the project. You can see the three note styles in Figure 10.49.

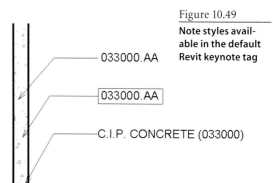

Figure 10.49

Note styles available in the default Revit keynote tag

The three styles are Keynote Number, Keynote Number—Boxed, and Keynote Text. Each of the notes shown in Figure 10.49 pulls information from the same text file that we discussed earlier in this chapter. You are simply using the flexibility of family types to report different values within the model from the same note. As with any other family, you can edit this family to change the note length, font style, or other attributes to match your office standards.

Adding Notes to a Wall Section by Material

As we discussed earlier in this chapter, there are three styles of keynotes: Element, Material, and User. With all of these styles, there are limits to what you can note within Revit. Understanding this is critical to successfully using the keynote system so you can optimize the value of your predefined notes.

Nearly all model elements in Revit can be keynoted; the only exceptions are detail lines, imports, and groups. This becomes a critical issue when you begin embellishing details within a model, drafting them in 2D with a drafting view, or importing standard details from CAD and looking to add keynotes to the CAD drawing. As a best practice, we recommend using detail components and embedding them into project families. *Detail components* are families created with 2D lines that can be dropped into any view to represent elements that are not modeled as 3D objects. An example would be blocking that appears over a window head. This is not something you would create as a model element, but it is still necessary to show in a section or detail (see Figure 10.50).

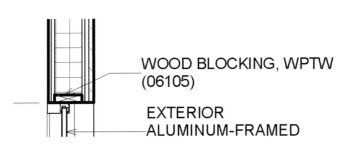

Once you've established your keynote style and made your adjustments to font size and type, it's time to add some notes to the drawing. Adding notes to a drawing from this point is quite simple:

1. From the Drafting tab of the Design bar, choose the Keynote tool.

2. Select Element, Material, or User from the list. For our example, select Material.

3. Move the cursor over the model—as you mouse over materials, Revit will try to identify what material is being used. If the material already has a note value defined, a floating note identifying the material will appear (Figure 10.51). From here, click to place the arrowhead of the note, click again to locate the joint in the leader, then click again to locate the text. If the material is unknown, Revit will show a question mark to tell you this material has not been identified in the project yet (Figure 10.52). Locate the note using the same method for materials that are already defined. Revit will then prompt you to select a value from the Keynotes table (Figure 10.53).

PLYWOOD (06105)

Roofs : Basic Roof : SIPS Roof

Once you've selected the note for a material, that same note will be applied every time you select that material with a keynote in every other view within the project.

By default, Revit does not include an arrowhead with any of the keynotes. There is no way to preset arrowhead styles for any of the notes. After you first insert a note into Revit, you will have to select the note to add an arrowhead. To do this, select the note and open its Element Properties dialog box, then select Edit/New. Here you can globally set an arrowhead style for any of the keynote family types. Most of the common arrowhead styles can be found in this Properties dialog box. Selecting one from the list shown in Figure 10.54 will change the arrowheads for all of the notes of that type within the project.

?

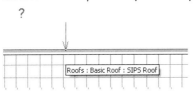

Roofs : Basic Roof : SIPS Roof

Figure 10.53

Choose a keynote value from the list.

Keynotes - [\\PSF\.Mac\Users\ekrygie\Documents\Mastering Revit 2008\Model\textnotes....]

Key Value	Keynote Text
⊞ 02870	[SITE FURNISHINGS] 2/04
02920	[LAWNS AND GRASSES] 2/06
02930	[EXTERIOR PLANTS] 2/06
⊞ 03300	[CAST-IN-PLACE CONCRETE] 8/02
⊞ 04810	[UNIT MASONRY ASSEMBLIES] 8/02
⊞ 05120	[STRUCTURAL STEEL] 2/01
⊞ 05310	[STEEL DECK] 5/03
⊞ 05500	[METAL FABRICATIONS] 2/02
⊞ 05511	[METAL STAIRS] 2/02
⊞ 05521	[PIPE AND TUBE RAILINGS] 2/02
⊞ 05530	[GRATINGS] 5/02
⊞ 05721	[ORNAMENTAL RAILINGS] 2/02
⊞ 06105	[MISCELLANEOUS CARPENTRY] 11/03
⊞ 07210	[BUILDING INSULATION] 2/06
07271	[SELF-ADHERING SHEET AIR BARRIERS] 8/04
⊞ 07412	[METAL WALL PANELS] 2/06
⊞ 07413	[INSULATED CORE METAL WALL PANELS] 2/06
⊟ 07540	[THERMOPLASTIC MEMBRANE ROOFING] 2/00
07540.AA	THERMOPLASTIC MEMBRANE ROOFING SYSTEM (075...
07540.AN	CRICKET (07540)
⊞ 07620	[SHEET METAL FLASHING AND TRIM] 11/00
⊞ 07720	[ROOF ACCESSORIES] 11/02

Keynote Text:

THERMOPLASTIC MEMBRANE ROOFING SYSTEM (07540)

[OK]   [Cancel]   [Help]

Figure 10.54

List of arrowhead styles

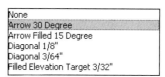

None
Arrow 30 Degree
Arrow Filled 15 Degree
Diagonal 1/8"
Diagonal 3/64"
Filled Elevation Target 3/32"

Once you've added a couple of notes, it's an easy process to continue noting the remaining materials in the wall section. The completed section with keynotes looks like Figure 10.55.

Figure 10.55

Fully material key-noted wall section

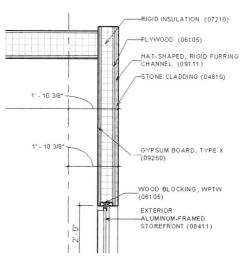

RIGID INSULATION (07210)

PLYWOOD (06105)

HAT-SHAPED, RIGID FURRING CHANNEL (09111)

STONE CLADDING (04810)

1' - 10 3/8"

1' - 10 3/8"

GYPSUM BOARD, TYPE X (09250)

WOOD BLOCKING, WPTW (06105)

EXTERIOR ALUMINUM-FRAMED STOREFRONT (08411)

2' - 0"

Adding Notes to a Wall Section by Element

Another way to keynote a drawing is to note by assembly, or within Revit, by element. Keynoting by element means that you are not noting the individual materials, as we did in our previous example, but the entire assembly at once. So, in lieu of noting individual layers of plywood and gypsum board, you are noting the entire wall assembly. The process to add the notes is similar:

1. From the Drafting tab in the Design bar, choose the Keynote tool.

2. Select the Element option from the flyout menu.

3. Move your cursor over elements in the model, and Revit will try to identify the element or assembly. If the element already has a note value defined, a preview note identifying the element will display. From here, click to place the arrowhead of the note, click again to locate the joint in the leader, then click again to locate the text. If the element is unknown, Revit will display a question mark to tell you this element has not yet been identified in the project. Locate the note using the same method as for elements that are already defined. After you set the text location, Revit will prompt you to select a value from the Keynotes table.

A wall section noted by element looks like Figure 10.56.

Figure 10.56

Wall annotated with element keynotes

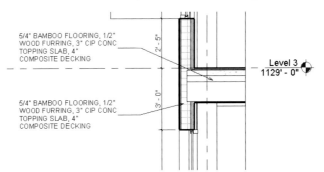

Element, material, and user notes in Revit are different entities and are allowed their own unique notes. You can note by material, by element, and by user within the same project.

Predefining Keynotes

There are a variety of other ways to add notes to a project without adding them directly in a view. Within the properties of elements and materials is a field to predefine a keynote. Putting a value in this field before annotating the drawings allows you to avoid selecting notes from the keynote list when you are actually annotating a view. All of the notes would be preselected. Depending on the note type, the location for these settings varies:

Element This value can be set in the properties of the various families in a Revit project. By selecting a wall, for example, you can open this wall's properties, then click Edit/New to reach the wall Type Properties. Under Identity Data, you can then define a keynote (Figure 10.57). Selecting this field, you will be presented with the same Keynote table that you'd receive if noting this element in a view. If the note is incorrect for this project or element, you have the option to change the note here as well.

Material This value can also be set in the Settings → Materials dialog box. By selecting a material from this list and then clicking the Identity tab, you can add keynote values directly to your materials (see Figure 10.58). You will again be presented with the familiar Keynote dialog box to select your materials.

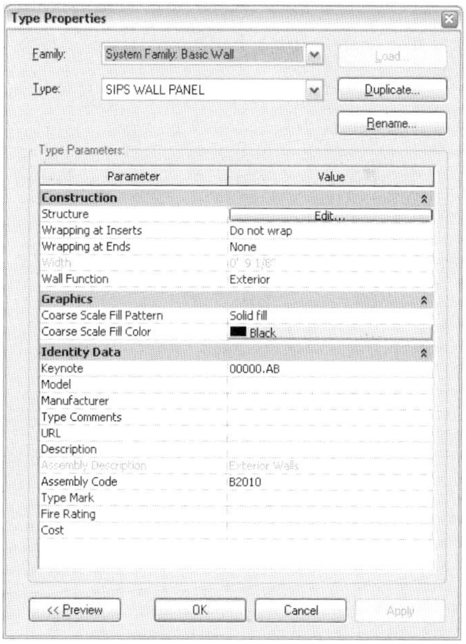

Figure 10.57

Type Properties of wall showing keynote value predefined

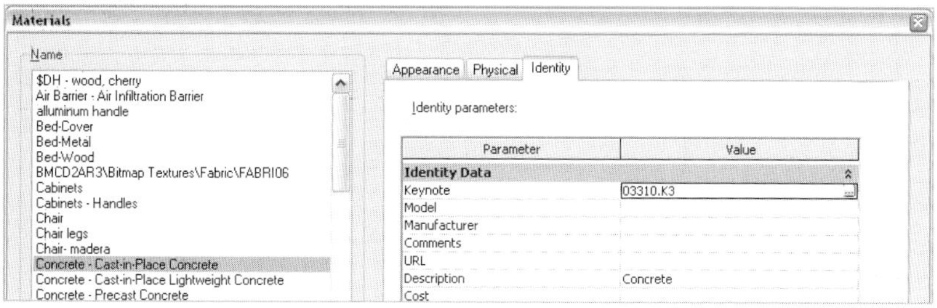

Figure 10.58

Defining keynotes for materials

User   User notes are view specific and cannot be predefined. While it is still only possible to annotate model elements and detail components with the user notes, this tool will allow you to note the same element with different notes in separate views. This can be dangerous to the consistency of your notes in your drawings if used inappropriately. The advantage to this note type, however, is if you need to note something differently in one view based on a unique condition. Some examples might be a material or color change in a special location, or a special flashing or sealant issue around a unique window condition. This means you don't have to re-create a new family type simply to add a different note.

Revit does not support more than one keynote.txt file per project. So if you want to include keynotes from different standards, you can simply add more to the one .txt file that you have, and they will all be available to be used.

CHAPTER 11

Construction Documentation

Now that we've discussed how to annotate a drawing, be it for presentation or production, we will review how to create the set of documents that will be used by the contractor and subcontractors to build the project.

In this chapter, we'll go into detail about preparing the construction document set. Topics we'll cover include:

- **Formatting your documents**
- **Creating schedules**
- **Using drafting views**
- **Understanding drafting tools**
- **Importing CAD details**
- **Reusing details from other projects**

Formatting Your Documents

When you begin documenting your project, most of your modeling should be more or less complete. That doesn't necessarily mean that you have all your views established or all your sections cut, but it's helpful if the majority of your building geometry is in place.

To illustrate, let's go back to the house we've been working on. By this point the geometry of the house should be well established; to begin the documents, you'll create a series of views of the model. You've already established some views in the model. Some were in the Revit template file, and you made others while creating the model. However, the views you currently have for the floor plans are set up for presentation purposes and are not suitable as construction documents. Therefore, we need to create new views, customize their appearance, and place them onto sheets to make digital or paper prints of them.

Laying Out Sheets

The following exercise will help get you started documenting the house. We will begin making some views and placing them on construction document sheets.

1. Open `Source_House.rvt` in the Chapter 10 folder on the book's companion web page, www.sybex.com/go/introducingrevit2009.

2. To start, you'll duplicate both Level 1and Level 2 using the Project Browser. To do this, right-click the view name, and choose Duplicate View → Duplicate. Doing so creates a new view called "Copy of (*ViewName*)." Repeat this step for the second view.

3. Rename the view Copy of Level 1 to **First Floor Plan** by right-clicking the view name and choosing Rename. Use the same process to rename the view Copy of Level 2 to Second Floor Plan.

The First Floor Plan view has a graphical appearance that doesn't match the Second Floor Plan view. Both views need to have a consistent graphical appearance showing the necessary information for a documentation set. To do this, you'll create a new view template using the Second Floor Plan view as a baseline. You can then apply this template to the first floor plan so the two views have a similar set of graphics.

Before making the view template, make some graphical adjustments to the Second Floor Plan view. First, turn on the Sections and Elevations annotations:

1. Open the view Second Floor and choose View → Visibility Graphics from the menu or press VG on the keyboard.

2. Select the Annotation Categories tab. Make sure the Sections and Elevations category check boxes are selected. Click OK.

3. In the Project Browser, right-click the Second Floor Plan view, and choose Create View Template from View.

4. Name the view template **Floor Plan**, and click OK. A dialog box appears that allows you to adjust any of the many properties available in View Templates. For now, we will accept the template as we set it, so click OK again.

5. Right-click the First Floor Plan view, and choose Apply View Template.

6. Choose Floor Plan from the list, and click OK. You have just unified the look of the First Floor and the Second Floor.

Next, you need to create some additional views of the model: sections and callouts. Follow these steps:

1. Open the Second Floor Plan view, and cut a wall section through the west end of the house, as shown in Figure 11.1. After creating this section, it will be pointed in the wrong direction. Using the Flip icon, flip the section cut to point in the other direction.

2. In the Section 3 view, create two callout views using the Callout tool on the View tab of the Design bar. One callout should focus on the south clerestory condition, and the other should focus on the northern window in the stairwell. See Figure 11.2 for callout locations. Rename the details you have just created **Detail 1** and **Detail 2**.

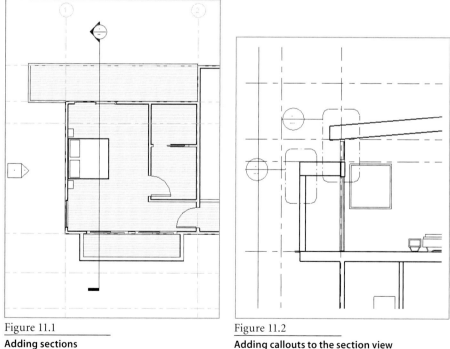

Figure 11.1

Adding sections

Figure 11.2

Adding callouts to the section view

To reposition the callout tag, select any of the callout lines and use the blue grips to reposition or resize the tag or the box.

Now that you have created the views needed to document your project clearly, you can begin laying them out on sheets. There is a sheet template located on the book's website, www.sybex.com/go/introducingrevit2009; we will use it as the basis for our sheet set. You need one sheet for plans; one for elevations; and one for details, sections, and 3D views. To use the sheet templates and create the sheets, follow these steps:

1. Right-click on Sheets in the Project Browser, and select New Sheet from the context menu. In the next dialog box, choose Load and browse to the file named Sheets-CD .rfa. Click OK.

2. The Sheet view will become your active view. Repeat this step two more times, so that you have three sheets in the project.

3. Rename the sheets as follows: **A100 Floor Plans**; **A200 Elevations**; and **A300 Sections & 3D views.** To do this, right-click the sheet name in the Project Browser and choose Rename to bring up a renaming dialog box. You can also rename the sheet directly in the view when the sheet is opened. Select the sheet and click the blue text of the sheet name or number, and the text becomes an active text field you can then edit. Be sure to change the sheet name as well as the sheet number when you're editing from the sheet itself (Figure 11.3).

When you add sheets, they appear in the Project Browser under the Sheets node.

As a next step we can begin adding views to the sheet itself. With a sheet view opened, you can drag a view from the Project Browser onto the sheet:

1. In the Project Browser, select a view (click and hold on the view name), and then drag it onto the sheet. A preview graphic of the view extents appears to aid in placement.

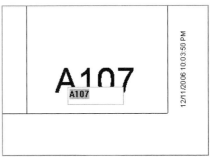

Figure 11.3

Modifying the sheet name within the view

2. When you get the view approximately where you want it, release the mouse button. The view drops into place.

Each view is assigned a unique number once it's placed on the sheet. This is referred to as the *detail number*, and it appears as a parameter of the view once it has been placed on a sheet.

For the next exercise, lay out the sheets with the following views on them:

- *A100*—First floor plan and second floor plan
- *A200*—North elevation and south elevation
- *A300*—Section 1, Section 3, and 3D View (1)

Notice that on sheet A100, the two plans don't fit on the sheet; see Figure 11.4. Obviously, it's vital to be able to produce drawings that read clearly and easily within the bounds of what will be the printed area. Revit provides control over the sizes of your views as they appear on the sheets, so it's easy to fix issues like this when they arise.

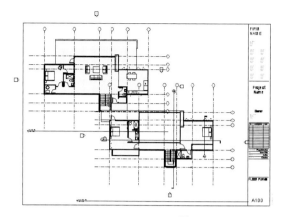

Figure 11.4

Plans initially don't fit on the sheet.

You can do this directly from the sheet, giving you real-time feedback about the view and its relation to the sheet:

1. Open Sheet A100. Mouse over one of the views on the sheet, and right-click.

2. Select Activate View.

3. Use the View Control bar to select Show Crop Region (![icon]). The light bulb in the icon turns yellow, indicating that the crop region is on. The view will now have a box surrounding the extents of the view with blue grips you can use to bring the extents of the view within the boundaries of the sheet. Once this is done, you can then right-click the view again and choose Deactivate View from the context menu. Note that while the crop region is still visible, it will not show when printed. You can then place the views on sheets in a more organized fashion similar to Figure 11.5.

To make minor adjustments to a view location, select the view and use the arrows on the keyboard to nudge it around. The tighter you're zoomed in on a view, the smaller the increment of movement.

4. Finish laying out the other two sheets. A200 and A300 should look like Figures 11.6 and 11.7, respectively.

In a typical, professional-looking sheet arrangement, especially when you have multiple views (plans or elevations) on a sheet, it's common to line up gridlines (in the vertical dimension on the sheet) and levels (in the horizontal). Revit automatically aligns the grids and levels between views on the sheet when you drag views onto a sheet. Click and drag a view—a green, dotted snap-alignment line appears when grids are aligned with grids in the other views (or levels with other levels). This comes in handy when you lay out a sheet with multiple wall sections and you want the levels to all be lined up relative to one another on the sheet.

Figure 11.5

Floor plans arranged

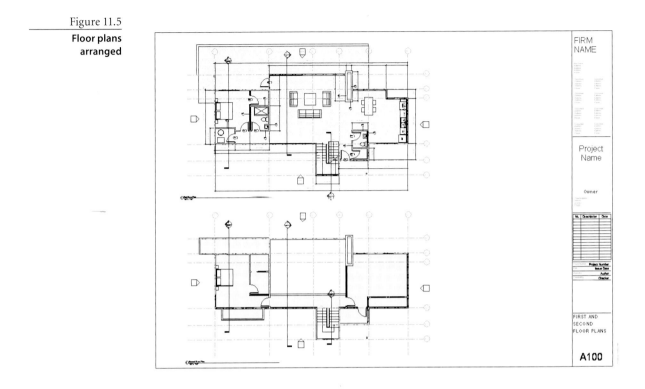

Figure 11.6

A200

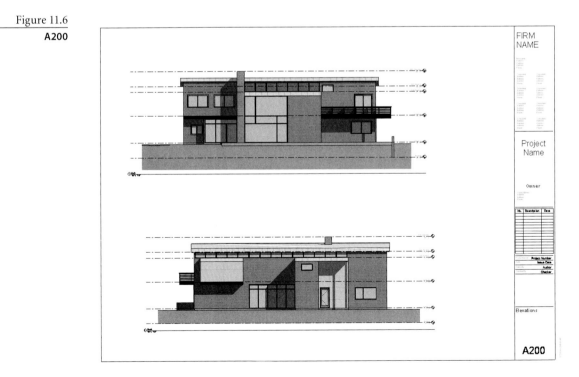

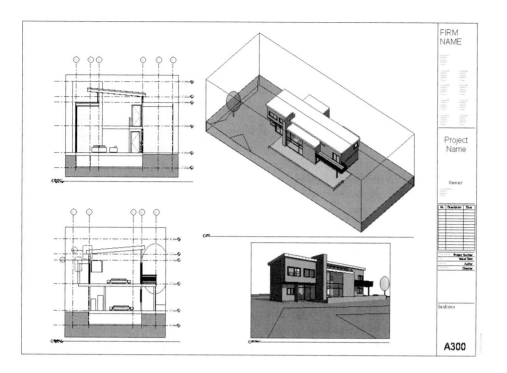

Figure 11.7

A300

Schedules

In Chapter 3, we explained that schedules are a live, textual view of the model. We also discussed the different types of schedules you can create and walked through a simple example. For your documentation, you need to know how to modify the graphical appearance of a schedule and filter out information you don't need to show.

Create and Customize a Schedule

When you create a new schedule, you're presented with a number of format and selection choices. These let you organize and filter the data for display in the schedule as well as set the font style and text alignment. Let's explore the options in the New Schedule dialog box.

> Revit is essentially a database of model objects that are loaded with information; thus many of the same functions available in database queries are available in Revit. If you're unfamiliar with database conventions, don't stress—you don't need to know about databases to run Revit successfully.

From the View tab in the Design bar, choose Schedule/Quantities to create a new schedule. The New Schedule dialog box (Figure 11.8) first prompts you to select the category of elements you want to schedule. You can provide a name for the schedule and choose which phase of construction the schedule represents. We've left the phase as New Construction, because that is what you're creating with the sample model.

Once you select the schedule you would like to create, you will be presented with another dialog box that contains the following tabs. These tabs are designed to help you format your data and its visual presentation:

Fields This tab lets you select the data that will appear in your schedule. For the wall schedule, it shows all the properties available in the wall family.

Filter This tab allows you to filter out the data you don't wish to show. You'll use this tab to restrict displayed data so that only information about the concrete walls in the project appears in the schedule.

Sorting/Grouping This tab lets you control the order in which information is displayed. It also allows you to decide whether you want to show every instance of an item or only the totals for a given family.

Formatting This tab controls the display heading for each field and whether the field is visible on the schedule. It's possible to add fields that are necessary for calculations or sorting but don't show on the printed copy of the schedule. Additionally, this tab can tell Revit to calculate the totals for any of the fields.

Appearance This tab controls the graphical aspects of the schedule, including the font size and type of text for each of the columns and headers in the schedule. It also allows you to turn the grids on and off or modify the line thickness for the grid and boundary lines.

The following example walks through the different options in the Schedule Properties dialog box while you create a new wall schedule. In this example, you'll create the schedule, filter out all but the concrete walls, and calculate the volume of recycled content in the walls based on the assumption that you're using 15 percent recycled content in all the concrete poured on the project. When you've finished, the schedule should look like Figure 11.9.

Figure 11.9

The completed schedule

	Concrete Walls				
		Wall Properties			
Wall Type	Width	Length	Area	Volume	Recycled Volume
Basic Wall: N1 - CIP CONC	0' - 8"	20' - 2"	62 SF	41.00 CF	6.15 CF
Basic Wall: N1 - CIP CONC	0' - 8"	9' - 0 7/32"	81 SF	53.88 CF	8.08 CF
Basic Wall: N1 - CIP CONC	0' - 8"	4' - 10"	94 SF	62.74 CF	9.41 CF
Basic Wall: N1 - CIP CONC	0' - 8"	15' - 0 5/8"	143 SF	95.33 CF	14.30 CF
Basic Wall: N1 - CIP CONC	0' - 8"	18' - 0"	150 SF	100.00 CF	15.00 CF
Basic Wall: N1 - CIP CONC	0' - 8"	18' - 2 3/8"	167 SF	111.03 CF	16.65 CF
Basic Wall: N1 - CIP CONC	0' - 8"	18' - 2 3/8"	167 SF	111.03 CF	16.65 CF
Basic Wall: N1 - CIP CONC	0' - 8"	56' - 6"	168 SF	111.98 CF	16.80 CF
Basic Wall: N1 - CIP CONC	0' - 8"	18' - 0"	202 SF	134.33 CF	20.15 CF
Basic Wall: N1 - CIP CONC	0' - 8"	18' - 0"	202 SF	134.70 CF	20.20 CF
Basic Wall: N1 - CIP CONC	0' - 8"	78' - 10"	235 SF	156.49 CF	23.47 CF
Basic Wall: N1 - CIP CONC	0' - 8"	22' - 0"	269 SF	179.41 CF	26.91 CF
Basic Wall: N1 - CIP CONC	0' - 8"	93' - 8"	279 SF	186.00 CF	27.90 CF
Basic Wall: N1 - CIP CONC	0' - 8"	29' - 4 15/16"	327 SF	190.11 CF	28.52 CF
Basic Wall: N1 - CIP CONC	0' - 8"	22' - 4"	304 SF	202.95 CF	30.44 CF
Basic Wall: N1 - CIP CONC	0' - 8"	18' - 0"	323 SF	215.22 CF	32.28 CF
Basic Wall: N1 - CIP CONC	0' - 8"	40' - 4"	338 SF	225.56 CF	33.83 CF
Basic Wall: N1 - CIP CONC	0' - 8"	35' - 4 17/32"	480 SF	320.29 CF	48.04 CF
Basic Wall: N1 - CIP CONC	0' - 8"	17' - 6"	530 SF	353.17 CF	52.98 CF
Basic Wall: N1 - CIP CONC	0' - 8"	7' - 4"	553 SF	368.67 CF	55.30 CF
Basic Wall: N1 - CIP CONC	0' - 8"	22' - 4"	619 SF	389.81 CF	58.47 CF
Basic Wall: N1 - CIP CONC	0' - 8"	7' - 4"	617 SF	411.44 CF	61.72 CF
Basic Wall: N1 - CIP CONC	0' - 8"	77' - 10 1/8"	906 SF	546.71 CF	82.01 CF
Basic Wall: N1 - CIP CONC	0' - 8"	36' - 3"	855 SF	570.08 CF	85.51 CF
Basic Wall: N1 - CIP CONC	0' - 8"	100' - 5 1/8"	954 SF	636.23 CF	95.44 CF
Basic Wall: N1 - CIP CONC	0' - 8"	17' - 8 3/4"	1032 SF	678.81 CF	101.82 CF
Basic Wall: N1 - CIP CONC	0' - 8"	83' - 11 13/3	1039 SF	692.45 CF	103.87 CF
Basic Wall: N1 - CIP CONC	0' - 8"	73' - 4 3/4"	1179 SF	786.28 CF	117.94 CF
Basic Wall: N1 - CIP CONC	0' - 8"	17' - 8 3/4"	1401 SF	933.74 CF	140.06 CF
Basic Wall: N1 - CIP CONC	0' - 8"	124' - 0 19/3	1444 SF	962.36 CF	144.35 CF
Basic Wall: N1 - CIP CONC	0' - 8"	148' - 5 13/3	4419 SF	2803.17 CF	420.48 CF
31	20' - 8"	1270' - 2	19537 SF	12764.98 CF	1914.75 CF

Follow these steps:

1. Open the Station.rvt file found in the Chapter 10 folder on the book's companion web page.

2. Navigate to the View tab, and choose Schedule/Quantities.

3. Choose Walls from the category menu, and name the schedule **Concrete Walls** (see Figure 11.10).

4. Click OK.

5. Select the fields to be scheduled (see Figure 11.11). The fields are parameters used by the category, and they all appear in the properties of the element being scheduled. Add a field by double-clicking the name of the field in the left pane or by selecting the field and clicking the Add button. Doing so moves the field from the left to the right column. Or, you can remove a field by selecting it in the right column and clicking Remove.

Figure 11.10

Starting a schedule

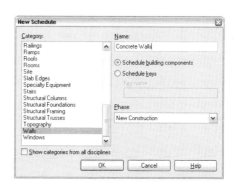

Figure 11.11

Fields tab

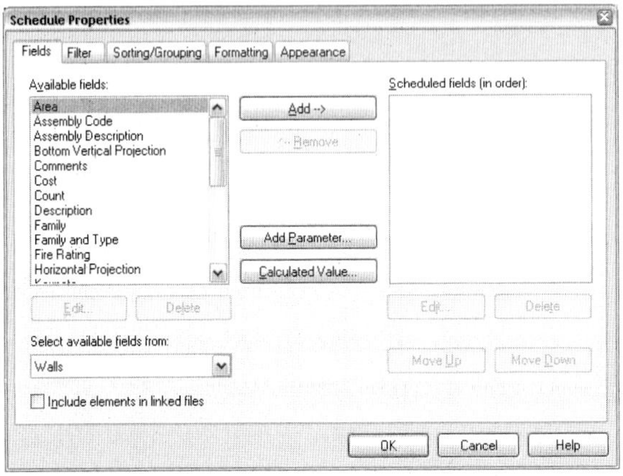

6. Choose the following fields for the schedule:

   Area

   Description

   Family and Type

   Length

   Volume

   Width

7. With a field selected, use the Move Up and Move Down buttons in the lower-right corner of the dialog box to sort the fields in the order you want them to appear in the schedule table. For example:

   Family and Type

   Description

   Width

   Length

   Area

   Volume

   There is no predefined field in Revit for recycled content, but Revit lets you create custom fields and custom formulas.

8. To make a new field to display information about the recycled content of your walls, click the Calculated Value button (Calculated Value...).

9. The Calculated Value dialog box opens (Figure 11.12). In this dialog box you can create new columns in your schedule based on relationships to other fields in the table. Name your new value **Recycled Volume.** For Type, choose Volume from the drop-down list; and in the Formula box, type **Volume*.15.**

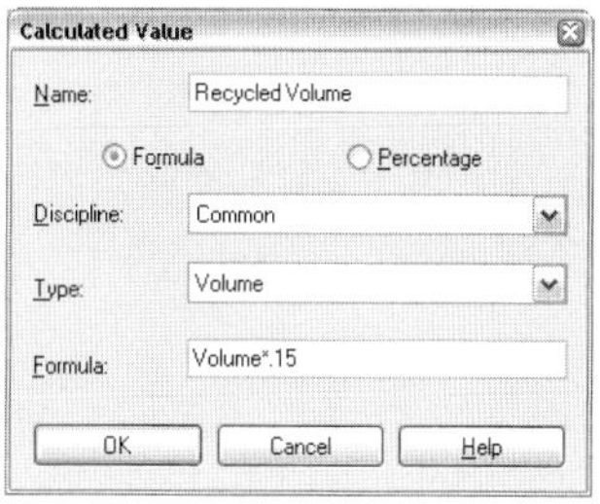

10. When you're done, click OK.

Figure 11.12

Adding a calculated value

TIPS FOR CUSTOM FIELDS

There are a few things to note when you create custom fields:

- You can't mix field types. This means you can't select a field type of Area or Number and take a percentage of volume. You need to calculate apples to apples.

- The formula area is case sensitive. This is also true for custom family types and other calculated Revit fields.

- You can't calculate with fields that aren't included in the schedule.

- Revit's Help menu lists valid formula syntaxes. You can enter integers, decimals, and fractional values in formulas using normal mathematical syntax, as shown in the following examples:

    - Length = Height + Width + sqrt (Height*Width)

    - Length = Wall 1 (11000mm) + Wall 2 (15000mm)

    - Area = Length (500mm) * Width (300mm)

    - Volume = Length (500mm) * Width (300mm) * Height (800 mm)

    - Width = 100m * cos(angle)

    - x = 2*abs(a) + abs(b/2)

    - ArrayNum = Length/Spacing

---

11. Choose the Filter tab (Figure 11.13). Because you want to show only the concrete walls, you need to filter out all the other walls in this schedule.

12. From the upper-left Filter By drop-down menu, choose Description.

13. The right Filter By menu allows you to select from a standard list of database queries: equals, doesn't equal, contains, doesn't contain, and so on. For this schedule, use the default value, equals.

Figure 11.13

Filter tab

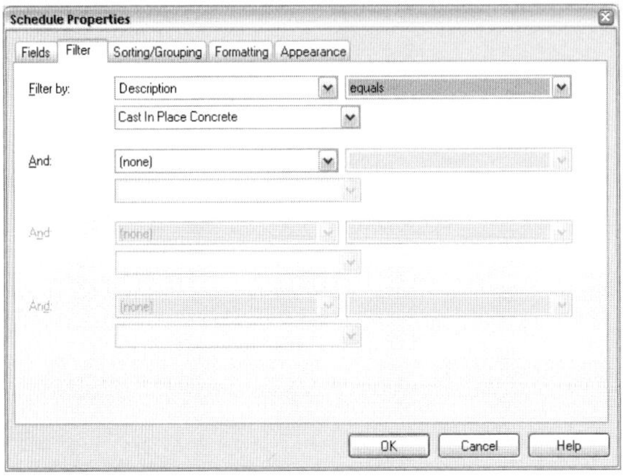

14. From the lower-left Filter By menu, choose Cast in Place Concrete. (This menu dynamically generates from the descriptions given in the properties for the element in question. In this example, wall properties are displayed.)

15. Select the Sorting/Grouping tab shown in Figure 11.14. Use these options to sort the walls first by Family and Type, and then by Volume.

16. Near the bottom of this tab, select the Grand Totals check box. Choose Counts and Totals from the drop-down menu at the right.

Figure 11.14

**Sorting/
Grouping tab**

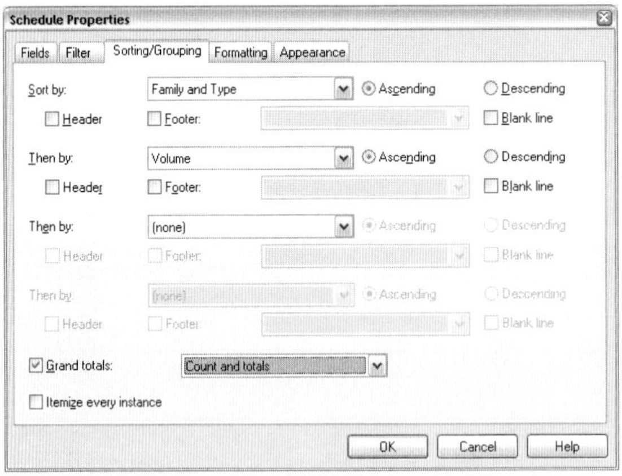

On this tab, choosing Counts and Totals means you're telling Revit to autocalculate a few things. First, you're counting all the instances of a type family in the model. You also have the option to report totals for those counted types. For example, you may have two sizes of fixed windows in a project. The count tells you how many of each type you have. The total gives you a sum of all the fixed windows, regardless of size. This count and total relate only to family or type quantities.

17. At the bottom of this tab is an Itemize Every Instance check box. Leave it deselected for now, which makes it a hidden field.

If you select Itemize Every Instance, a separate line will appear on the schedule for each instance of an object type in the model. This may be useful when you're listing every door or window, but it can make for a long schedule.

18. Select the Formatting tab shown in Figure 11.15. Change the Heading value of the Family and Type field to Wall Type. To do this, select Family and Type in the Fields list, and type **Wall Type** in the Heading box.

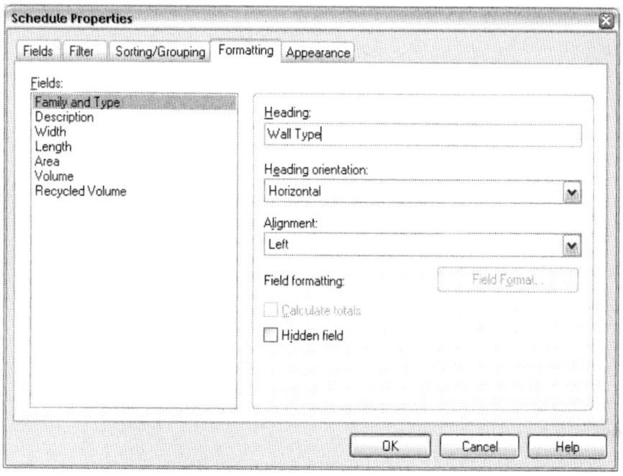

Figure 11.15
Formatting tab

19. Select Description in the Fields list, and select the Hidden Field check box.

20. Select each of the remaining fields (Width, Length, Area, Volume, and Recycled Volume), set their alignment to Right, and select the Calculate Totals check box. This option tells Revit to add a list of other values together that aren't type related (like the calculation in step 15). This gives you the ability to calculate values between similar fields within Revit and return customized but accurate data. So, in English, this means that you can customize your schedules in a variety of ways and know they are always reporting accurate and current information.

You can select fields individually, or you can select them all by holding down the Ctrl key and clicking each field name.

21. Select the Appearance tab shown in Figure 11.16. On this tab, you define gridlines, outlines, header text, and body text. Select the Bold check box to the right of Header Text. The rest of the settings are fine, unless you feel like experimenting with fonts and size.

22. Click OK. Revit will generate a schedule that shows all the information you asked for from the model. At the bottom of the schedule, the total for each of the fields is displayed.

Figure 11.16

Appearance tab

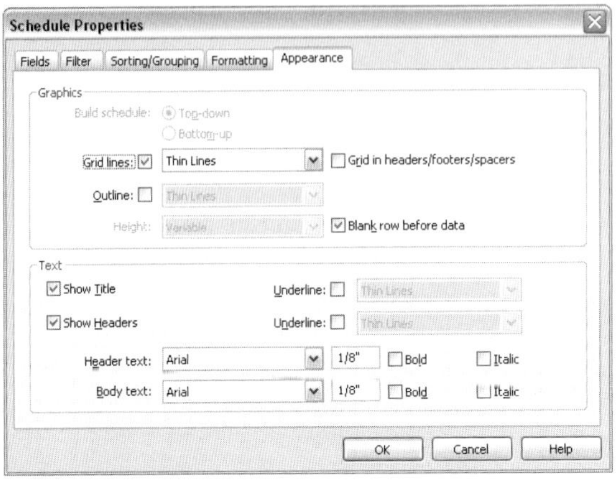

Additional Formatting

You can do some additional formatting after you create a schedule. By selecting multiple headers, you can group them and add secondary tier headers. Let's combine Width, Length, Area, and Volume:

1. Click in the Width header. Holding down the left mouse button, drag your cursor to the left or right, selecting additional headers until you've selected all four (see Figure 11.17).

2. Click the Group button on the Options bar.

3. Revit groups all four headers together. Add a title for the new grouping: **Wall Properties** (Figure 11.18).

Figure 11.17

Grouping schedule headers

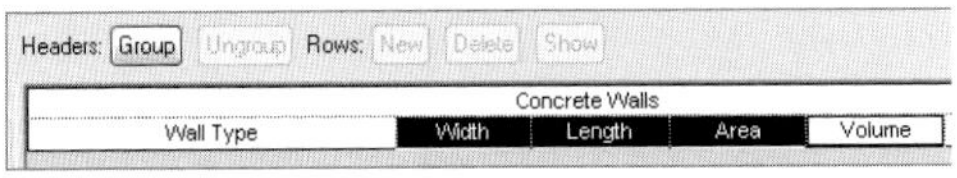

Figure 11.18

Adding headers to schedules

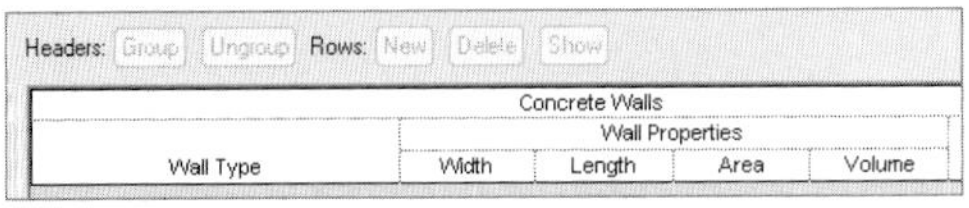

Finding Elements in the Model

Not only do Revit schedules report information about elements in the project but they also can be used to control elements. If you decide to exchange one wall type for another, you can do so by clicking in the schedule—under wall types, in this example. A menu appears, listing all available types currently in the model, and you can choose the type you want. Again, this automatically changes the instance of the wall to another wall type in all views in which the wall is present.

The schedule you just created lists all concrete walls; you can use the schedule to locate any of these walls in the model. To do this, select a wall from the schedule list. In the Options bar, you can choose to delete or show the element you've selected. Be aware that the Delete option entirely removes that element from the model and from every single view in which it appears. This is the essence of Revit: you don't need to manually seek all views in which this wall appears to delete it, because the element really exists once and only once in the model.

When you choose Show, Revit opens any view the element can be displayed in, zooms in on that element, and highlights it in red. This powerful tool lets you find the location of any model element in the project.

The schedule is not only filled by rows automatically generated by the tool—you can also can add new rows to the schedule manually. There are many cases in which this might be useful, such as when you make room schedules and you want to predefine room names before adding the tags to the model.

> Coordinated documentation is a key value of Revit. After you create a schedule, it doesn't require manual updating. Any time you add or remove content from the model, the schedule dynamically updates itself, even if it's placed on a sheet. A change you make anywhere in the model will be propagated everywhere that change is relevant.

View Templates for Schedules

Revit allows you to save a schedule that you've carefully prepared as a view template and apply it to other schedules. This is useful in cases when you have many schedules in a project and you need them to look alike to maintain visual continuity by using the same font and graphical conventions. To create a schedule view template, right-click the schedule in the Project Browser, and choose Create Template from View 2. Then give the template a name.

The Schedule View template allows you to standardize all the font types, styles, and any other settings found on the Appearance tab in your project. Maybe you've already created schedules using various graphical styles. It's never too late to apply a view template and tidy things up. To apply a schedule template to a previously created schedule, follow these steps:

1. Right-click the schedule in the Project Browser, and choose Select Apply View Template.

2. Select the template you wish to apply, and click OK.

Placing and Handling Schedules on Sheets

To place a schedule on a sheet, follow the same steps you use to place a view on a sheet. Drag and drop and then adjust and nudge until you get the correct layout. Once you've placed your schedule on a sheet, you can start to take advantage of Revit's productivity tools.

Traditionally, schedules have been time-consuming and extensive exercises in data entry and table manipulation. Schedules are often long lists that are hard to manipulate and that need to be updated whenever new content is added to a project. Few applications have an intelligent way of doing all this. For example, splitting a schedule usually requires cutting, copying, and a lot of rework to achieve the needed appearance and coordinate the data. Revit makes this process easy by putting graphical controls directly onto a schedule once it's on a sheet. Click the Split icon (⌄), and the schedule splits in half. Drag the blue control at the bottom of the schedule to move rows back and forth across the split. If you need to un-split the schedule, drag one of the split sections on top of the other one, and they merge back together. All graphic edits of the schedule, such as changes in column width, propagate to all split segments of the schedule.

Let's practice by placing a schedule on a sheet in the `Station.rvt` file where you created the Concrete Wall schedule:

1. Create a new sheet by right-clicking the Sheets group from the Project Browser and choosing New Sheet.

2. Select the Presentation: Presentation sheet.

3. Drag the Concrete Walls schedule from the Schedule list in the Project Browser onto the sheet in the View window.

4. When you drop the schedule onto the sheet, it appears too long for the sheet; the text in each cell is returned and wrapped in the cell, further adding to the schedule length (see Figure 11.19). This isn't the look you're aiming for. To modify it, grab the blue arrows at the top of the schedule header, and drag them to the right to enlarge the width of each column. Doing this makes the schedule wider and also shortens the column.

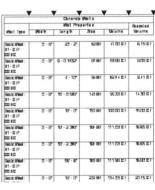

Figure 11.19

Adding a schedule to a sheet

5. Unfortunately, even though the column has been shortened, it still doesn't fit on the 11″ × 17″ sheet you've placed it on. Fortunately, Revit lets you split a schedule into multiple segments. To do this, click the blue squiggle that appears in the center of the schedule on the left or right side (shown in Figure 11.20). This splits the schedule in the center and adds a new header to the new column.

Figure 11.20

Splitting a schedule

> You can split a schedule as many times as needed to fit it onto a sheet.

6. To finally locate the schedules on the sheet, you can drag each set of columns independently by grabbing the blue cross icon in the center of the schedule. (These individual segments can't be placed on separate sheets.) The finished schedule on the sheet should look like Figure 11.21.

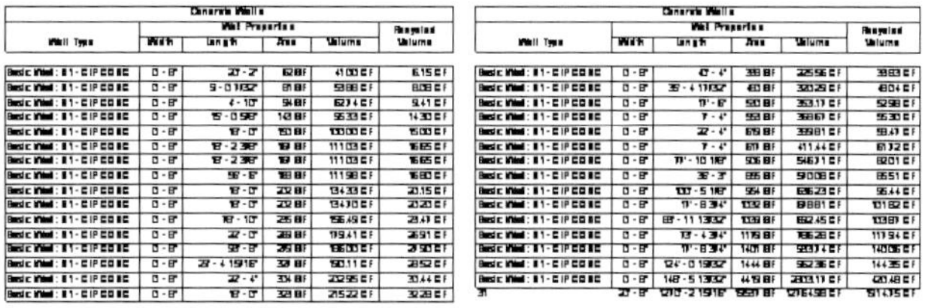

Figure 11.21

The schedule on a sheet

In addition to letting you split a schedule into separate segments, Revit allows you to rejoin the segments into a single schedule:

1. Select the blue cross at the middle of the second segment.

2. Drag it over the first segment of the schedule. Your schedule is complete and displays in its original form.

> A new feature in Revit 2009 is the ability to schedule railings.

Drafting Views

Because it isn't feasible, or even reasonable, to model every single construction detail in 3D, Revit provides the means to draft 2D information. Revit's drafting views are strictly 2D views used for drawing details for a construction document set. Some examples where it might be useful to move from the 3D model to 2D geometry are for things like window jamb, head, and sill details; or reusing details taken from past projects or from manufacturers who supply details in 2D. In our own practice, for teams just starting with Revit, it's a good rule of thumb to figure on creating any drawing at 1 ½″ = 1′-0″ or larger as only 2D. This will give you some flexibility starting out in Revit to fine-tune your family making skills.

When placed on a sheet, drafting views have the same intelligent referencing as other views. This lets you produce coordinated drawings. Even though drafting views present only 2D details, because they're in Revit, they can be tied parametrically to sheets, so all the references are dynamic.

To create a new drafting view, follow these steps:

1. Go to the View tab of the Design bar and choose Drafting View ().

2. A dialog box opens prompting you for a detail name and scale (Figure 11.22).

3. Using the Scale drop-down menu, choose from a list of standard and custom view scales.

4. Click OK. A new node, Drafting Views (Detail), is added to the Project Browser (see Figure 11.23). This new drafting view is primed for either drafting a new detail or importing existing CAD details.

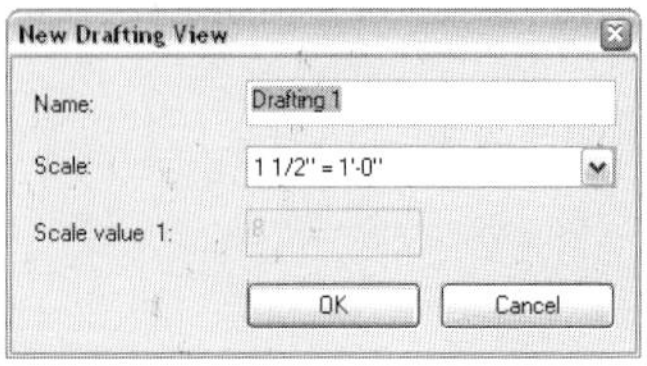

Figure 11.22

New Drafting View dialog box

Drafting Tools

The drafting tools available in Revit are similar to what you might find in any CAD application. You can draw lines, arcs, and circles and create groups of 2D lines to use repeatedly. Lines can be drawn, extended, moved, copied, mirrored, arrayed, and trimmed—everything you'd expect to be able to do to lines.

Figure 11.23

Drafting Views node

Figure 11.24

Drafting tools

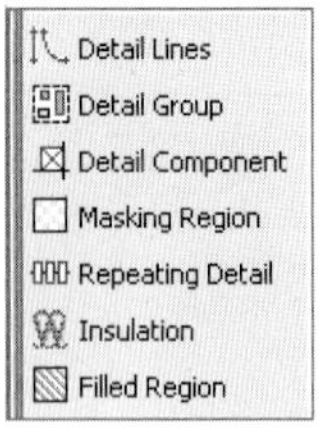

- Detail Lines
- Detail Group
- Detail Component
- Masking Region
- Repeating Detail
- Insulation
- Filled Region

To demonstrate Revit's drafting tools, you'll work on the house model (from the book's web page, www.sybex.com/go/introducingrevit2009) for the remainder of this chapter. Open the file Source_House_Begining Detailing.rvt, and find the Detail 2 view that you created earlier. This is the detail through the window at the clerestory. For the time being, you'll ignore the flashing and focus on the linework.

Several different drafting tools are available in Revit. You access them from the bottom of the Drafting tab of the Design bar (see Figure 11.24). We'll explore them in the order in which they appear on the tab, from top to bottom, and you'll use them on the callout detail.

Detail Lines

Detail lines are the most common drafting tool available in Revit. These are view-specific lines that you can draw in any view and use to create 2D details. When you activate the Detail Lines tool ( ), it lets you use the Type Selector to choose from existing line styles in Revit, including ones that have been imported from any other Revit families or CAD files (Figure 11.25). Line styles are defined by line weight, color, and pattern.

If you're drawing something with lines that represents an object, consider creating a detail component.

Figure 11.25

Line styles in the Type Selector

If no existing line style conforms to your needs, if you want to edit the graphic properties of a line style, or if you want to delete existing line styles, use the Line Styles dialog box (choose Settings → Line Styles).

The Options bar for detail lines shows all the drawing styles and line-shape choices available in Revit (Figure 11.26).

The Draw and Pick Lines tools are similar to the tools used to create walls. The Draw tool (the default tool) allows you to choose any of the drawing options from the nearby button menus.

The Pick Line tool (also selected by default) is the most commonly used tool. It's illustrated in Figure 11.27. The second tool, shown as a rectangle in Figure 11.27, is dynamic and always appears as the tool most recently used from the flyout menu represented by the third button shown in the Options bar in Figure 11.26. Here is a list of all the drawing tools and their uses:

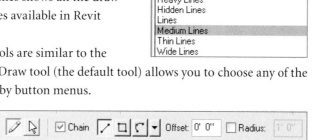

Figure 11.26

Options bar for detail lines

Figure 11.27

Pick Line options

Line This is a simple line-creation tool. By default, when you choose the second point of your line, Revit automatically begins a new line from that point. You can disable this feature by deselecting the Chain check box in the Options bar. The flyout contains all the drawing shapes.

Rectangle This tool draws all four sides of a rectangle or square. It can only draw vertical and horizontal lines.

Polygon This tool draws multisided shapes. When this tool is selected, a box on the Options bar lets you select the number of sides you want for your shape. If you want a rectangle that is nonorthogonal, use the Polygon tool and enter **4** for the number of sides.

Circle This tool draws circles by radius.

Arc Passing Through Three Points This tool draws an arc using the following sequence of points: first point, last point, midpoint.

Arc from Center and End Points This tool draws an arc using the following sequence of points: center point, start point, end point.

Tangent Arc This tool draws an arc from a starting point. You must select a point in the view to begin the tangent arc.

Fillet Arc Selecting this tool prompts you to choose two nonparallel lines and create a fillet arc between them.

Spline This tool draws a spline. The points of the spline can be edited after the line has been drawn, but you can't fillet or trim a spline.

Ellipse This tool draws ellipses by letting you locate the center and then the major and minor radii.

Partial Ellipse This tool draws a half segment of an ellipse using the following sequence of points: start point, end point, radius.

In addition to these tools, a check box next to the Line button allows you to chain your lines together by pairing the end point of one line with the start point of another.

Lines

The Lines tool (⬛) (not to be confused with the Detail Lines tool) is found on the Basics and Modeling tabs in the Design bar.

Lines are model elements (as opposed to detail/annotation elements) and appear in every view applicable. This means if you draw a line in an elevation view, it appears in every 3D view, elevation view, detail view, and so on, where that portion of the eleva-

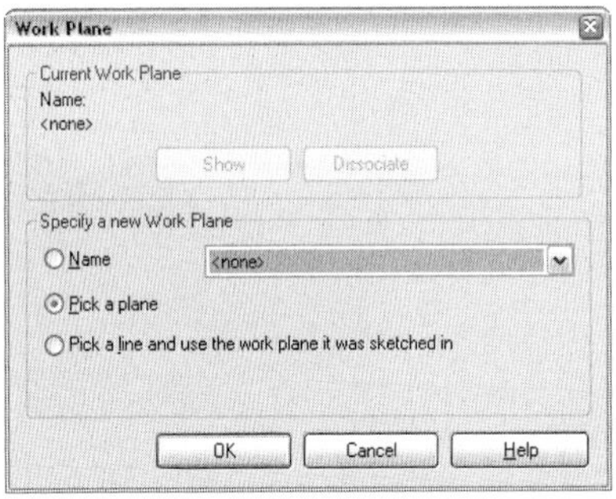

Figure 11.28

Choosing a work plane

tion is visible. The lines use all the same draw commands as the Detail Lines tool; however, they're drawn on a 3D work plane in the model.

If the view you're in isn't an active work plane, then when you select the Lines tool, it will ask you to define or select a work plane by displaying the dialog box shown in Figure 11.28.

Here, you can either use the Name option to choose a work plane that is already defined, use the Pick a Plane option to choose a face (such as the face of a wall or floor) to draw on, or use the Pick a Line and Use the Work Plane It Was Sketched In option, which we hope is self-evident.

> You may be wondering, "When do I use lines, and when do I use detail lines?" Use *detail lines* when you're drawing things in 2D that will appear only in the view they're created in. Some examples would be linework in an elevation or something drawn in a drafting view. Use *lines* when you want the same line to appear in all views but you don't necessarily need a 3D modeled element to communicate the design intent. Examples for the use of lines are control joints or gaps between panels in a façade.

> Keep in mind that if the line occurs on a predictable module, it may be helpful to create a filled region.

Detail Groups

Detail groups are similar to blocks in AutoCAD. They're collections of 2D graphics that you'll probably want to repeat again and again in the same or different views. A classic example is wood studs or blocking. You can easily and quickly set up a group and use that group over and over in the model. Doing so helps control consistency throughout the drawing.

To make a detail group, create the detail elements you'd like, select all the elements, then group them using the Group command: Edit → Group → Create Group.

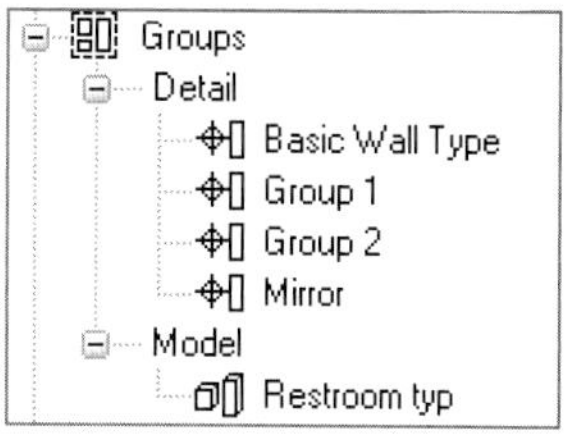

Figure 11.29

Groups in the Project Browser

Once a group is created, you will be prompted for a group name. We suggest that you name the group rather than accepting the default name Revit wants to give it (Group 1, Group 2, and so on).

To place a detail group, use the Detail Group button (⬛ Detail Group   ) in the Drafting tab. Then, use the Type Selector to choose which group you want to place, or you can expand the Groups node in the Project Browser and insert a group by name (Figure 11.29).

Detail Components

Detail components represent various small-scale building components such as screws, blocking, or metal studs, and are parametric 2D families. They're similar to detail groups but are created in the Family Editor and can be designed with dimensional variation built right into the family. In other words, a single detail component can make a full range of shapes available in a single component. Because they are families, this also means they can be stored in your office library and shared across projects easily.

To add a detail component to your drawing, select the Detail Component button (▱ Detail Component   ) from the Drafting tab in the Design bar and choose one from the Type Selector.

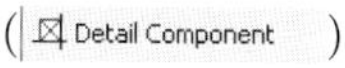

If you need to load a new component, click the Load button in the Options bar, and browse to the Detail Components folder. Revit has a wide range of common detail components in the default library.

To make a new detail component, use the Family Editor, and choose File → New Family → Detail Component.rft. Now you can begin drawing drafting lines, as you did in the project, and then save the file as an independent family that can be loaded into any project. We'll go a bit deeper into how to make families in Chapter 13.

A detail component is an incredible feature, not to be underestimated. Not only can you insert detail components into a project, but you can also insert them into 2D and 3D families and set them to show only at fine levels of detail. One way to use a detail component is to insert it into a family and use it to demonstrate a higher level of detail when the family is cut in section. An example is the shims and silicone in a window head that you don't necessarily want to model, but that you do want to show in a wall section or detail.

Masking Regions

A *masking region* is designed to hide portions of the model that you don't want to see in the view. Affectionately referred to as "white-out," a Masking Region imposes a 2D shape on top of the model that masks elements behind it.

> The masking region obscures only the model and other detail components. It can't mask annotations.

To add a masking region to your view, click the Masking Region button (□ Masking Region) on the Drafting tab.

This takes you to Sketch mode, where you can draw a closed loop of lines. When you draw a masking region, you can assign the boundary lines different line styles—check the Type Selector to make sure you're using the line style you want displayed. One of the line styles that is particularly useful for the Masking Region tool is the Invisible Line style. It allows you to create a borderless region—ideal if you want to truly mask an element in the model.

Figure 11.30

A masking region

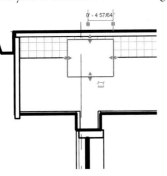

Each line can be given its own line style, making it possible to create a shape with different boundary line representations. A masking region is shown in Figure 11.30.

To edit a masking region, select the region, and choose the Edit button from the Options bar. Doing so brings you back to the Sketch mode and lets you edit the region.

Adding to the Detail

Now that you have a better understanding of detail components and masking regions, let's make an example on the model we have been using. You will be adding a gutter to the roof.

1. Select the Detail Component button, and choose the 4″ × 4″ gutter that has been preloaded into this model.

2. Open the view Detail 2, select the Detail Component button from the Design tab, and choose Gutter Bevel Section 4″ × 4″ (15cm × 15cm) from the Type Selector.

3. Use the Mirror tool to flip the gutter. Be sure to uncheck Copy in the Options bar. After mirroring the gutter, align it with the roof edge (Figure 11.31).

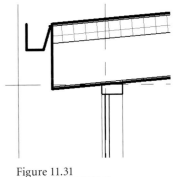

Figure 11.31

Adding a gutter

You also need to add a fascia board, which is something you didn't model with the Roof family. But before you do that, you need to mask some of the rigid insulation in the roof in order to build the fascia board back in from the roof edge:

Figure 11.32

Adding a fascia board

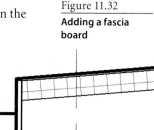

1. Use the Masking Region tool to draw a box at the roof edge. Make the box using four medium lines, and make it 1″ (2.5cm) wide. Bring it to the underside of the roof sheathing, and run it just past the bottom of the soffit, as shown in Figure 11.32.

2. Use the detail component Nominal Cut Lumber-Section 2×4 to build out the window heads. You can use the spacebar to rotate the component during placement.

3. Although you could use a detail component to place blocking above the window head, let's use detail lines instead. Select the Detail Lines tool and a medium line from the Type Selector.

4. Draw a box from the window head to the bottom of the rigid insulation.

5. Using a thin line, draw a line from corner to corner in the box. The finished detail looks like Figure 11.33.

If you decide to move or change those lines you've just drawn, you want them to all move together. This is a great use for groups. By selecting the window head and the blocking, you can use the Group command to group those elements into one unit. Another way to group a selection of elements is using the Group Tool located in the toolbars at the top of the interface. Figure 11.34 shows the elements grouped together.

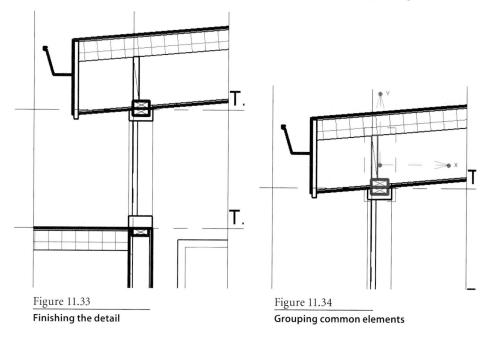

Figure 11.33

Finishing the detail

Figure 11.34

Grouping common elements

Creating a Repeating Detail

Repeating details are a common occurrence in architectural projects. Two-dimensional representations of masonry walls, metal decking, and roof tiles all comprise a series of repeating elements. Most of these elements aren't modeled as 3D components in Revit but are represented with symbolic detail components.

You create repeating details in Revit by selecting the Repeating Detail button (▦ Repeating Detail) on the Drafting tab of the Design bar.

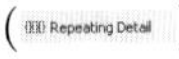

This tool takes a single detail component and arrays it along a straight line at regular intervals. Let's open the properties of a repeating detail to get a feel for how it's laid out. Figure 11.35 shows the Type Properties dialog box for a brick repeating detail.

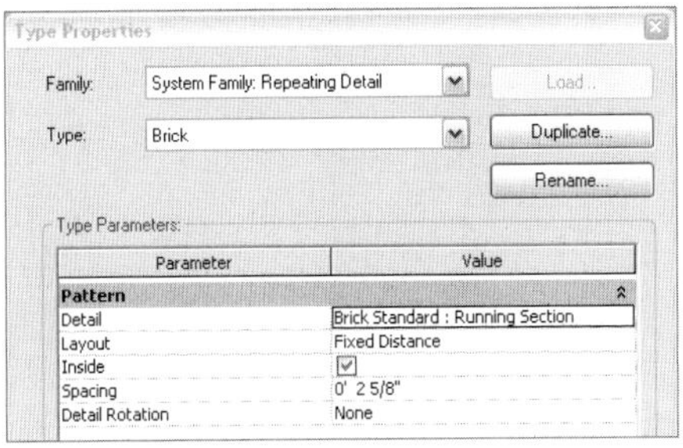

Figure 11.35

Repeating detail properties

When you select a repeating detail, the Type Selector is activated so you can select any repeating detail you've already loaded in the project. Repeating details are similar to families in that they have types and properties. If you don't have the repeating detail that you want loaded, it's easy enough to create one on the fly. All you need is a detail component that you wish to repeat.

Repeating detail placement is similar to placement of a line—the repeating detail has a starting point, an end point, and repeating 2D geometry in between. Let's make one to demonstrate this feature:

1. Click the Repeating Detail tool on the Drafting tab.

2. Choose the Properties button next to the Type Selector.

3. Click Edit/New.

4. Click Duplicate.

5. Give your new repeating detail a name.

6. Now, you need to select a detail component from the Revit library or use one you created on your own with the Detail field in the Type Properties dialog box.

The default repeating detail in Revit is a running brick pattern. If you look at it carefully, it consists of a brick detail component and a mortar joint (see Figure 11.36).

When you create a repeating detail layout, measure the distance between the beginning of the brick and the end of the mortar joint to understand the module on which the detail will repeat. When the detail component is inserted, it acts like a Line tool and allows you to pull a line of brick, as shown in Figure 11.37. This line can be lengthened, shortened, or rotated like any other line.

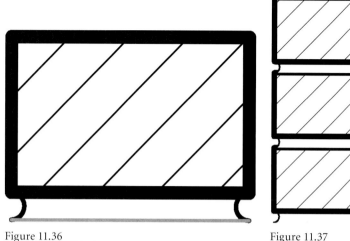

Figure 11.36

A repeating detail singular unit

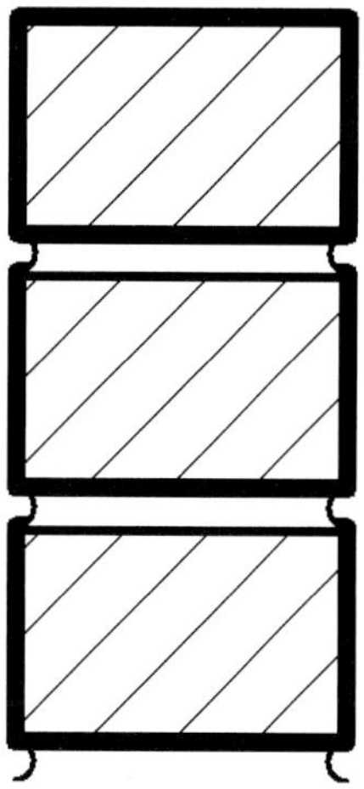

Figure 11.37

A repeating detail in the drawing view

If you're making a repeating detail from a component that isn't loaded in your project, you won't find it listed under the Detail item in the Properties dialog box. You first need to load it in your project and then make it a repeating detail component.

Let's take a closer look at the various options you can set in the Type Properties for a repeating detail (Figure 11.38):

Detail Here you can select the detail component you wish to have repeated.

Layout This option offers four different modes:

> **Fixed Distance** The path drawn between the start and end points when drawing the repeating detail is the length at which your component repeats at a distance of the value set for spacing.
>
> **Fixed Number** Here you can set how many times a component repeats itself in the space between the start and end points (the length of the path).

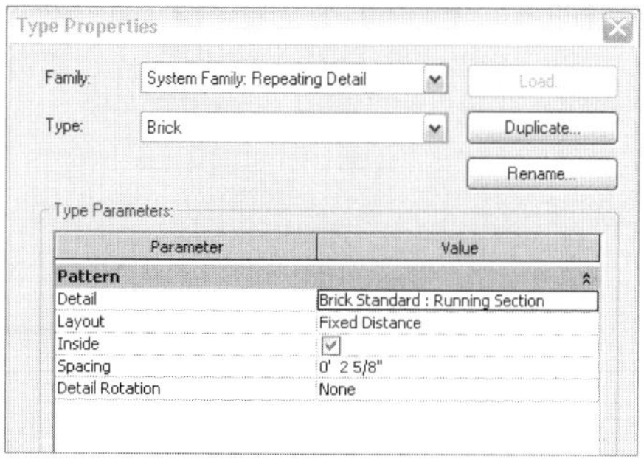

Figure 11.38

Type Properties for a repeating detail

> **Fill Available Space** Regardless of the value you choose for spacing, the detail component is repeated on the path using its actual width as the spacing value.
>
> **Maximum Spacing** The detail component is repeated using the set spacing, and the number of repeated components is set so that only complete components are drawn. Revit creates as many as will fit on the path.

Inside This check box adjusts the start point and end point of the detail components that make up the repeating detail.

Spacing This value is active only when Fixed Distance or Maximum Spacing is selected as the method of repetition. It represents the distance at which you want the repeating detail component to repeat. It doesn't have to be the actual width of the detail component.

Detail Rotation This allows you to rotate the detail component in the repeating detail.

Custom Line Types

You can use the Detail Component tool to create custom line types (lines with letters or numbers for various services such as fireproofing, rated walls, fencing, and so on). Note that when you create a detail component, you can't use text for the letters but need to draw them using lines.

Figure 11.39 shows the creation of a detail component in the Family Editor and the final result used as a repeating detail in the project environment.

Figure 11.39

Making a custom repeating detail

Insulation

The Insulation tool ( ) works just like a repeating detail component but is specifically designed as a symbolic representation for batt insulation. Due to the frequent use of this pattern, Revit provides a ready-made tool just for insulation. When drawn, it has two blue grips that let you change its length. The element properties of the insulation include only two changeable parameters:

Width This parameter is used to control the width of the insulation that is used. The Width parameter is also available in the Options bar when insulation is selected and is specific to each instance of insulation added to the model. Changing the width of one instance of insulation will change only that instance (see Figure 11.40).

Insulation Bulge to Width Ratio This parameter is used to control the density of the circles used in the insulation line, making the circles for the insulation head wider or flatter.

In most cases, you'll have two lines representing the space in the wall where the insulation needs to fit. Revit allows you to place the insulation using the centerline of the insulation as a location line.

Figure 11.40

The insulation Options bar

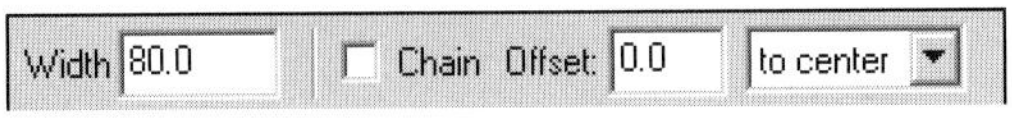

| Width 80.0 | ☐ Chain Offset: 0.0 | to center ▼ |

Adding Insulation

Now, let's add some insulation to your detail:

1. Select the Insulation tool from the Drafting tab.

2. In the Options bar, set the width to 3½″ (10cm).

3. Draw in the insulation below the windowsill. The finished detail will look like Figure 11.41.

Filled Region

The Filled Region tool (<img> Filled Region) is a 2D drafting tool that can be applied for many different purposes.

It can help you color surfaces or areas for graphic representations during the conceptual or design-development phase. It also can be a useful tool to document details and show material texture. Figure 11.42 shows how filled regions are used to communicate different functional zones in section.

A filled region consists of a boundary, which can use any line type, and a fill pattern that fills the area defined in the boundary. Figure 11.43 shows a filled region used with a hatch pattern.

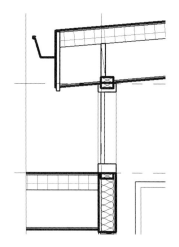

Figure 11.41

Adding insulation to the detail

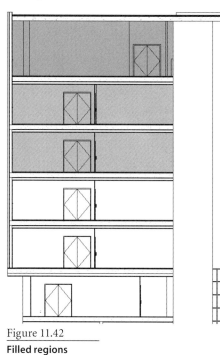

Figure 11.42

Filled regions

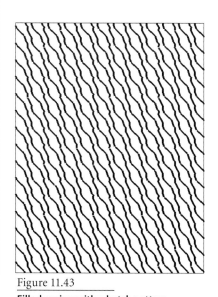

Figure 11.43

Filled region with a hatch pattern

Filled regions can also be transparent or opaque to show or hide what is behind them. Figure 11.44 shows two filled regions: the one at left is opaque, and the one at right is transparent.

Figure 11.44

Transparent and opaque filled regions

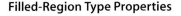

Filled-Region Type Properties

Filled region type properties define how the fill appears. This includes pattern, pattern color, and transparency (see Figure 11.45).

Figure 11.45

Type Properties for a filled region

Should you want to change the line style of the region boundary, you need to edit the region and then change the line style in Sketch mode. The Edit button appears in the Options bar when a filled region is selected.

For each filled region that has a different pattern, transparency, or other variation in appearance, you need to make a new filled region type. Remember that type properties propagate to all instances of the type, so making a change to one type may affect many instances in many different views. If you want to make a filled region with a new pattern, be sure to duplicate an existing type before you start changing type parameters.

Revit lets you define different line styles for each boundary segment of a filled region. This can be handy depending on how you're using the filled region. For example, if you're using the filled region with an earth hatch to cover the foundation, you might want a heavier line around the footings and slab and a lighter one in other areas.

The effective use of filled regions depends on the fill patterns used in them. Let's review in more detail some basic aspects of fill patterns:

- Fill patterns can be drafting or model patterns.

- Drafting fill patterns are visible only in the view in which they're created; they aren't visible in 3D view. Drafting view fill patterns are scaled specific to the view. So, a pattern with ¼″ cross-hatching will always show with the lines ¼″ apart, regardless of the scale of the view.

- Model patterns represent the material characteristics of an element (brick, stone, and so on) and do appear in 3D view. These patterns are model based and will not change their dimensions based on scale. So, if you have a standing seam metal roof pattern of vertical lines 16″ apart, they will always measure 16″ apart. In a ¼″-scale view, they will print twice as far apart as in a ⅛″-scale view.

> Revit comes with a nice selection of both drafting and model patterns, but, as with any library, it's never enough. You'll often want to create patterns or reuse patterns from other projects or applications. Patterns can be imported from any AutoCAD .pat files as well. Specify whether the pattern is model or drafting.

Show/Remove Hidden Lines

In visual communications between architects and engineers, when one element obscures another, either partially or fully, the hidden element is usually represented with dashed lines. Often, just a portion of an element is hidden. In the CAD world, it can take a lot of work to explode a block, split lines, and change many of the line styles to a hidden line type.

Revit has a special tool, called the Show/Remove Hidden Lines tool, for recognizing obscured elements and representing the portion that is hidden with dashed lines while still maintaining the complete object. This tool isn't located on the Drafting tab; it is a part of the Tools toolbar (see Figure 11.46).

Figure 11.46

Show Hidden Lines tool

You select the Show Hidden Lines tool (⬚),  click the element that obscures the object, and then click the element that is obscured. The hidden portion of the element becomes dashed. If an element is obscured with more than one element, keep repeating this operation until you get the desired look. Because Revit is a parametric engine, when you relocate or delete the obscuring element, the hidden element responds intelligently to those changes.

The first image in Figure 11.47 shows an I-beam hidden by another beam. The second image shows the results after the first iteration of the Show Hidden Lines tool, when the second beam is selected as an obscuring element and the I-beam is selected as an obscured element.

Figure 11.47

Using the Show Hidden Lines tool

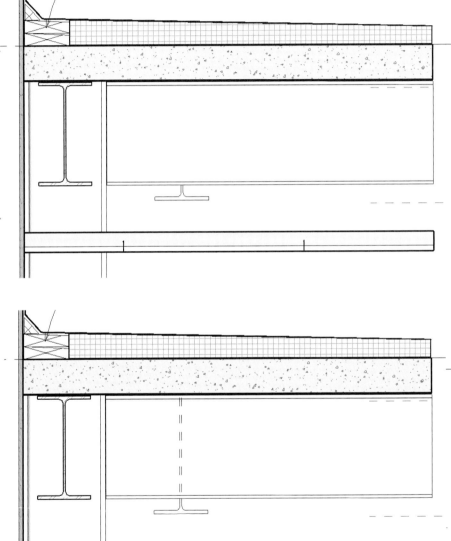

The Show Hidden Lines tool applies to 2D and 3D elements in all possible combinations (detail over detail, detail over model, model over detail, model over model).

Next to the Show Hidden Lines tool is the Remove Hidden Lines tool, which resets the graphic display of the elements so they look like they did before you applied the hidden line mode. This is the second button in Figure 11.46.

Importing CAD Details

In Chapter 7, we discussed how to import a CAD file into Revit. Existing libraries of CAD details or details you receive from a manufacturer can also be imported directly into a Revit project. If you're working with someone who only produces details using CAD, you can incorporate their work into your Revit model without disrupting workflow.

To prepare a CAD file for import, we recommend that you delete all the superfluous data in the file before importing it. If your import contains hatches or annotations that you don't intend to use in Revit, delete them first as well in the application where those have been created (AutoCAD as an example).

We also recommend that you import only one detail at a time so you can take better advantage of Revit's ability to manage sheet referencing. If you have a series of details organized in a single CAD file that you'd like to import into Revit, isolate each detail by saving it as a separate file, and then import them into separate drafting views within Revit.

> Every time you explode a CAD file in Revit, you add objects to the database. An inserted CAD file is one object. An exploded CAD file consists of many objects—maybe thousands of objects. For the best performance, explode CAD files as rarely as possible.

Reusing Details from Other Projects

There are many times in a project workflow when you want to grab details made in other projects and reuse them. So far we have covered how to do this using CAD files from other projects and from manufacturers' websites. This workflow is also possible using details created from other Revit projects. We will also talk about how to take our active project file and export key details to our library. In this section, we will discuss how to pull details out of a Revit file and put them into our active project.

Exporting Details from Revit Projects

As you create more and more details in Revit, you will inevitably want to save some of them to your office's standard library so that you can reuse them in other projects and save the invested work. With Revit, you can save a view out of a project and create a separate .rvt file that contains only that view. That file can then be incorporated into new projects. For example, if you have a 3D model detail that you embellished with 2D components and invested time making it and would like to save that work for future projects, you can save it as a Revit file.

Right-click any drafting view in the Project Browser and choose Save to New File. It might take Revit a minute to compile the view content, but you will be presented with a dialog box asking you for a file location to save the view. The default filename will be the same as the view name in the project. To bring views from that file into another project, open the other project, then choose File → Insert from File → Views. Choose the file you saved; then a dialog box (see Figure 11.48) will open and you can choose which views to bring into your project.

Figure 11.48

Exporting a view from Revit

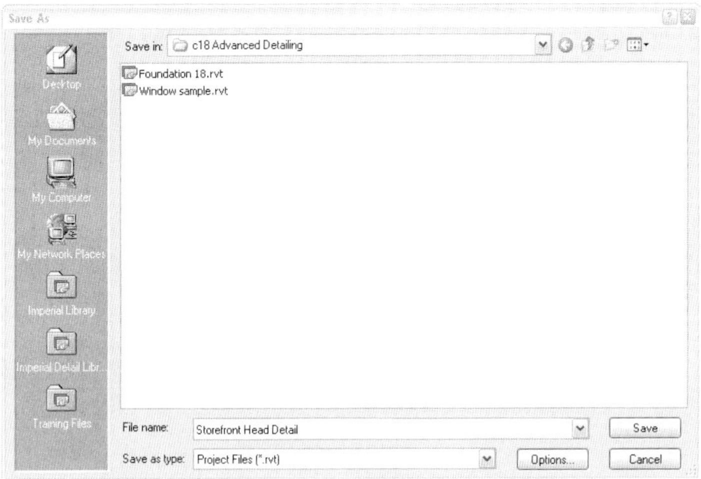

Once the view is exported, it is like any .rvt file. Opening the view directly will allow you to edit and manipulate any of the elements you exported in the view. You will also see a streamlined version of the Project Browser (Figure 11.49) with only the relative views present. These Revit files can be kept in a project library for later use.

The second way to export a view from Revit is to navigate to File → Save to Library → Save Views. This will open a dialog box of all of the exportable views from the project file. Here, you can select any number of views to be simultaneously exported into separate library files (Figure 11.50). This is a great way at the end of a project to export all of the detail views you would like to keep in a project library. Select the desired views by checking the appropriate boxes and click OK.

Figure 11.49

Streamlined Project Browser of saved Revit views

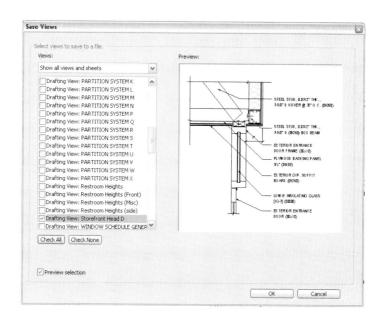

Figure 11.50

Multiple views can be saved as separate Revit files.

Importing Views into Revit Projects

To import any of these files into a new project, navigate to File → Insert from File → Views. This will allow you to navigate to your library containing your exported details. Choosing the exported detail file opens a dialog box (Figure 11.51) that allows you to select the view.

Figure 11.51

Inserting a view into a different project

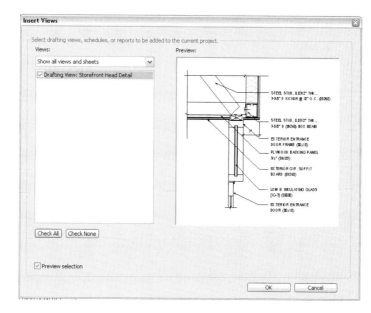

Notice that the view is described as its location within the Project Browser (Drafting View) and its view name (Storefront Head Detail). Selecting this view and clicking OK will merge the view into your current project (Figure 11.52). The view will appear in the location called out by the view name. In this case, you can find this view located in the Project Browser under Drafting Views.

Figure 11.52

The imported view merged into a new project

- Ceiling Plans
- 3D Views
- Elevations (Building Elevation)
- Drafting Views (Callout)
  - **Storefront Head Detail**
- Area Plans (Gross Building)
- Area Plans (Rentable)
- Legends

Another way to insert content into Revit is to use only the drafting views from exported files and not import any of the model components. This can be useful in many examples where you might want to take a doorjamb detail or a window head condition. In these instances, the detail might be strictly 2D, so you aren't going to import any of the 3D model information. Or you might have a wall section where some of the elements are drawn in 2D and 3D. You might only want the 2D information (the drafting lines, detail components, and annotations, for example) because you plan to reuse those in a new section in a different project.

To import the 2D content into your view, open the view you want to import into and choose File → Insert from File → 2D Elements. The resulting dialog box will look similar to the one for importing the full view but with some slight differences (Figure 11.53).

Unlike the Insert view, you can only choose one view at a time to insert. There is also an option to transfer the view scale with the view elements. Selecting this check box will reconfigure the view you are inserting into to match the view that you have inserted.

Select the drafting view and click OK. This will bring all of the 2D elements in the selected view into your active view. You can repeat this command multiple times in the same view window if you need to repeat the content.

Figure 11.53

Inserting 2D content from another Revit file

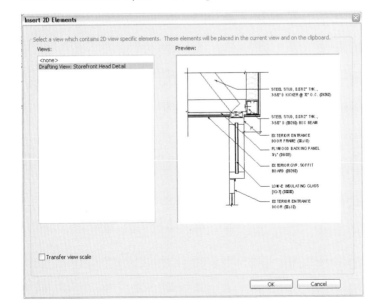

CHAPTER 12

Printing

We've reviewed how to create building elements, generate views, and get these views onto sheets. We also covered how to export the information you create in Revit so that it can be used by other downstream applications.

In this chapter, we'll review paper printing as well as some lightweight digital outputs (PDF and DWF). We'll also look at how to take advantage of Autodesk Design Review in conjunction with Revit as a way to exchange digital markups. We then offer some best practice tips on printing. Topics we'll cover include:

- Printing your documents

- Revit printing tips

- Publishing your BIM data

Printing Your Documents

In this section, we'll discuss a few of the specific settings and commands you'll use to print from Revit. If you've been working in the Windows environment, you'll find that printing from Revit is straightforward, because it's very similar to other Windows-based applications.

Print

Selecting File → Print brings you to the dialog box shown in Figure 12.1. All the features for printing are found here.

Figure 12.1

Print dialog box

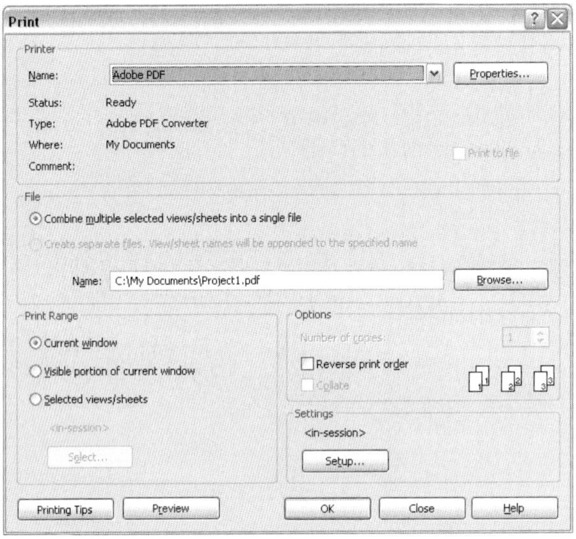

Print to File

Printing to a file allows you to create a printing or plot file (.prn or .plt) that can then be sent to a printer independently of the software in which it was created. Creating a .plt or .prn file means you can print many copies of the drawing set, at any time, without having to interrupt your workflow while you print. To print to file, select the Print to File check box below the Properties button.

Selecting the Create Separate Files. View/Sheet Names Will Be Appended to the Specified Name option creates a separate file for each view or sheet in the selection (Figure 12.2). This option is sometimes more practical for printing large sets. If paper runs out or any interruption happens during the printing process, you don't lose any time and can continue printing the remainder of the sheets later. By contrast, if you're printing from a single file, you'll need to start the print job over.

Print Range

In this section of the Print dialog box, you define exactly what you want to print. It includes these options:

Current Window This option prints the full extent of the open view, regardless of what extents of that view are visible currently on your screen. For example, if Figure 12.3 is what you see in Revit, Figure 12.4 will be the output when Current Window is selected.

Visible Portion of Current Window This option prints only what you see in the frame of the open window. It's a substitute for Windows' Print → Page Range → Selection command, which Revit doesn't currently support.

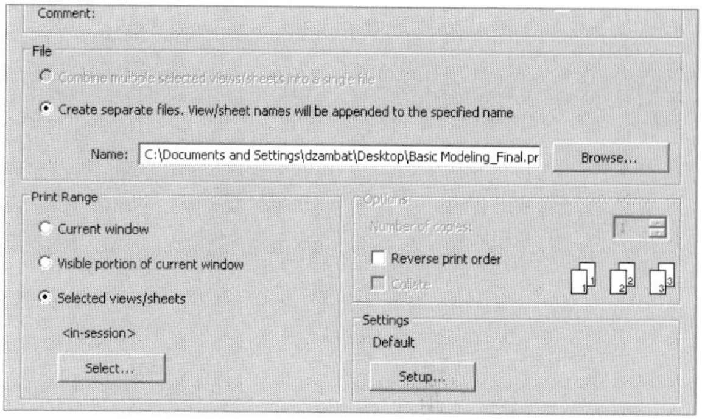

Figure 12.5 shows a Revit screen (what you see), and Figure 12.6 shows what will print if you select Visible Portion of Current Window.

Figure 12.2

Multiple sheets and views can be printed at once.

Figure 12.3

3D view zoomed out for printing

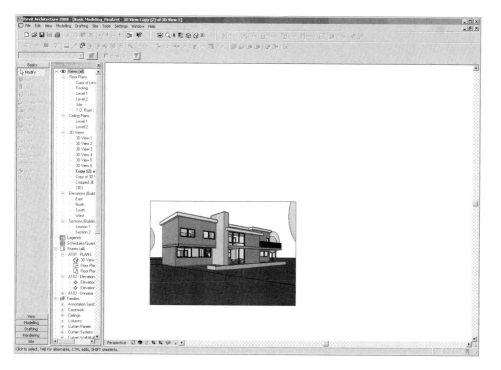

Figure 12.4

**Output when
Current Window
is selected**

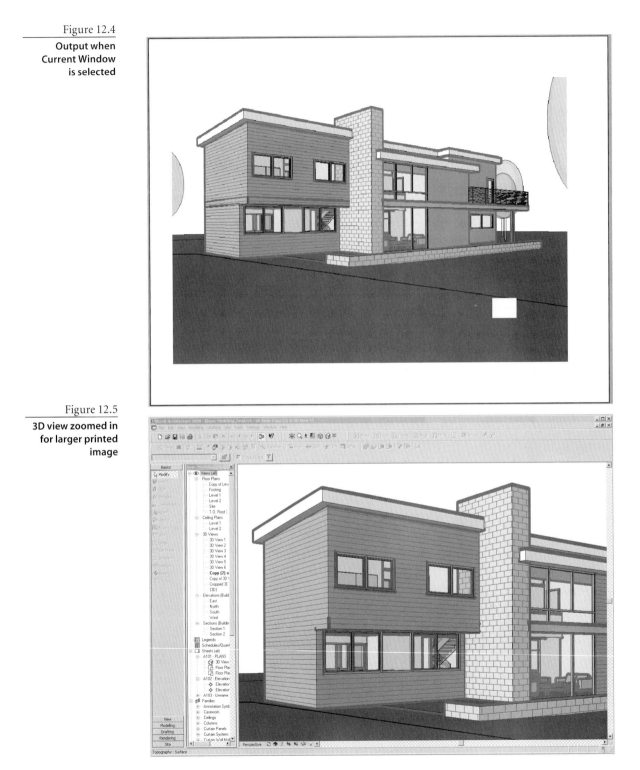

Figure 12.5

**3D view zoomed in
for larger printed
image**

Figure 12.6

Output when Visible Portion of Current Window is selected

Another way to print what you see on your screen is to use the PrintScreen key, typically found at the upper right of a Windows keyboard. Pressing this key copies a full image of the screen to the Clipboard. From there, you can paste it into Photoshop or another image application. If you want to print only the active window and not your entire desktop (an example would be a dialog box or just the Revit window), use Alt+PrintScreen—use this if you have a dual-monitor configuration so as to limit your print screen to the active application frame.

Selected Views/Sheets This option allows you to define a reusable list of views, sheets, or any combinations of views and sheets. This way, you can essentially batch-print a job by sending large quantities of sheets to the printer in one shot and save these selections for later print jobs. Figure 12.7 shows the View/Sheet Set dialog box.

This dialog box lets you pick any view or sheet to include in the View/Sheet Set. If you only want to include sheets in a set, use the Show options at the bottom of the dialog box to cull the list.

Figure 12.7

**The View/Sheet Set
dialog box**

This is a great tool to help define print lists. Some examples of what you might want to use these selections for would be a 100 percent construction document package or a specific set of presentation sheets.

> These check boxes only control what you see in the sheet/view list. They don't control what will or won't be printed.

Print Setup

The printing environment is set up using the Print Setup dialog box (Figure 12.8). Here you set up a printer and settings for printing. You can save these settings with a name so that they can be reused in later sessions of Revit. These settings can also be transferred to other Revit projects if need be, using the Transfer Project Standards tool located in the File menu. Let's take a look at some of the printing options available to you.

> To transfer print settings from one project to another, open both in the same session of Revit, and choose File → Transfer Project Standards.

Hidden Lines Views

Views in Revit can be displayed in four graphic modes: wireframe, hidden-line, shaded, and shaded with edges. The most commonly used type of view is hidden-line. You'll choose this type for floor plans, sections, and elevations, and sometimes even for 3D.

Revit lets you select whether you wish to print this type of view with vector processing or raster processing of the hidden lines. Vector is faster; however, you need to be aware of some nuances when working with hidden-line views. For example, transparent glass material prints transparent with raster processing but opaque with vector processing.

Figure 12.8

The Print Setup dialog box

Figure 12.9 shows a perspective in hidden-line mode printed using raster processing. Figure 12.10 shows the same perspective printed with vector processing. Note that you can't see through the glass using this setting.

If you have many views on a sheet, even if only one of them is an image or a shaded view, Revit automatically changes the printing to raster processing.

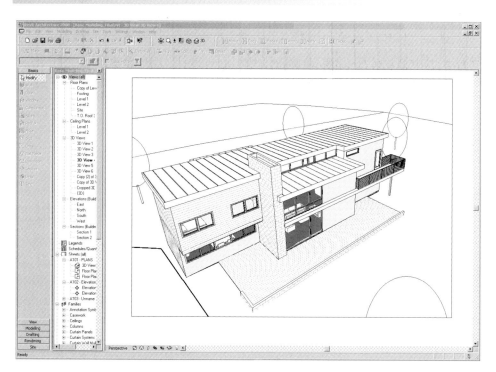

Figure 12.9

Raster print example

Figure 12.10

**Vector print
example**

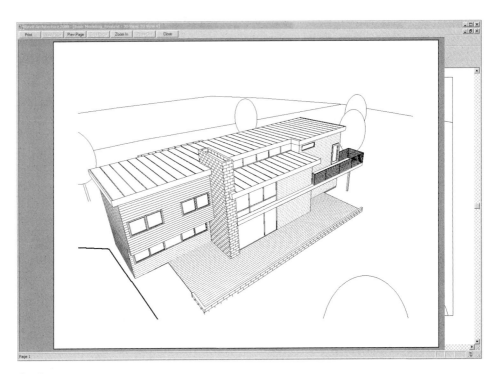

Options

The Options pane is at the lower left in the Print Setup dialog box. It includes these options:

View Links in Blue View links are hyperlinked tags that lead you from one view to another or from a sheet to a view. They appear blue in Revit and print black by default, but you can specify to print them in blue, which is how they appear on the screen.

Hide Ref/Work Planes; Hide Scope Boxes; Hide Crop Boundaries These three check boxes let you decide whether to print various Revit-specific graphics, including reference planes, scope boxes, and crop boundaries.

Hide Unreferenced View Tags During the course of a project, you may create a lot of elevation tags, section flags, or detail callouts for working purposes that you don't wish to be printed in the final documents or placed on any sheet. Such view tags are referred to as *unreferenced*, and Revit gives you the option to not print them.

In Figure 12.11, note the section lines, callout views, and crop region in the floor plan.

Figure 12.12 shows that when you select Hide Crop Boundaries and Hide Unreferenced View Tags, some features from the view don't appear on the print. These will not show up in the Print Preview either.

Figure 12.11

The view as it appears in Revit

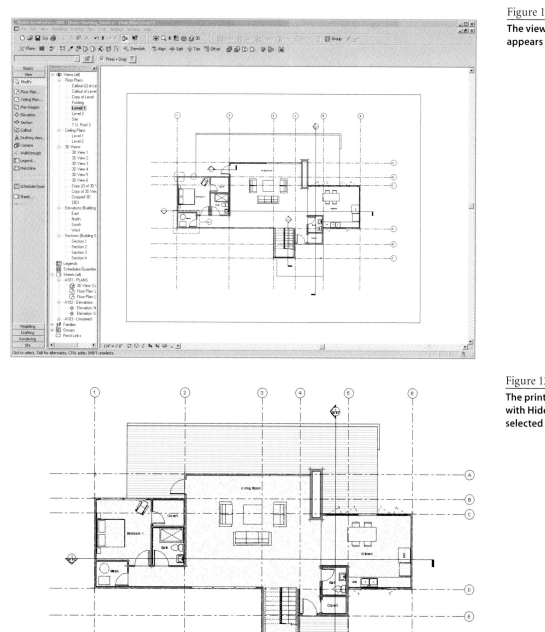

Figure 12.12

The printed view with Hide options selected

Revit Printing Tips

Here are some helpful, specific hints about printing from Revit. These tips will help you to optimize your print performance whether you are printing to a paper or digital format:

- When you're plotting large-format sheet sizes to plotters such as the HP DesignJet or OCE printer, change the plotter's settings so the data is processed in the computer. (This is probably handled through the printer's advanced settings menu. Each printer has its own command sequence.)

- Be sure the Far Clip Plane is active for the view and set to a reasonable distance. (View Properties → Far Clip Plane should be on in each view.) Having a distant clip plane can significantly slow your printing process.

- Hatches and other types of fill patterns when used extensively or in high density can affect performance. (The Sand fill pattern is an example.) If possible, turn them off, or exchange them for less performance-intensive patterns.

- Level of detail can affect performance. If you don't need to print in Fine view, reduce it to Medium or Coarse.

- A DWG, when mistakenly inserted in all views, can affect printing speed. If you notice that your elevation or section prints slowly, the reason may be a DWG that is imported into that view but shows as a single line and thus is unnoticeable. This will happen if you insert a DWG in a plan view, but are printing and elevation or section view. You can check which DWGs are showing by opening the Visibility/Graphics dialog box, clicking the Imported Categories tab, and deselecting the Show Imported Categories in This View check box.

- For general performance improvements, including when you're printing, Revit has a 3GB switch functionality. You can learn about it by navigating to the Knowledge Base area of the Autodesk website. Go to www.autodesk.com/support, and choose Autodesk Revit Building. The 3GB switch document is linked on the resulting page.

- Offices have a finite number of printers. Set up each of your plotters and printers in your Revit template. That way, you don't have to re-create them for each new project.

- Set up some standard sheet sizes: 11″ × 17″, 8½″ × 11″, Size E1, and Full Size E1 are some standard architectural sheets. Add these to your template as well.

Publishing Your BIM Data

The construction process goes through many iterations and exchanges of information among different parties. Exchanging a full-blown data-rich building information model is not always required, and not everyone on the project team will be using Revit. Many team members just need to see a drawing to approve or mark up some changes and send it back to you. Some team members may be using dial-up Internet connections or older computers that can't handle big downloads effectively (or at all). You may also not be ready to share your intellectual property with the world in the form of editable drawings. Finally, you may be concerned about unauthorized appropriation or editing of your documents by others. This is where using lightweight digital output comes into play.

You need to be able to share drawings and documentation in a safe, noneditable, lightweight form that can be viewed by others outside the world of Revit. This is the problem that some new publishing technologies are trying to solve.

Design Web Format (DWF)

Design Web Format (DWF) is Autodesk's solution for publishing intelligent data in a light, easy, and secure way while preserving the power of the information embedded in the design documents. DWF files are highly compressed, and are capable of transmitting big design models via e-mail or other limited-transfer technologies.

DWF Publishing Options

You can publish a Revit project as a DWF file and send it to various stakeholders in the building process. With the latest version of Autodesk Design Review (we will discuss Design Review in more detail later in this chapter), it is possible to view and even mark up these files. Microsoft Vista also has an embedded DWF viewer, so the receiver won't have to install a separate DWF viewer, as required with machines running Windows XP or earlier.

Revit has a built-in DWF publisher, so you don't need to install any additional drivers in order to create DWFs. There are two ways to publish a DWF from Revit:

Figure 12.13

Publish DWF options

- 2D DWF (good for sending out 2D sheets and individual drawings)

- 3D DWF (good for creating a 3D representation of your BIM model)

Choose File → Publish DWF (see Figure 12.13) to view the options.

DWF EXPORT OPTIONS

Revit is a BIM modeler with tons of information embedded in it about each element within the model. Much of this information is also published into the DWF format. You can send model and room data with the DWF or choose not to. This option is available under File Publish → 2D or 3D DWF. Choose the Options button (Figure 12.14).

When you select the Model Elements option in the DWF Export Options dialog box, all the property information about the model elements in the view that is being exported is published to DWF. This allows anyone viewing the DWF to select an object in that view and see its properties. Some examples of these properties are area, length, family name, and so on.

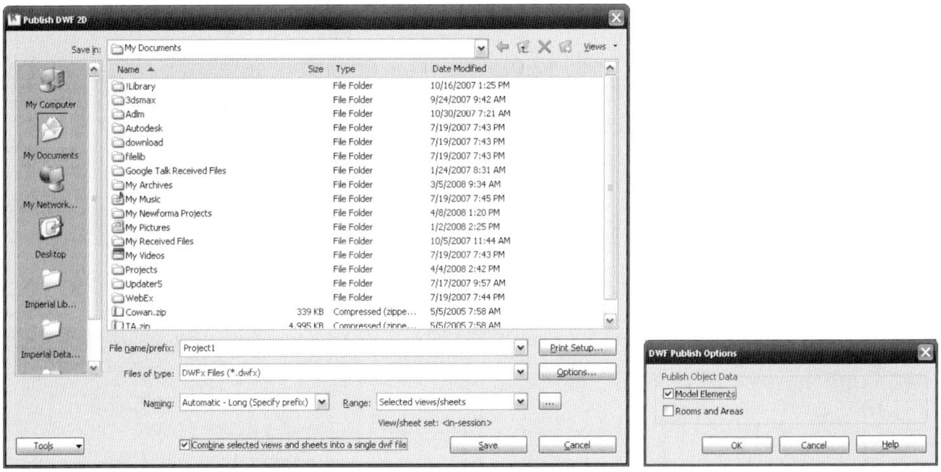

Figure 12.14

The Publish dialog box and DWF Export Options dialog box

Selecting the Rooms and Areas check box publishes additional information that isn't included in Model Elements, because in Revit, rooms and areas are objects rather than physical elements. Room area and perimeter are two examples. This information can be helpful, especially to facility managers to whom you may be sending your DWFs.

EXPORTING A VIEW OR SHEET AS A SINGLE FILE

When publishing to DWF, you can make separate DWF files for each view or publish all views into one DWF file. To do so, select the Export Each View or Sheet As a Single File check box in the Export dialog box. Note that even though DWF is a lightweight format, depending on the size and complexity of the project you're dealing with or the number of sheets (or views) you want to publish, a DWF can be large; you may want to consider splitting it into a few separate DWFs.

Publishing to 2D DWF

When you publish to 2D DWF, the information is published in 2D flat drawings, regard-less of the view type. This means that perspective and axonometric views are published as flat images. Figure 12.15 shows a 2D DWF. Note that although the drawing is technically in two dimensions, it retains its visibility settings and element properties.

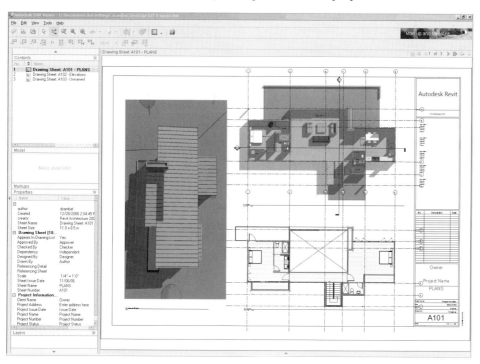

Figure 12.15

A 2D DWF

Publishing to 3D DWF

Publishing a 3D DWF creates a full-blown 3D DWF model. When it is opened with a DWF viewer, you can spin the model around, turn visibility of separate elements on and off, slice the model in sections, make elements transparent, and review the model in a variety of ways. Figure 12.16 shows some of this functionality.

The cross-section tool lets you slice the model in any direction and reveal the exterior. You not only see the 3D information and can easily move around and review parts of the building, but you can inspect the properties of any element available in the model.

Sharing digital models using 3D DWF has proven to be of special value for construc-tion companies. It both facilitates design visualization in the field and allows builders to do a constructability review in the office before problems arise in the field. Also, 3D DWFs are useful to owners because they effectively convey the future look and feel of their building.

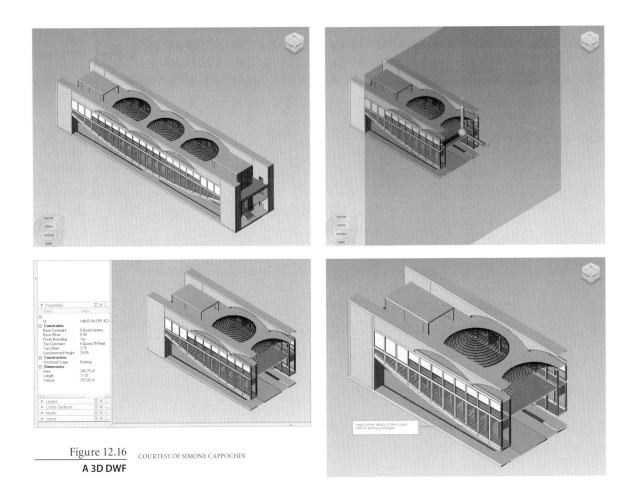

Figure 12.16

COURTESY OF SIMONE CAPPOCHIN

A 3D DWF

Marking Up Drawings with Design Review

Autodesk Design Review is a free application created by Autodesk that allows you to review, mark up, and track changes to 2D and 3D designs. These comments are stored in the DWF file, and even show up in your Revit file by linking in a DWF file. (www.autodesk.com/designreview). This is a very light-weight application that can be easily downloaded, installed, and used by all the stakeholders on the project team.

In the Design Review application, when you select a Revit element, for example a wall in the 3D view (Figure 12.17), it displays all its properties in the left pane. Viewing models and querying element properties is just one advantage of this tool. The DWF environment opens up new, intelligent ways to share information, propose revisions, and discuss document changes to the BIM model.

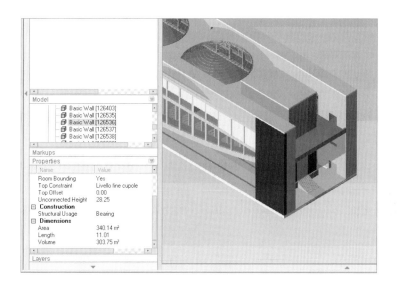

Figure 12.17
DWF element properties

In a time-honored scenario, an architect prints and sends a set of physical drawings to their engineer. The engineer reviews them, physically marks with a red pen the necessary changes, and sends the drawings back to the architect. The architect reviews the revised drawings and re-creates the changes in their digital files. This process is repeated throughout the life of the project. Not only is there a lot of room for error with all the transposing of information, but a lot of money is spent on printer paper, postage, and shipping. The transmission of black-and-white, smeared facsimiles or poor penmanship can result in misinterpreted information. Using DWF reduces costly errors and omissions in your communications with team members and clients. Let's review how you can leverage these tools.

A WORKFLOW SCENARIO: MARKING UP A 2D DWF FROM A REVIT MODEL

In Revit, the architect opens the sheet they wish to send to a consultant, then publishes it to 2D DWF, and sends it via e-mail.

> Markup functionality only works with Revit sheets—make sure you are publishing sheets and not views when working with the DWF mark-up features.

The consultant opens the DWF in Design Review, reviews the drawings, makes a markup with desired changes directly in the digital file, and sends the DWF back to the architect (e-mail again). Figure 12.18 shows a sample marked-up DWF.

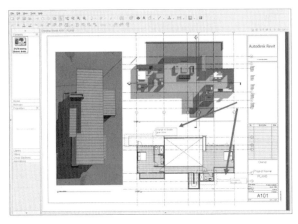

Figure 12.18

A marked-up DWF

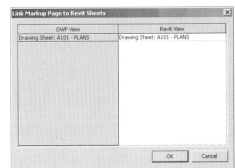
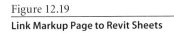

Figure 12.19

Link Markup Page to Revit Sheets

The architect links the DWF markup (File → Import/Link → Link DWF Markup Set) into the Revit file from which the DWF was originally generated. The red markup shows up on the correct sheet and in correct position, as shown in Figure 12.19.

Figure 12.20

Element Properties dialog box for a markup

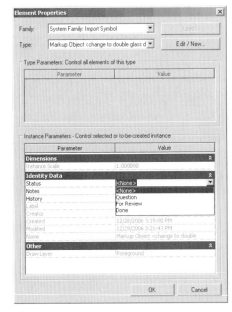

Each linked markup has a defined status (None, Question, For Review, or Done), which is shown in the Element Properties dialog box for each markup (Figure 12.20). When initially linked, the default status is None, but it can be changed to another status after an initial review. Thus, the architects in the team can track whether a certain change request has been executed or is still under review or discussion.

Marking Up 3D DWF files

Design Review lets you mark up and add comments not only to 2D DWF files but also to 3D DWF files. The process is the same: you select the Markup tool from the toolbar, click the spot that you want to comment on, and type in the text box that opens (see Figure 12.21).

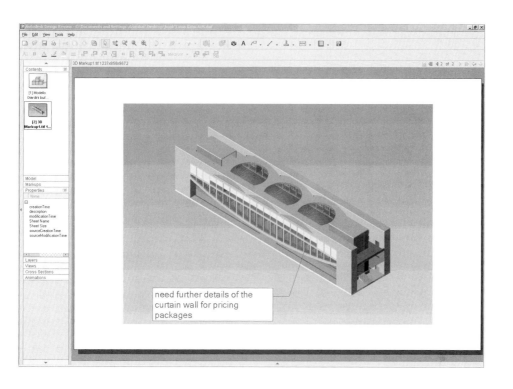

Figure 12.21

With Design Review, markups can even be added to 3D views.

Collaborating through a digital publishing mechanism is of value for many participants in the building industry because it allows for shorter review cycles; faster decisions;
better communication of information; better visualization of projects; and better tracking, archiving, and documenting of change orders.

Publishing to PDF

Portable Document Format (PDF) is an Adobe-created document format. The main uses
of PDF in the past were securing documents the originator didn't wish to have edited and
putting content into a manageable file size for digital transfer. Today, PDF is also commonly used to transfer drawings among team members and reprographic companies.
(A reprographic company can create large-format copies, which does pages at $30'' \times 42''$
(Arch E1) or other large-format sheet sizes.)

Revit supports printing to PDF through the use of printer drivers. You need at least
one PDF driver installed on your machine to be able to print to PDF. If you do not own a
copy of Adobe Acrobat (Adobe's PDF creator), there are other solutions currently on the
market that also make PDFs. PDF995 (www.pdf995.com) is an inexpensive solution that can
be installed on any workstation. For server-based solutions allowing multiple people to
print via PDF to a networked printer, JawsPDF is also available (www.jawspdf.com).

Another printing format to consider adding is EPS. This offers fantastic vector resolution and is great if you need to open for further postproduction in Photoshop. Getting EPS files out of Revit requires a PostScript driver. Printing is very, very fast. More information can be found at:

`www.adobe.com/support/downloads/product.jsp?product=pdrv&platform=win`

Or check out the Autodesk User Group International (AUGI) post at:

`http://forums.augi.com/showthread.php?t=36877&highlight=eps`

CHAPTER 13

Advanced Topics

This chapter touches on three topics in Revit that are beyond the basics. These topics are explored in more detail in our *Mastering Revit Architecture 2009* (Sybex, 2008) book, but knowing the fundamentals about them early on can be useful as you gain more experience with Revit.

In this chapter, we will review the basics of the Family Editor, using the Design Options tool, and worksharing. The Family Editor allows you to create and edit components in Revit. The Design Options tool allows you to make design iterations within Revit. And worksharing lets you divide the model so more than one person can work on it at the same time. Topics we'll cover include:

- Understanding families

- Using design options

- Worksharing—the multi-user environment

Understanding Families

Within Revit, components and other content are referred to as *families*. Some types of these elements can be created and edited on the fly within the project environment, and some are created and edited outside of a project file. Revit comes with a built-in family-editing application called Family Editor that is tailored for making all types of content, from doors and windows, to annotation symbols, to stand-alone furniture. Creating your own content is a critical aspect of working on projects, and thus creating families is a critical aspect of working with Revit, because families make up a vast amount of what goes into a model. Family editing is a relatively complex workflow involving using geometry, understanding constraints, and adding parametric variability into your components. Those topics can't be covered in one chapter, but we will cover the basics so that you can at least get started.

All elements in Revit are considered *families*. When you open Revit, a standard set of architectural objects and annotation symbols are already created and ready to use—these are all families. Families can be accessed a number of ways:

- In the Project Browser Families node, where you can find all loaded families in the project.

- In the Type Selector when an element is selected.

- By choosing File → Load from Library → Load Family. Here you'll find all the available default families that exist outside of the project, in an external library that you can load in the project. You can also browse from this location to any custom location where you have saved families that you've created.

- At www.autodesk.com/revitarchitecture. Click Data and Downloads, and then click Templates and Libraries. You can download thousands of families created for different geographic regions.

Revit uses three types of families:

- System families

- In-place families

- Component families

We'll discuss these next.

System Families

System families are created in the context of a Revit project, on the fly. You can create a new type of system family only by duplicating an existing family and then changing its properties. Here is a list of families that fall into this category:

- Walls

- Roofs

- Stairs
- Floors
- Ceilings
- Ramps
- Mullions

To create a new system family, select the one that is most similar to the one you need, duplicate its type, rename it, and modify it. Let's use a wall as an example:

1. Activate the Wall tool. From the Type Selector, select a wall that has similar properties to the wall you need to create. If none is similar, it's easiest to use a generic wall.

2. Click the Properties button, then click the Edit/New button, and click the Duplicate button.

3. You're prompted to give the new wall type a name. Rename the wall to reflect your design intent.

4. Start editing the wall by clicking the Edit button under Structure. Doing so opens another dialog box where you can add and modify layers of the wall structure. By clicking the fields for Function, Material, and Thickness, you can change the values (see Figure 13.1).

Using the Preview button at the bottom of this dialog box, you can switch the preview of the wall structure from Plan to Section.

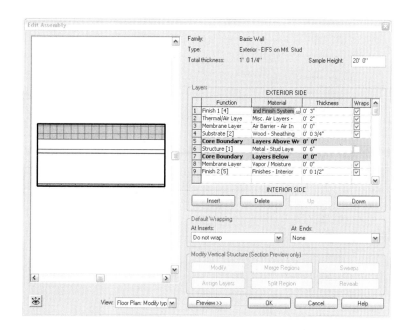

Figure 13.1

Modifying wall types

In-Place Families

In-place families are built in the context of your project using the Family Editor Design bar. This allows you to model geometry using your project as a reference. These families are useful for one-off objects that are highly specific to your project and unlikely to be reused in other projects. Usually they are connected with some complex geometry or have complicated shapes, or are tightly coupled with specific geometry in your project.

You create in-place families by clicking Create on the Modeling tab of the Design bar (⊫ 🔏 Create...) or selecting Create from the Modeling menu. Revit then lets you draw whatever you want and assign that to whatever category of element you wish. For example, if you are making a free-form wall, you assign the family to the category Wall, then create your geometry using Revit's form-making tools (Extrusion, Blend, Sweep, Revolve, Swept Blend). Having the elements belong to a correct category is important later in the process for correct reporting in the building database (scheduling) as well as for controlling the visibility of those elements.

The list of available categories you can assign the geometries to is a fixed list—if no category maps to what you intend to create, use the Generic Model category. So, if you are creating a custom fireplace, you will not find a Fireplace category in Revit; in that case, use the Generic Model category. As soon as you make a new in-place family, you will be asked to choose your category, as shown in Figure 13.2. You can always change the category later, if need be, by returning to the dialog box by choosing Settings → Family Categories and Parameters.

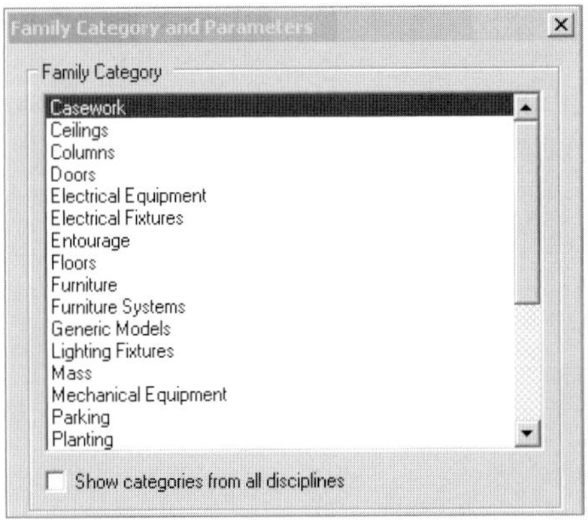

Figure 13.2

Family Category and Parameters dialog box

The in-place family is good for creating nonstandard element types such as slanted and tapered walls, unusual roof shapes, and furniture or other building elements that must conform to specific geometry in your model (a bench along a curved wall, for example). Figure 13.3 shows an in-place wall that follows the shape of a site and has a nonorthogonal profile. That said, try to use in-place families sparingly. Duplicating an in-place family makes unique elements within the model. If an element is becoming repetitive, it should be replaced with a family.

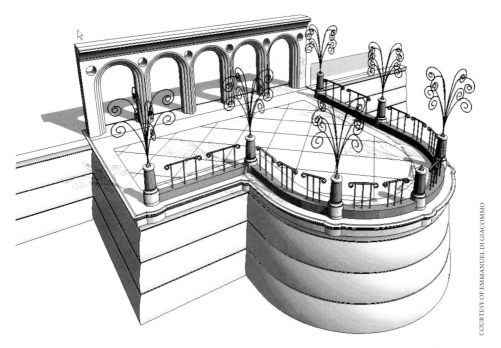

Figure 13.3
Sample in-place wall

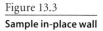

COURTESY OF EMMANUEL DI GIACOMMO

Component Families

Component families, also called *standard families*, are created and can be modified in an environment outside the Revit project, called the Family Editor. The fact that these types of families aren't created directly within the project environment allows some diversification of the project workflow and can help to minimize the number of users working directly in a project file on large projects.

Component families can include doors, windows, furniture, plumbing fixtures, light fixtures, entourage, columns, annotations, title blocks, massing families, structural elements, electrical equipment, site equipment, plants, profiles, and so on. Some examples are shown in Figure 13.4.

You will periodically need to open the Family Editor to create a new family. To do so, select File → New → Family. Often, however, you are working within a project and need to change a family already inserted into that project. To edit a family that is being used in your project, select the family, and then click the Edit Family button in the Options bar. You'll find yourself in the Family Editor environment.

Figure 13.4

Component family examples

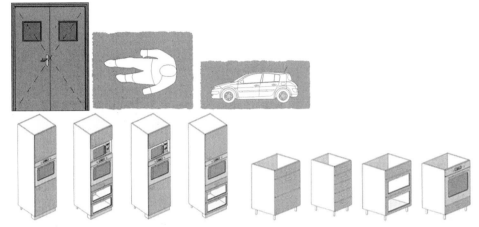

Because this is an introductory book about Revit, we won't explain the Family Editor in detail (it deserves an entire, separate book), but we would like to explain its basic principles. The Family Editor is designed to do two primary tasks:

- Create a new element
- Modify an existing element

The Family Editor is a unique design environment (see Figure 13.5), but it isn't separate software that you have to install. It's an integral application that is automatically installed with Revit. The Family Editor resembles the Revit project environment but is tailored for specific modeling tasks. It has only one Design bar in which relevant tools are located.

Figure 13.5

The Family Editor

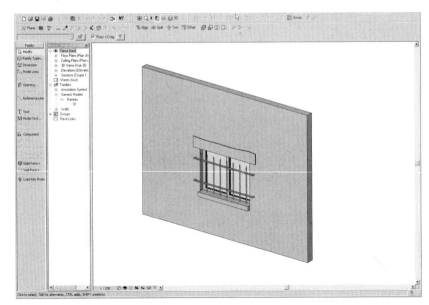

You can open the Family Editor several ways:

- When editing a family directly from within a project
- By opening an .RFA file from Windows Explorer
- By selecting File → New → Family (to create a new family)

When you create a new family, you're prompted to select a template. The templates are predefined files that are set up for the purpose of creating specific content that will behave according to the characteristics of the element to be created. For example, the window template looks different from the door template. The next section discusses templates in more detail.

Family Templates

If you're creating a table, you need to start with the furniture template. If you wish to create a sink, you start with a plumbing fixture template. To create a new door, select a door template. You get the idea. The available templates for modeling elements are listed in Figure 13.6 and can be found in your Libraries folder, located at `C:\Documents and Settings\All Users\Application Data\Autodesk\RAC 2009\Imperial Library` or `C:\Documents and Settings\All Users\Application Data\Autodesk\RAC 2009\Metric Library`.

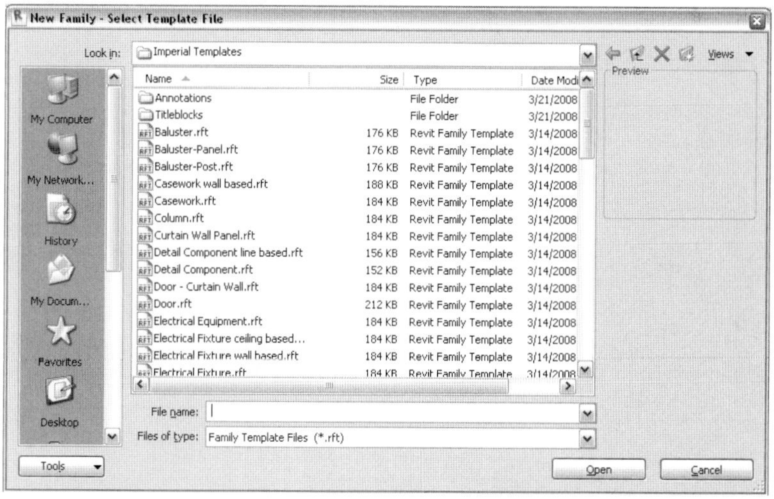

Figure 13.6
Family types

> The family templates are different for metric and U.S. customary content. Make sure you select the correct ones when you install Revit.

The family templates are grouped in three categories:

- Model templates (the one you see listed when you open this dialog box)
- Annotation family templates (tags, keynotes, and so on)
- Title block families (you can create custom title blocks per project or company)

Selecting a correct template before you create a family is essential. A correct template does the following:

- Categorizes the family you create. This ensures that your family is located in the Project Browser and has a graphic appearance that's consistent with other elements of the same category.
- Lists that family in the correct Type Selector when elements are selected.
- Schedules the family according to the type you selected.
- Enables content-specific parameters and behaviors.

If you want to create a window but you choose the door template, your window won't have the parameters necessary to interact properly with the model. If you wish to create furniture but you select a generic family template, your furniture piece won't schedule when you schedule your furniture, and so on.

> **Rule number one:** Decide whether your component will be a hosted or nonhosted element. Try to use hosted geometry only if the geometry you are hosting to needs to be cut. Examples of this would be windows or doors.
>
> **Rule number two:** Select the correct template.
>
> **Rule number three:** Choose a good insertion point. The default insertion point of a family will be the center of the green crosshairs that appear in the family template.

If none of the categories match what you're hoping to create, use the generic family template.

Templates are provided for each category; some additional family templates are also provided. Depending on the type of element, you'll notice that some templates are *host based*. (Light fixtures can be wall based, ceiling based, floor based, and so on.) Make sure you select the one that will make your element behave appropriately. Figure 13.7 shows some hosted families.

> You *can* change the family type after the creation of the family. To do that, open the family in the Family Editor and choose Settings → Family Categories and change the family to a new category. This will categorize your element correctly for scheduling.

Parametric and Nonparametric Family Types

You can create 2D and 3D families in the Family Editor that can be either parametric or nonparametric.

Figure 13.7

Floor-based and wall-based lighting fixtures

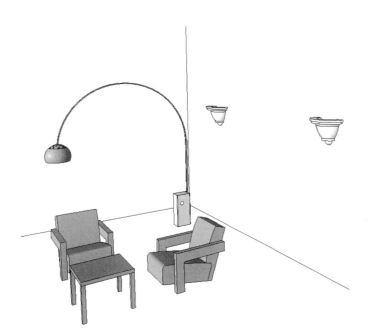

Parametric families allow variation in size and material to be captured and edited as parameters. Many types of parametric variations can be stored in a single family as types. An example of a parametric object is a table that is produced in four different sizes and two different wood types, or a window that is manufactured in 20 different sizes. Figure 13.8 shows a parametric family in two different sizes: as the family is changed, the table size and chair count increase or decrease.

Figure 13.8

A parametric family

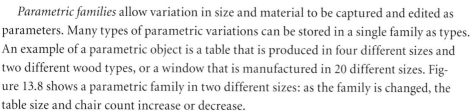

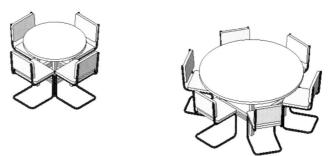

Nonparametric families do *not* provide changeable dimensions; they may provide variation in material, if anything. An example is a furniture family that is produced in only one size (a Le Corbusier chair or a designer lamp as an example). You can't buy it in other sizes, and thus there is no need for parametric properties. Note that you can make any family parametric at any time by adding a parametric dimension to it. Nothing in the family template limits a family to being nonparametric. Figure 13.9 shows a sample non-parametric family.

Figure 13.9

Example of a non-parametric family

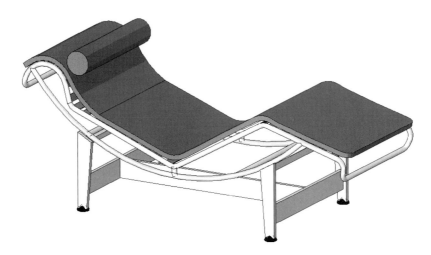

A possible scenario for nonparametric families can involve using content previously made with other software applications and importing it into the Family Editor. Revit allows you to import 2D as well as 3D DWG or SKP files (SketchUp files). Revit reads these file types, and you can leverage them to extend your Revit library with elements you've created

Figure 13.10

Example of a non-parametric family

with other software packages. Figure 13.10 shows an imported wind turbine that was built in SketchUp and imported into a Revit Family. It can then be placed in your Revit models like any other family, with one exception—you cannot control faceting or the level of detail. If it's a complicated family, it's probably best to create it starting in Revit.

Levels of Detail and View Visibility

Families in Revit let you control the visibility of their individual parts based on the view's detail level. (You can change the detail level in the model using the View Control bar.) When you're working in the Family Editor, you can select any elements and choose Vis-ibility from the Options bar. The Family Element Visibility Settings dialog box (Figure 13.11) allows you to change the elements' visibility using three levels of detail: Coarse, Medium, and Fine. If all levels of detail are selected, then the element appears all the time, in each possible level of detail. You can also make elements appear in different types of views: plan, front/back, and left/right. Elements are always visible in 3D views, provided all levels of detail are selected.

If you make a simple table or a chair, you'll probably view the table as a rectangle in all three

Figure 13.11

Family Element Visibility Settings dialog box

levels of detail. If you make a door family, however, you'll want to change the display at different scales. Figure 13.12 shows the three levels of detail. Note that the table doesn't change; the walls get two different representations, and the door has three.

Revit families are flexible: you can choose to display only certain elements of the family in one level of detail and a more complicated presentation in another. It's up to you—you have full control.

Family Types

The Family Editor allows for the creation of *family types*. These are typically objects created by manufacturers that come in a variety of standard sizes and finishes. Rather than creating 60–70 families that are the same shape and material but have many dimensional variations, with Revit, you only need to model one family and create types for each variation. You can then add these types to a *type catalog* (a simple comma-delimited .txt file) that makes types of that family, as shown in Figure 13.13.

Once the family is loaded into the project environment, you can select all available types in the Project Browser or using the Type Selector.

You can design Revit families that use simple mathematical formulas to determine rules of behavior. For example, a shelving family can be set up so that when a shelf spans longer than 20″ (50cm), it gets another support, as illustrated in Figure 13.14.

All the different family templates let you use custom fields and formulas, so there is no limit to what you can create.

Visual Control

Each family belongs to a category, but you can create additional subcategories in the Family Editor to provide a richer set of controls over the visual and graphic appearance of geometry in the family. A door family, for example, can have several meaningful subcategories: door leaf, handle, hardware, opening direction, frame, and so on. You can control visibility of each of those subcategories by selecting and deselecting them.

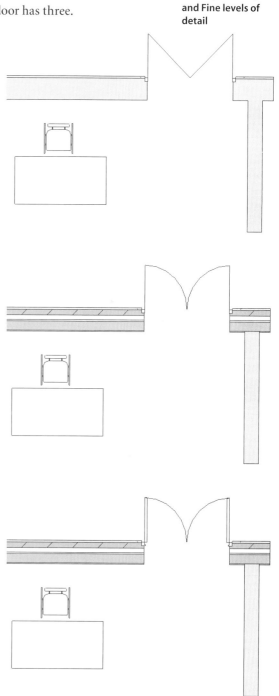

Figure 13.12

Top to bottom: Coarse, Medium, and Fine levels of detail

Figure 13.13

A family using a type catalog

Figure 13.14

Formulas in families allow for smart behavior.

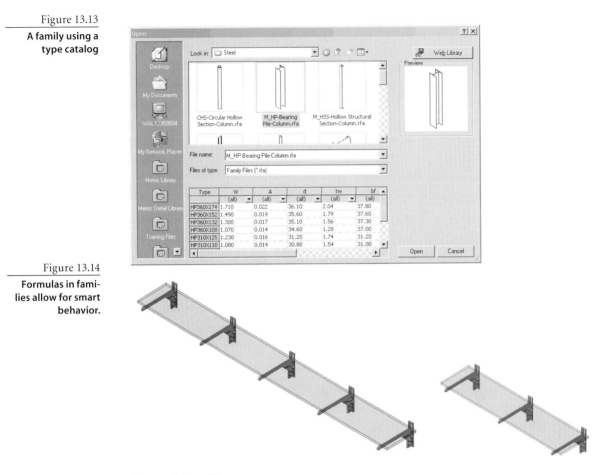

Nested Families

Revit lets you combine multiple families into one family. Imagine a door that incorporates a fixed transom window above it. These can be created as two separate families initially but combined into one to be inserted into the project. Nesting one family into the other, rather than using two, simplifies placement and design management in the final project. Revit also allows you to match the parameters so that when you change the width of a door, the transom window width changes, too. Figure 13.15 shows a door with a nested transom: rectangular and arched. Both are separate families combined into one family.

Figure 13.16 shows the dependency of the width of the door and the transom; any changes to one apply to the other automatically.

All these behaviors are defined by you, the user. No other software lets you do this without knowing some form of programming language. Similar to the previous example, Figure 13.17 shows a two-pick brise soleil family with exchangeable lamellas that are nested.

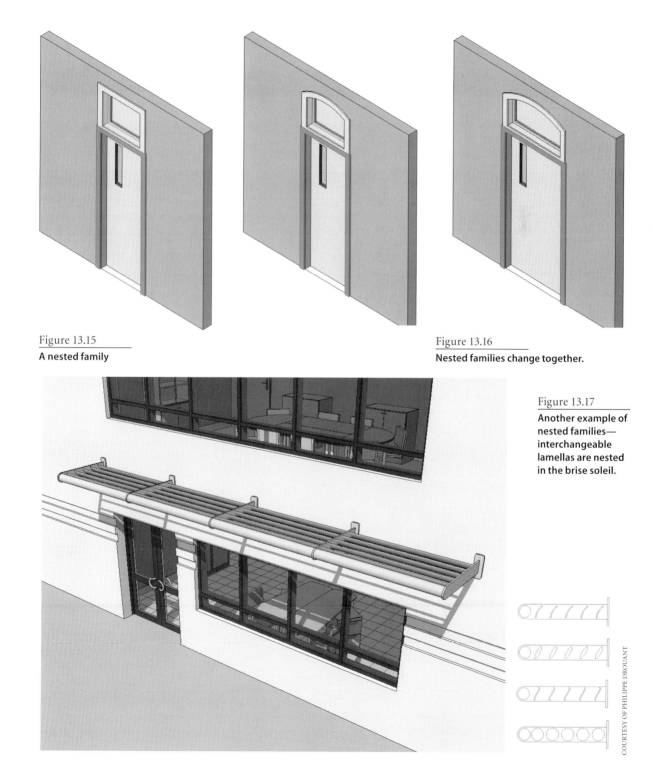

Figure 13.15

A nested family

Figure 13.16

Nested families change together.

Figure 13.17

Another example of nested families— interchangeable lamellas are nested in the brise soleil.

COURTESY OF PHILIPPE DROUANT

The Family Editor supports shared families: you may have one family repeating as a nested family in many different families (a handle can be used on various types of doors, windows, and so on). These families can be shared so that when one changes, all others change, regardless of the host in which they're nested.

The Revit Family Editor allows for complex families, from both a geometrical and a behavioral aspect. Figure 13.18 shows some complex nested families that you can create in Revit.

Figure 13.18

Complex nested families

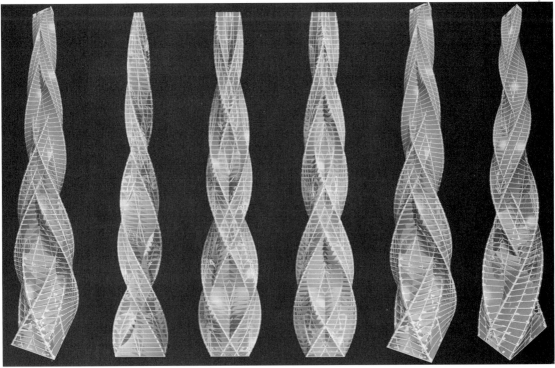

COURTESY OF PHIL READ

Historical architecture is no challenge for Revit; extremely complex content has been created using the Family Editor all around the world. Figure 13.19 shows an example of some historical windows.

Upgrading Families

Regardless of which version of Revit you use to create families, you can always open them in a version that is the same or higher. Revit automatically upgrades families from previous releases. Note that once a family has been upgraded and saved, you can't reopen that family in an older version of Revit.

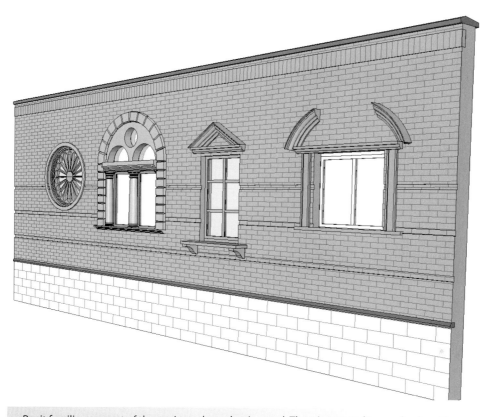

Figure 13.19

Historical content can be easily created in Revit.

Revit families are part of the project where they're used. There's no need to send out archive packages or extra libraries when you share the project with someone else. The families are an integral part of the Revit project.

Using Design Options

Design iteration is an integral part of a design process, and as architects we're all familiar with the need for and importance of working through multiple solutions. Design alternatives, schemes, options, versions—whatever you may call them—happen throughout the life of a project. During initial feasibility studies, deciding how to best orient functional program elements relative to the site is common and often involves myriad schemes. Comparing and estimating cost becomes a key factor as well. For each proposal, what is the associated cost? For example, when you move into a more detailed design and want to iterate through a series of entry-canopy options, countless sketches and ideas are processed, and the ability to visualize and analyze multiple solutions is essential to making decisions. Regardless of the stage in the process, you often need to create several design variations.

A typical method for making multiple design schemes, if you're working with a legacy CAD application, is to create one initial design and then make copies of it. Each copy becomes a separate file that is used to explore an alternate design solution independently. Although this approach can work well initially, the downstream effects can be difficult to manage. Integrating ideas from one file to another, maintaining a common set of references, and even something as mundane as file-naming schemes can be tedious and error prone.

Revit has a tool specifically designed to address this problem: *Design Options.* To examine the Design Options tool, we'll use Figure 13.20, which shows variations of balcony solutions.

Figure 13.20

Design options for balconies

The Design Options Interface

You won't see the Design Options toolbar the first time you open Revit. To display the Design Options tools, right-click above the Options bar, and choose Design Options from the flyout menu that opens. Figure 13.21 shows this option and the toolbar that appears as a result.

Because this book is an introduction to Revit, we won't go into the use of design options in depth, but we'll cover the principles behind this tool. Let's briefly explore a scenario for design options. Let's say you need to create various schemes for laying out interior partitions and desks in an office. You want to make two options, which are shown in Figure 13.22: an area with private offices and an open office plan.

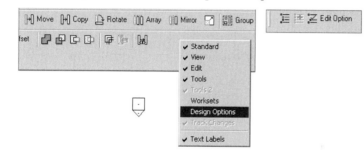

Figure 13.21

Making the Design Options toolbar visible

Figure 13.22

Two design options

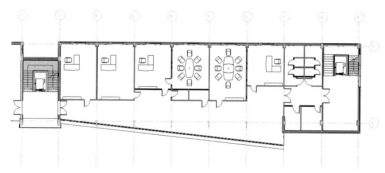

Option 1: Office area with private offices

Option 2: An open office plan

It's possible to create both of these options in one Revit file. You can move elements from option to option on the fly. You can generate views that show the two options simultaneously for comparision and place these views on sheets to present them for review. You can even schedule each of the options for economic review. Here are some steps describing a design options workflow in Revit:

1. Open the Design Options dialog box by clicking the Design Options button on the toolbar (▤). It will be the only button active.

2. To create a new option set, click New in the Option Set section of the dialog box. Option sets control subsets of options. For example, if you want two different entry canopies, the option set will be for entry canopies, and the options will be for Canopy A and Canopy B.

3. Create Option 1 and Option 2 within that option set by clicking New in the Option section of the dialog box. Your option set and options should look like Figure 13.23 when you're finished.

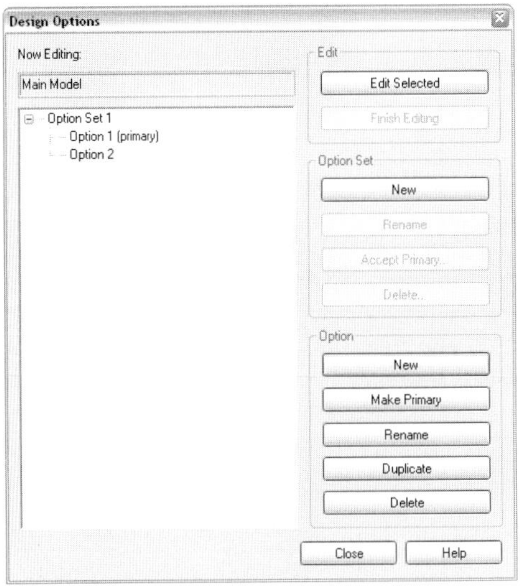

Figure 13.23

Design Options dialog box

4. Click Close to exit the dialog box.

5. Next, create a duplicate view for comparison. Duplicate any view, and then go to Visibility/Graphics Overrides. You will see a new tab, Design Options—open that tab. Change the Design Option from Automatic to Option 2.

You can make as many option sets with as many options in the same model as you need.

Setting Your Views

You can customize each view to show various design options. Note that only one option from each option set can be viewed at a time. Once you've created design options, a new Design Options tab shows up in the Visibility/Graphic Overrides dialog box. From here, you can specify which option you want to appear in the view. To have the same view type show two different options, you must duplicate the view and in the Visibility/Graphic Overrides dialog box change the design option that you want to display. Figure 13.24 shows the option sets in the Visibility/Graphic Overrides dialog box.

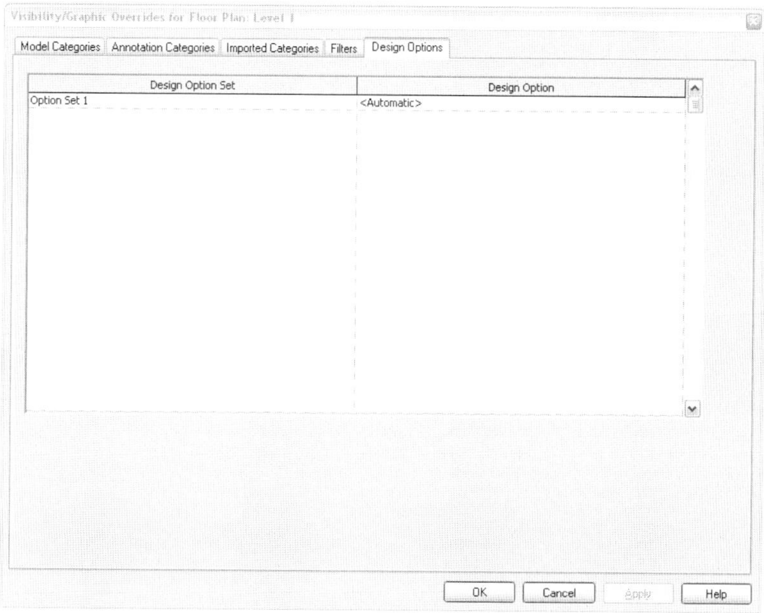

Figure 13.24

The Visibility/ Graphic Overrides dialog box controls option visibility.

By default, the first option you created will be set to Primary, and that will remain so unless you specify otherwise. To change the primary option, open the Design Options dialog box, select an option, and click the Make Primary button. So, if the first option you created is Option 1, then that will be the primary option and this option will be displayed automatically in each view (see the Automatic setting in Figure 13.23). To change the option you want displayed by default in a view, you can change which option is primary. To see secondary options, use Visibility/Graphic Overrides and change from Automatic to whatever option you want to see.

Figure 13.25

Activating a design option

Creating the Elements in the Options

To add elements to an option, click the Edit Option button on the Design Options toolbar, and select the option you want to work in. Figure 13.25 shows these selections for the example we've set up.

Once you're in the proper view with the correct option set and visibility selected, you can start designing for that option. You can tell when an option is active for editing in two ways:

- You can't select elements outside the option set.

- The Edit Option button on the toolbar appears to be pressed.

In real practice, you'll probably start with one design and then realize you want to study some iterations of an element of that design. As an example, let's consider a canopy. If you've already modeled a canopy, but you want to study some design iterations on it, you need to create design options. When you do, be sure to move the current canopy design to one of those option sets. If you don't, you'll see multiple canopies overlaying each other in your views.

With no design options active, select all the elements for an option, and click the Add to Design Option button (⊞). Move the elements to one design option by selecting the appropriate check boxes shown in Figure 13.26. To remove an element from a design option, select the element and click the third button (⊞).

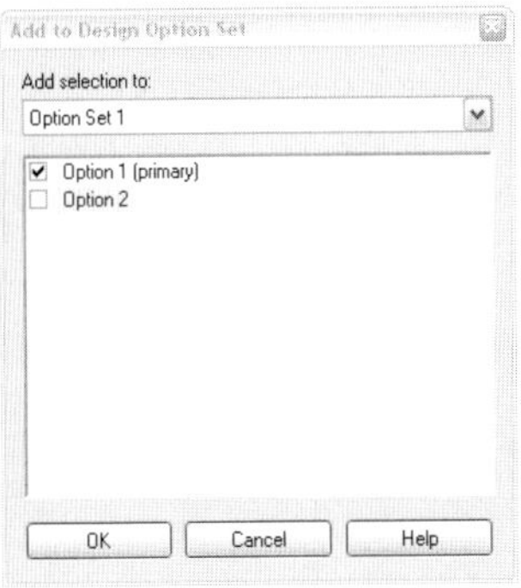

Figure 13.26

**Adding elements to
a design option**

You may want a quantity overview showing how much material one option uses versus the other. You can generate a schedule that reports information about elements in each specific option. To define what the schedule reports relative to what is visible in the model, edit the visibility of the schedule. In the Element Properties dialog box of a schedule, click the Edit button to open the Visibility/Graphic Overrides dialog box.

Revit won't report double or triple entities of all options for quantity calculations. It reports quantities for only one design option at a time.

Once you've decided on a solution, make the option with which you want to continue the design the primary option (see Figure 13.27). You can do this by clicking the Make Primary button in the Design Options dialog box. Then, click the Accept Primary button. This eliminates all the other options and merges your chosen option back into the model.

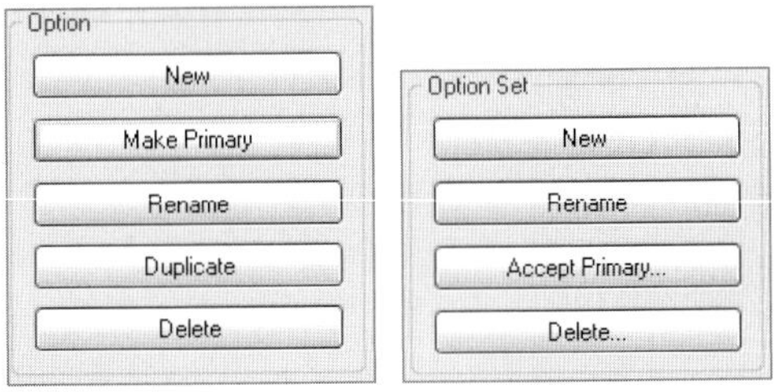

Figure 13.27

Make Primary and Accept Primary

Worksharing—the Multi-User Environment

Most projects involve more than one person working at any given time. Often, many people work in tandem to meet deadlines and produce construction documents. Keeping with the theme of an integrated single-file building model, Revit allows for this workflow without breaking apart the model. A complex model can be edited by many people at once using what is called *worksharing*.

There are various ways that you can share work across a team with Revit:

- File linking
- Borrowing elements
- Worksets

We covered the idea of linked file-sharing methodology in Chapter 7.

In this section, we'll focus on the other two methods of sharing.

Borrowing Elements

This methodology allows team members to work on the same file and take ownership of elements to work on. When elements aren't taken by anyone, they're free to be taken and then edited. When a team member needs to work on an element that belongs to someone else, that member gets a message that the element belongs to someone and can then send a notification to the current owner of the element requesting access. The owner of the element can then grant permission to take ownership—*relinquishing* elements, as it's called in Revit.

Worksharing Using the Worksets Methodology

A *workset* is a collection of building elements (floors, roofs, walls, windows, and so on) that can be edited by one team member at a time (if the whole workset is checked out) or by multiple team members (if only individual elements are checked out). You need to understand some core concepts about worksharing before you begin.

> Once you enable worksharing in a model, you can't undo it. Remember that. We suggest that you make a copy of your file before you enable worksharing so you keep an unshared version as a backup.

By default, worksharing isn't enabled when you start a project. You share your work by first enabling worksets, then creating a *central file*. Each user then navigates to the central file and creates a local copy by dragging and dropping the file to a location on their local computer. All work is done from this copied—but still associated—local file. This enables every user to open his or her own file simultaneously. The elements in each separate file are tied to an ownership rule managed by the central file, making it impossible for you to edit an element in your local file if that same element is owned by someone else.

Revit is a database. In effect, you're taking permissions of one or more elements from the central database file and copying changes (and permissions) to the central file. If one user has ownership over an element, no other user can edit that element until its permissions and changes are reconciled with the central file.

Worksets also let you put collections of elements into a container, which is useful for turning off the visibility of elements that aren't being worked on. When you enable worksharing, a new tab appears in the Visibility/Graphics Overrides dialog box for the worksets. You can turn on or off any workset in any view and make those settings part of your view templates.

Worksharing Basics

The other team members can view the elements of any workset but can only edit them using element borrowing.

Worksharing is designed to accommodate any division of labor you see fit. There are no inherent restrictions in how you use worksharing to accomplish work. For example, if you want to break up a team and have one group work on the exterior shell and one work on the interior core, this isn't a problem. At any point in a project, you can create or remove worksets.

By default, the Worksets toolbar isn't activated in Revit. To turn it on, right-click in a blank area of the toolbar and select Worksets from the flyout menu.

You can start worksharing in two ways:

Figure 13.28

The Worksets toolbar

- Choose File → Worksets from the main menu.

- Click the Worksets button on the Worksets toolbar, shown in Figure 13.28.

Figure 13.29

Activating worksets with a project

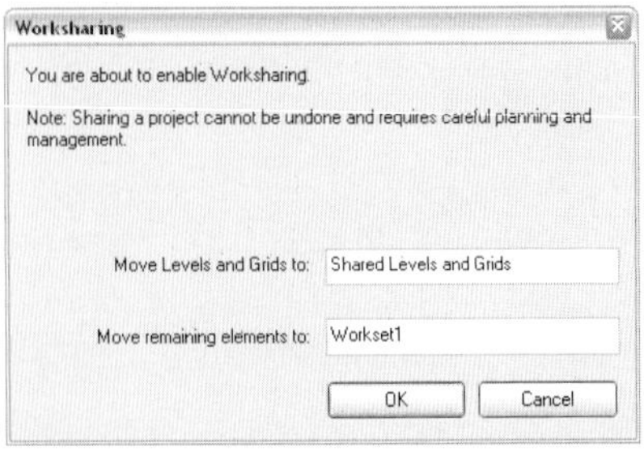

Either of these actions opens a dialog box (Figure 13.29) telling you that you're about to enable worksharing and that what you're doing can't be undone. By default, Revit creates two worksets: one contains the levels and grids; the other contains geometry and is named Workset1.

Three other types of worksets are created automatically:

Views worksets Each view in a project has a dedicated view workset. It contains the view's definition and any view-specific elements (text, dimensions, and so on). View-specific elements can't be moved to another workset.

Family worksets For each loaded family in the project, an automatic workset is created.

Project standards worksets This automatic workset covers project settings like materials, line styles, and so on.

Once you've activated the worksets, you'll see the dialog box shown in Figure 13.30. Here, you can add and remove worksets.

Figure 13.30

Worksets dialog box

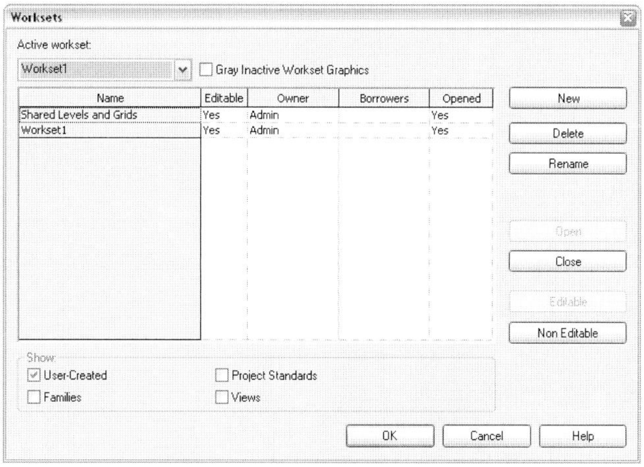

When you activate worksets, you're the owner of all of them. This is what the Yes value in the Editable column means.

> The activation of worksets is usually done by the team's project manager, who creates this first workset setup, creates user worksets, and assigns people to work on the project.

Workset Organization

It's important that you think of your project as a holistic building when dividing into worksets. Some good examples of worksets are Shell and Core, Exterior Skin, and First Floor Interior Partitions. Technically once you have activated worksharing, you do not need to add any more worksets than the ones Revit has generated. This is because Revit will automatically manage ownership of elements on a per-element basis and relinquish ownership automatically when you save to a central file. Worksets should be used to help define visibility and division of labor within the team.

Workflow

There is always one central file that spawns local files and manages element ownership. This is the file that changes are saved into and from which you get updated versions of the model as you work. Work can be done directly in the central file, but that isn't a suggested workflow.

To begin using worksharing, follow these steps:

1. Activate worksets.

2. Save the file as a central file. To do so, choose File → Save As, and click Options. In the resulting dialog box (Figure 13.31), select the Make This the Central Location after Save check box and finish by clicking OK.

3. Make local copies of the central file.

4. Draw the basic layout, exterior shell, and so on.

5. Create worksets.

6. Move elements into worksets (select the element, open the Element Properties and under Worksets change the workset to which it needs to belong).

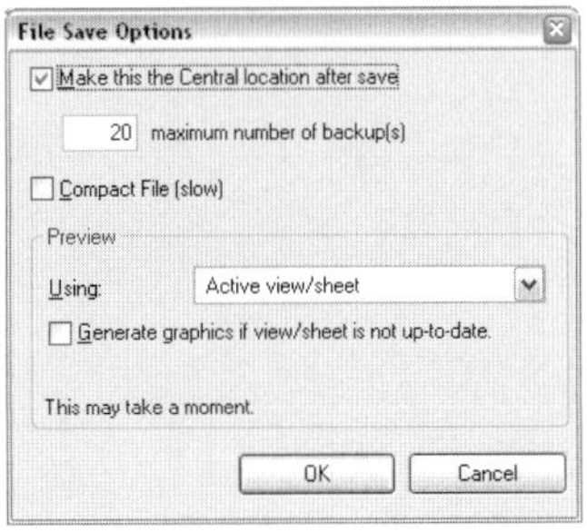

To use the central file, you go against everything any IT manager ever yelled at you for: you make a local copy of the central file and work directly off your C drive. Although this approach is a bad idea for most work, for the Revit database, it does a couple of good things:

Figure 13.31
Saving a central file

- It allows more than one user to make changes to the file.

- It's more responsive as the file gets larger, because your access speed to your hard drive is faster than most networks.

You can make a local copy by dragging and dropping the central file to your desktop or anywhere on your C drive. Open that file. You'll originally see the message shown in Figure 13.32, alerting you that you have a local copy of a central file. Revit maintains the link between your local copy and the central file provided you don't move the central file from its location on your network.

Figure 13.32
Warning about creating a local file

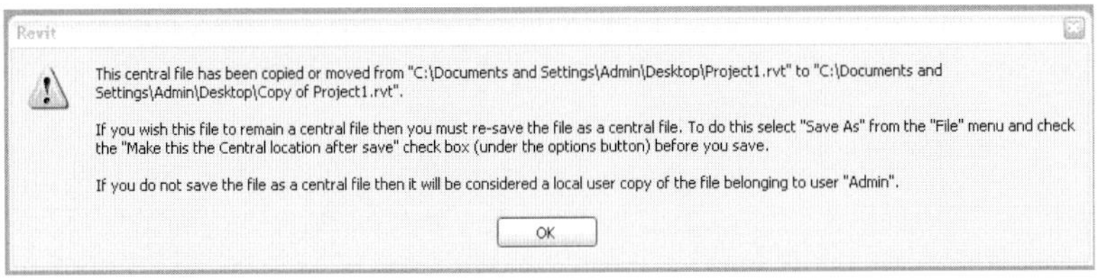

Once you're in a worksharing environment, every element added to the file belongs to a workset. Try to keep model elements in a workset other than shared levels and grids, because these worksets may be locked down at some point to avoid accidental movement of key datums. To make sure you're placing elements in the proper workset, check the

Figure 13.33
Workset field on the toolbar

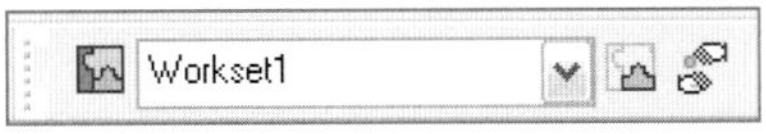

Worksets toolbar (see Figure 13.33). The workset shown in this box is the workset your elements will be drawn on.

A helpful toggle in the Worksets toolbar is the Gray Inactive Workset button (🔳). It grays out all elements that aren't in the active workset, helping you identify which elements are in the workset you're working on. This is a temporary view state and doesn't affect print output.

> Create a filter that applies a graphic override based on the active workset. Now you can quickly identify which elements are on which workset.

Saving Shared Work

There are two ways to save your work when you're using a workshared file:

Save The Save tool only saves the work you've done on your local copy; the work isn't shared. This is useful when you're in the design phase and trying different designs, and you aren't ready to share your work with others.

Save to Central Next to the Save tool is the Save to Central button (🔳). Use it to commit your work to the central file. When you do so, your work appears in the central file and becomes available to the entire team. Saving to central also acquires the changes that others have made and loads them into your model. You can also do this using File → Save to Central.

Loading Work from Other Team Members

It's possible to update your model from the central file without committing your changes to central. Think of this process as getting an update of the model. To do so, choose File → Reload Latest. Your file gets the latest changes saved from the central file and brings them into your local file.

CHAPTER 14

Tips and Troubleshooting

This chapter is designed to give you some tips and tricks about how to keep your project file running quickly and smoothly. Listed here are some pointers to keep you from getting into trouble and some solutions if you do. Topics we'll cover include:

- **Optimizing performance**

- **Using best practices**

- **Dealing with file corruption**

Optimizing Performance

It should make sense that a small file on a good network runs the quickest. Depending on your hardware configuration, typical file sizes can run a large gamut. We've seen them range from 30MB to 200MB. Much of that variation depends on the level of detail you've put into your model, the presence of imported files (like other 3D files or CAD files), and the overall complexity of your model. However, there are a number of things you can do to be proactive about keeping your model performance optimized. Here are a few we recommend:

Use the 3 GB switch. Revit now supports Microsoft XP's 3GB switch. Windows XP allows any given application access to only 2GB of RAM at a given time; if the application needs more, it get the rest from virtual memory. Microsoft's switch (which is available in XP Service Pack 2) allows you to change that 2GB limit to 3GB. To find out how to do this, visit www.autodesk.com/support, choose Revit Building from the menu, and read the support article on enabling the 3GB switch. Of course, you need more than 2GB of RAM in your workstation for this switch to do you any good.

More information on RAM and virtual memory can be found at the Autodesk knowledge website. Visit this site for details: http://usa.autodesk.com/adsk/servlet/ps/item?siteID=123112&id=8018971&linkID=9243099.

Don't explode imported CAD files. A CAD file imported into Revit is a collection of objects that is managed as single entity. If you explode a CAD file, the single object immediately becomes many—and becomes that much more data for Revit to track. If you're unfortunate enough to explode a hatch pattern, one object becomes many thousands. If you're importing DWG files, leave them unexploded as much as possible. If you need to hide lines, use the Visibility/Graphic Overrides dialog box to turn layers on and off. Explode *only* when you need to change the imported geometry, and start with a Par-

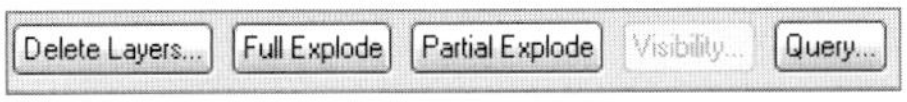

Figure 14.1

Import explode options

tial Explode. Figure 14.1 shows the tools available in the Options bar when you select an imported or linked DWG file.

Another option is to change the DWG file directly in CAD—delete lines and layers you don't need, then reimport.

Delete or unload unused DWGs. Often, you import a DWG as a reference, but then you don't need it later in the process. It's easy to forget, but if you no longer need an import, go ahead and delete it by selecting it in the view and deleting it. This will delete the import in all views.

Close unused views. Keeping the number of open views to a minimum helps the model's performance. Choose Window → Close Hidden Windows often (Figure 14.2), because it's easy to have many views open at once, even if you're concentrating on only a few views. Once you reduce your open views to just two or three, you can take advantage of the view switch toggle: press Ctrl+Tab, and you'll cycle through your open views. Press Ctrl+Shift+Tab to reverse the view cycle.

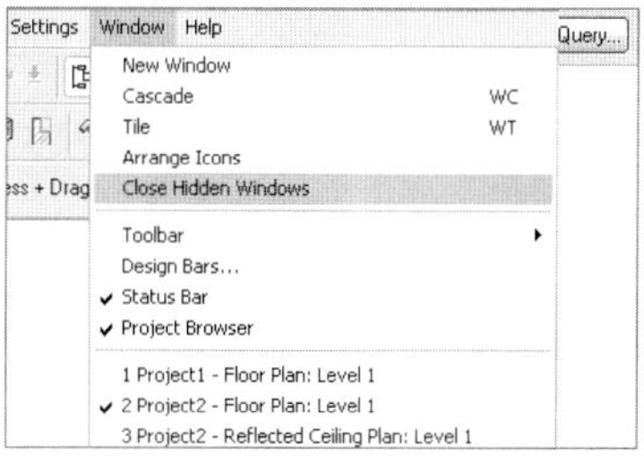

Calculate room volumes only when necessary. You can turn on room volume calculation by choosing Settings → Room and Area Settings. Check Compute Room Volumes (shown in Figure 14.3) only if you need room tags or a schedule to display volumetric information. Don't forget to switch off this option after you print or view the information. Otherwise, the volumes will recalculate each time you edit something in the model, and this can affect the overall performance of your file dramatically.

Figure 14.2

Close hidden windows that you're not using.

Best Practices

The following Best Practices will not only help you keep your project files running smoothly but they will also keep frustration levels with poorly performing files low.

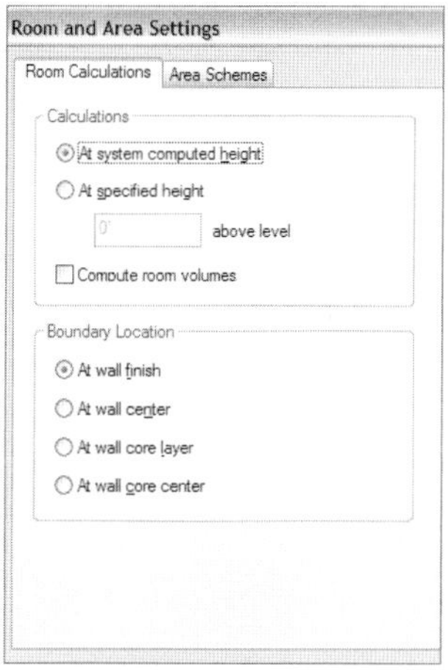

Worksharing files: Make a new local copy once a week. Sometimes in a workshared environment, your local copy can begin to perform poorly but others on your team don't have the same problems. If this is the case, we recommend that you make a new local file. Local files can become problematic because of any of the things that commonly cause issues with large files in a networked environment. As a general practice, it's a good idea to make a new local copy once a week.

Figure 14.3

Do not compute room volumes unless necessary.

Use graphics card options to improve drawing performance. In the Settings → Options Graphics tab, make sure you have both Use OpenGL Hardware Acceleration and Use Overlay Planes to Improve Display Performance checked (Figure 14.4). Deselecting the overlay planes check box can cause significant degradation in performance—we recommended you never deselect this option.

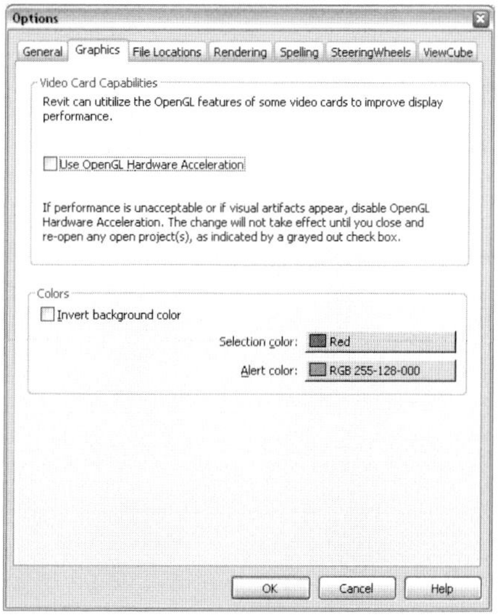

Figure 14.4

Enable video card options for better performance.

Import or link DWGs in one view only. Importing in all views can seriously affect performance. Figure 14.5 shows the Link (Instead of Import) check box in the Import or Link dialog box. Linking is better than importing if you don't need to edit the geometry.

Figure 14.5

**Import into
one view.**

Watch out for imported geometry. Although Revit has the ability to import files from a number of other sources, you should exercise caution when doing so. If you're importing a 60MB NURBS-based Rhino file into your model, expect your Revit model to grow in size and react a bit slower than it did before. Delete unneeded imports to reduce file size and improve overall performance.

Purge unused elements. Revit has a built-in tool that allows you to purge unused families and content. This is a good way to reduce file size, improve performance, and minimize the list of things you need to search through when adding content in the project. Loaded but unused families can make your file grow quickly. To purge, choose File → Purge Unused. If your file is very large, it may take a few minutes to run this command before you see the dialog box shown in Figure 14.6. Here, you can opt to keep or purge families individually.

Some Revit families can only be removed from the project with the Purge command. You will notice with elements such as dimensions and text notes, there is no way to delete a family type from the Properties dialog box. To get rid of unused types, use Purge. Everything included in the Other Styles group falls into this category.

Figure 14.6

**Use the Purge
Unused dialog box
to reduce file size.**

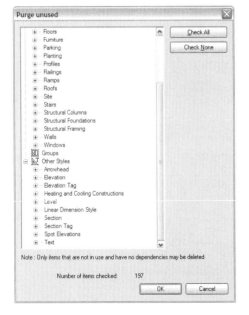

This is typically *not* a good idea at the beginning of a project, because your template may contain families that you intend to use but haven't yet inserted (such as wall types).

Manage the amount of information shown in views. Learn to manage the amount of information needed in your views. Don't show more than you need to show in a view either in depth or in your level of detail. Here are a few easy ways to keep your views opening and printing smoothly:

Minimize the level of detail. Set your detail level (in the View Control bar) relative to the scale you're viewing. For example, if you're working on a 1/32″ (1:50) plan, you probably don't need Detail Level set to Fine—it will cause your view performance to suffer needlessly.

One project was taking upward of 20 minutes to open plan views. As you can imagine, this was very frustrating for the users, especially when you opened those views accidentally. As it turned out, the views were set to a 1/16˝ scale and a fine level of detail. For the elements in the plan, none of them showed any significant information at this level of detail. By setting the View Detail to Coarse, they were able to reduce the time to open those views to under two minutes. We further optimized view performance by modifying complex families in the view to show less detail at a coarse level.

Minimize view detail. This goes along with the level of detail, but this tip is more user based than tool based. If you're printing a 1/32˝ (1:50) drawing, make sure you're showing the proper level of detail in the view. Even if Detail Level is set to Coarse, do you really need to show balusters in an elevation on your railing at that scale? They will print as a thick, black line. Turning them off in this view will help improve not only your printing speed but also the quality of the resulting printed sheet.

Minimize view depth. View depth is a great tool to enhance performance. It's especially valuable in section views. A typical building section is shown in Figure 14.7. The default behavior causes Revit to regenerate all of the model geometry the full depth of that view every time you open the view. To reduce the amount of geometry that needs to be redrawn, drag the section's far clip plane (the green dashed line when you highlight the section) in close to the cutting plane.

Figure 14.7

Minimize section Far Clip Offset.

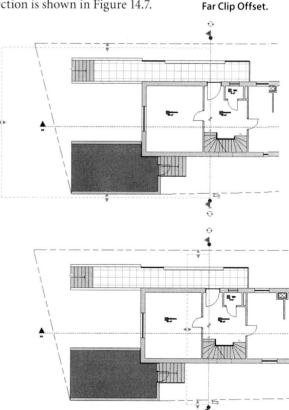

Turn off shadows. Shadows can help you make beautiful presentations, give a sense of depth in façades, and show the effect of the sun in a site-plan view; however, shadows are performance intensive and can significantly slow a view's time to open, print, or regenerate as you pan and move around in it. Make sure you turn shadows off whenever you don't need them.

Open only what you need. One of the benefits of having worksets is that you don't have to turn them all on at once. When you open the project, go to the Workset dialog box. There, you can highlight a workset and click the Close button (see Figure 14.8). Doing so drops that workset from active memory and gives you better performance. Remember, if worksets are closed, you can't do anything with them. If a workset isn't visible, it won't print. To print a current copy of the whole model, you'll need to turn the worksets back on.

Figure 14.8

Worksets can be closed to reduce the amount of memory used to open a file.

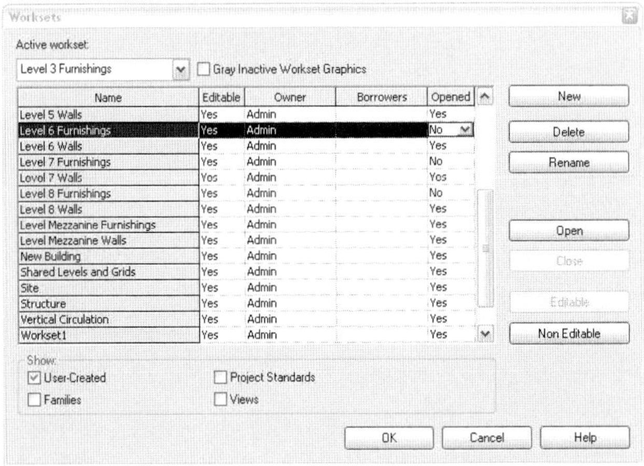

Break up your model. For larger projects, or campus-style projects, you can break up your model into smaller submodels that are referenced together. You can also do this on a single building. If you decide to divide your project, make your cuts along lines that make sense from a holistic-building standpoint. Don't think of the cuts as you would in CAD, but think about how the actual assemblies will interact in the building. As an example, don't cut between floors 2 and 3 on a multistory building unless you have a significant change in building form or program. Here's a list of some good places to split a model. See Figure 14.9 for an example:

- At a significant change in building form or massing
- At a significant change in building program
- Between separate buildings on the site
- At the building site

Consider printing paper, DWFs, or PDFs. Printing big Revit files can sometimes take a long time. Enabling raster printing speeds up printing, although there is a trade-off compared to the quality that vector printing offers. Depending on the printer, you may get better line quality by going to a DWF or PDF first, then printing your physical sheets. Experiment on a few sheets to see what your printer responds to best before sending your entire set. Printing a digital set first will also give you a record copy of what you have just printed as well as a quick way to make additional copies later if needed.

Figure 14.9

Splitting up a model can improve performance.

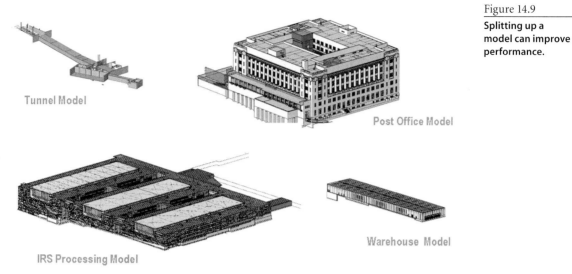

Tunnel Model

Post Office Model

IRS Processing Model

Warehouse Model

Model just what you need. Don't fall into the trap of overmodeling. Just because you *can* doesn't mean you *should*. Be smart about the level of detail you choose to model based on the complexity and size of your project. Some data is just easier and better to show in a 2D detail rather than as 3D model data. The amount of information you model or do not model should be based on your project size and complexity, your timeframe, and your comfort level with the software.

Don't overconstrain. User-defined relationships and constraints are important to embed in the design to help keep important dimensions constant. However, if you don't need to lock a relationship, don't. Even though the option to lock all alignments is available, it's often not necessary to do so. Overconstraining the model can cause problems later in the project process when you want to move or modify an element and you now need to figure out (or remember) what you locked and where to allow the particular element to be moved or modified.

Fix an overconstrained object. If you keep encountering a dialog box telling you the model is overconstrained and this is impeding your workflow, you can delete the constraint. If it is a simple element (such as a wall with no openings or sections), it might be easier to simply delete and redraw the troubled object.

Assign proper view detail. It is possible to create families in Revit with a seemingly infinite amount of detail. Use the Visibility tool found in the Family Editor. Make sure when creating families that you are setting the elements within the family to the right level of detail. Setting elements to Coarse, Medium, or Fine can keep your families from looking like blobs in Coarse view and quicken your screen-refresh times.

Close Revit with an empty view. To avoid long opening times for really large files, establish an office standard that you always close your last view as a drafting view or legend that is empty, or maybe contains only some text with the project name. This way, when Revit first opens the project it will need much less processing time. By default, Revit always opens with the view from when the project was last saved. We've seen some nice-looking "project pages" made with a drafting view using text and some simple instructions.

File Corruption

If your file becomes corrupted and begins to crash frequently, there are a few things you can do to help fix the problem before you call Revit Support in a panic. To proactively avoid this issue, focus on the previous tips before you begin having problems. Otherwise, here are some suggestions on what to do when you get into trouble:

Audit the file. Auditing the file will review the data structures and correct problems that are found within the model. An audited file won't look any different when the audit is completed; however, it should (ideally) not crash. This is not a cure-all, by any means, but it can help you get out of a tight spot when necessary.

Get everyone out of any worksets and local files, and have them relinquish their permissions. Open the file using File Open. The resulting Open dialog box lets you browse to a project location. Select your project and before clicking the Open button to open the file, select the Audit check box in the lower-right corner (shown in Figure 14.10). Revit gives you a warning before performing an audit on your file. The audit itself can take several minutes to complete. When this process is finished, save the project with a new name or in a new file location; don't save this file over the old Revit file. Saving over an existing Revit file can sometimes lead to instability. When you're finished, have everyone make a new local file, and you can get back to work.

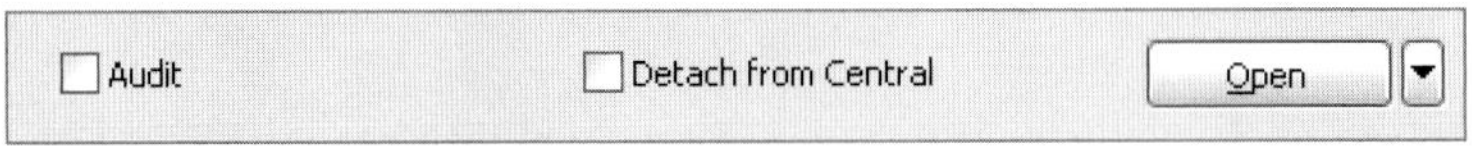

Figure 14.10

The Audit option is located in the File Open dialog box.

Review warnings. Each time you make something that Revit considers a problem, a warning is issued. If you ignore warnings, they will accumulate if left unresolved. Think of all these errors as unresolved calculations. The more there are, the more your computer will have to struggle with trying to resolve them. Revit provides an interface where you can review all the warnings in the project and fix problems.

Try to read and react to the warning that Revit sends. You don't have to do it when you're under a tight deadline or when doing so will interrupt your work. But once a week, you should spend 30 minutes reviewing the warnings, as this can improve your model's overall performance. You can find the list of warnings in your file under Tools → Review Warnings (Figure 14.11).

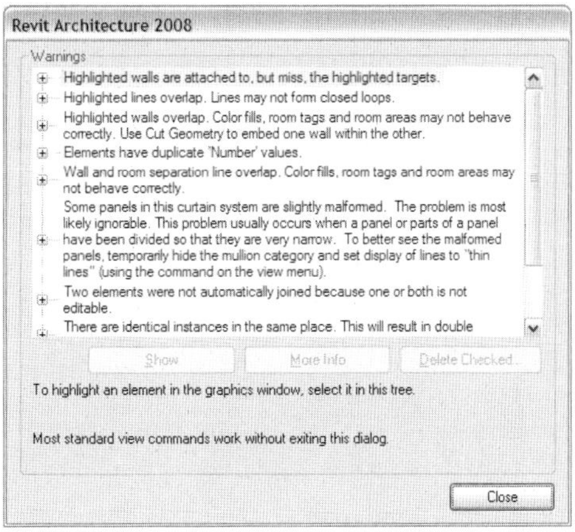

Purge unused elements. We referred to this earlier in the "Best Practices" section: Purge can also be used to get rid of poorly built families that might be wreaking havoc in your file.

Figure 14.11

Review warnings in this dialog box.

Index

Note to the reader: Throughout this index **boldfaced** page numbers indicate primary discussions of a topic. *Italicized* page numbers indicate illustrations.

U

V